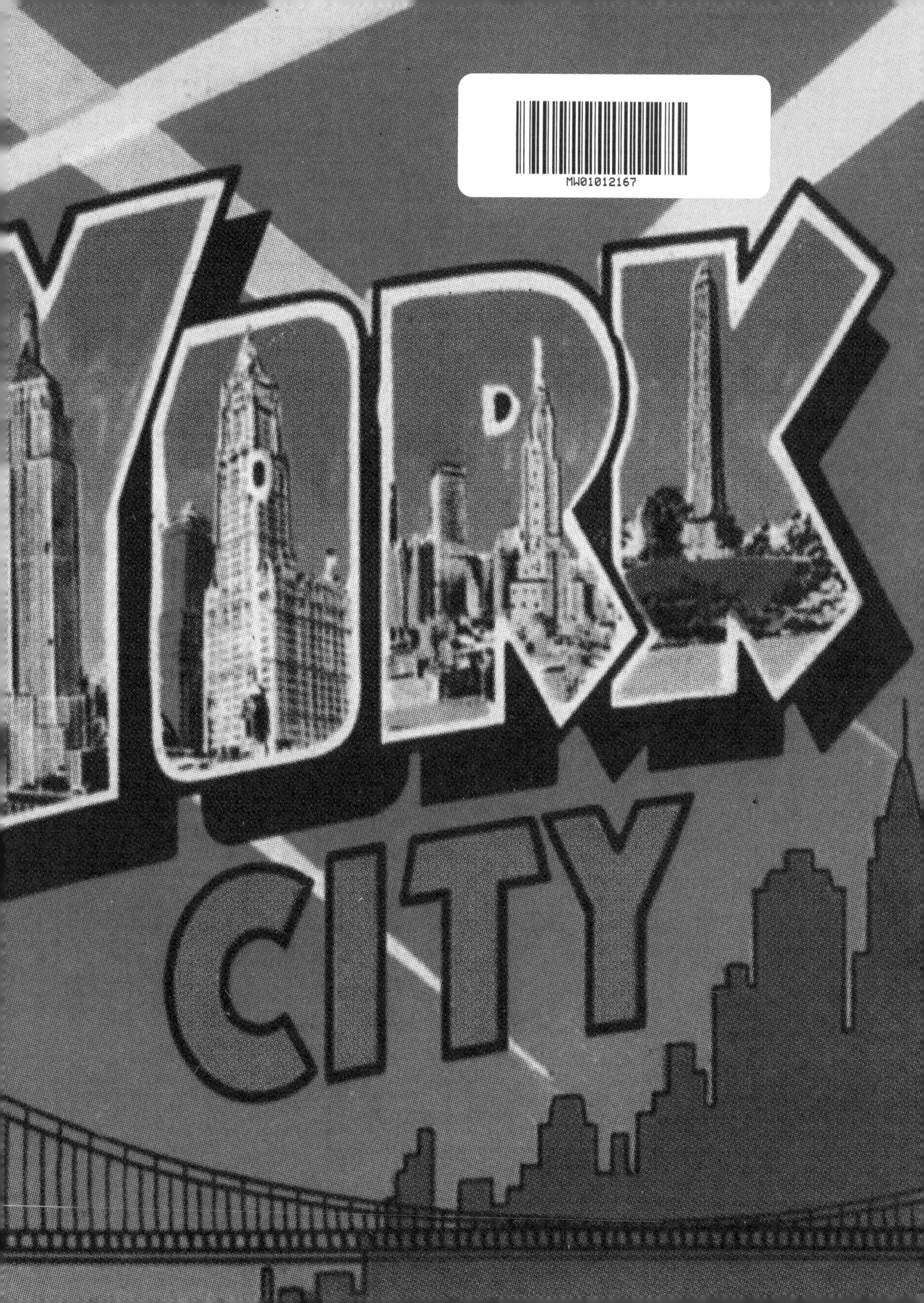
ORK
CITY

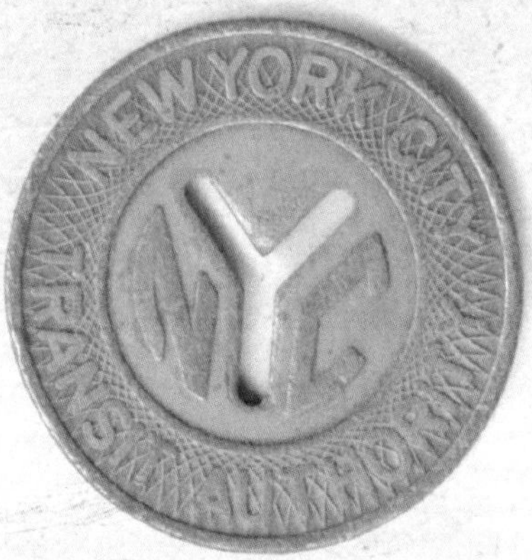
NEW YORK CITY

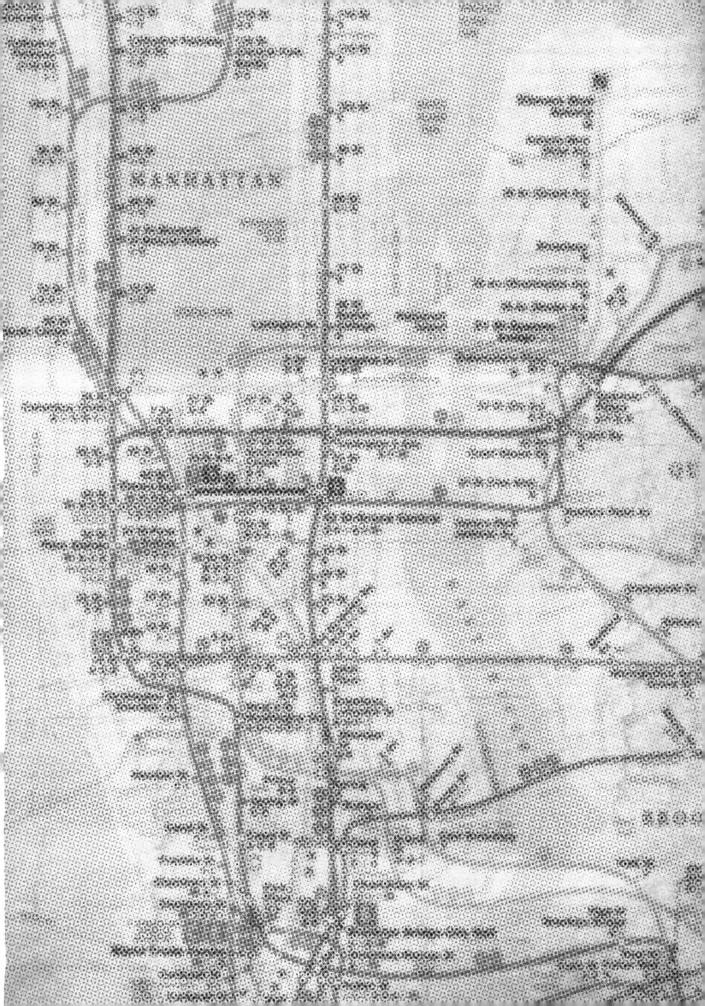

Drawn to New York

www.peterkuper.com
Introduction

Design by
Peter Kuper
Production
assistance
Minah Kim,
Edwin Vazquez
and Hilary Allison.

Published by
PM Press
PO Box 23912
Oakland, CA 94623
510-658-3906
info@pmpress.org

First edition April, 2013
ISBN: 978-1-60486-722-0
LIBRARY OF CONGRESS
CONTROL NUMBER 2012954996
Printed in Singapore

DIARIO DE
OAXACA
PETER KUPER
A SKETCHBOOK JOURNAL OF TWO YEARS IN
MEXICO

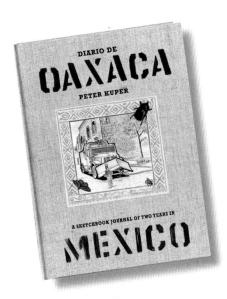

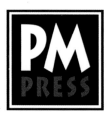

Also by the author
from PM Press:
Diario de Oaxaca
A Sketchbook Journal of
Two Years in Mexico
ISBN: 978-1-60486-071-9 $29.95

ABOUT PM PRESS

PM Press was founded at the end of 2007 by a small collection of folks with decades of publishing, media, and organizing experience. PM Press co-conspirators have published and distributed hundreds of books, pamphlets, CDs, and DVDs. Members of PM have founded enduring book fairs, spearheaded victorious tenant organizing campaigns, and worked closely with bookstores, academic conferences, and even rock bands to deliver political and challenging ideas to all walks of life. We're old enough to know what we're doing and young enough to know what's at stake. For more information please visit us at **www.pmpress.org**

Some of the material in *Drawn to New York* originally appeared in *World War 3, SP Revista de Libros, The New York Times, Nozone, The New Yorker, The Village Voice, New York Press, Fantagraphics Books, Speechless, Blab!, Heavy Metal, Poz, New York Magazine, MTV, Fortune, Oporto Festival, Scenario magazine, N.Y. Mix, Forbes, Esquire, the MoCCA festival, Pulse!, Road Strips* and *Aperture.*

Drawn to New York

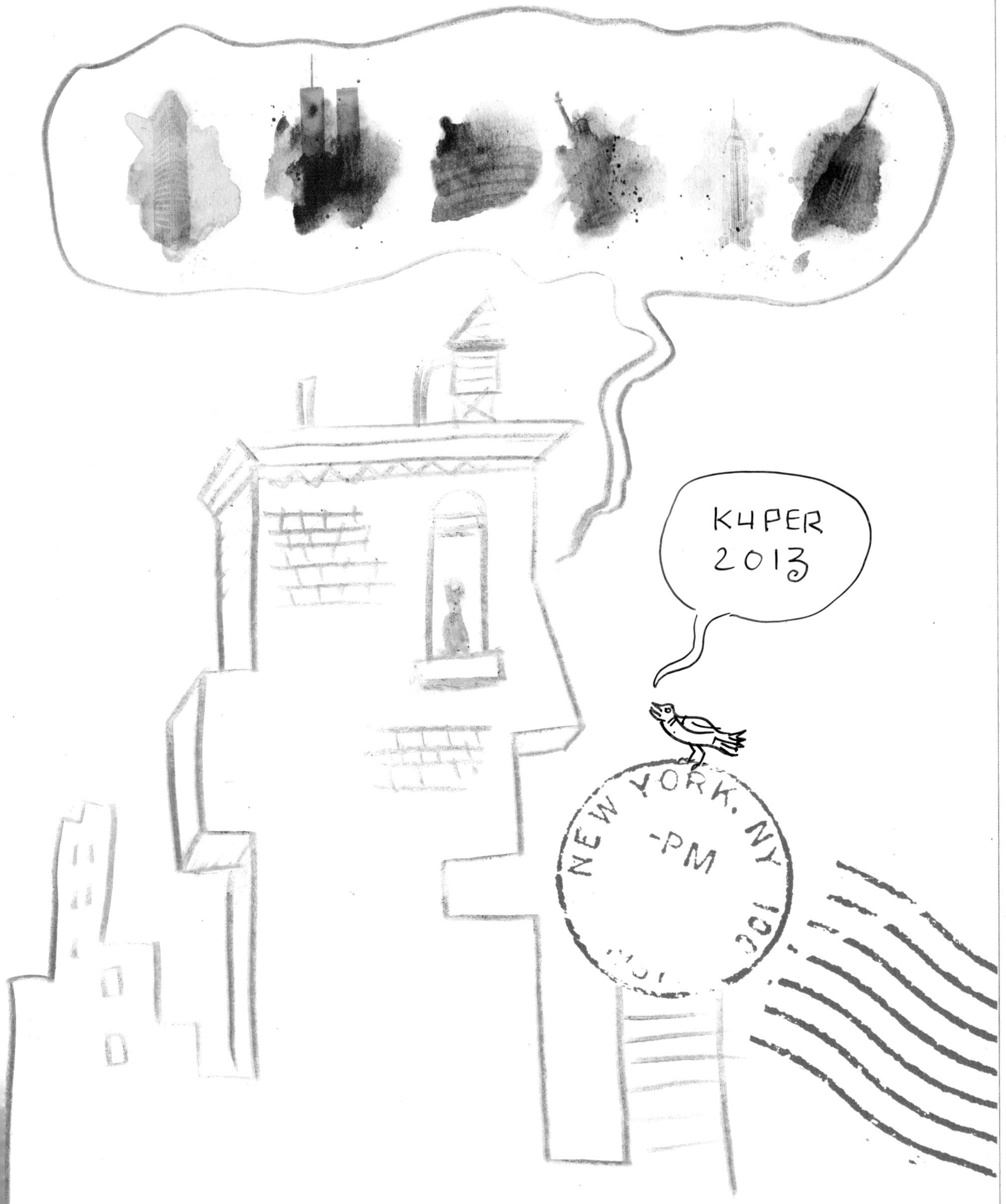
K4PER
2013
NEW YORK. NY
PM

Dedicated to the memory of Boris Aplon:
actor, uncle and my guiding light to Manhattan.

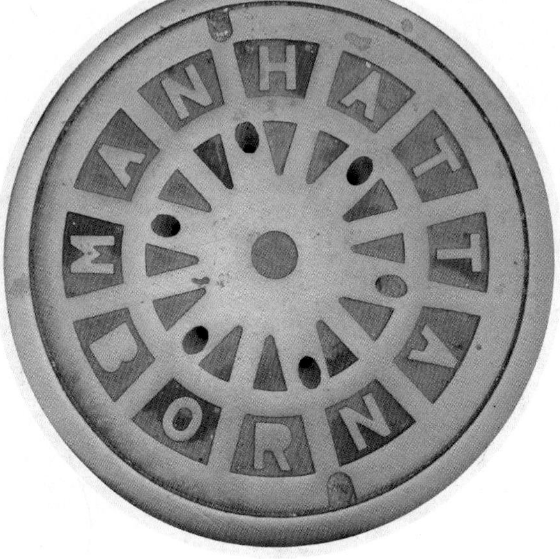
MANHATTAN BORN

Thanks to Emily and Betty Russell,
Jim Rasenberger, Kate Kuper and Rocky Maffit
for their sharp editorial advice.
Eric Drooker for his eloquent intro,
Junot Díaz for the kind words,
John Thomas for his legal insight,
Minah Kim, Hilary Allison and Edwin Vazquez
for art assistance and book production,
Craig, Ramsey and all the great people at PM Press,
Francisco, Diego, and Eduardo at Sexto Piso for a launch pad,
all my co-conspirators at *World War 3*
and the many friends and family who helped make
New York City my home: David and Betsy Klein, John and Jim
Zimmerman, Martha, Leslie, Jan, Seth, Tony, Rose, Steve,
Janet, Molly and Philip, Scott and Elena, Alan and Ginger,
Holly, my daughter Emily and about eight million other people.

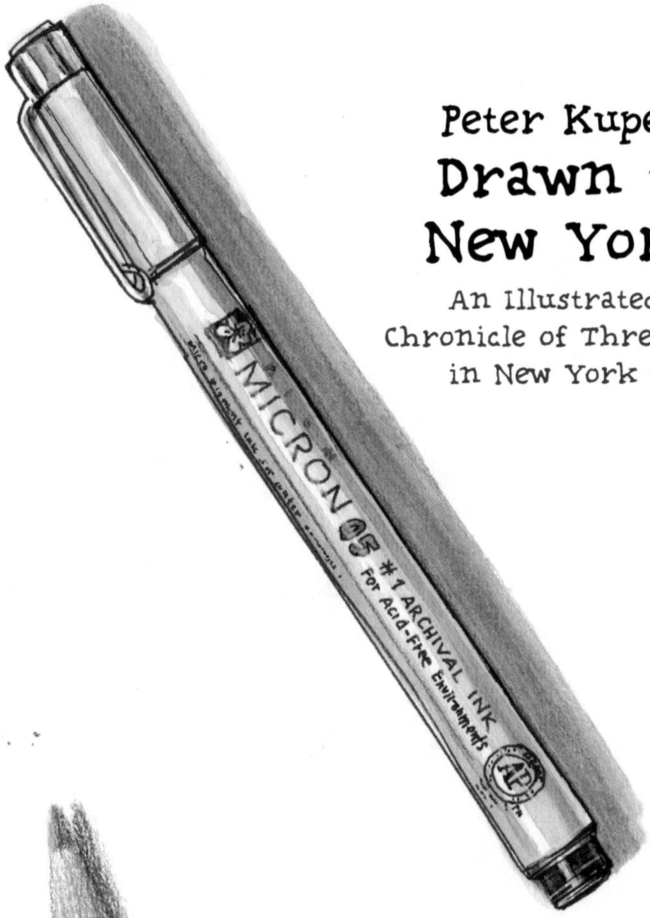
MICRON 05
#1 ARCHIVAL INK
For Acid-Free Environments

Peter Kuper

Drawn to New York

An Illustrated Chronicle of Three Decades in New York City

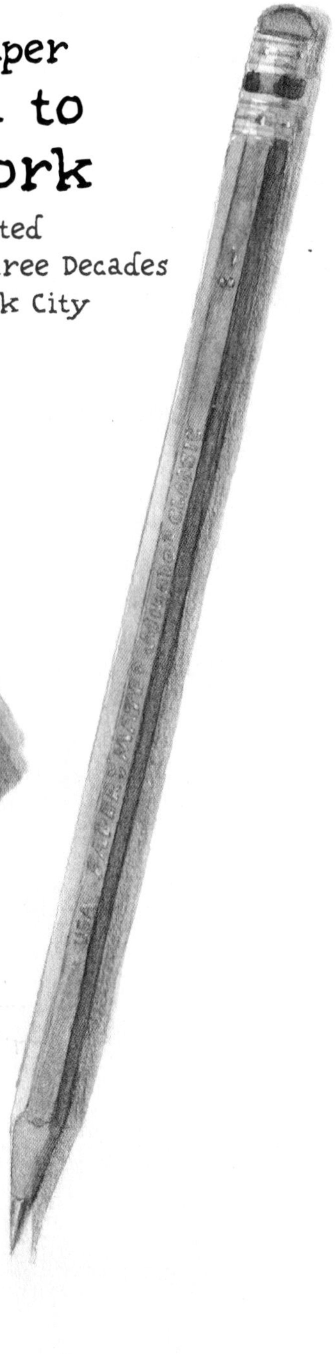

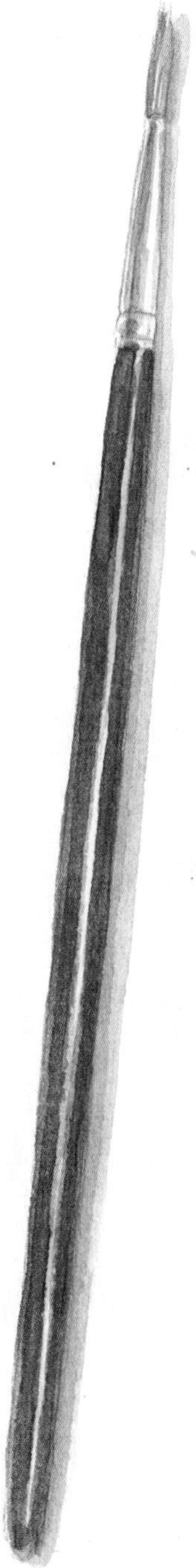

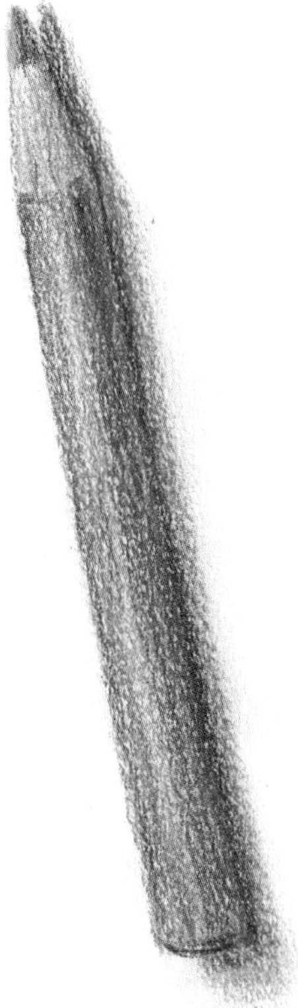

Introduction by
Eric Drooker

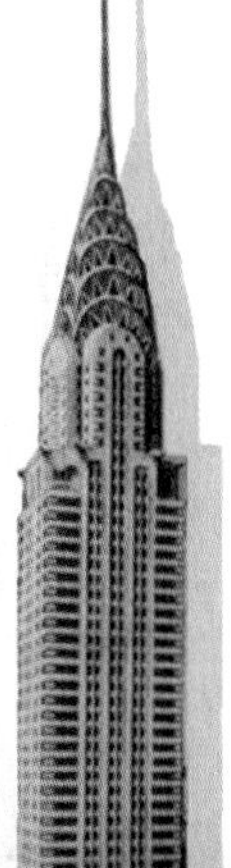

PM PRESS

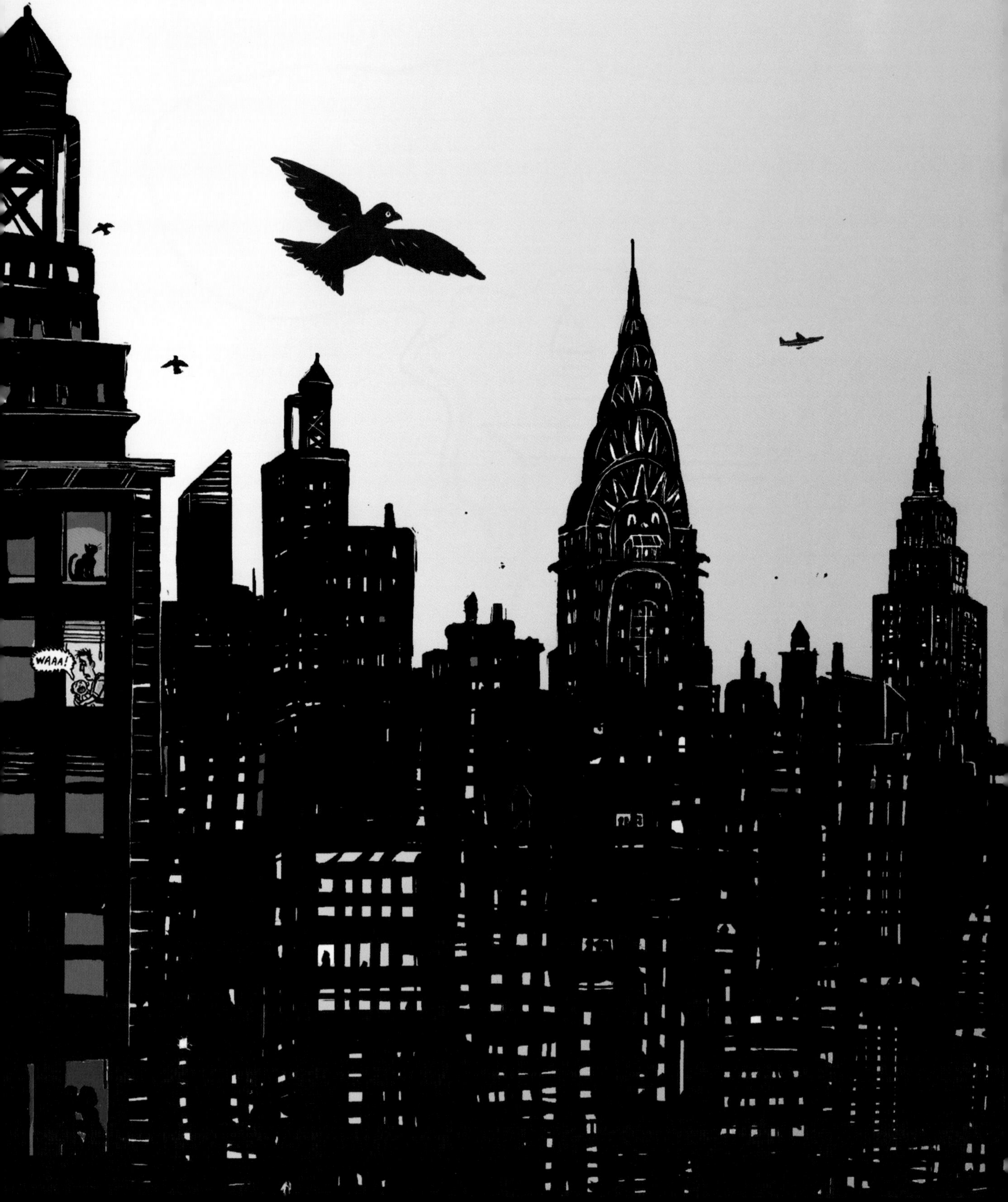
WAAA!

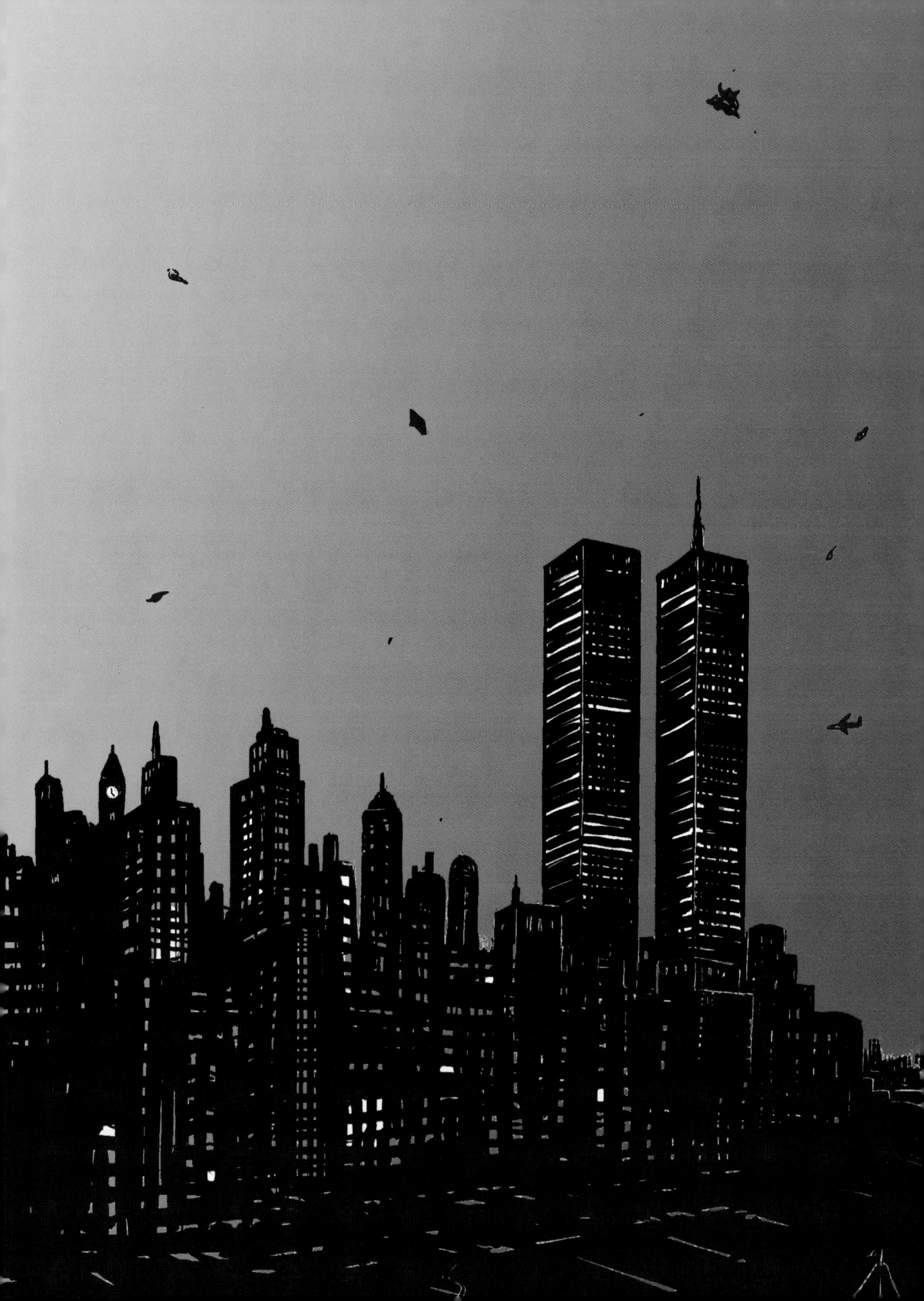

INTRODUCTION BY A NATIVE

Like moths to a flame, millions are drawn to New York . . . but why?

What's the attraction to the big city—the eternal Babel—with its
endless confusion of tongues? What's all the hubbub?
What is it that draws so many people—particularly artists—to Gotham?
Is it the buildings? The lights? The sound? The fury?
The wailing sirens at 3 A.M.? The incessant rumble
of nonstop express trains on rusted subway tracks?

Or is it simply the seduction of anonymity in the big city . . .
a chance to reinvent oneself in the rush hour crowd?
Many come as a career move, hoping to be discovered by others . . .
or at least to find themselves.
(Having been born and raised in Gotham, I realized I would need to
leave New York in order to lose myself . . . but that's another story.)

At the tender age of eighteen, Peter Kuper packed his midwestern bags
and left Cleveland's flatlands for good. When he arrived in Gotham's
vertical landscape, his eyes opened wide at the tall, dark, multifaceted
muse who would haunt and inspire him for decades.

As a cartoonist and graphic novelist, Kuper's art reflects the
sequential grid that is Manhattan. Each window tells a story,
and the rows of squares and infinite right angles form a map
of one man's journey through the modern labyrinth.

When viewed as a whole, as in this volume, Kuper's concrete visions of
New York amount to an epic love poem—an homage to his adopted city.
One feels a deep urban vertigo when gazing at his strips of the megacity he now
calls home. Through Kuper's paintbrush and pen, Gotham's screaming
whirlpools of cement, bulletproof glass, aging tenements and deafening rhythms
have made it onto the page intact.

-Eric Drooker

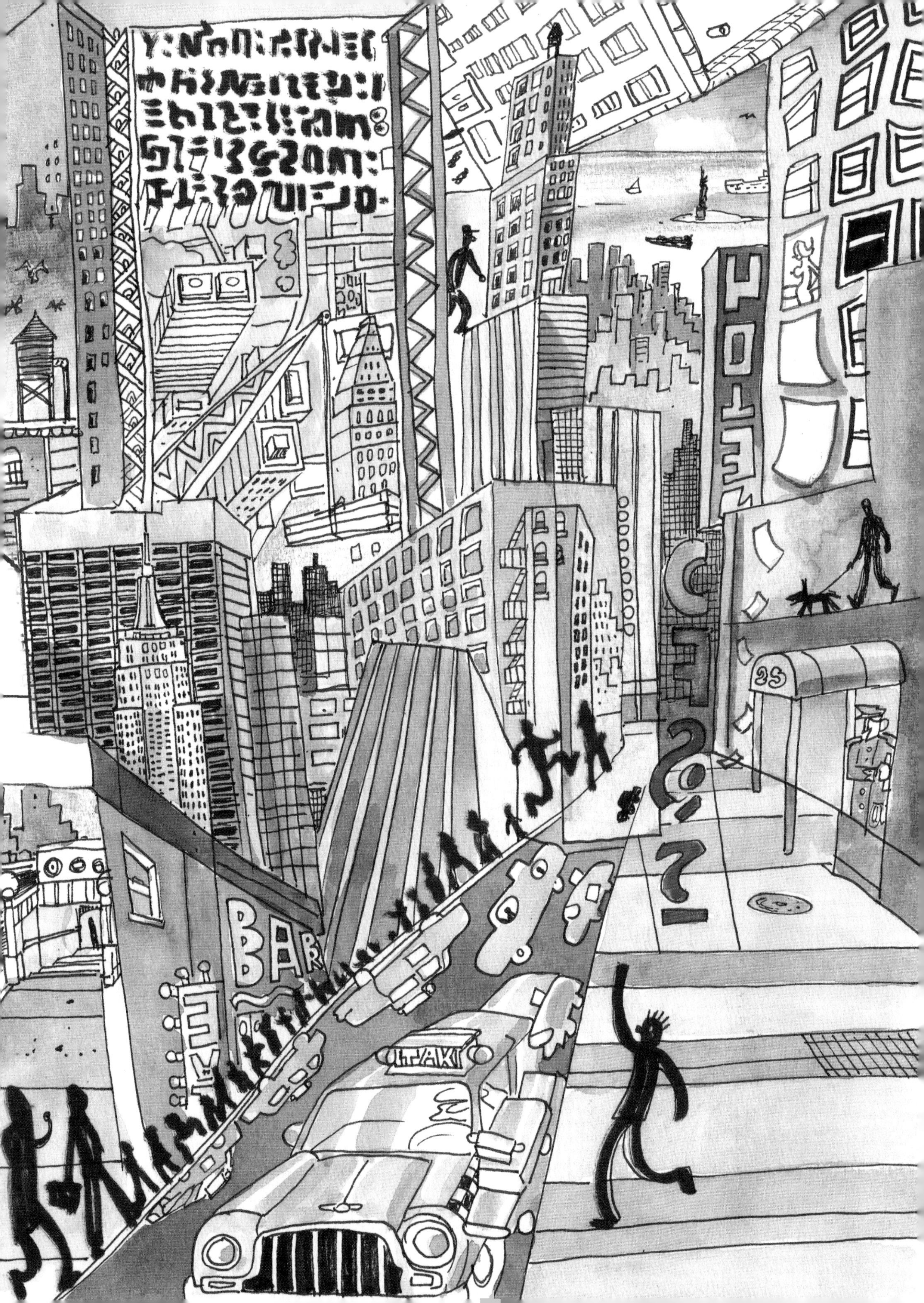
25
BAR
TAXI

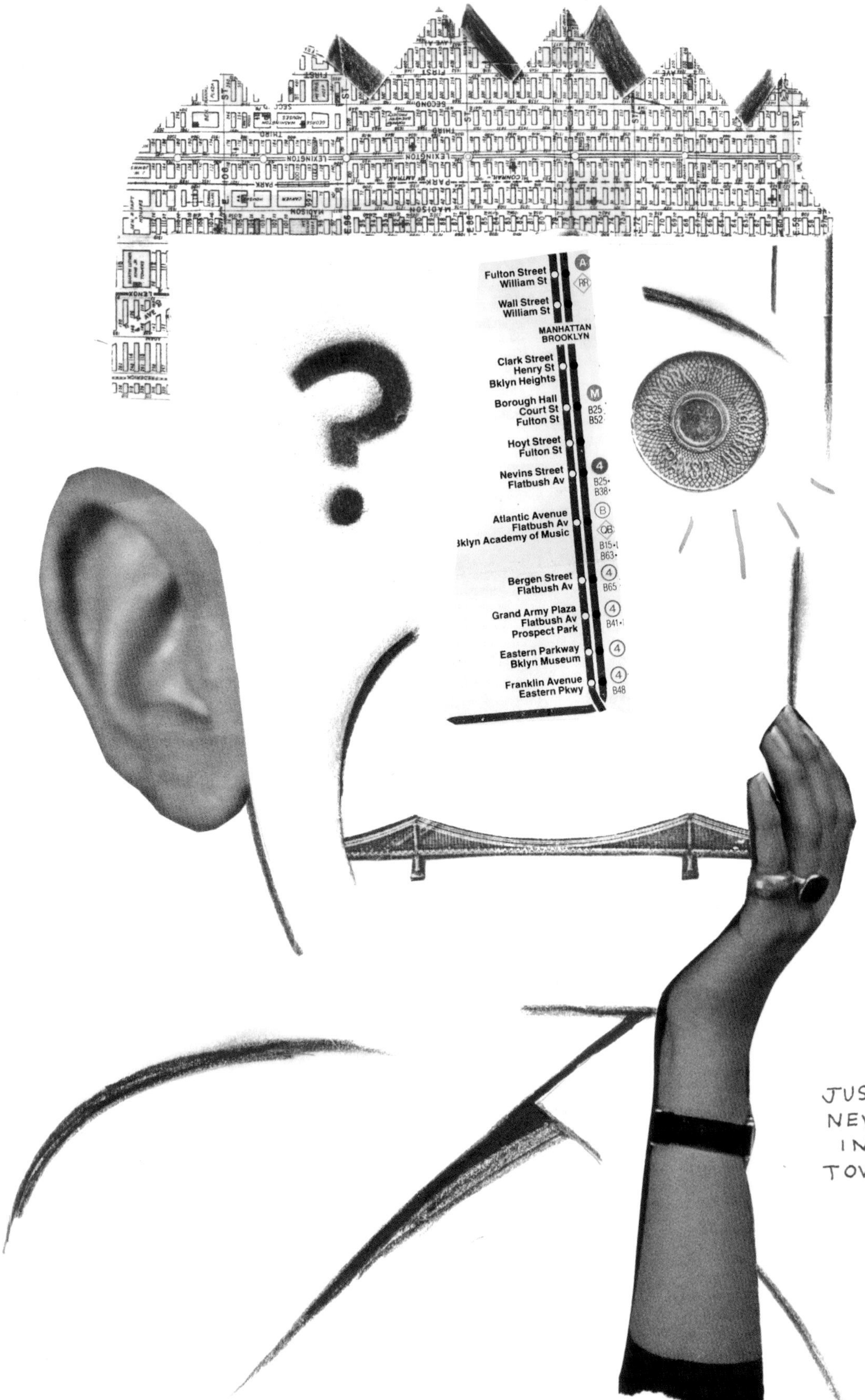
Fulton Street
William St
Wall Street
William St
MANHATTAN
BROOKLYN
Clark Street
Henry St
Bklyn Heights
Borough Hall
Court St
Fulton St
Hoyt Street
Fulton St
Nevins Street
Flatbush Av
Atlantic Avenue
Flatbush Av
Bklyn Academy of Music
Bergen Street
Flatbush Av
Grand Army Plaza
Flatbush Av
Prospect Park
Eastern Parkway
Bklyn Museum
Franklin Avenue
Eastern Pkwy
FIRST
SECOND
THIRD
LEXINGTON
PARK
MADISON
LENOX

JUST
NEW
IN
TOWN...

PREFACE

"Don't you see the rest of the country looks upon New York like we're left-wing, communist, Jewish, homosexual pornographers? I think of us that way sometimes and I live here."

-Woody Allen

I first visited New York in the summer of 1968, when I was nine. My uncle had the role of Lazar Wolf, the butcher, in the Broadway musical *Fiddler on the Roof*. He brought my family in from Cleveland, Ohio to see it and put us up in a hotel steps away from Times Square. Here was my first Broadway play and we got to go backstage to meet all the actors—*thrilling!* From there he took us to Maxwell's Plum, a famous dessert joint (long since demolished). After our ice cream sundaes, as we stood out front sweating in the humid night, my father pointed out an inebriated driver nodding in his car while waiting at a red light. In front of him was an ESSO gas truck, with "Highly Flammable" emblazoned on its back bumper. The light changed and traffic began creeping forward. Only the drunk driver sat stationary, now passed out on his steering wheel. Between gas truck and drunk was a man in a Pontiac trying to exit his parking space. Behind the drunk a line of taxis began beeping angrily. Roused briefly by the blaring horns, the drunk slumped forward and in doing so, slammed his foot on his gas pedal, plowing into the bumper of the Pontiac. His wheels spun and smoked as he pushed the Pontiac sideways, clearing his path towards the gas truck. My father flew into action, sprinted to the drunk, and dragged him out just before he could push past and meet exploding destiny.

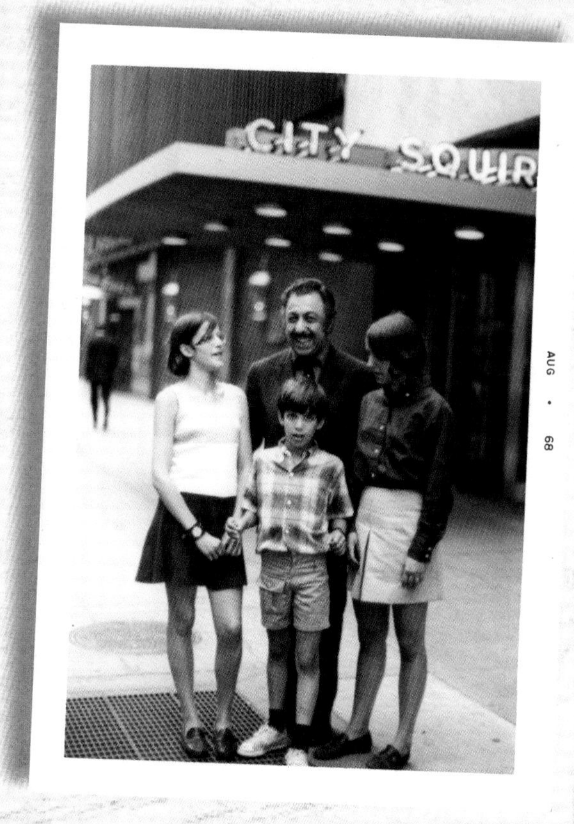

CITY SQUIR
AUG • 68

WITH MY UNCLE BORIS
AND SISTERS, KATE AND HOLLY, IN 1968

Clearly, New York was a dangerous place where terrible things could happen, but also a place that could turn ordinary people into superheroes. On that sweltering August night, amid the roaring swirl of Manhattan's manic energy, I decided I wanted to move to this city as soon as possible.

It took ten years, but on June 22nd, 1977, I stepped off a train at Grand Central ready to become a New York animator. I had visited during spring break and gone door to door to animation houses offering to do anything art-related. This would be my entry point, which would quickly lead to me becoming a star cartoonist-animator. The plan wasn't exactly formed, but amazingly I got a job offer working at Zander Studios that summer on a feature-length Raggedy Ann movie.

In the summer of 1977, New York City was bankrupt. Times Square was run-down and dangerous at night, subways were decrepit, with floor-to-ceiling graffiti and no air-conditioned cars in the underground roast. A garbage strike left mountains of uncollected trash and evil-looking rats scurrying underfoot. A serial killer, Son of Sam, terrorized the city and when a blackout hit in July, looters tore up the town.

I was in heaven.

When I finally got past the secretary at Zander's to see the studio boss, he looked at me with a blank expression. The job offer had vanished, since *Raggedy Ann* was completed and the animation industry was in a downward turn. He shook my hand and told me to call him in six weeks. I called him every six weeks until he stopped answering his phone.

Though I never did become an animator, New York opened the door to the world of illustration and cartooning. It wasn't by accident that the earliest comic strip creators and illustrators migrated to New York and created thriving industries. This was where the work was, but just as important, this was where their inspiration bloomed, and so has mine.

New York has changed tremendously since I arrived, something every-one who's ever lived here could be quoted as saying—no matter when they came. This city *is* change. That's its glory—it's a perpetually unfinished canvas, offering up possibility to each successive wave of artists.

Drawn to New York is a portrait of this city I love, both its darkness and light. Instead of a chronological narrative, I've juxtaposed the city's surface glitter with its darker underbelly—homeless people in Times Square and skaters in Central Park, the devastation of 9/11 and the bustle of daily life. This book is a reflection of thirty-four years on twelve miles of island with eight million people in a city whose story is ever being written.

-Peter Kuper
New York, NY
January, 2013

MASKS OF THE URBAN JUNGLE

Car alarm at 3 A.M.

Parking space hunt

Crazy taxi driver

The city *NEVER* sleeps

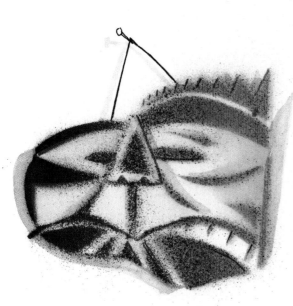

Bad street-cart
hot dog

Unidentified odor

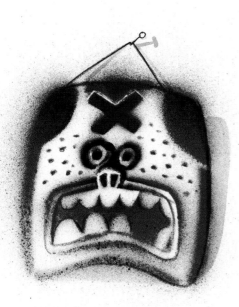

Flu season on the
Subway

Summer in
Central Park

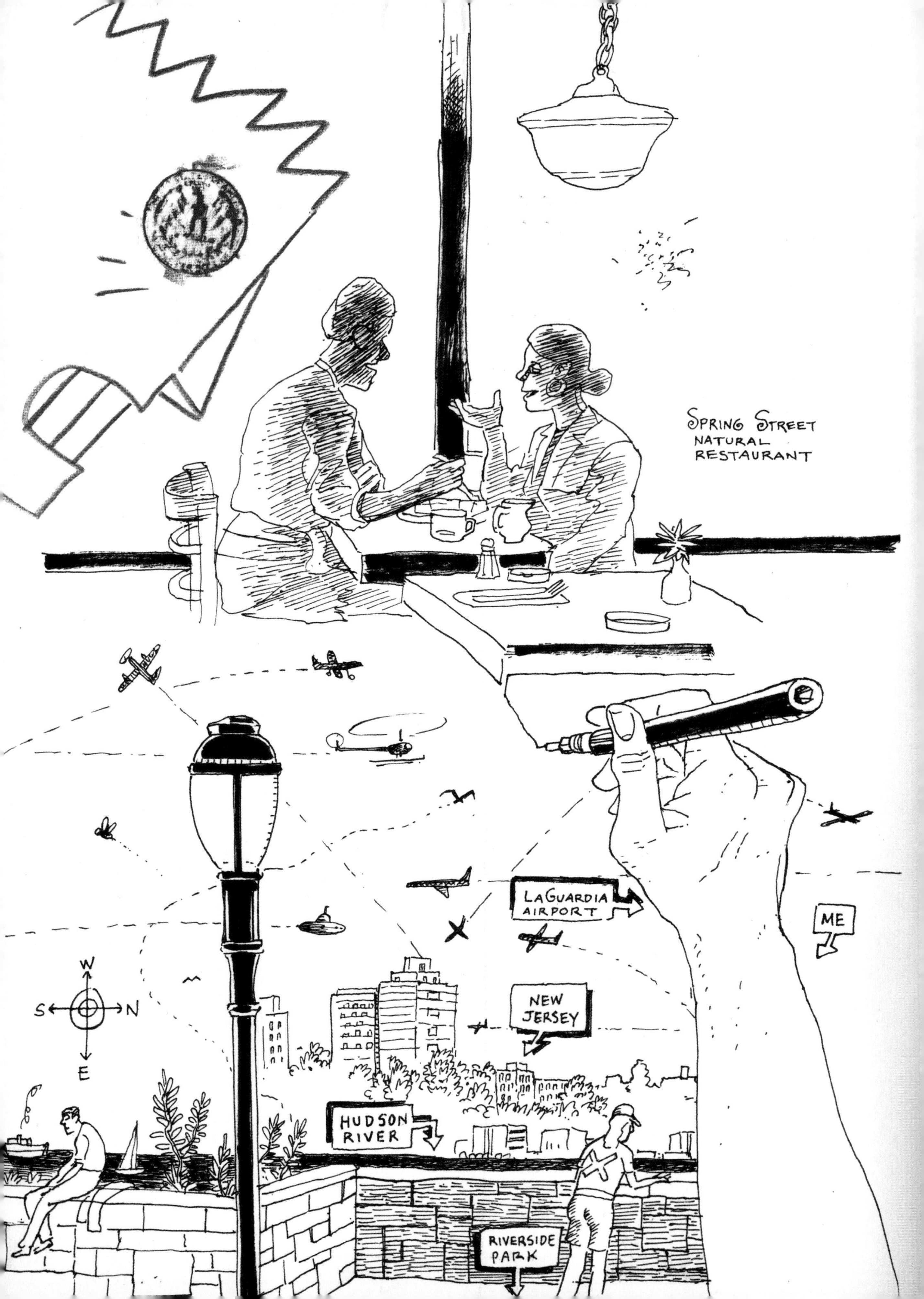
SPRING STREET
NATURAL
RESTAURANT
LaGUARDIA
AIRPORT
ME
W
S
N
E
NEW
JERSEY
HUDSON
RIVER
RIVERSIDE
PARK

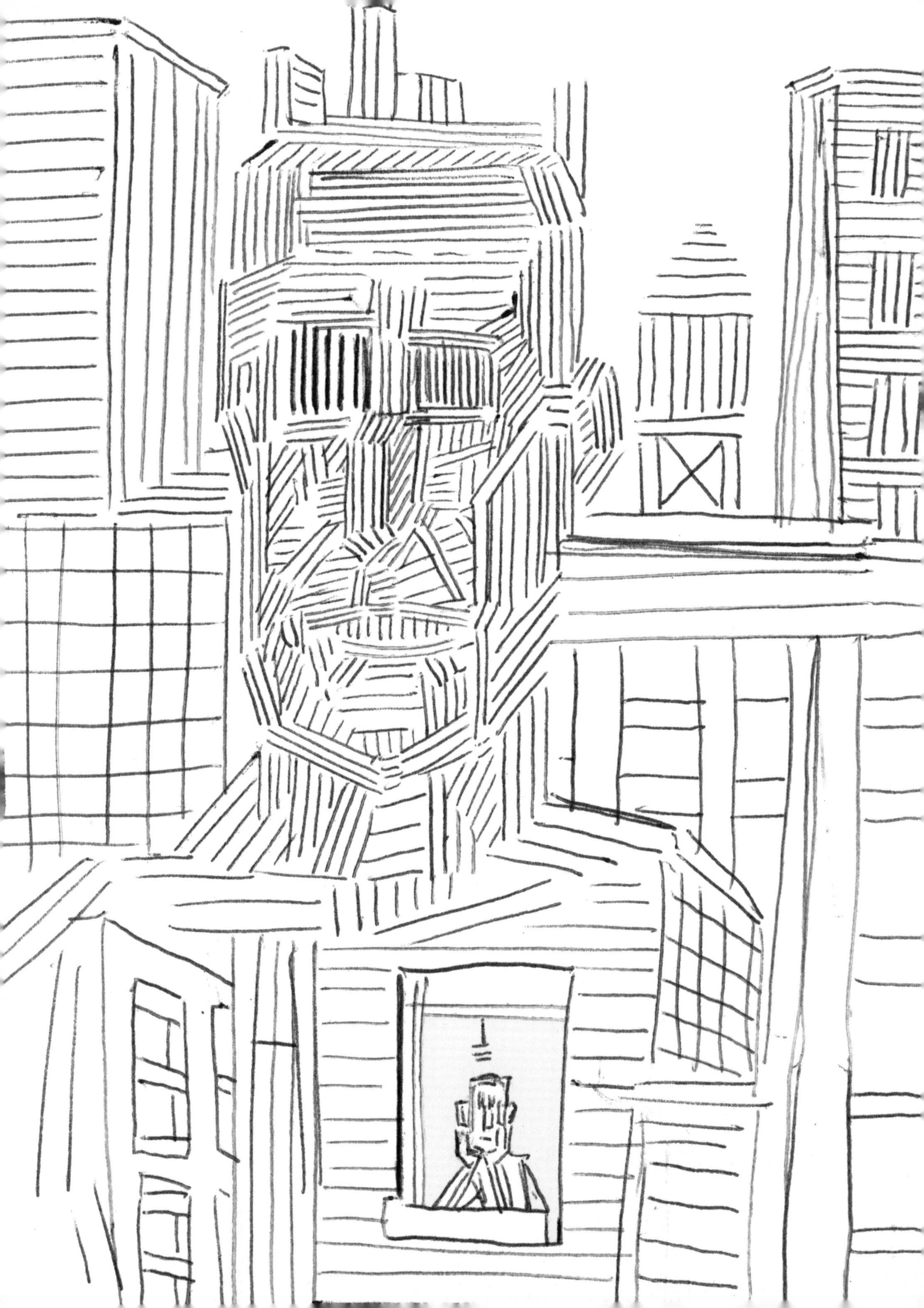

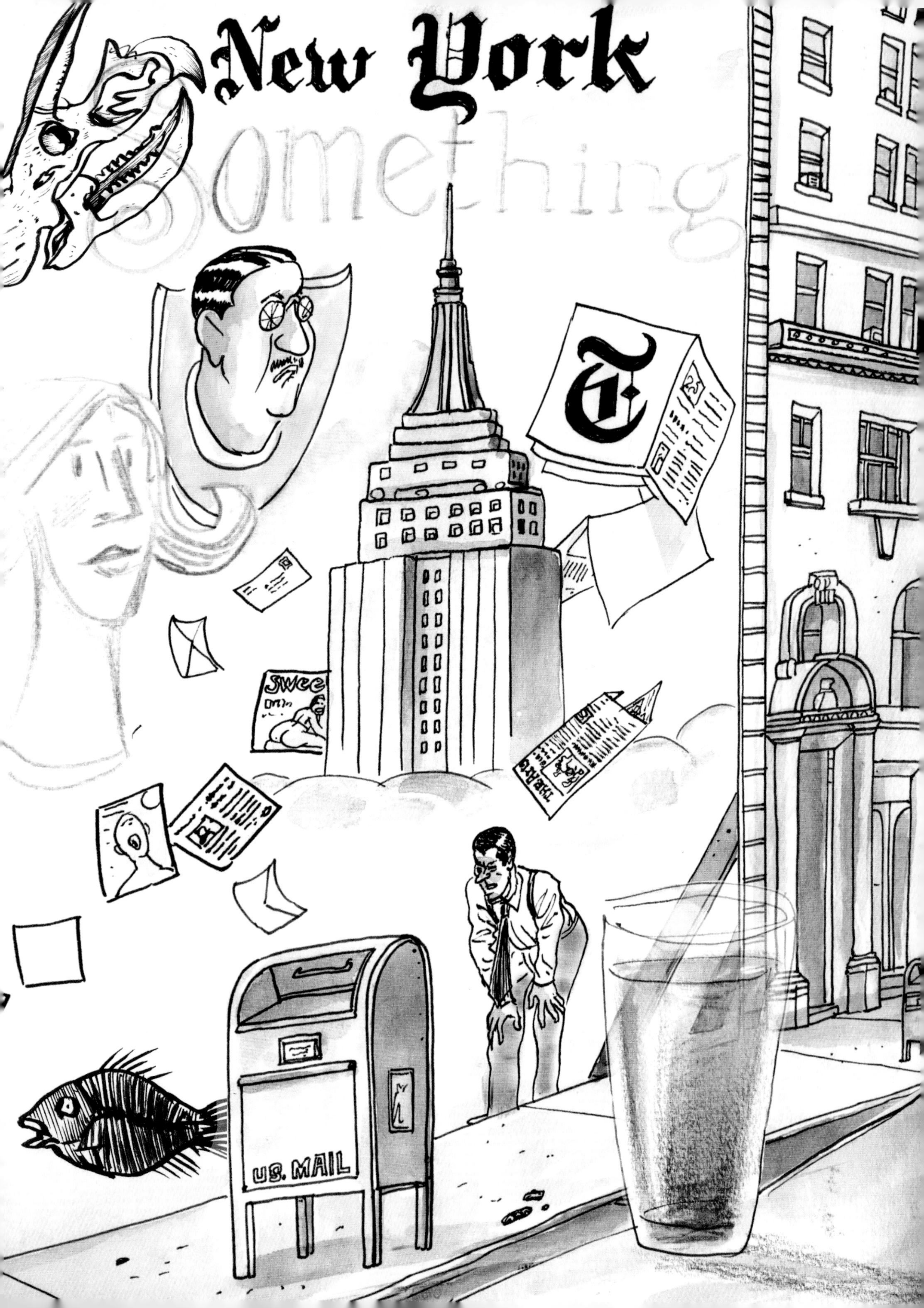
New York
Something
SWEE
U.S. MAIL

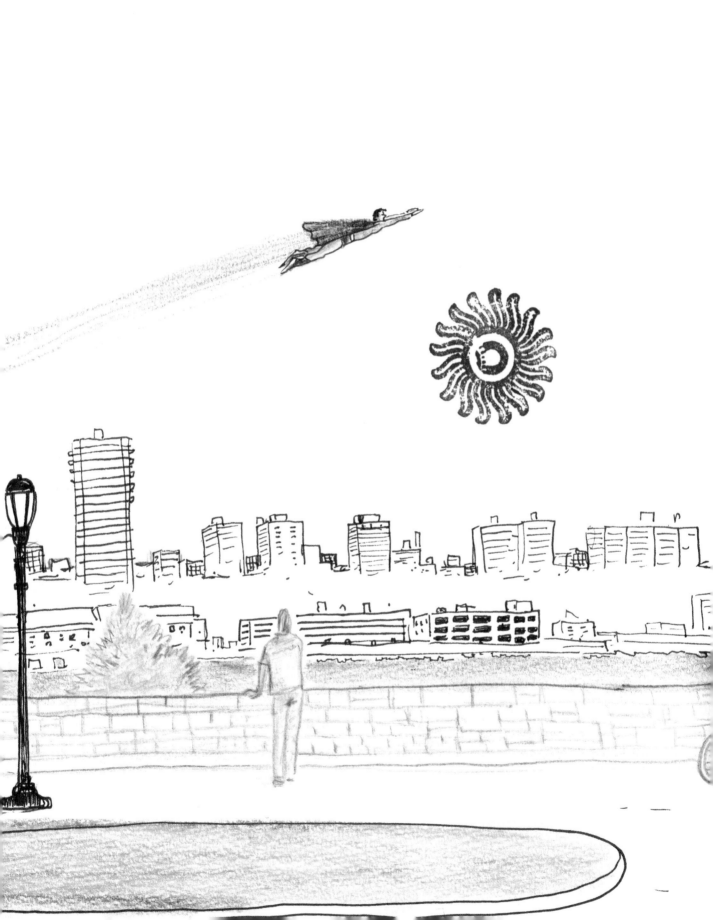

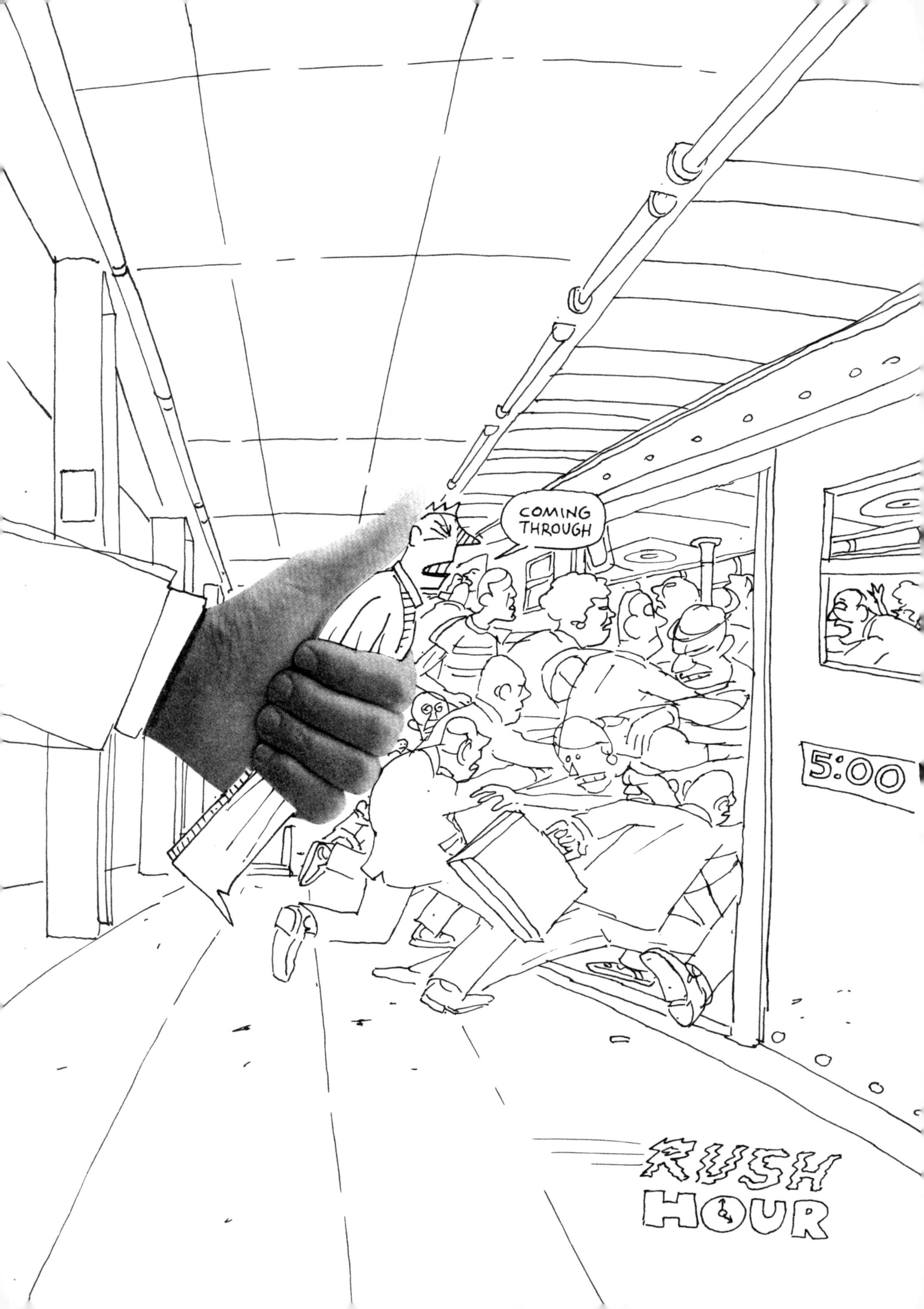
COMING THROUGH
5:00
RUSH HOUR

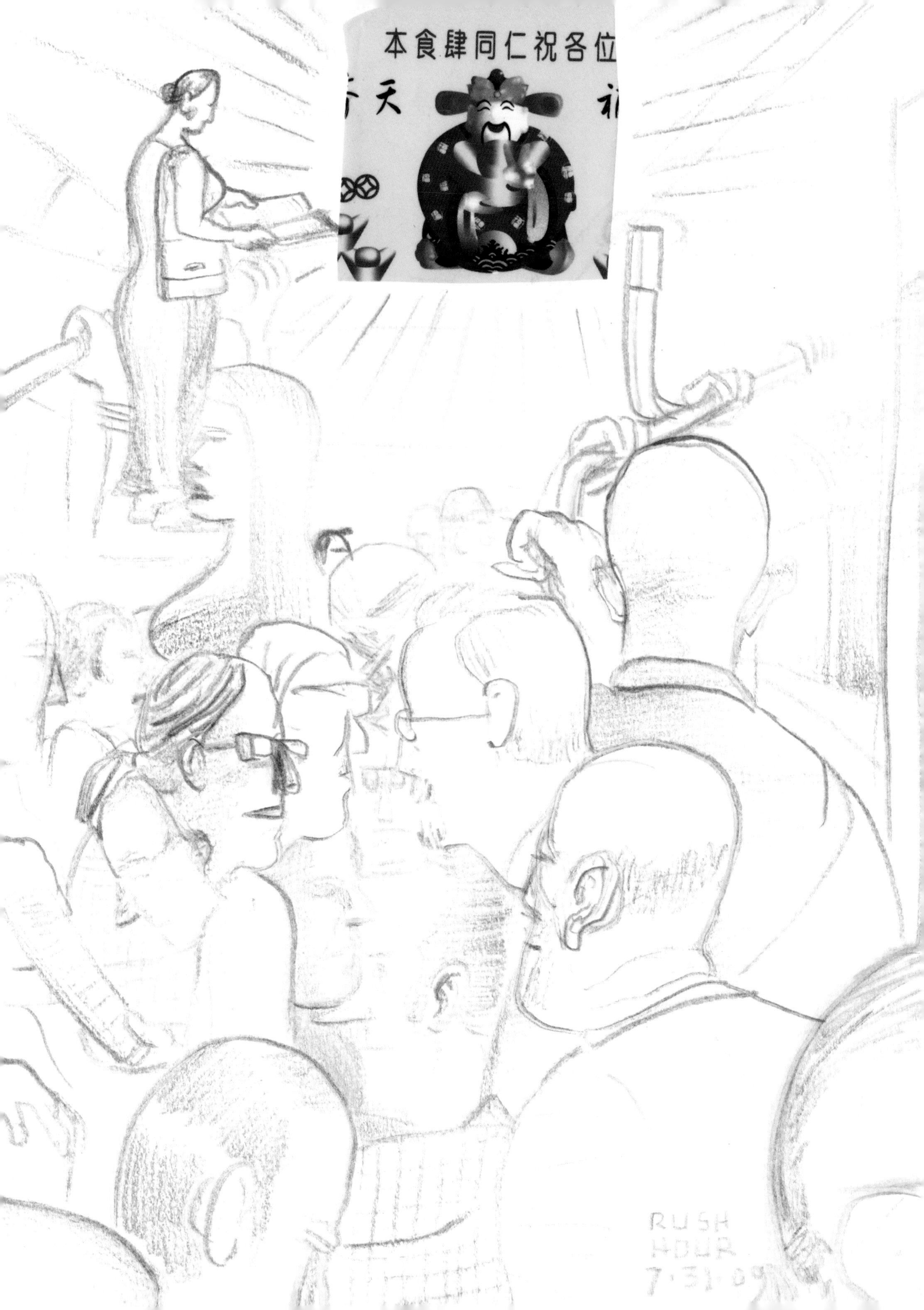
本食肆同仁祝各位
天
RUSH
HOUR
7·31·09

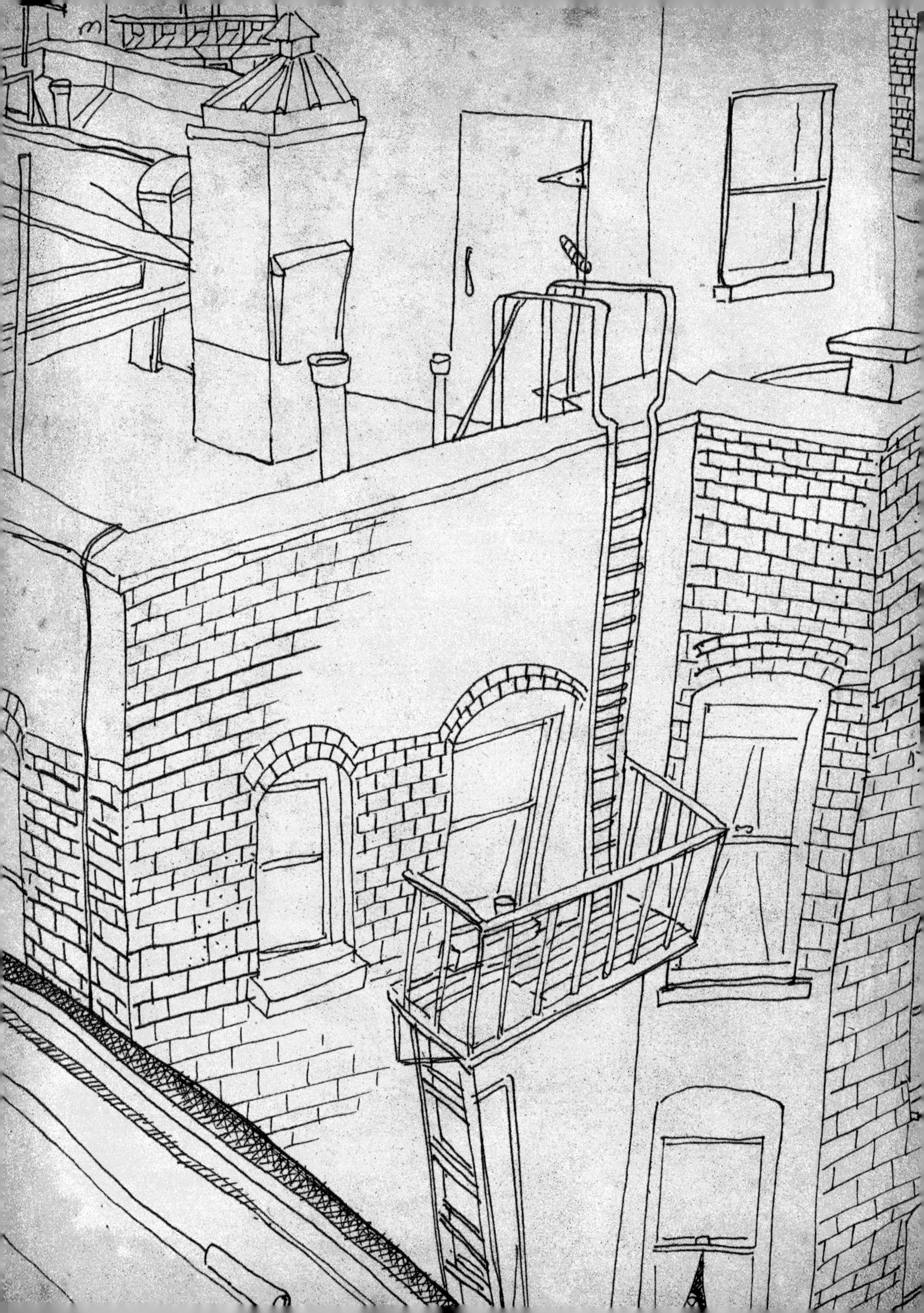

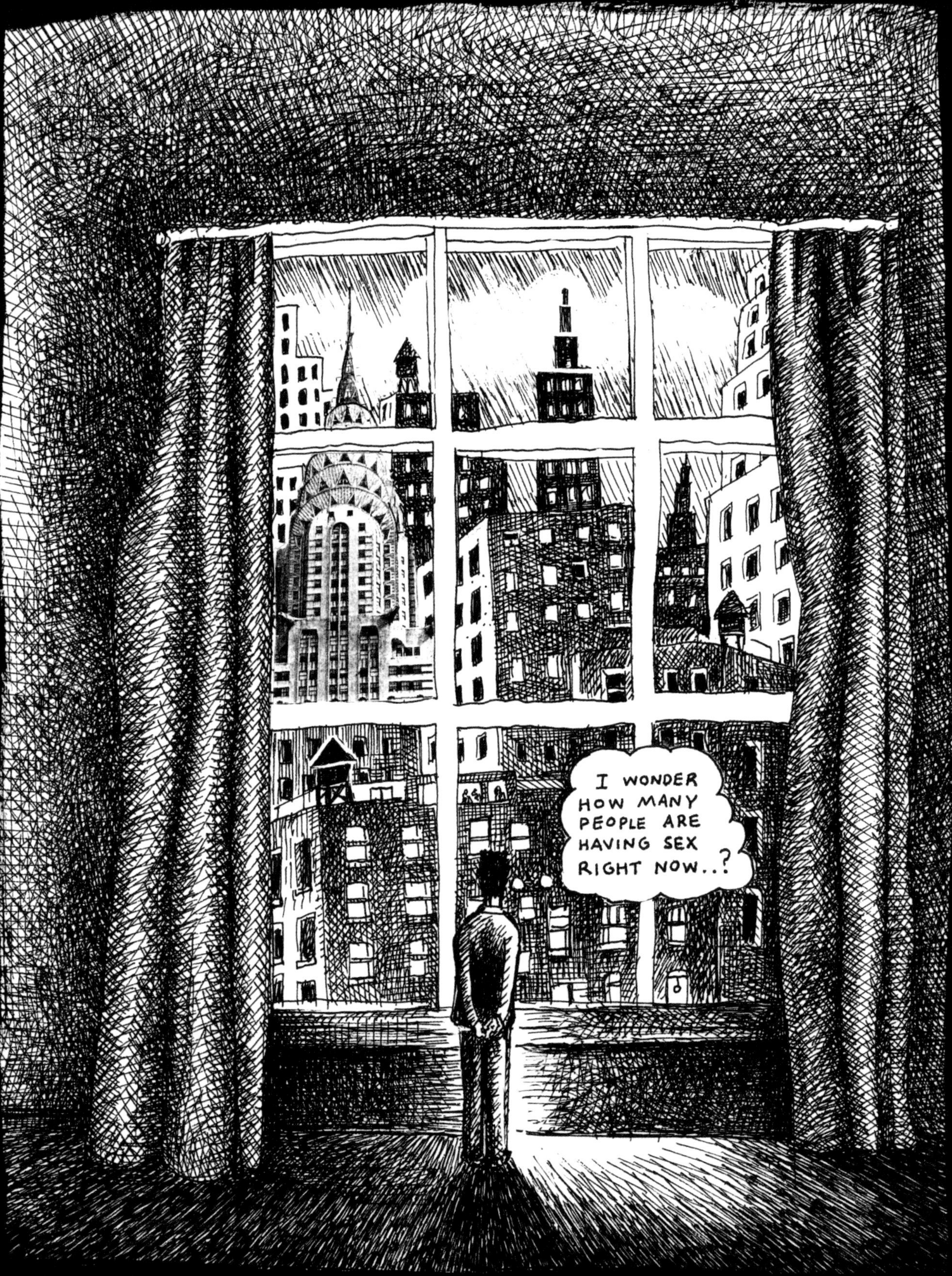
I WONDER HOW MANY PEOPLE ARE HAVING SEX RIGHT NOW..?

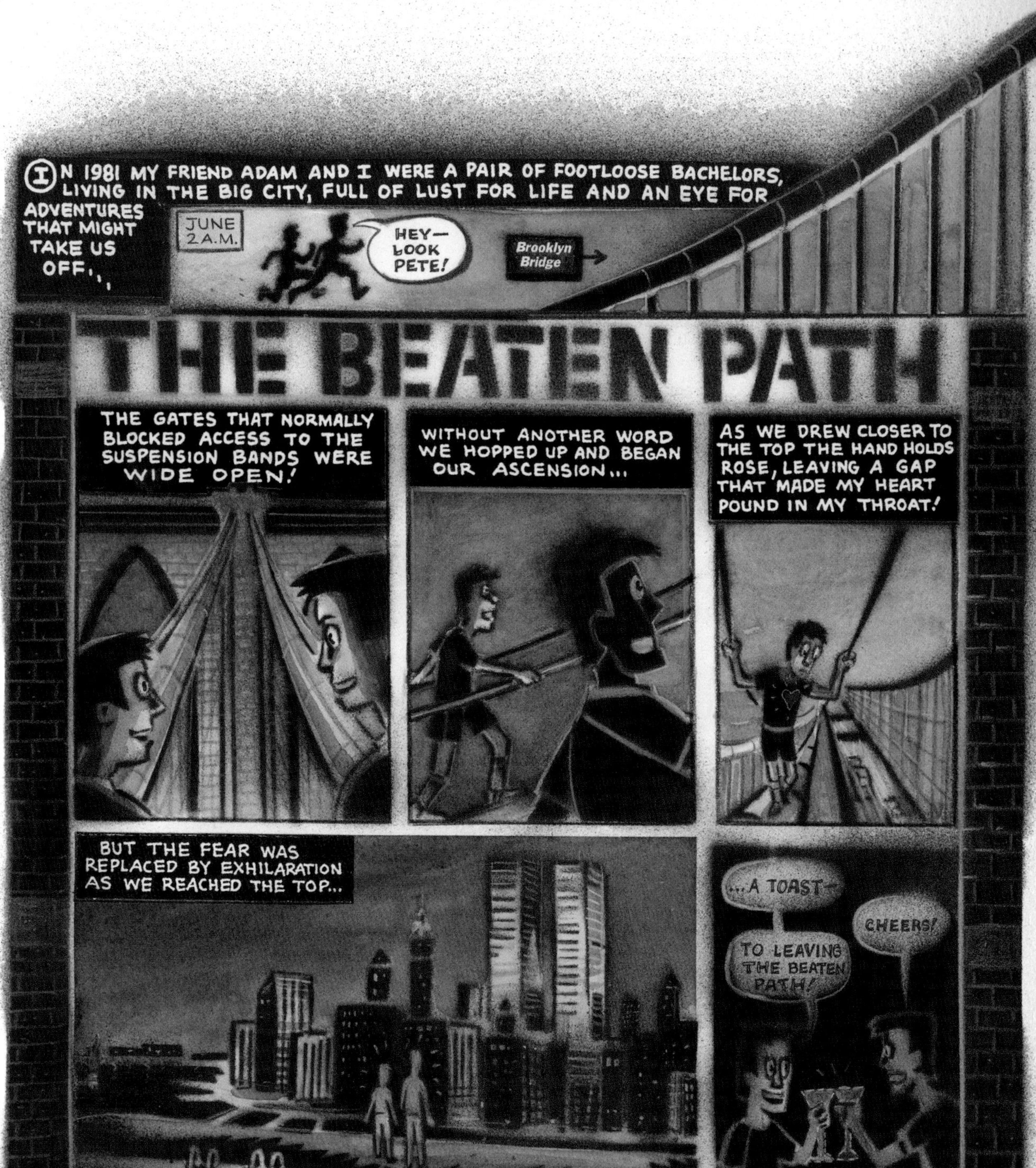
In 1981 my friend Adam and I were a pair of footloose bachelors, living in the big city, full of lust for life and an eye for adventures that might take us off...
JUNE 2 A.M.
HEY— LOOK PETE!
Brooklyn Bridge
THE BEATEN PATH
THE GATES THAT NORMALLY BLOCKED ACCESS TO THE SUSPENSION BANDS WERE WIDE OPEN!
WITHOUT ANOTHER WORD WE HOPPED UP AND BEGAN OUR ASCENSION...
AS WE DREW CLOSER TO THE TOP THE HAND HOLDS ROSE, LEAVING A GAP THAT MADE MY HEART POUND IN MY THROAT!
BUT THE FEAR WAS REPLACED BY EXHILARATION AS WE REACHED THE TOP...
...A TOAST—
TO LEAVING THE BEATEN PATH!
CHEERS!
INVISIBLE CHAMPAGNE
© 1995
PETER KUPER

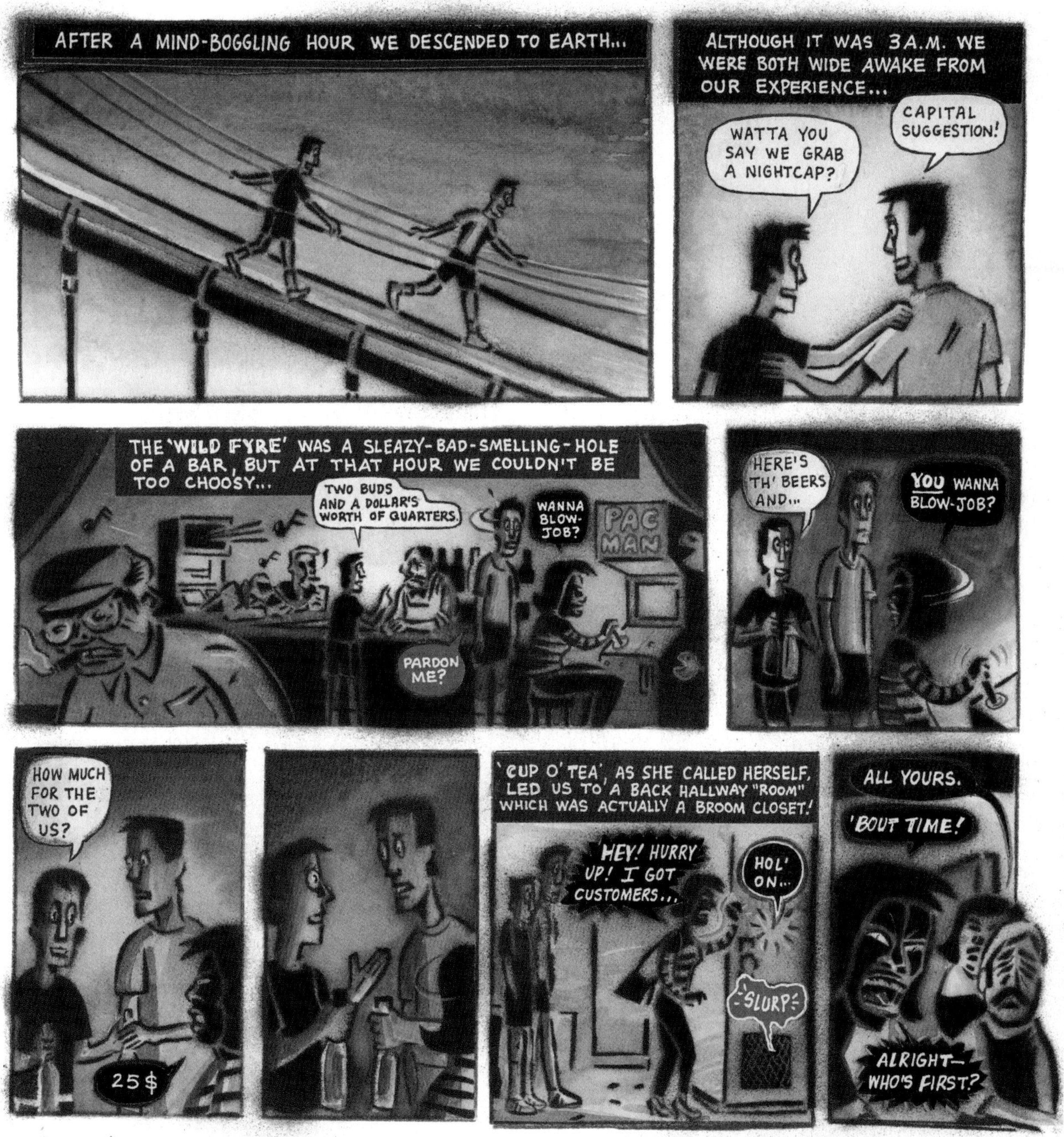
AFTER A MIND-BOGGLING HOUR WE DESCENDED TO EARTH...
ALTHOUGH IT WAS 3 A.M. WE WERE BOTH WIDE AWAKE FROM OUR EXPERIENCE...
WATTA YOU SAY WE GRAB A NIGHTCAP?
CAPITAL SUGGESTION!
THE 'WILD FYRE' WAS A SLEAZY-BAD-SMELLING-HOLE OF A BAR, BUT AT THAT HOUR WE COULDN'T BE TOO CHOOSY...
TWO BUDS AND A DOLLAR'S WORTH OF QUARTERS.
WANNA BLOW-JOB?
PAC MAN
PARDON ME?
HERE'S TH' BEERS AND...
YOU WANNA BLOW-JOB?
HOW MUCH FOR THE TWO OF US?
25 $
'CUP O' TEA', AS SHE CALLED HERSELF, LED US TO A BACK HALLWAY "ROOM" WHICH WAS ACTUALLY A BROOM CLOSET!
HEY! HURRY UP! I GOT CUSTOMERS...
HOL' ON...
SLURP
ALL YOURS.
'BOUT TIME!
ALRIGHT— WHO'S FIRST?

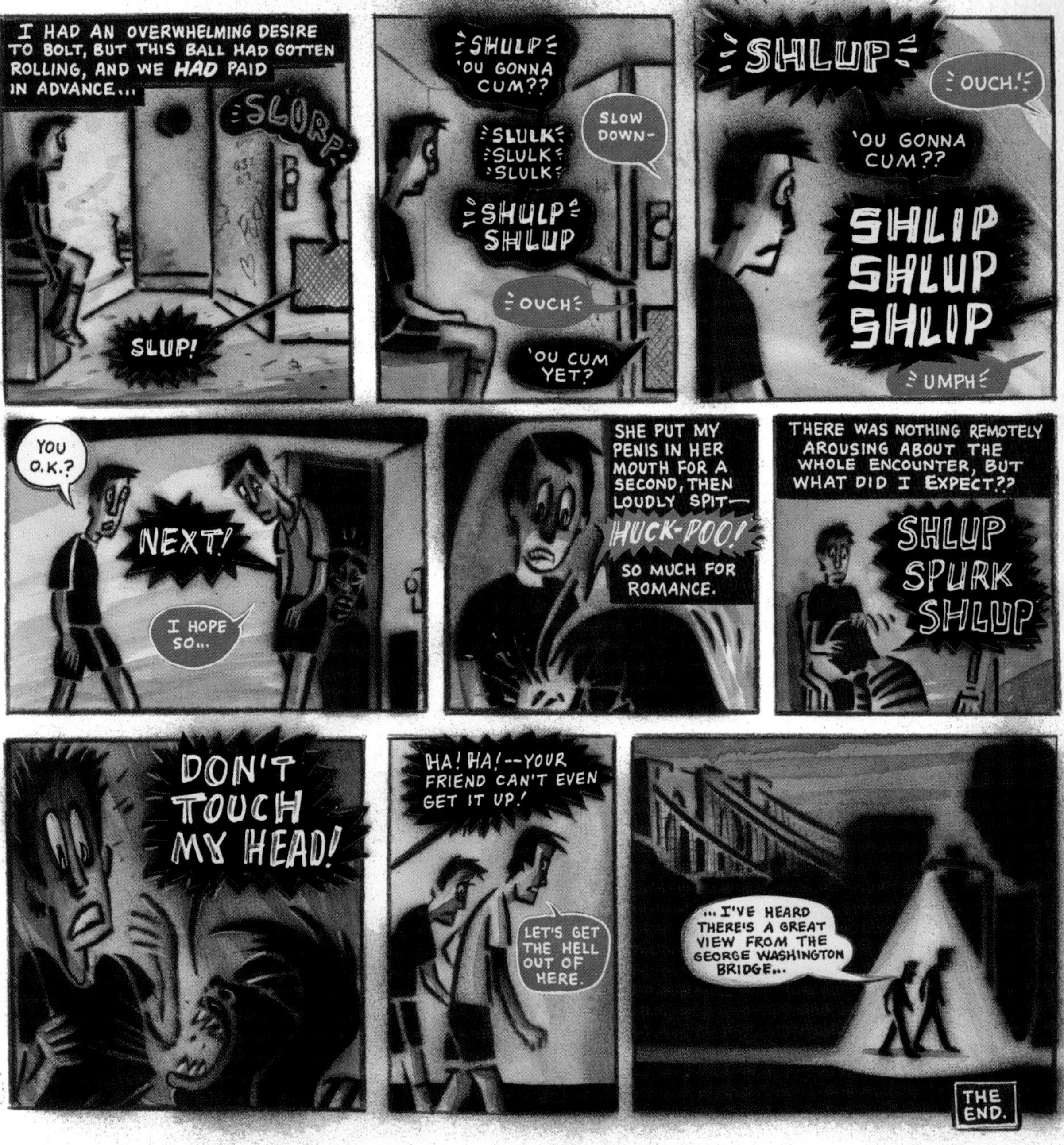
I HAD AN OVERWHELMING DESIRE TO BOLT, BUT THIS BALL HAD GOTTEN ROLLING, AND WE HAD PAID IN ADVANCE...
SLORP
SLUP!
SHULP
'OU GONNA CUM??
SLULK SLULK SLULK
SLOW DOWN-
SHULP SHLUP
OUCH
'OU CUM YET?
SHLUP
OUCH!
'OU GONNA CUM??
SHLIP SHLUP SHLIP
UMPH
YOU O.K.?
NEXT!
I HOPE SO...
SHE PUT MY PENIS IN HER MOUTH FOR A SECOND, THEN LOUDLY SPIT—
HUCK-POO!
SO MUCH FOR ROMANCE.
THERE WAS NOTHING REMOTELY AROUSING ABOUT THE WHOLE ENCOUNTER, BUT WHAT DID I EXPECT??
SHLUP SPURK SHLUP
DON'T TOUCH MY HEAD!
HA! HA!--YOUR FRIEND CAN'T EVEN GET IT UP!
LET'S GET THE HELL OUT OF HERE.
...I'VE HEARD THERE'S A GREAT VIEW FROM THE GEORGE WASHINGTON BRIDGE...
THE END.

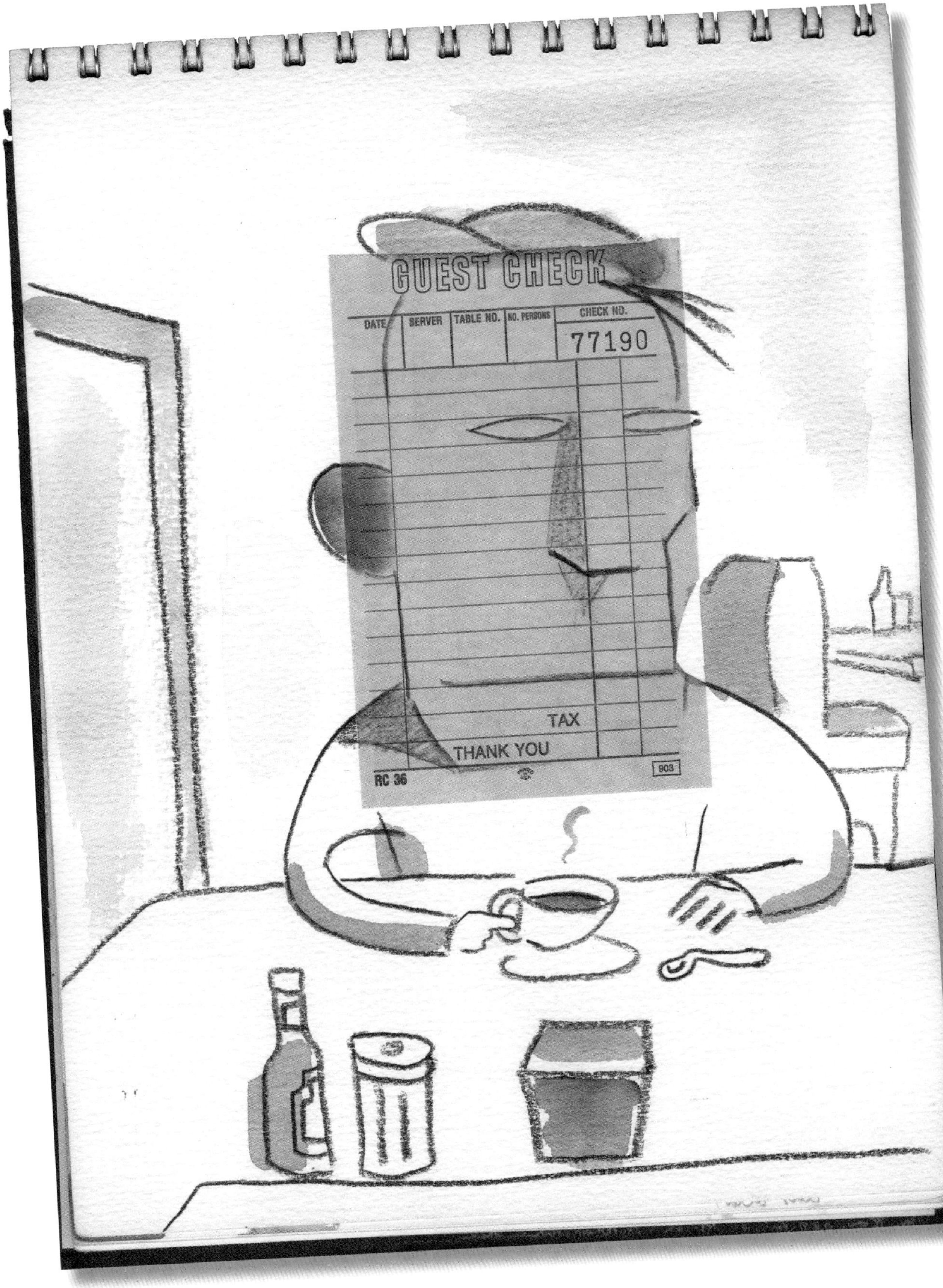
GUEST CHECK
DATE
SERVER
TABLE NO.
NO. PERSONS
CHECK NO.
77190
TAX
THANK YOU
RC 36
903

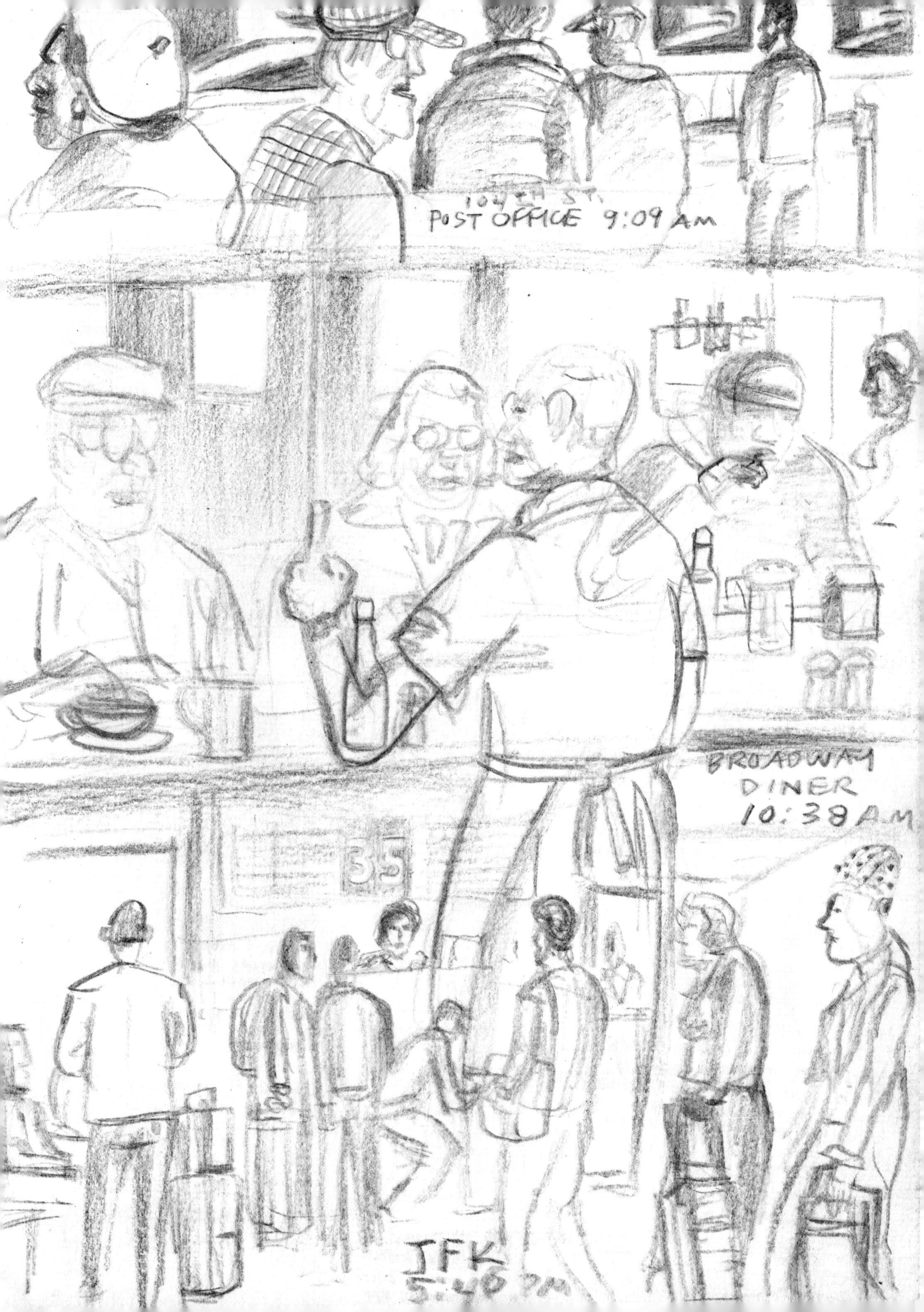
104TH ST.
POST OFFICE 9:09 AM
BROADWAY
DINER
10:38AM
35
JFK
5:40 PM

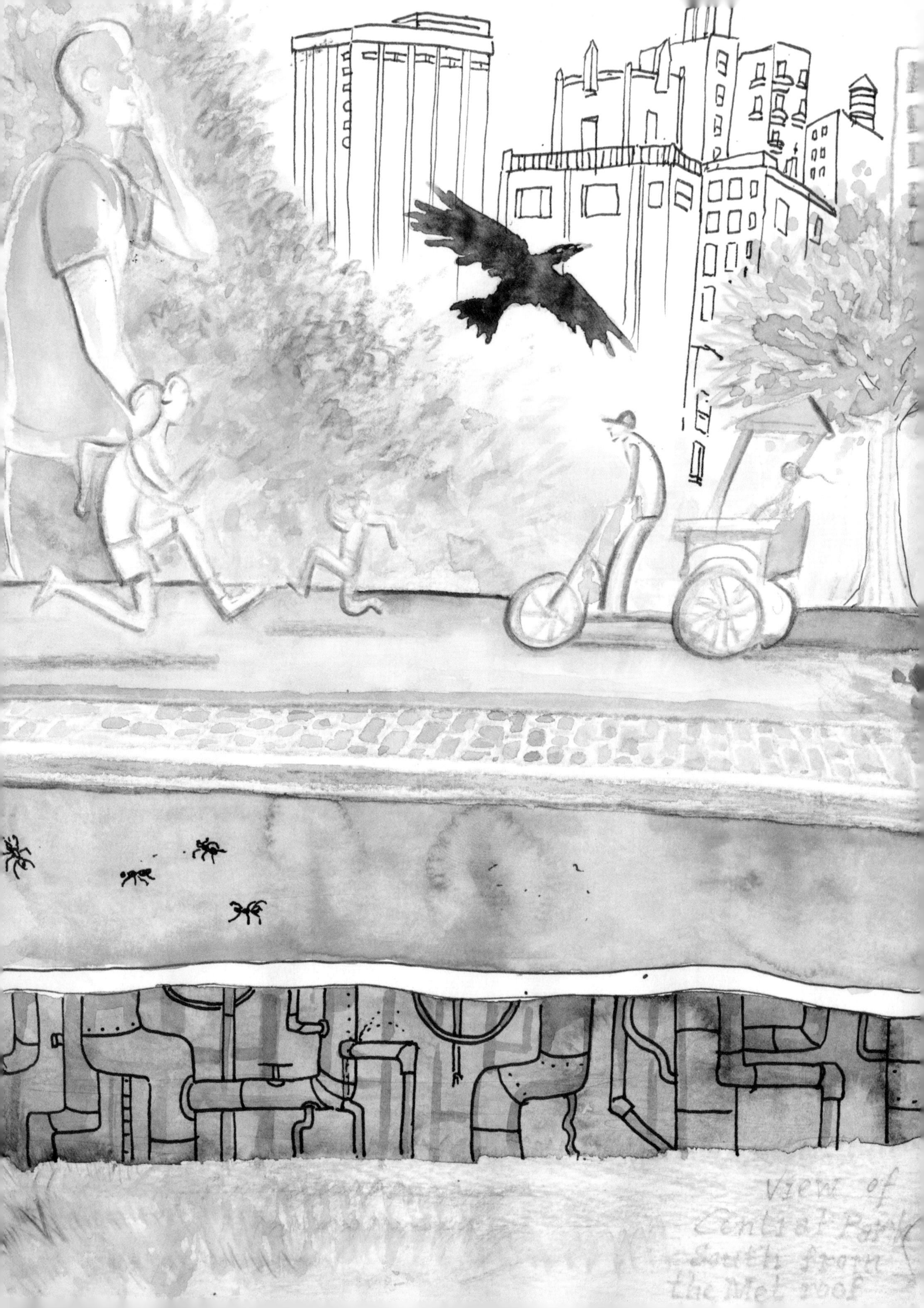
View of
Central Park
South from
the Met roof

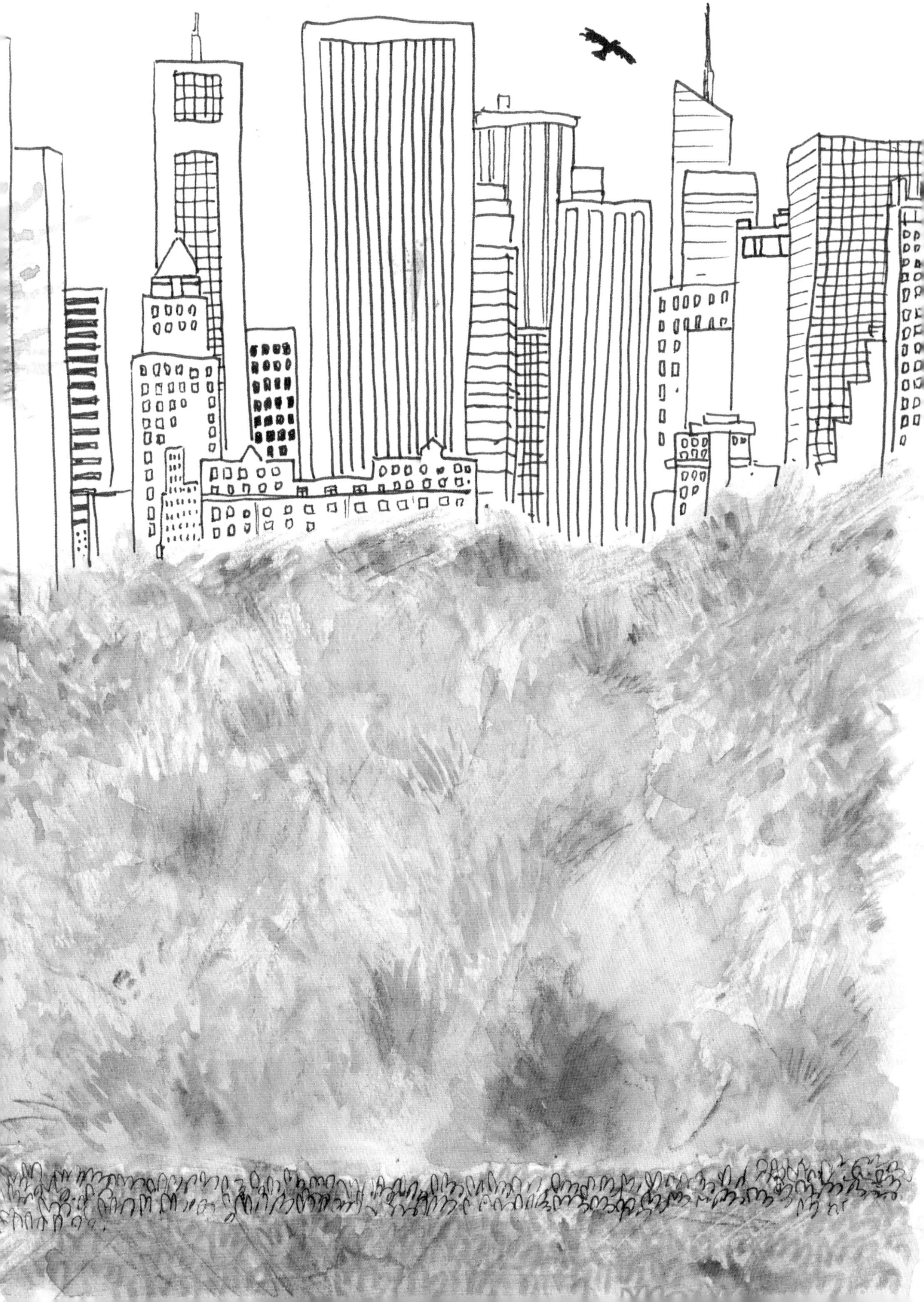

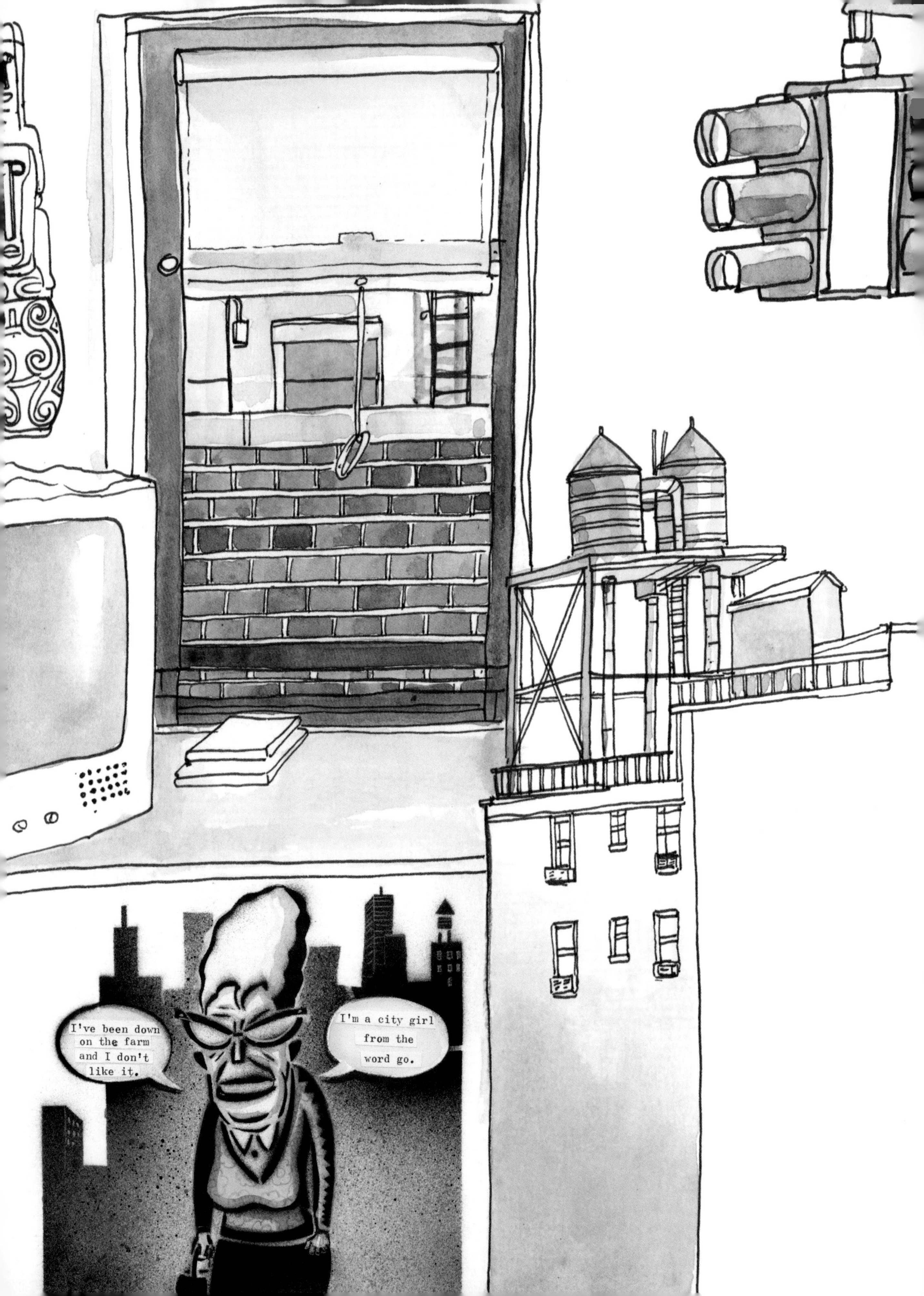
I've been down on the farm and I don't like it.
I'm a city girl from the word go.

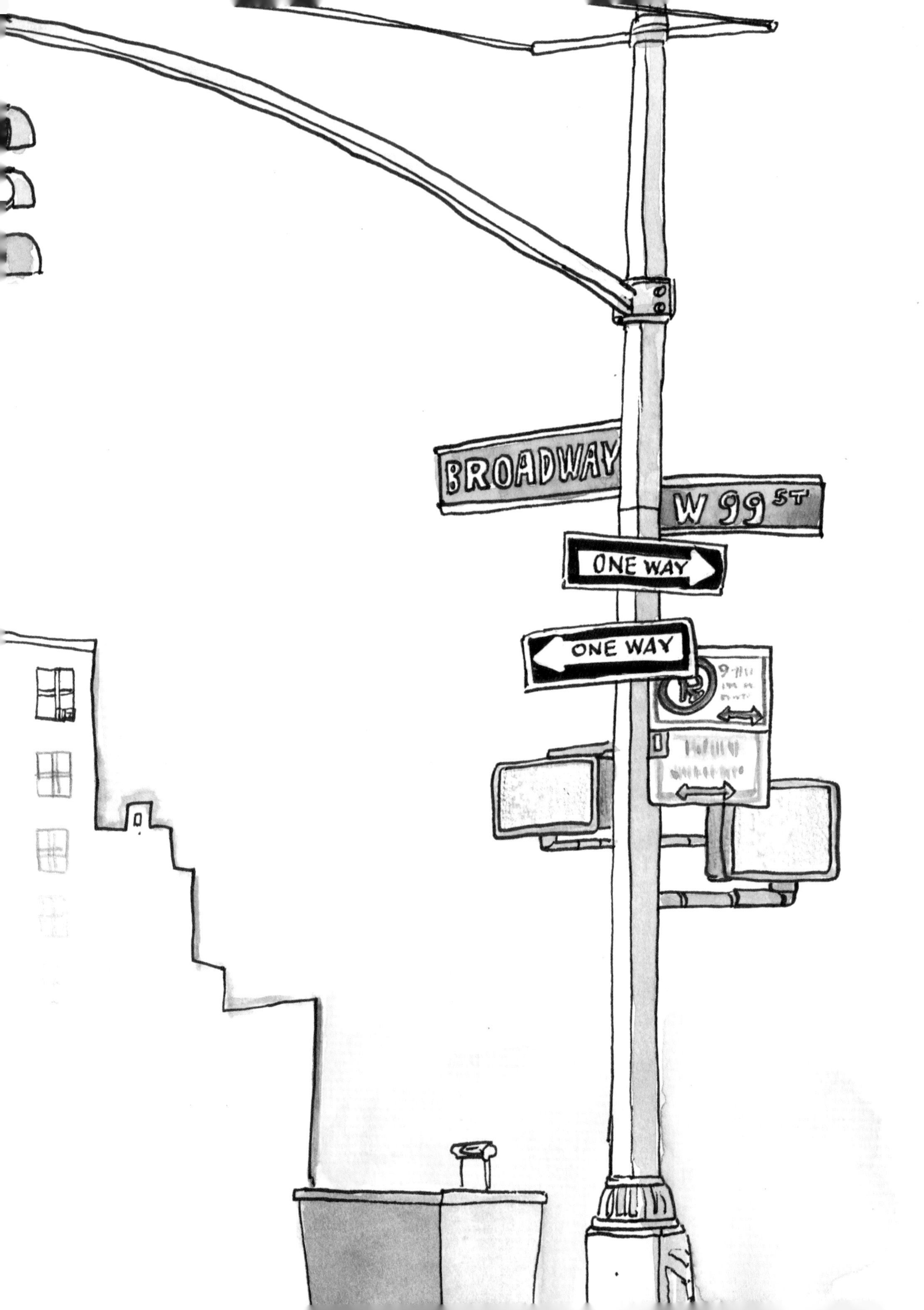
BROADWAY
W 99 ST
ONE WAY
ONE WAY

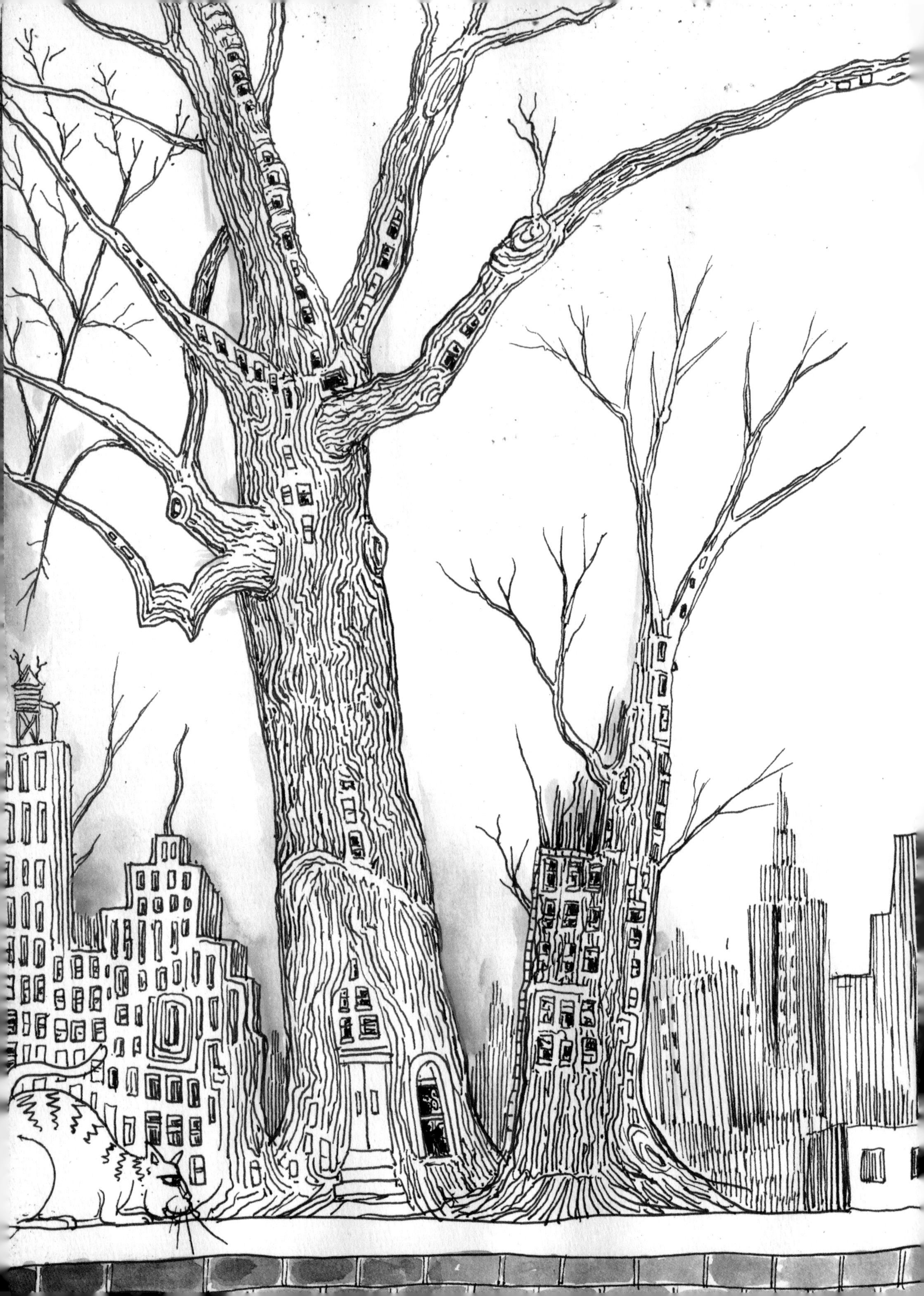

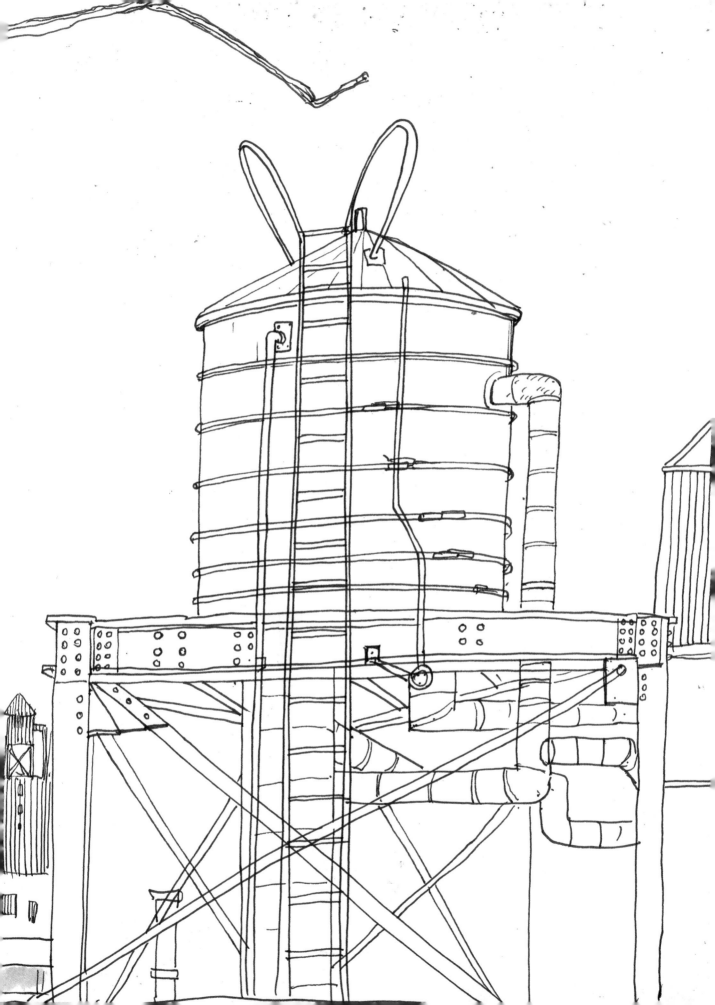

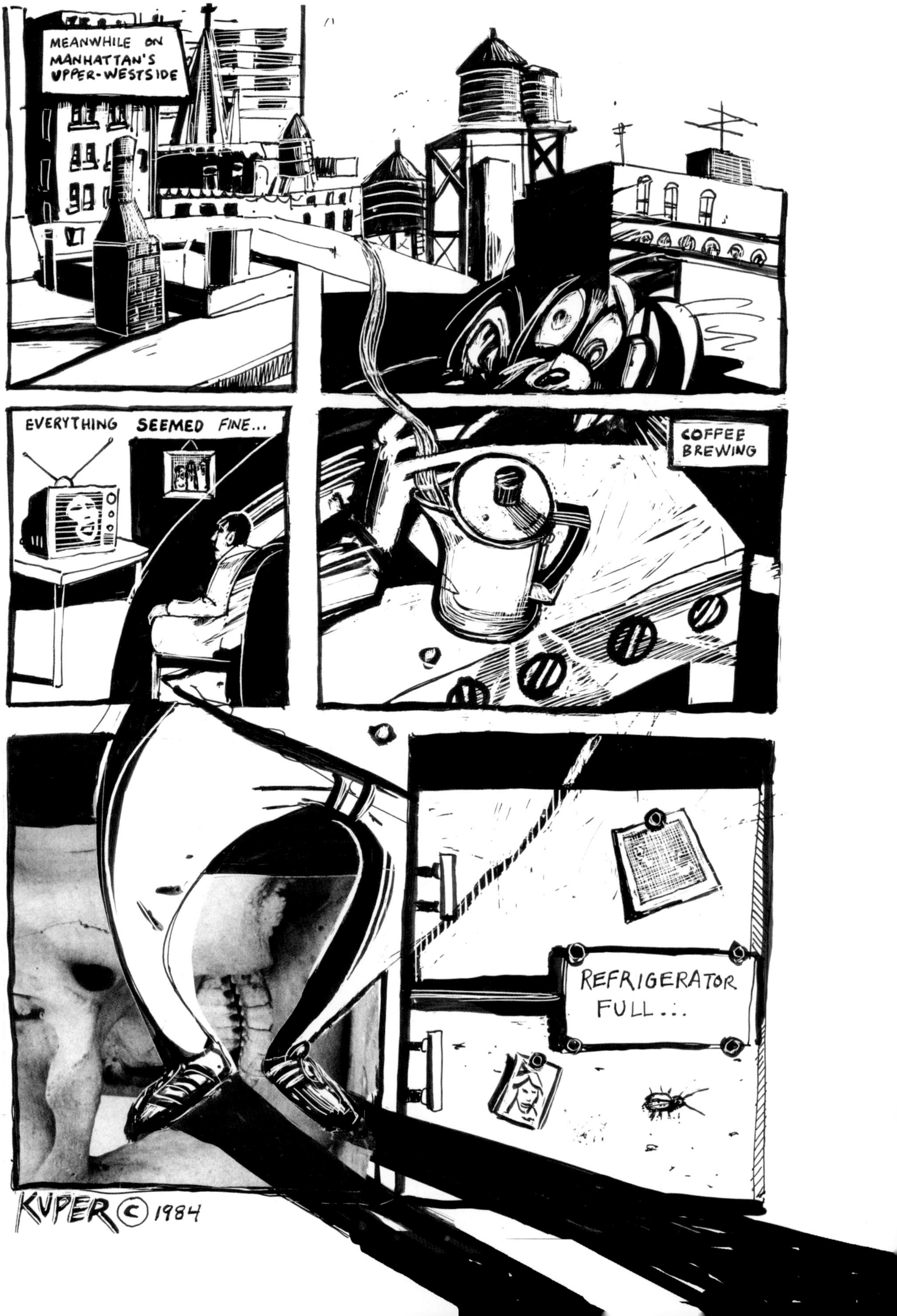
MEANWHILE ON MANHATTAN'S UPPER-WESTSIDE
EVERYTHING SEEMED FINE...
COFFEE BREWING
REFRIGERATOR FULL...
KUPER © 1984

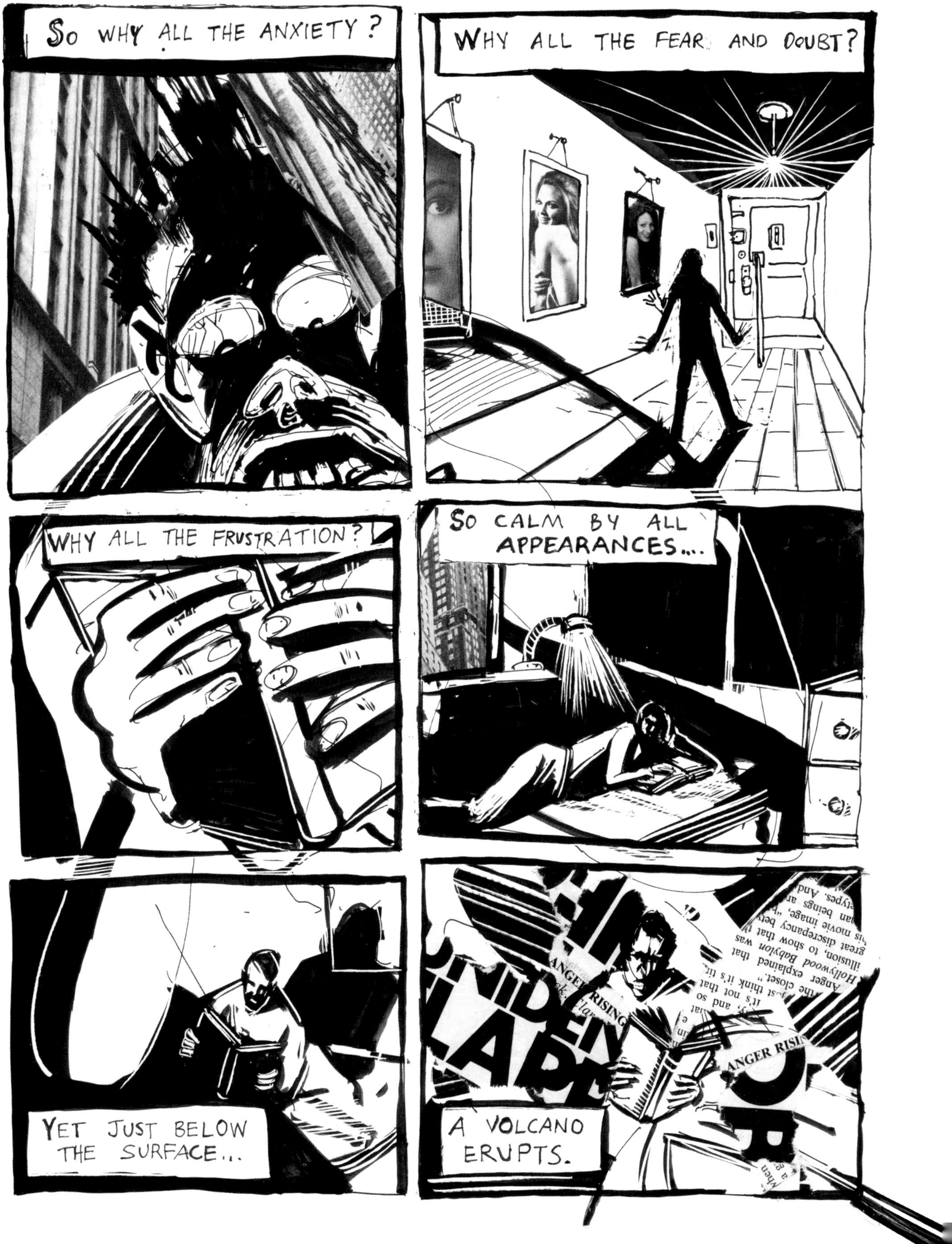
So why all the anxiety?
Why all the fear and doubt?
Why all the frustration?
So calm by all appearances....
Yet just below the surface...
ANGER RISING
A volcano erupts.

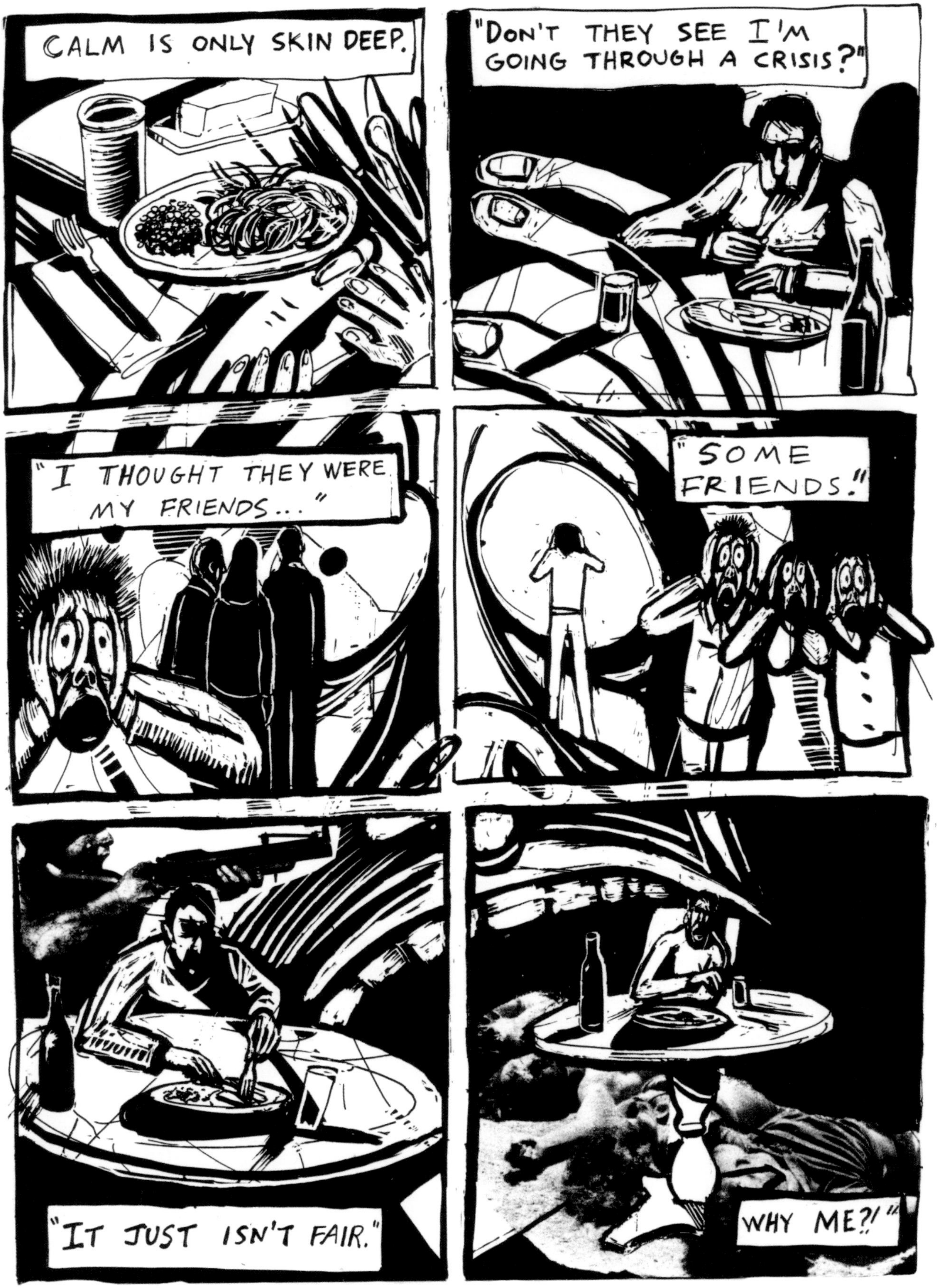
CALM IS ONLY SKIN DEEP.
"DON'T THEY SEE I'M GOING THROUGH A CRISIS?"
"I THOUGHT THEY WERE MY FRIENDS..."
"SOME FRIENDS!"
"IT JUST ISN'T FAIR."
WHY ME?!"

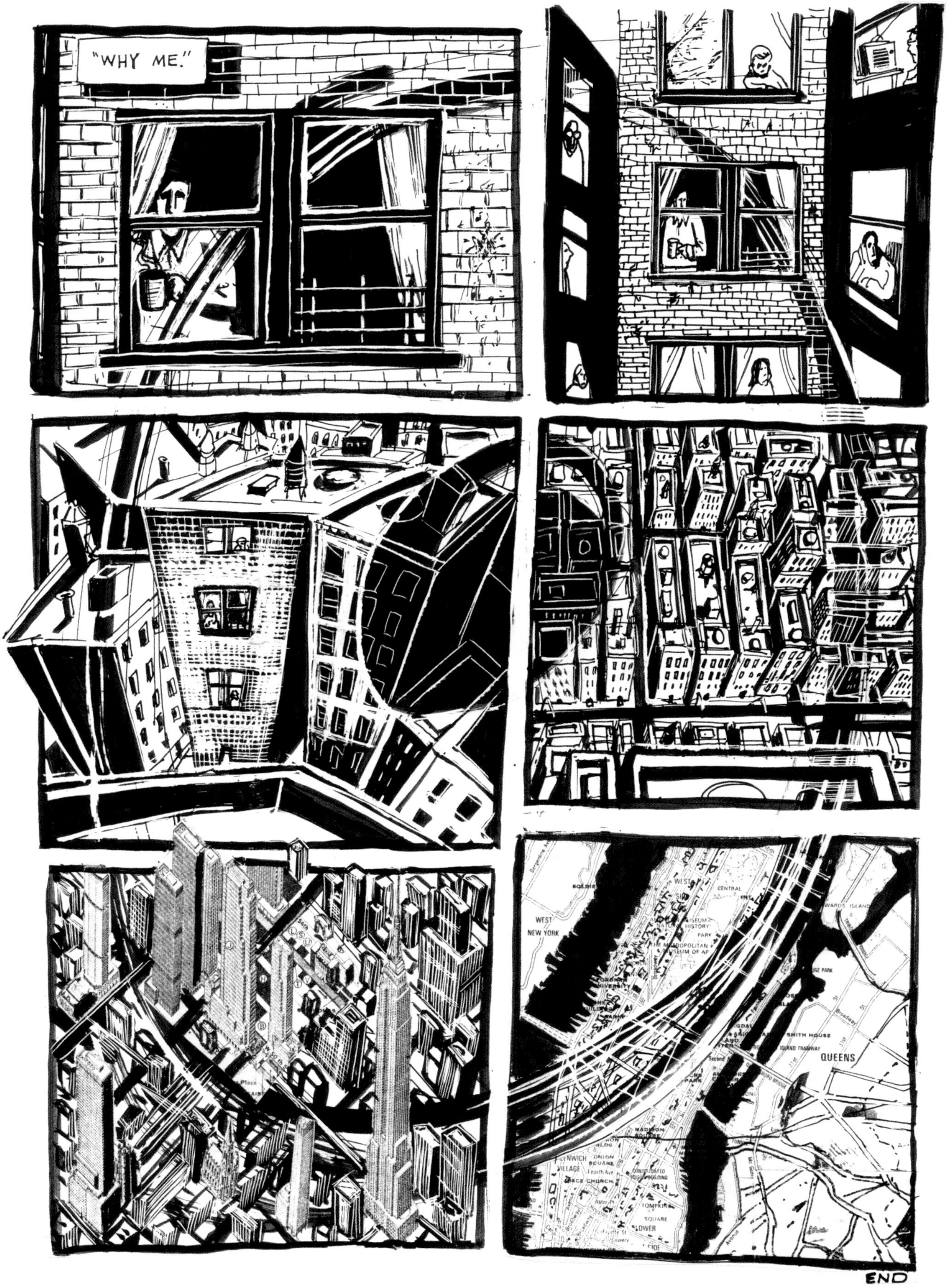
"WHY ME."
WEST
NEW YORK
WARDS ISLAND
QUEENS

END

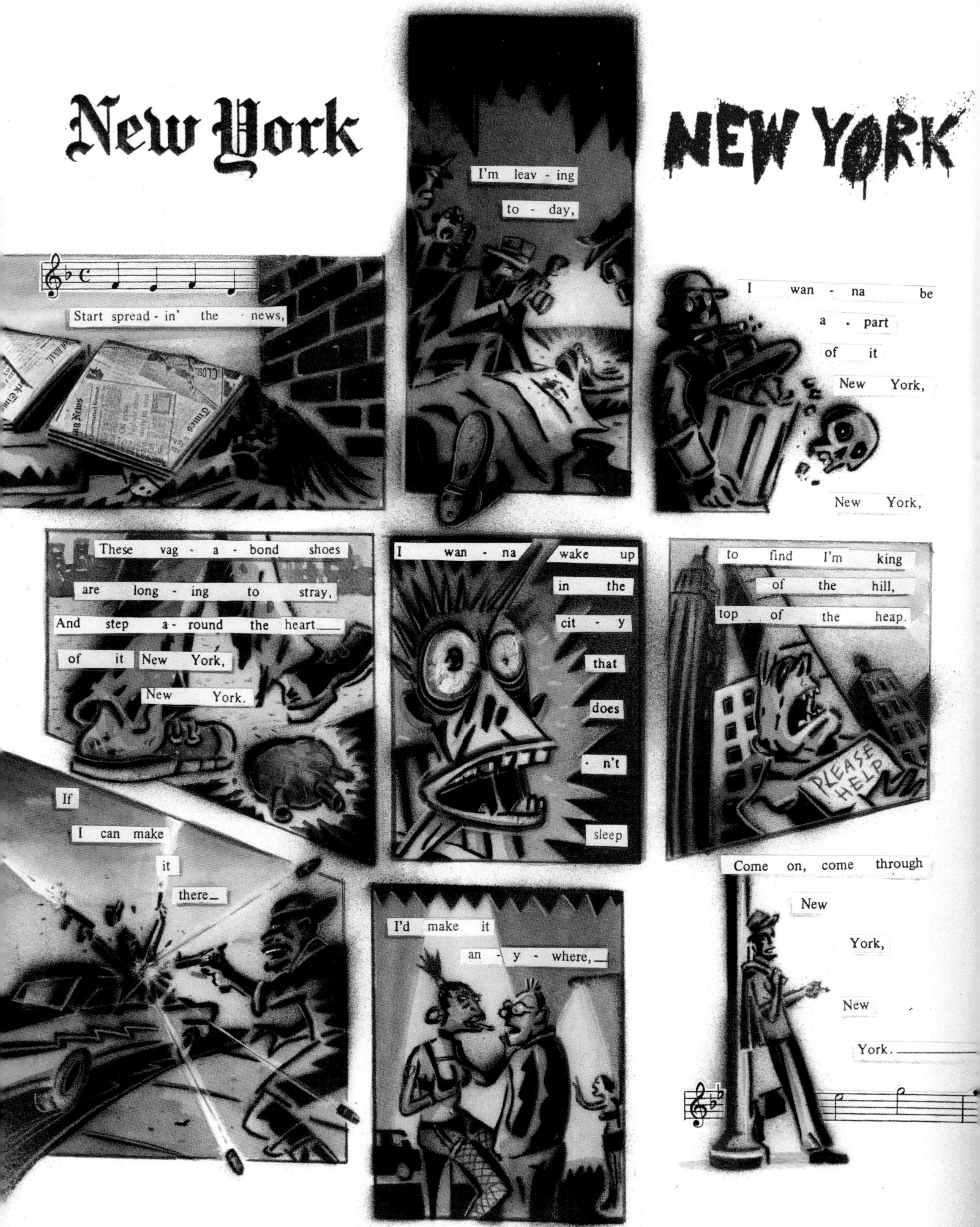
New York
NEW YORK
Start spread - in' the news,
I'm leav - ing
to - day,
I wan - na be
a part
of it
New York,
New York,
These vag - a - bond shoes
are long - ing to stray,
And step a - round the heart
of it New York,
New York.
I wan - na wake up
in the
cit - y
that
does
n't
sleep
to find I'm king
of the hill,
top of the heap.
PLEASE HELP
If
I can make
it
there
I'd make it
an - y - where,
Come on, come through
New
York,
New
York.

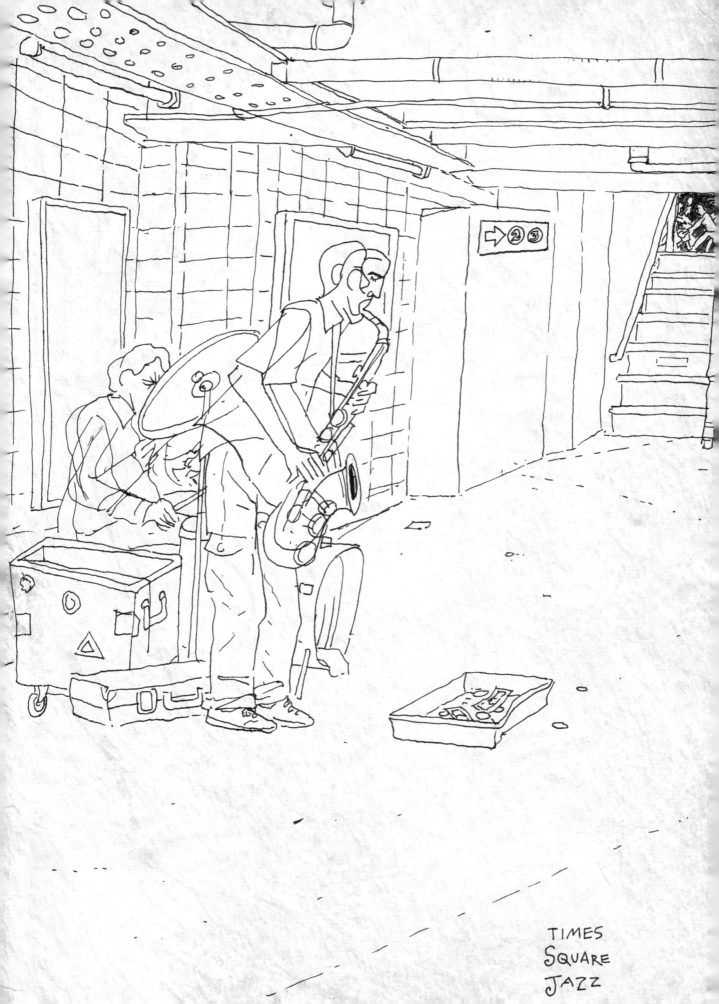

TIMES
SQUARE
JAZZ

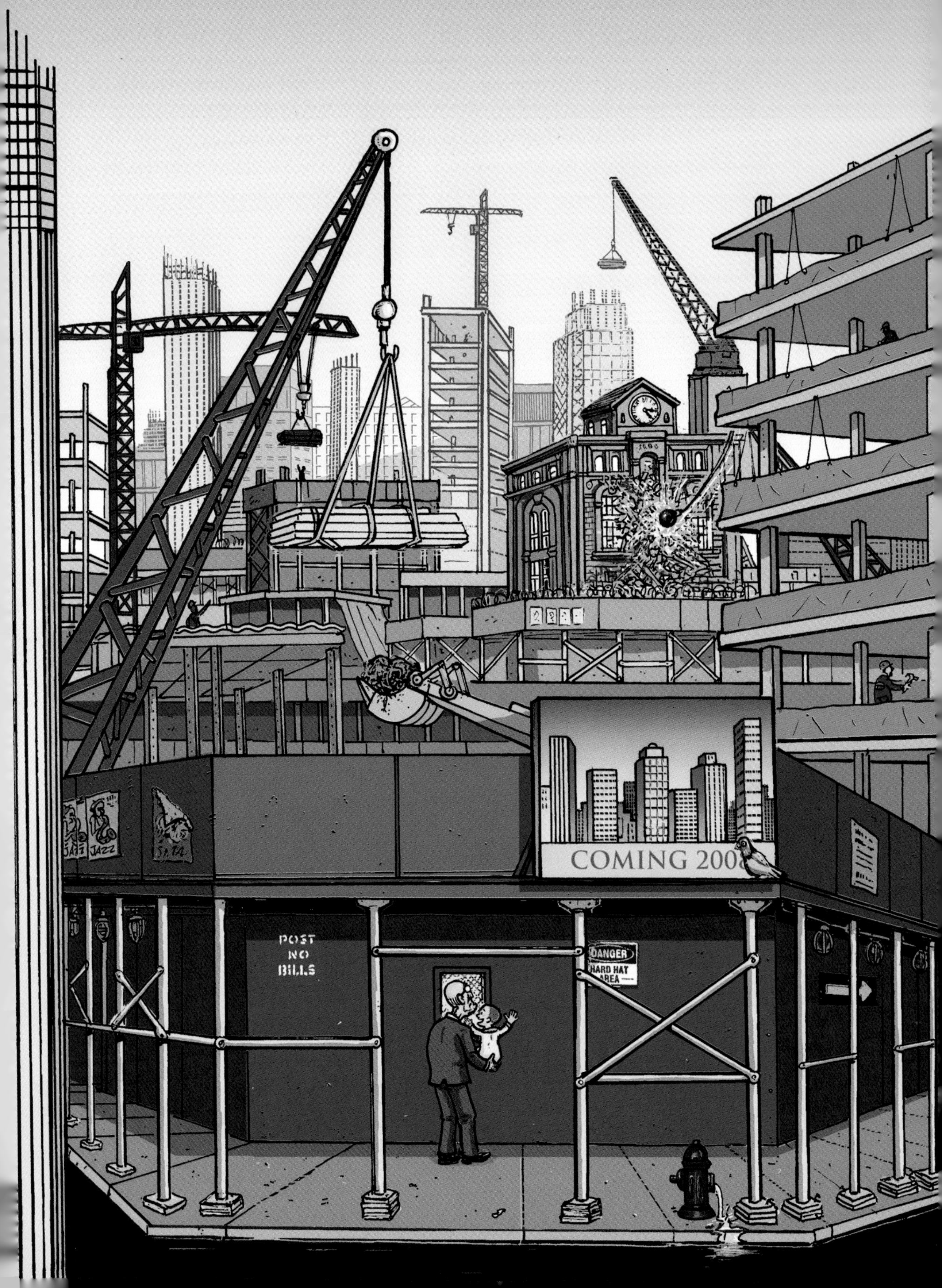
COMING 200
POST
NO
BILLS
DANGER
HARD HAT

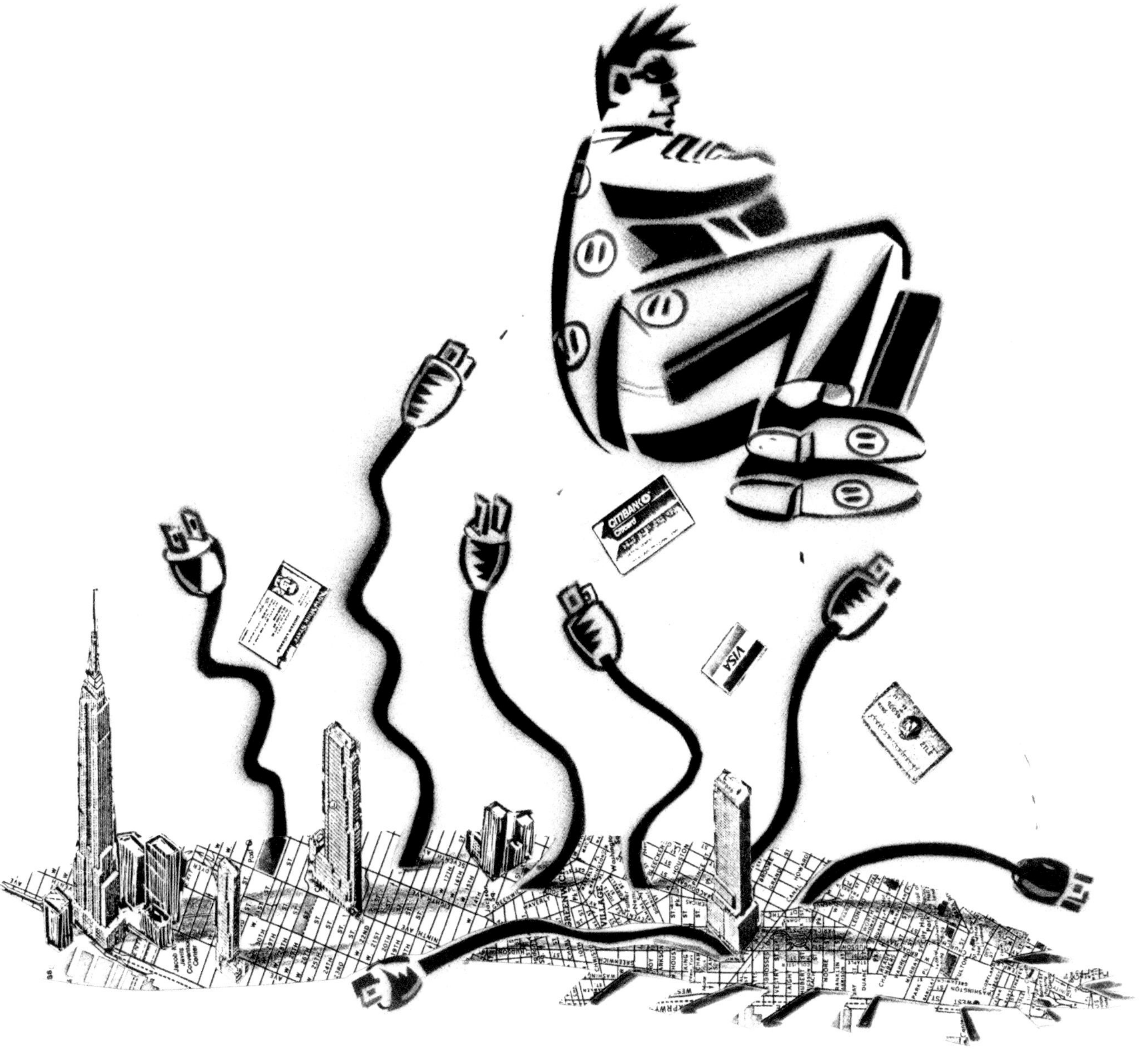
CITIBANK
VISA

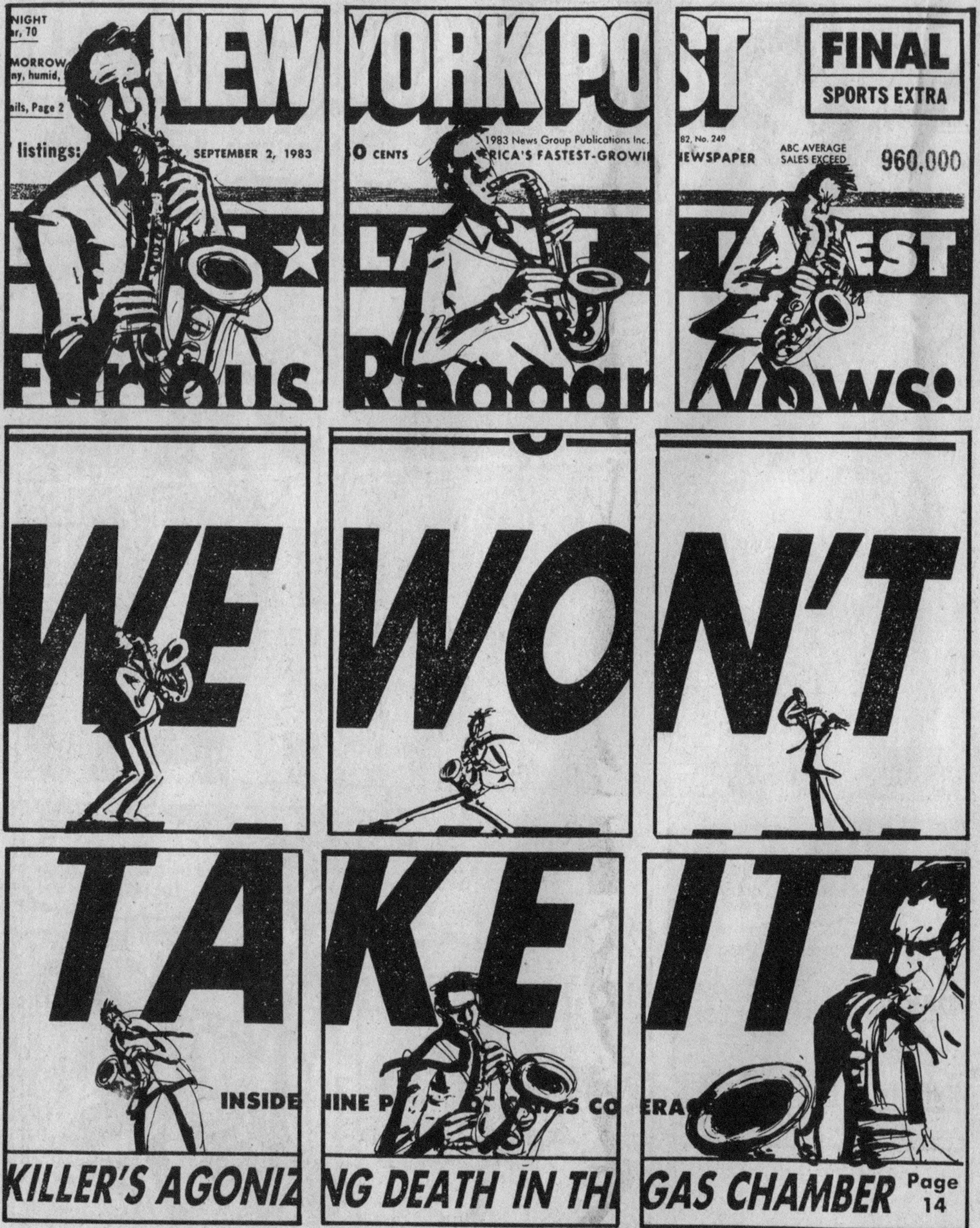

NIGHT
ar, 70
MORROW
ny, humid,
ails, Page 2
listings:
NEW YORK POST
FINAL
SPORTS EXTRA
SEPTEMBER 2, 1983
1983 News Group Publications Inc.
82, No. 249
CENTS
RICA'S FASTEST-GROWI
NEWSPAPER
ABC AVERAGE
SALES EXCEED
960,000
WE WON'T
TAKE IT!
INSIDE NINE P
KILLER'S AGONIZ NG DEATH IN TH GAS CHAMBER
Page 14

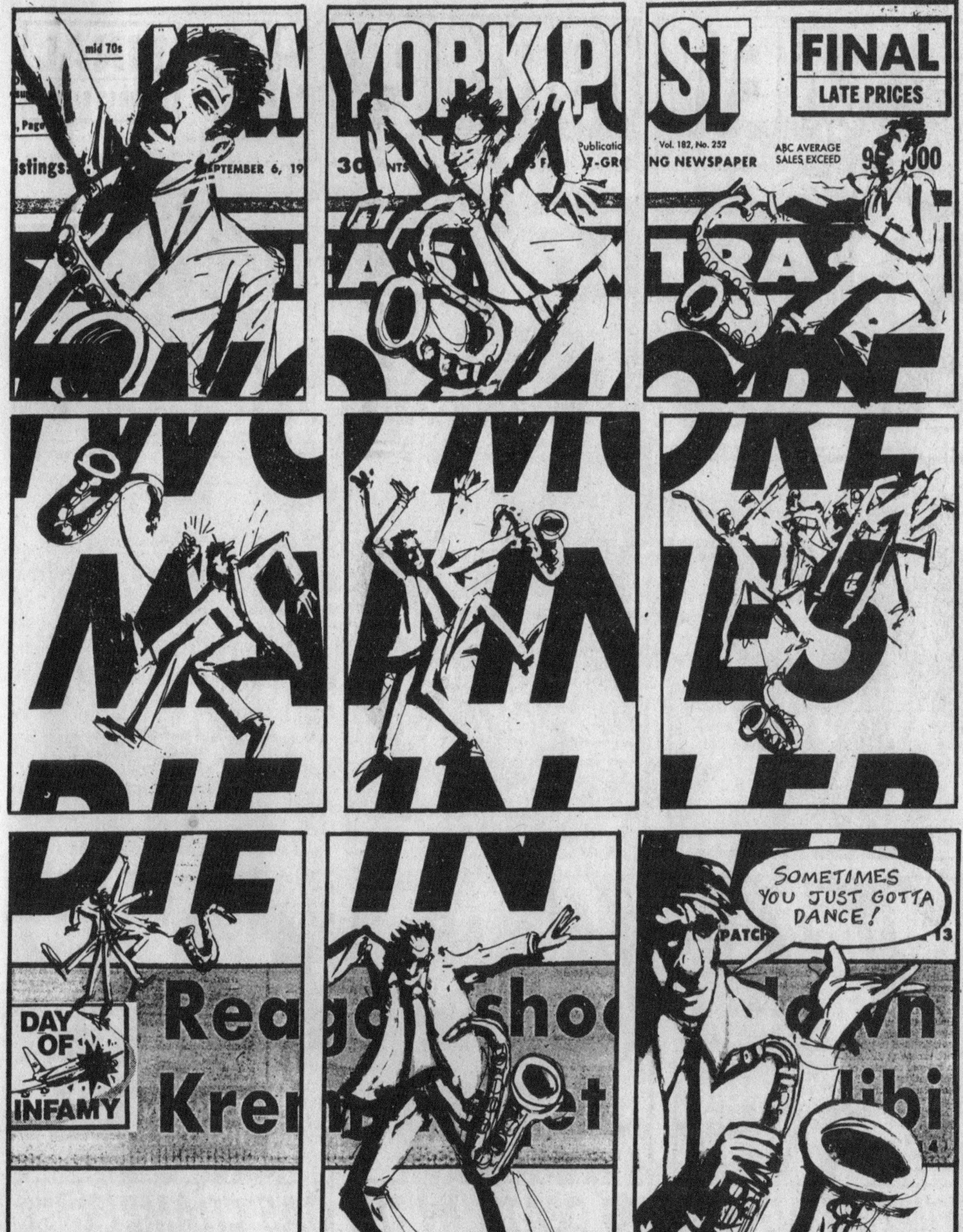
mid 70s
YORK
FINAL
LATE PRICES
Vol. 182, No. 252
ABC AVERAGE
SALES EXCEED
NEWSPAPER
DAY OF INFAMY
SOMETIMES YOU JUST GOTTA DANCE!

DEDICATED TO BOB ROCKWELL

© PETER KUPER
1983

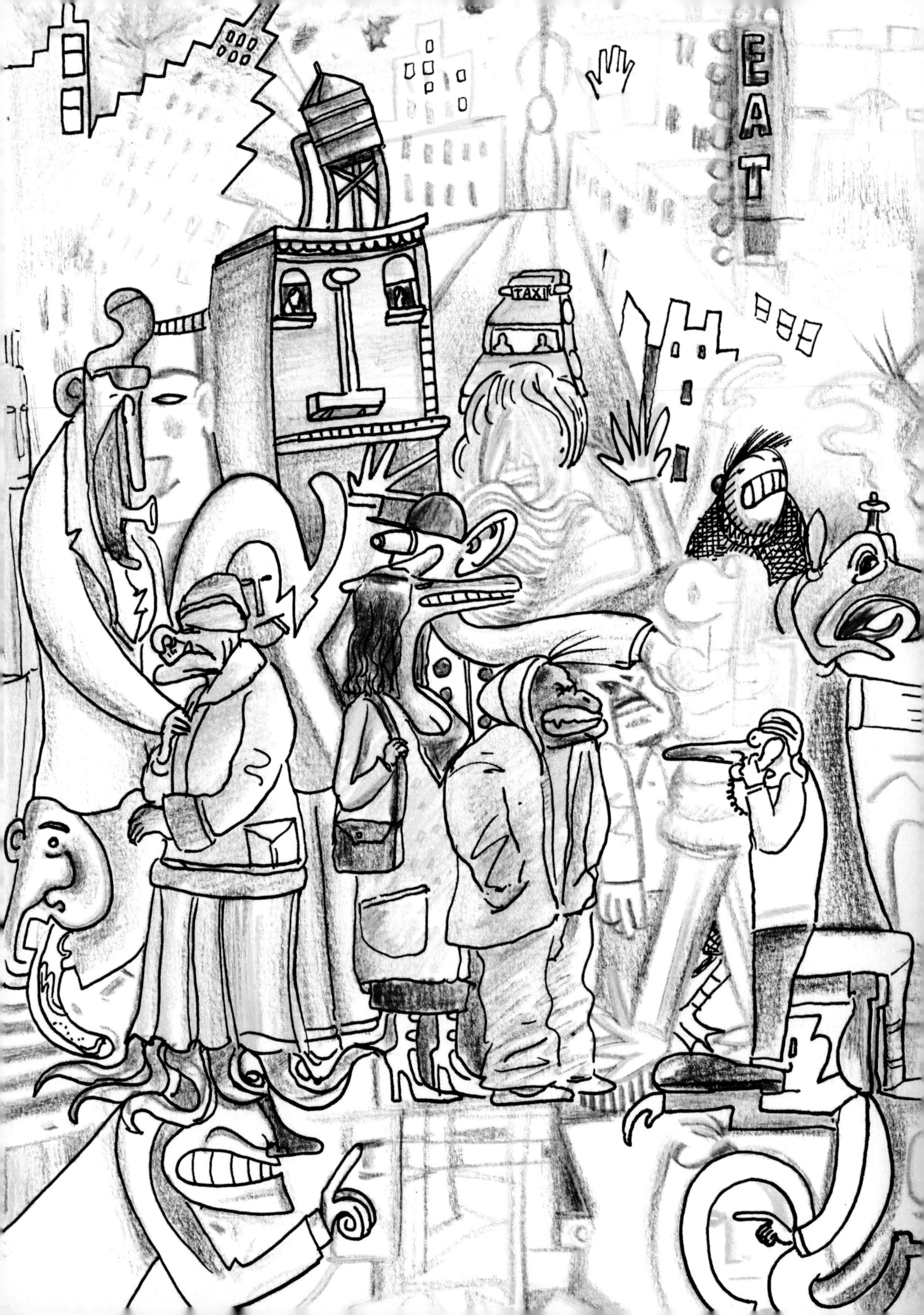
EAT
TAXI

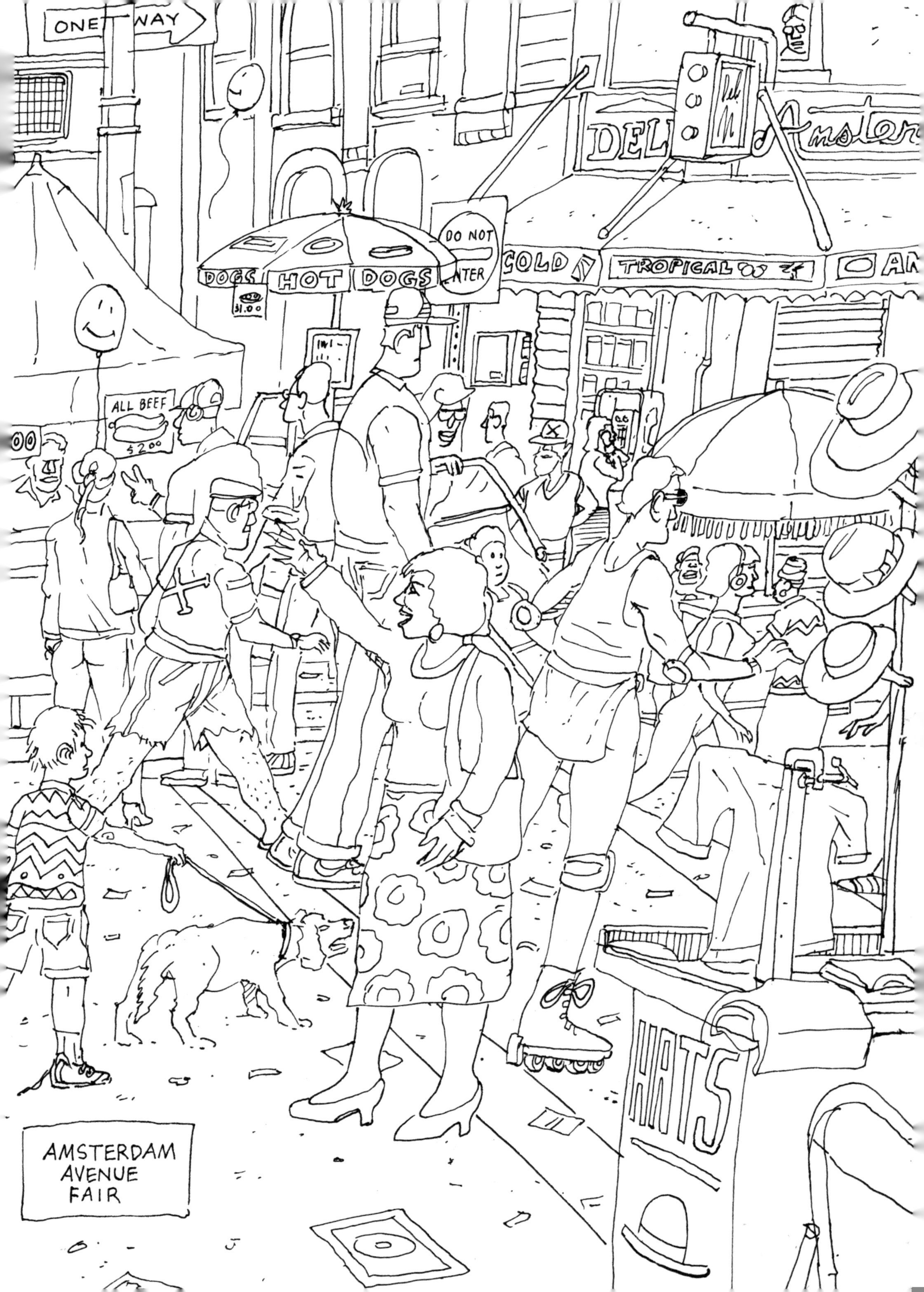
ONE WAY
DELI
DO NOT ENTER
DOGS HOT DOGS
$1.00
ALL BEEF
$2.00
COLD
TROPICAL
HATS
AMSTERDAM
AVENUE
FAIR

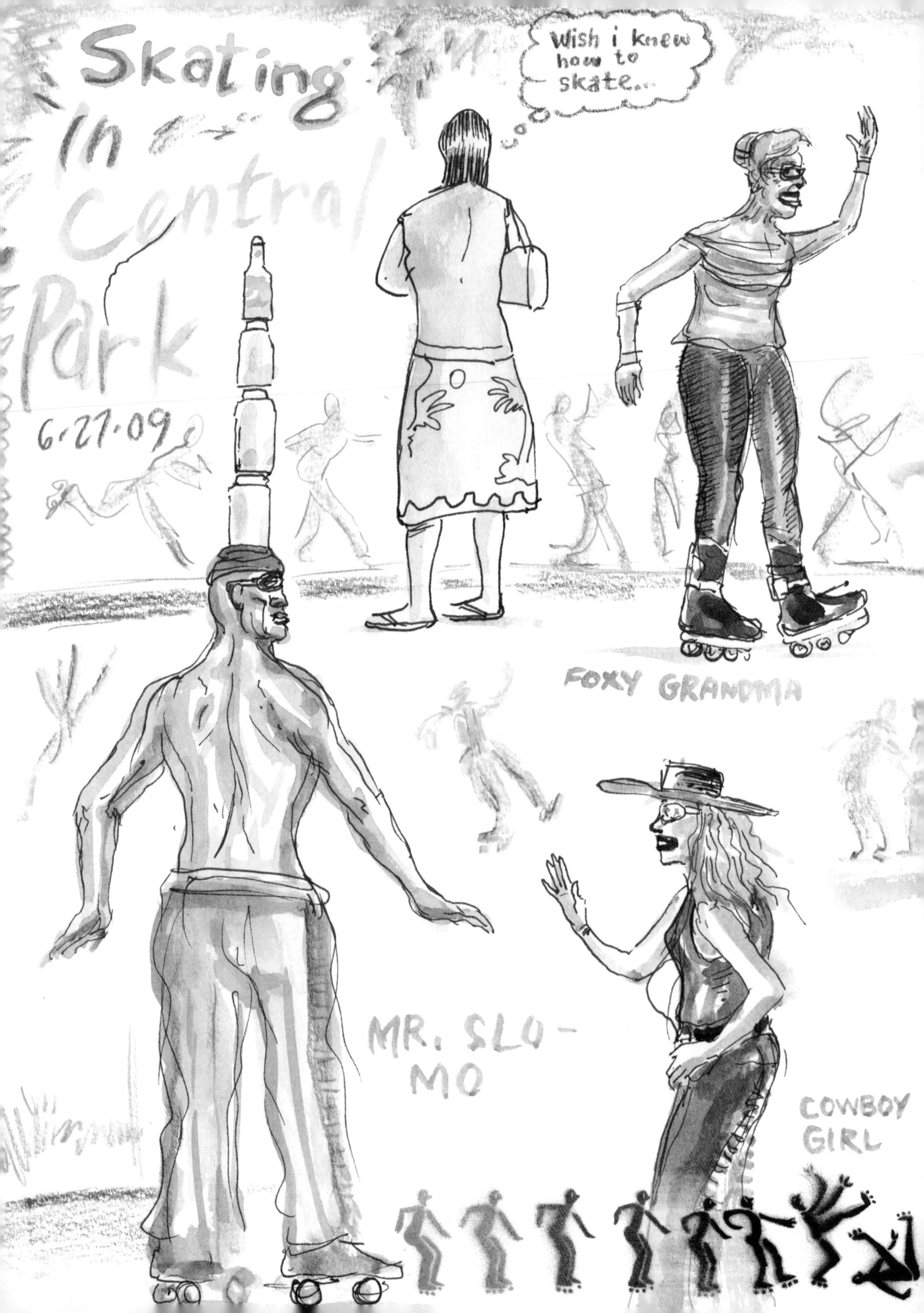
Skating In Central Park
6.27.09
Wish i knew how to skate...
FOXY GRANDMA
MR. SLO-MO
COWBOY GIRL

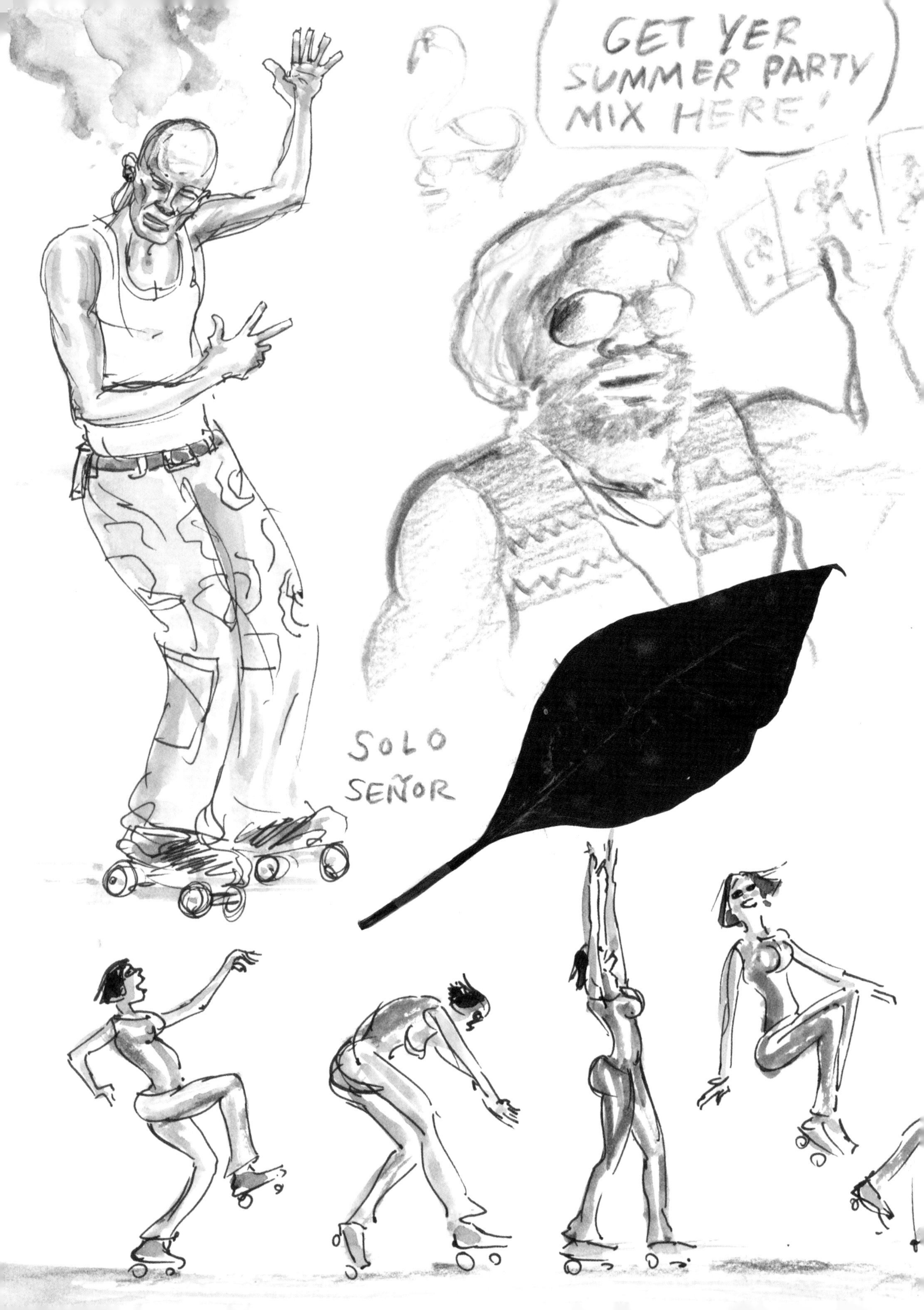
GET YER SUMMER PARTY MIX HERE!
SOLO SEÑOR

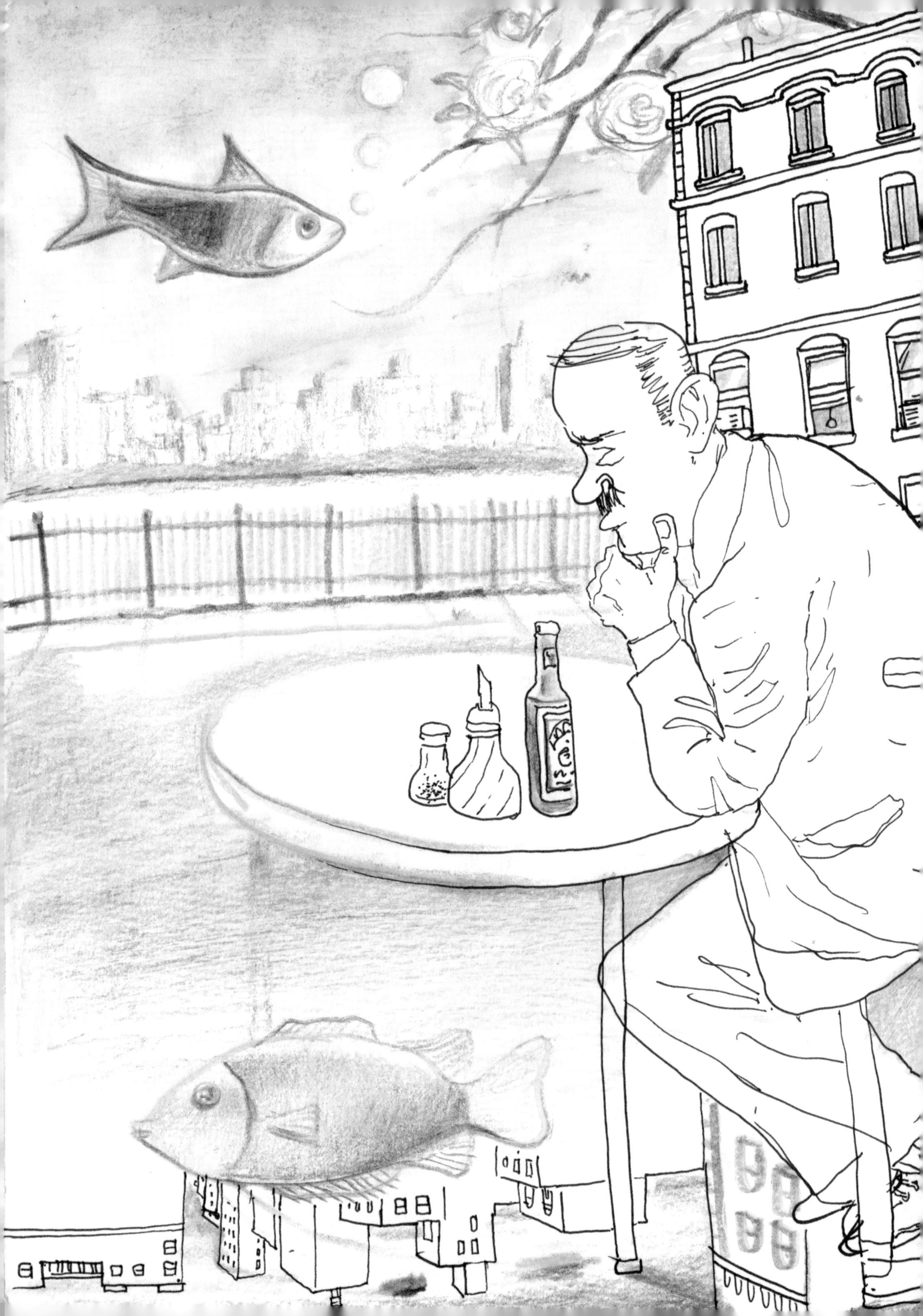

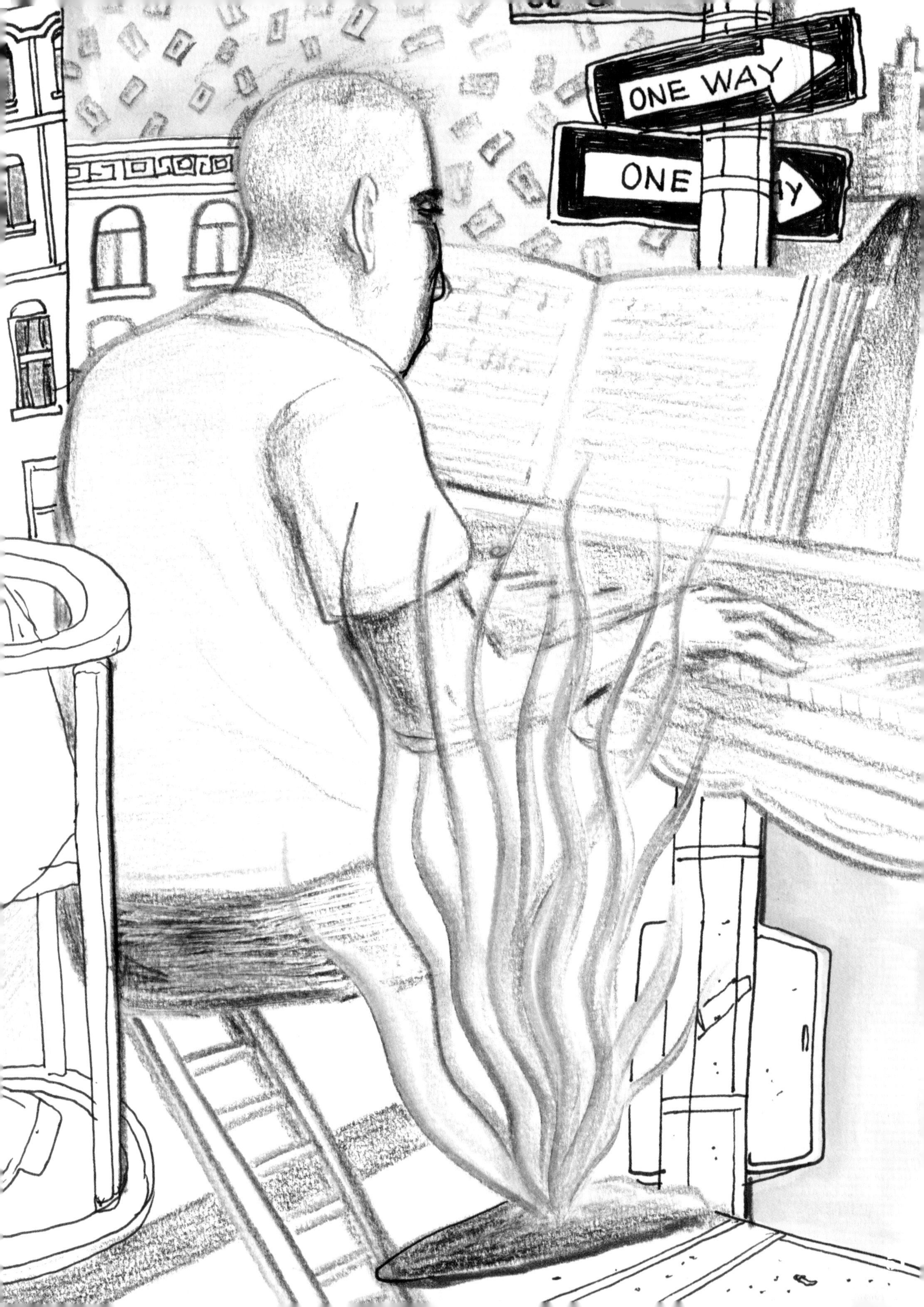
ONE WAY
ONE

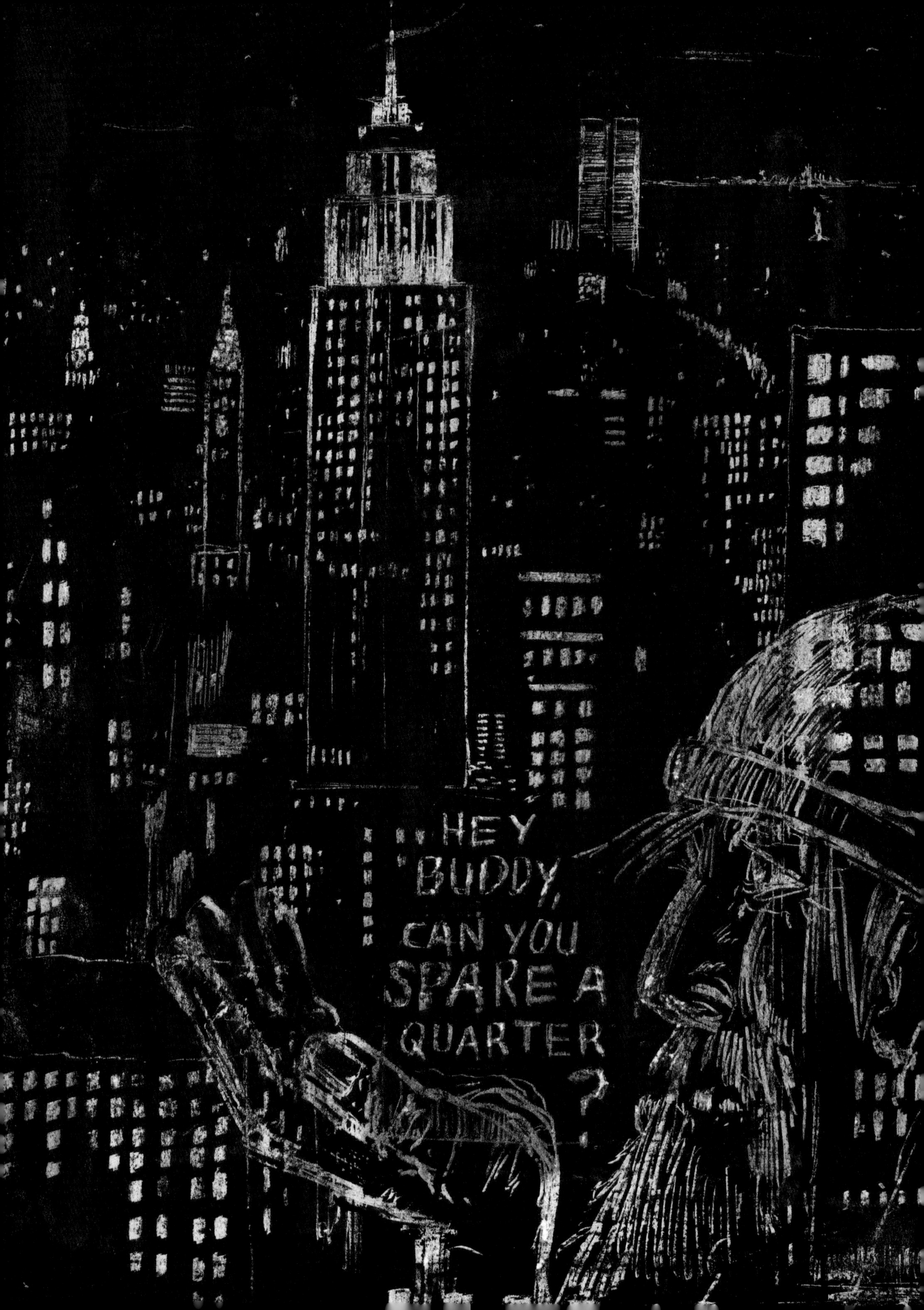
HEY BUDDY, CAN YOU SPARE A QUARTER ?

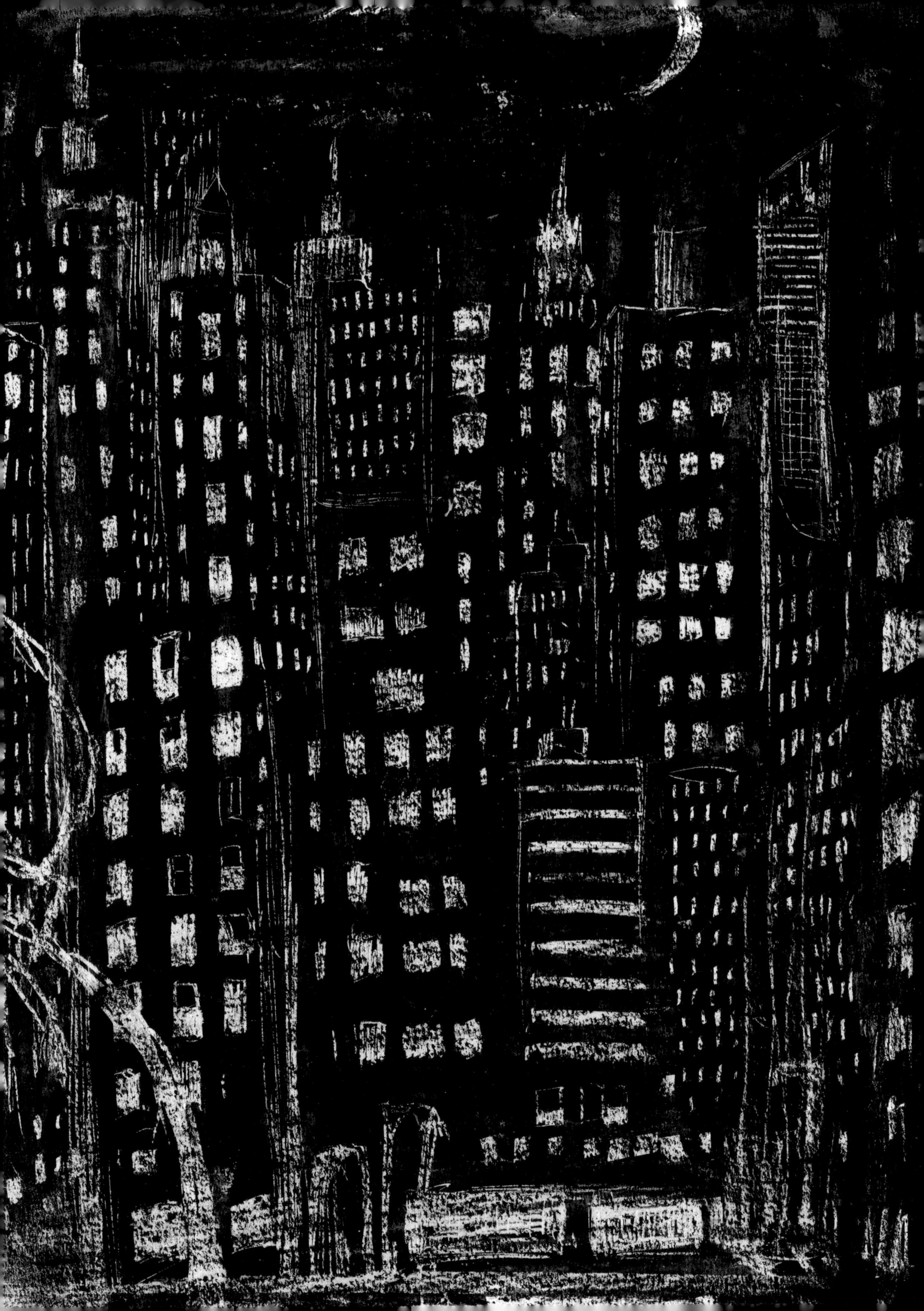

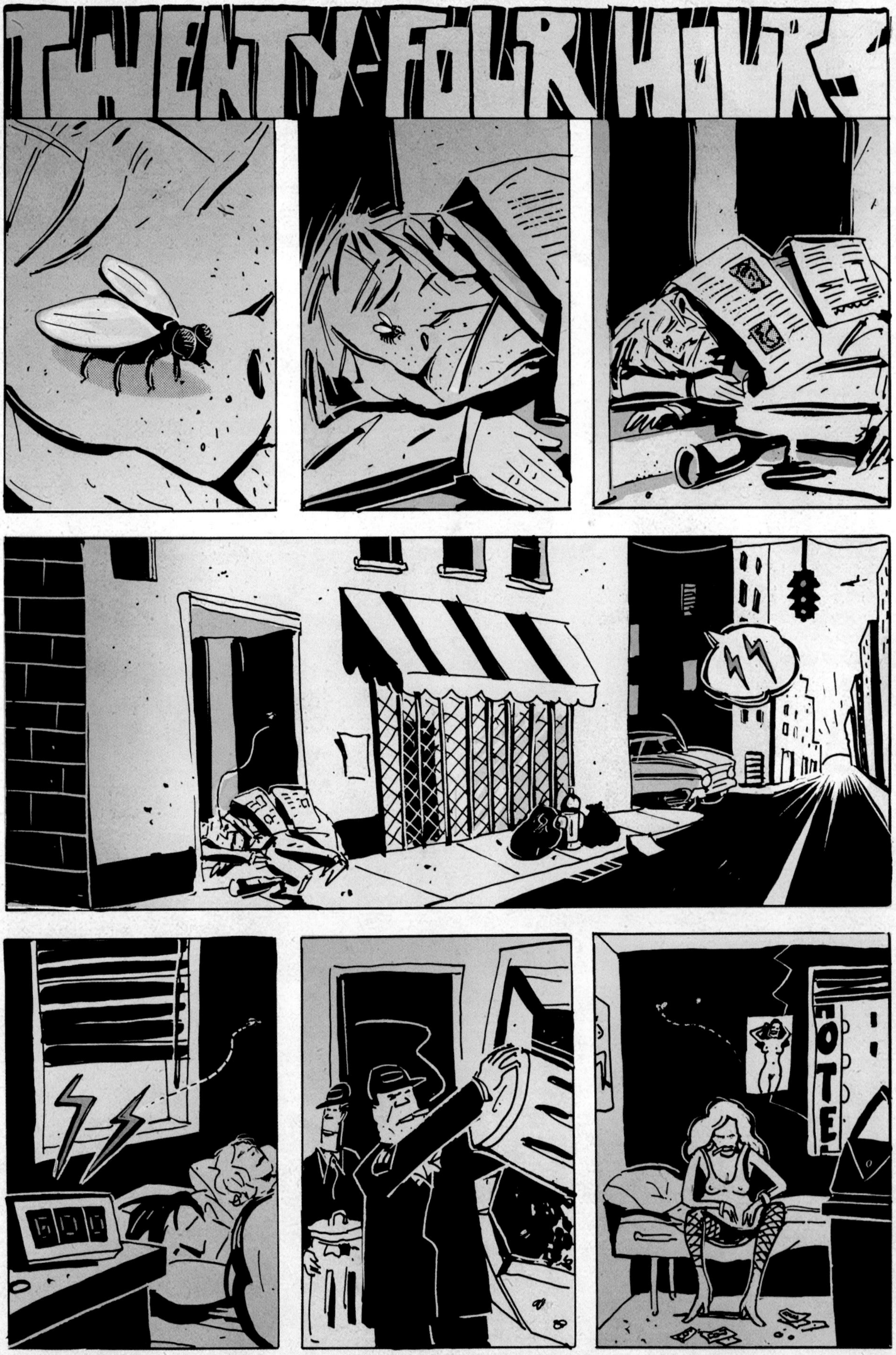
TWENTY-FOUR HOURS
HOTE

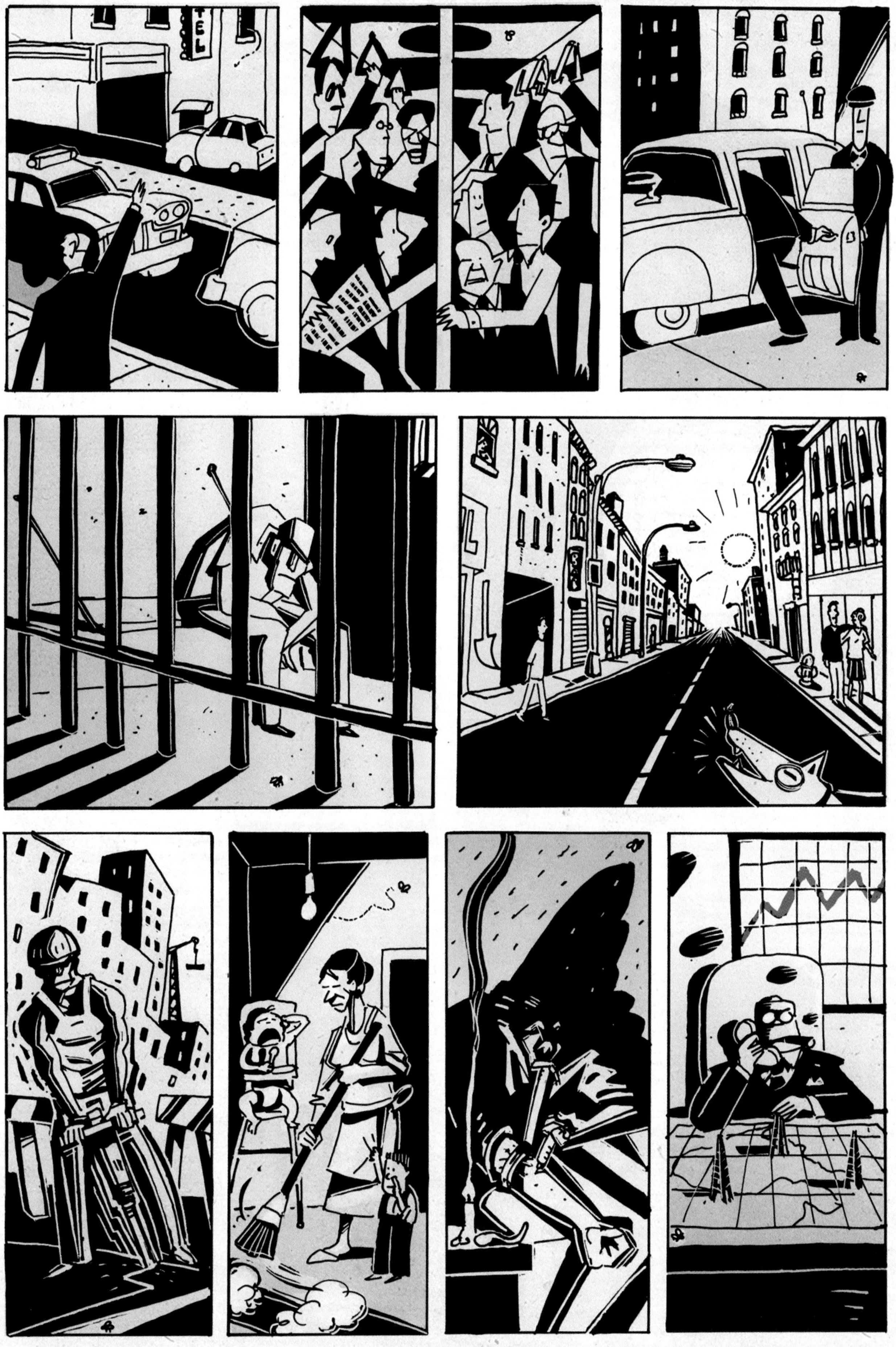

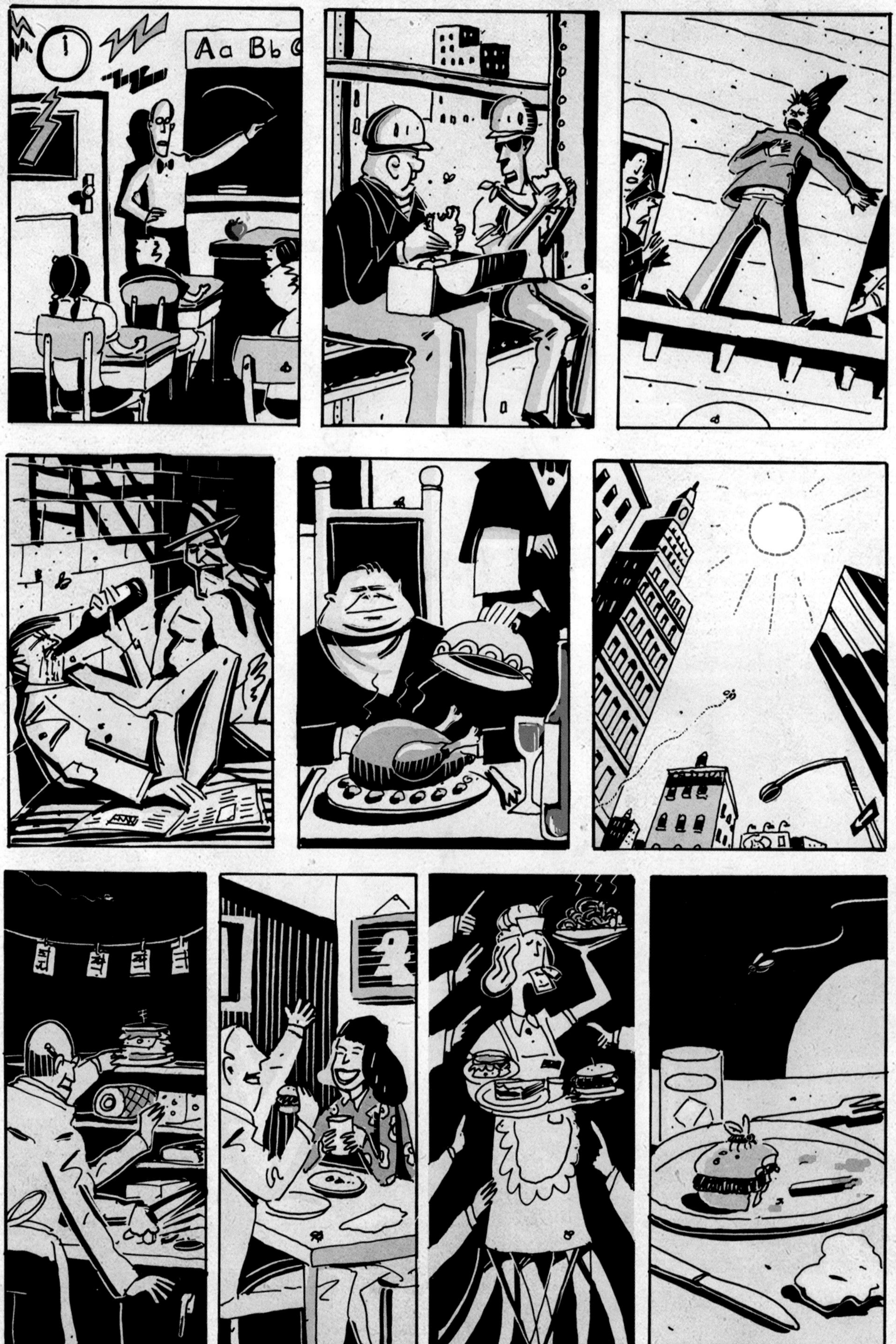
Aa Bb

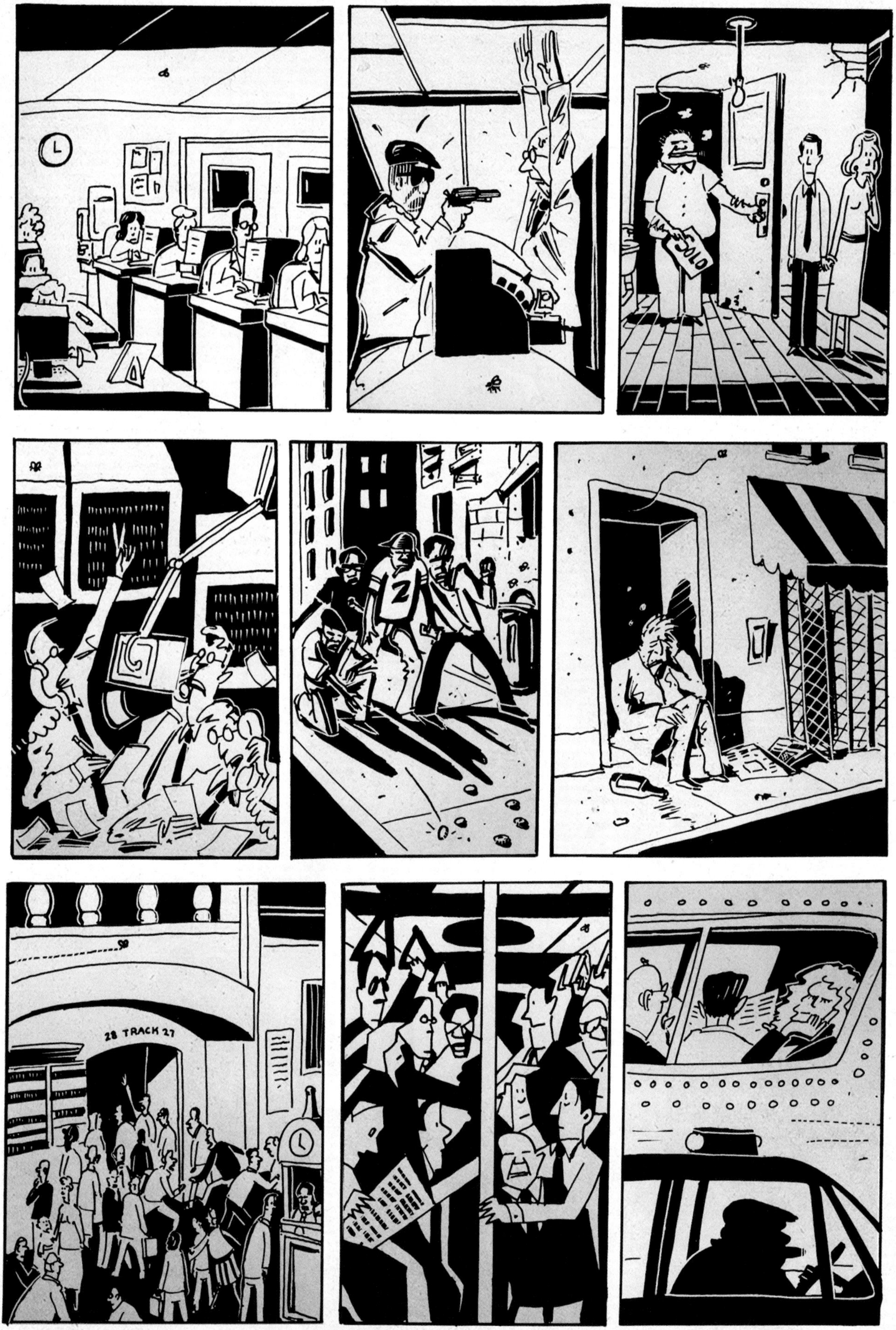
SOLD
28 TRACK 27

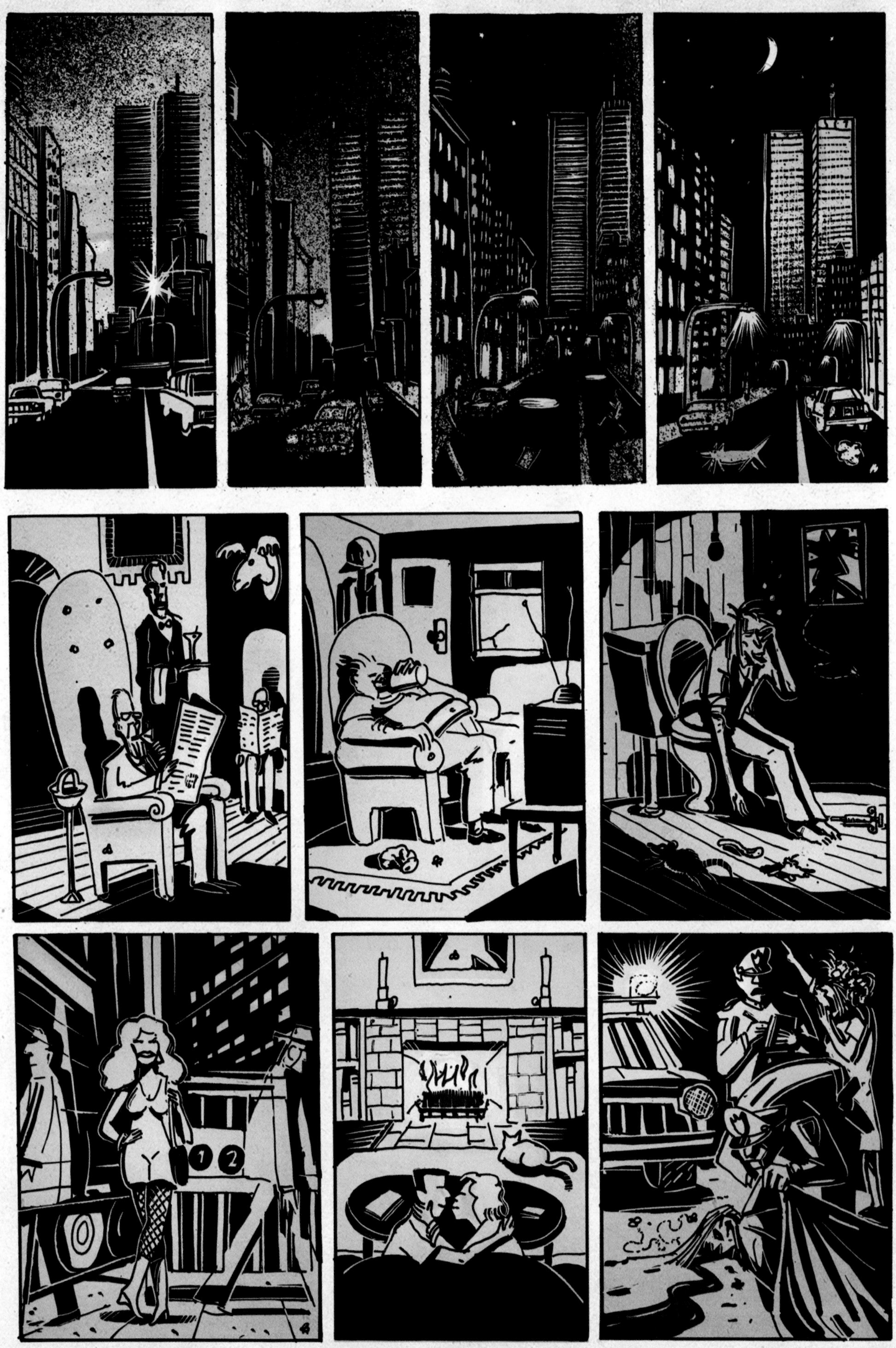

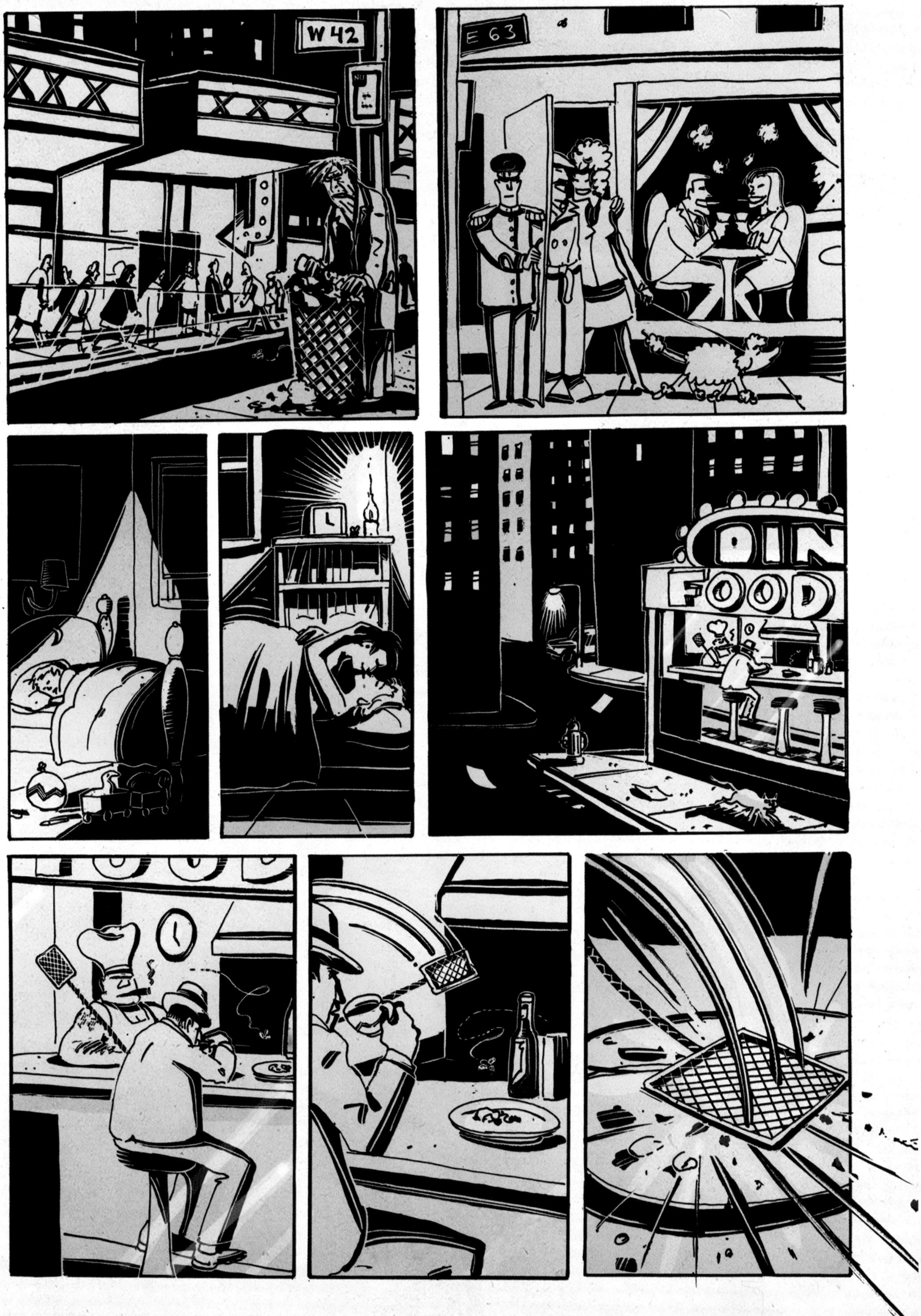
W 42
E 63
DIN
FOOD

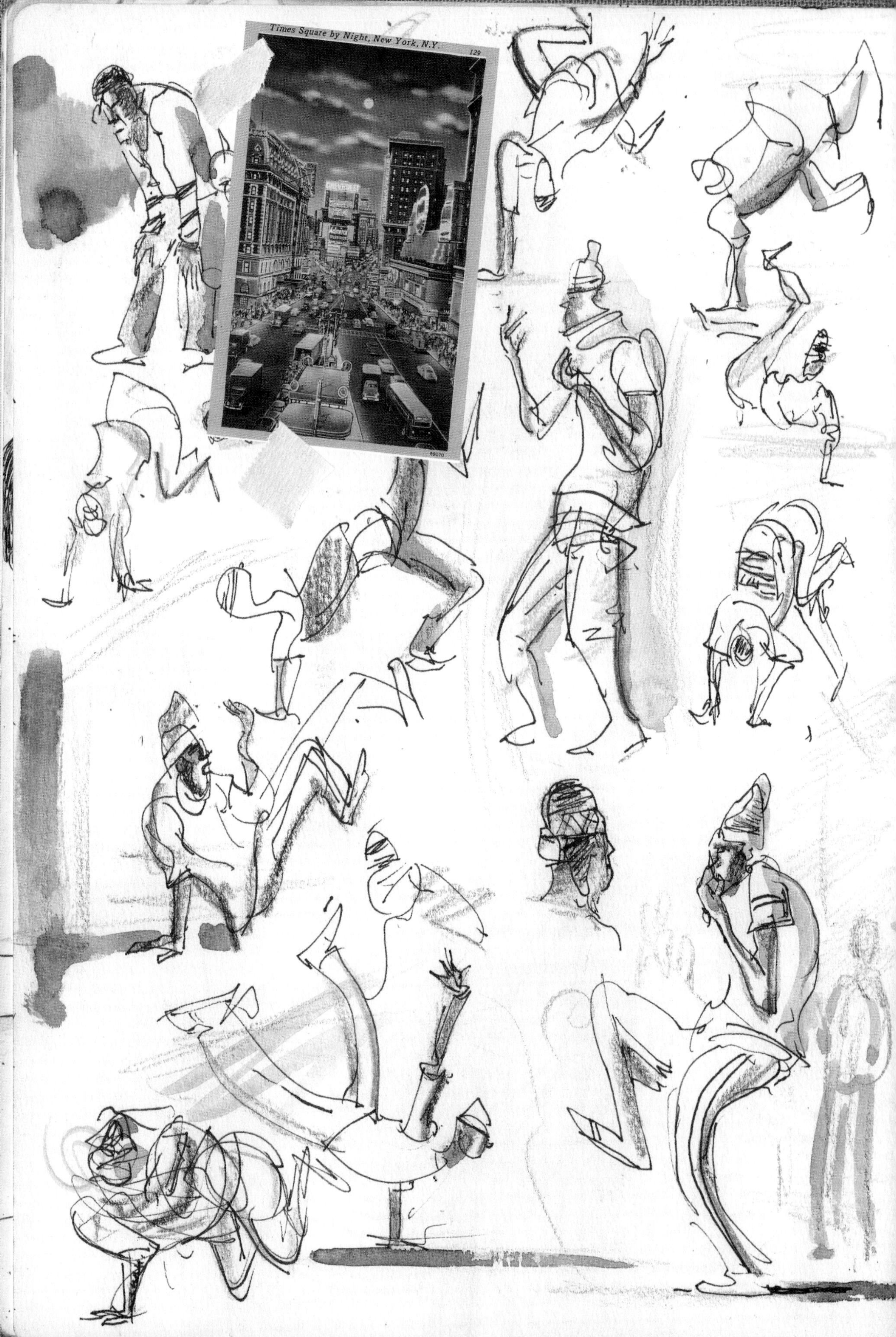
Times Square by Night, New York, N.Y.
129
89070

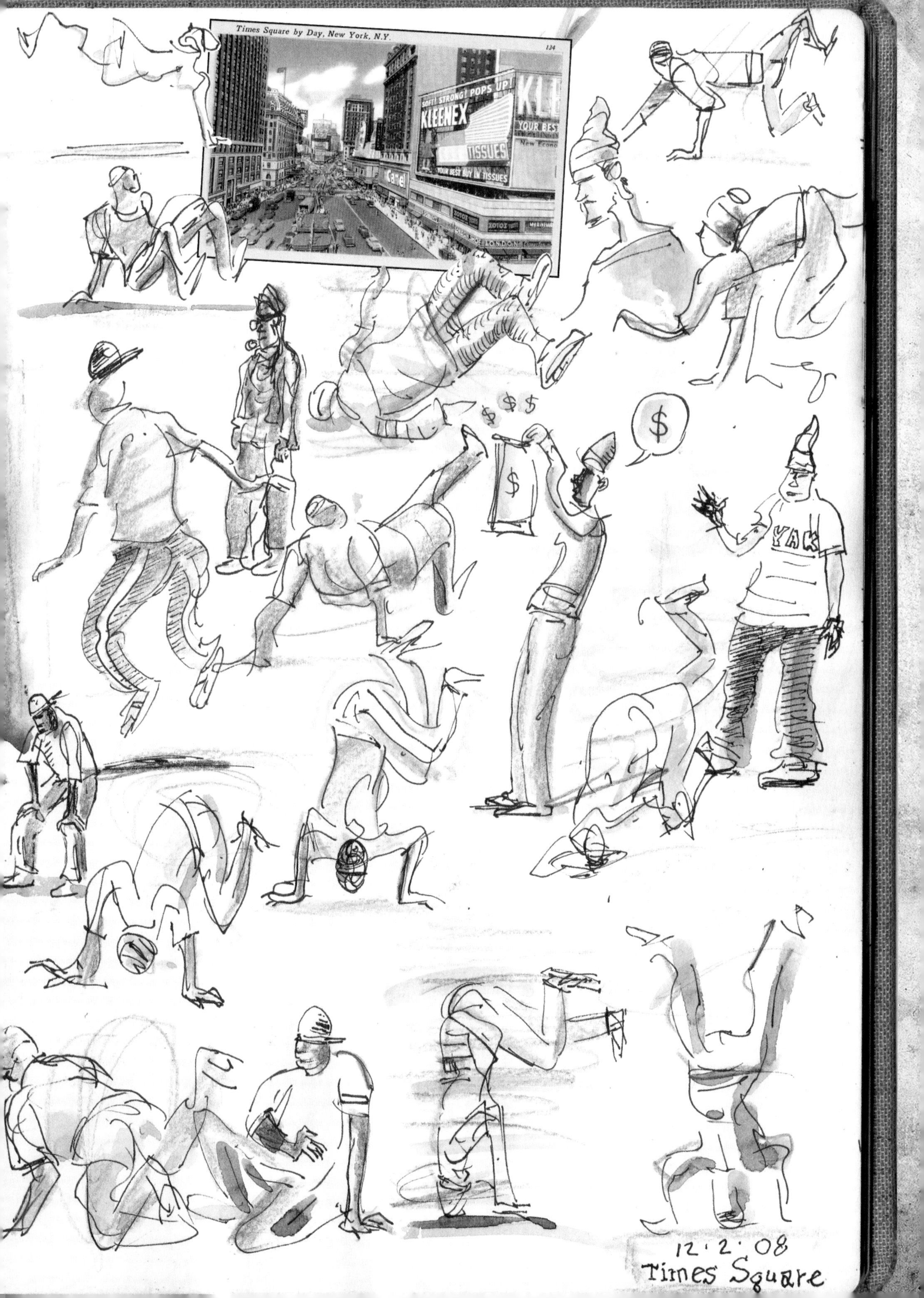
Times Square by Day, New York, N.Y.
134
SOFT! STRONG! POPS UP!
KLEENEX
TISSUES
YOUR BEST BUY IN TISSUES
Camel
$ $ $
$
$
YAK
12·2·08
Times Square

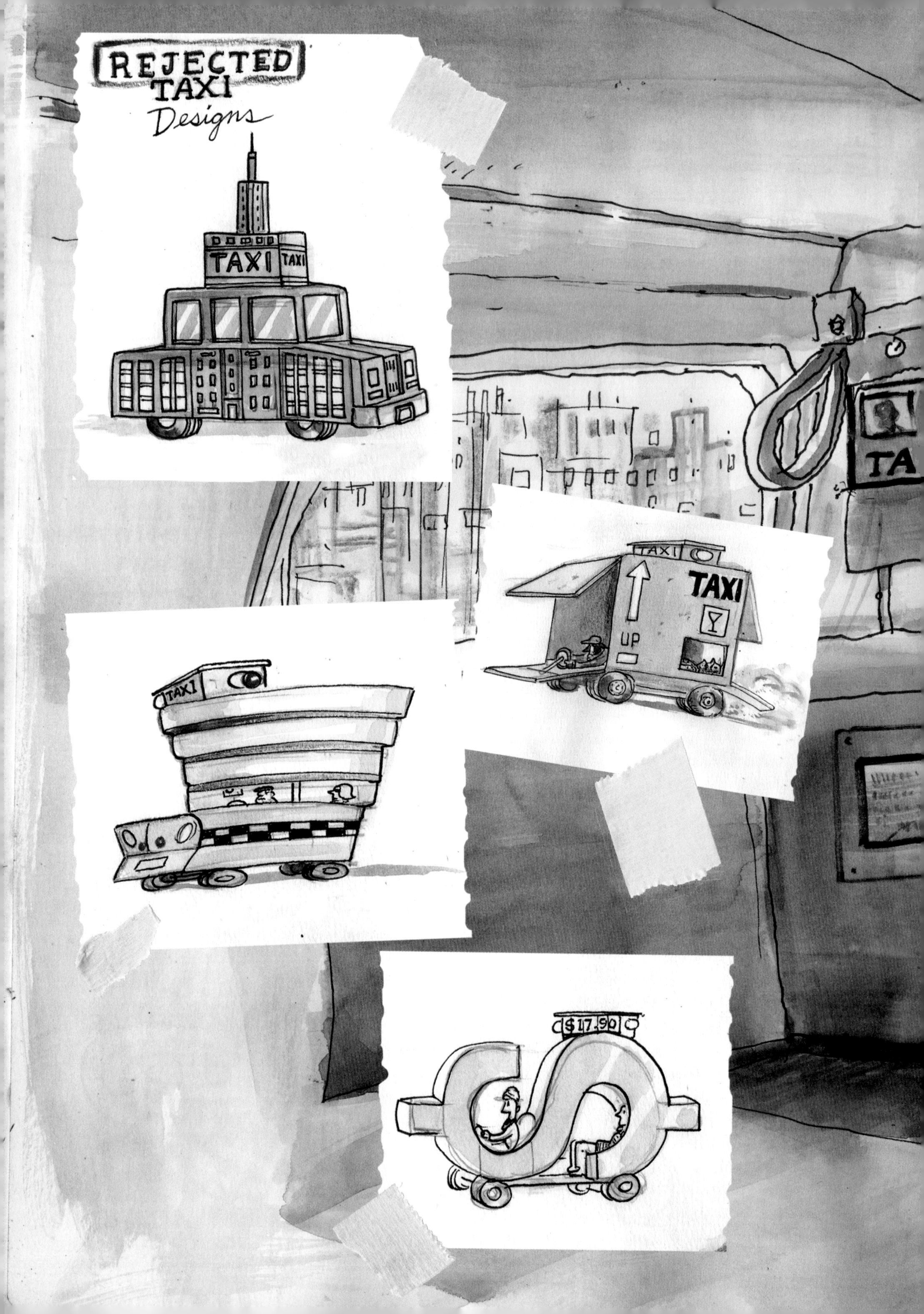
REJECTED
TAXI
Designs
TAXI
TAXI
TAXI
TAXI
UP
TAXI
$17.90
TA

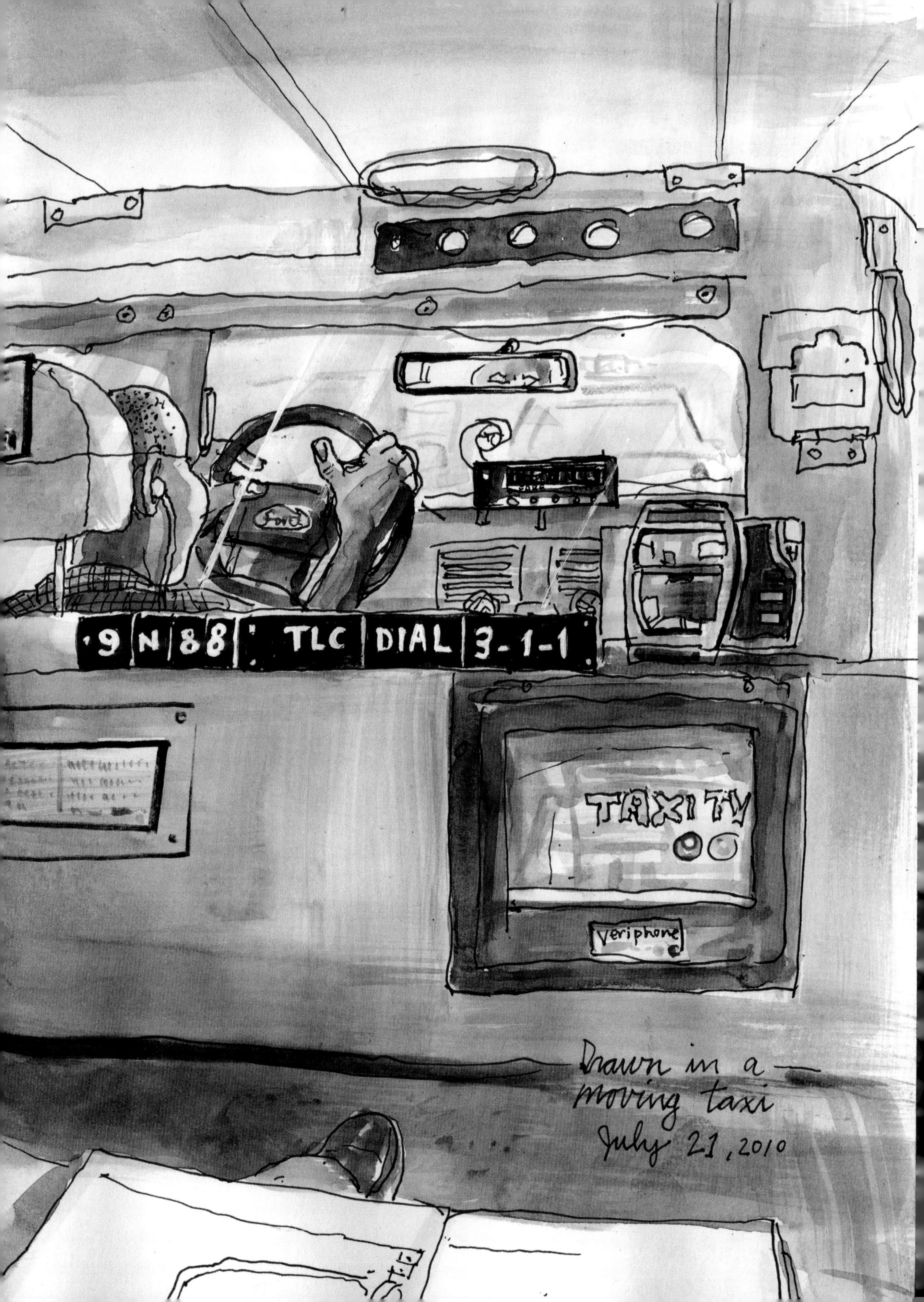
9 N 88
TLC
DIAL 3-1-1
TAXI TV
veriphone
Drawn in a moving taxi
July 21, 2010

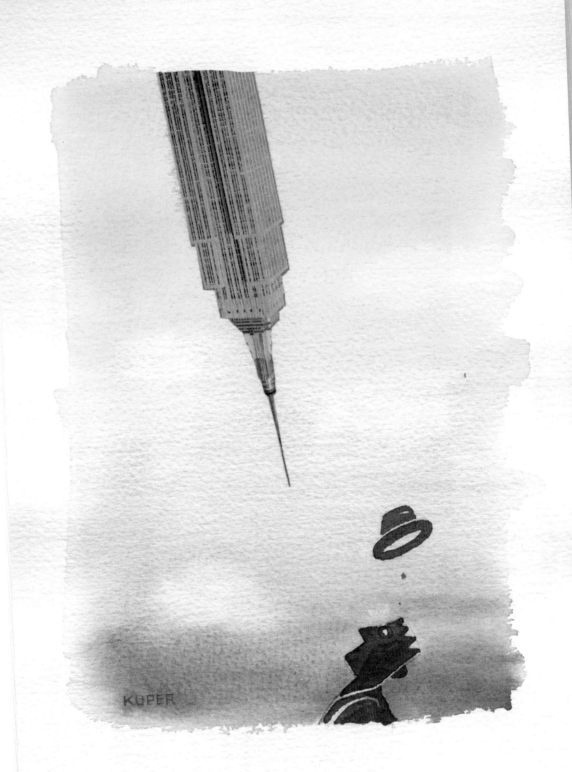

KUPER

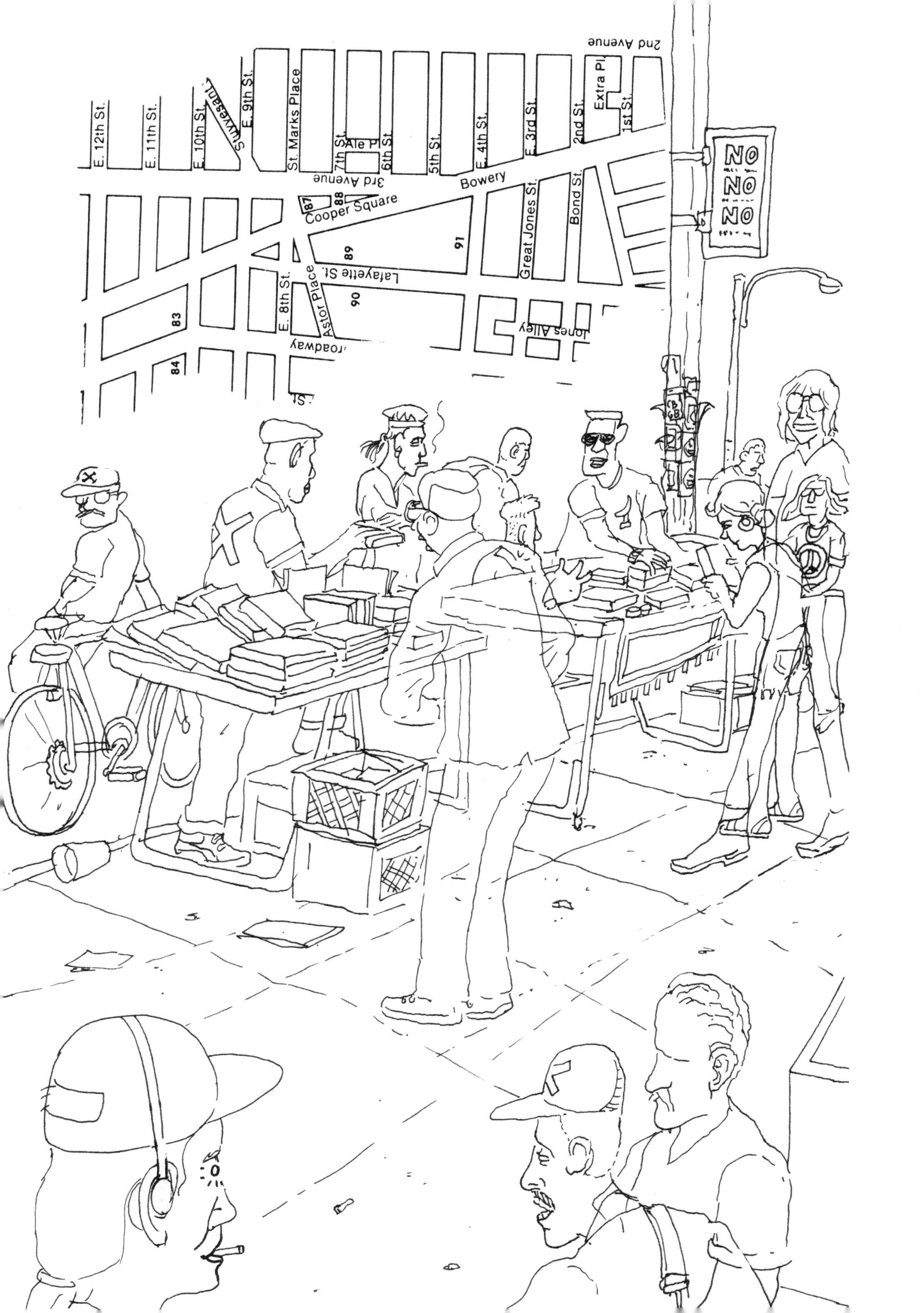
2nd Avenue
E. 12th St.
E. 11th St.
E. 10th St.
Stuyvesant
E. 9th St.
St. Marks Place
7th St.
Ale Pl
6th St.
5th St.
E. 4th St.
E. 3rd St.
2nd St.
Extra Pl.
1st St.
3rd Avenue
Bowery
87
88
Cooper Square
89
91
Great Jones St.
Bond St.
Lafayette St.
E. 8th St.
Astor Place
90
83
84
Jones Alley
roadway
NO
NO
NO

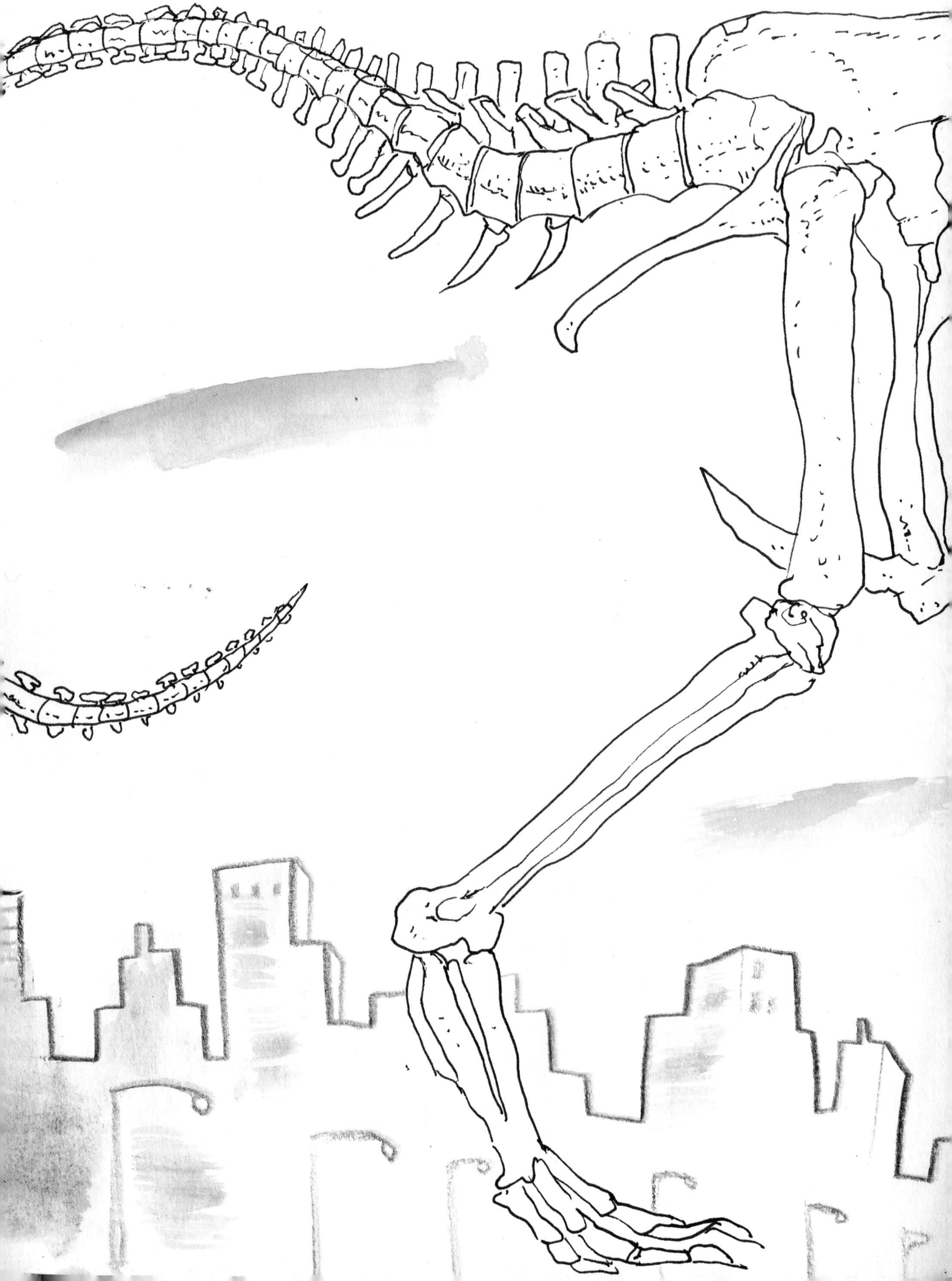

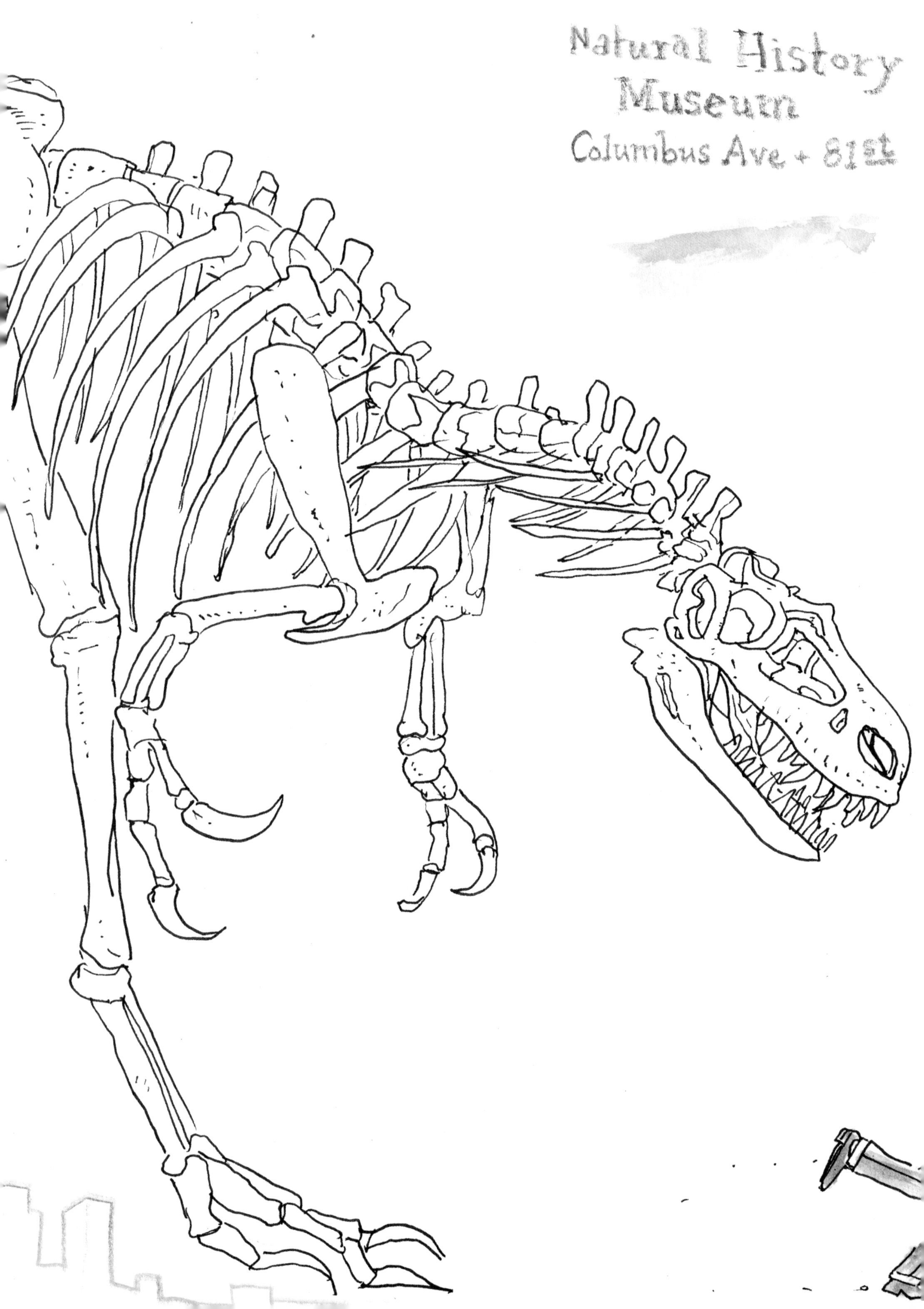
Natural History
Museum
Columbus Ave + 81st

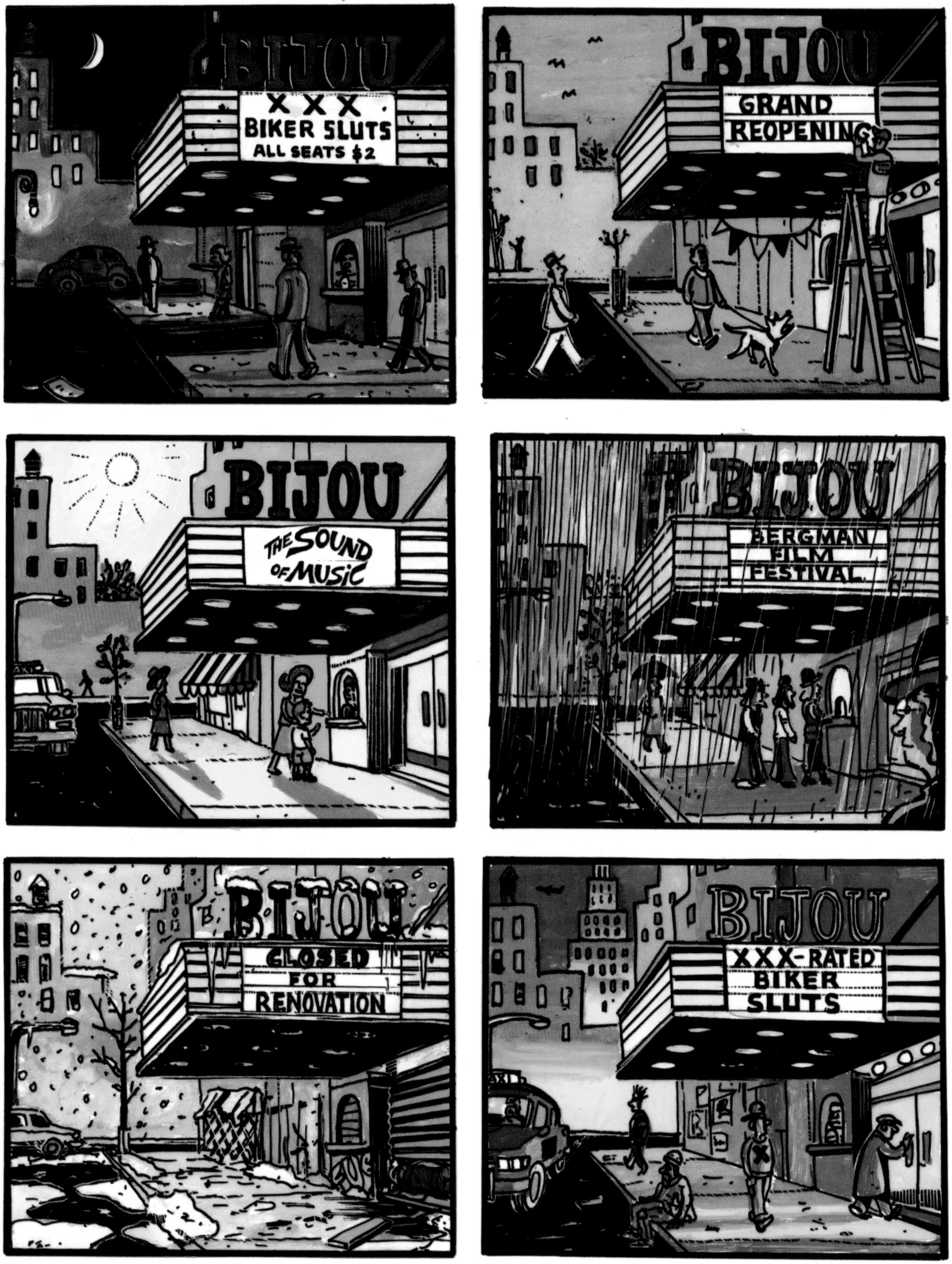
BIJOU
XXX
BIKER SLUTS
ALL SEATS $2
BIJOU
GRAND
REOPENING
BIJOU
THE SOUND OF MUSIC
BIJOU
BERGMAN
FILM
FESTIVAL
BIJOU
CLOSED
FOR
RENOVATION
BIJOU
XXX-RATED
BIKER
SLUTS

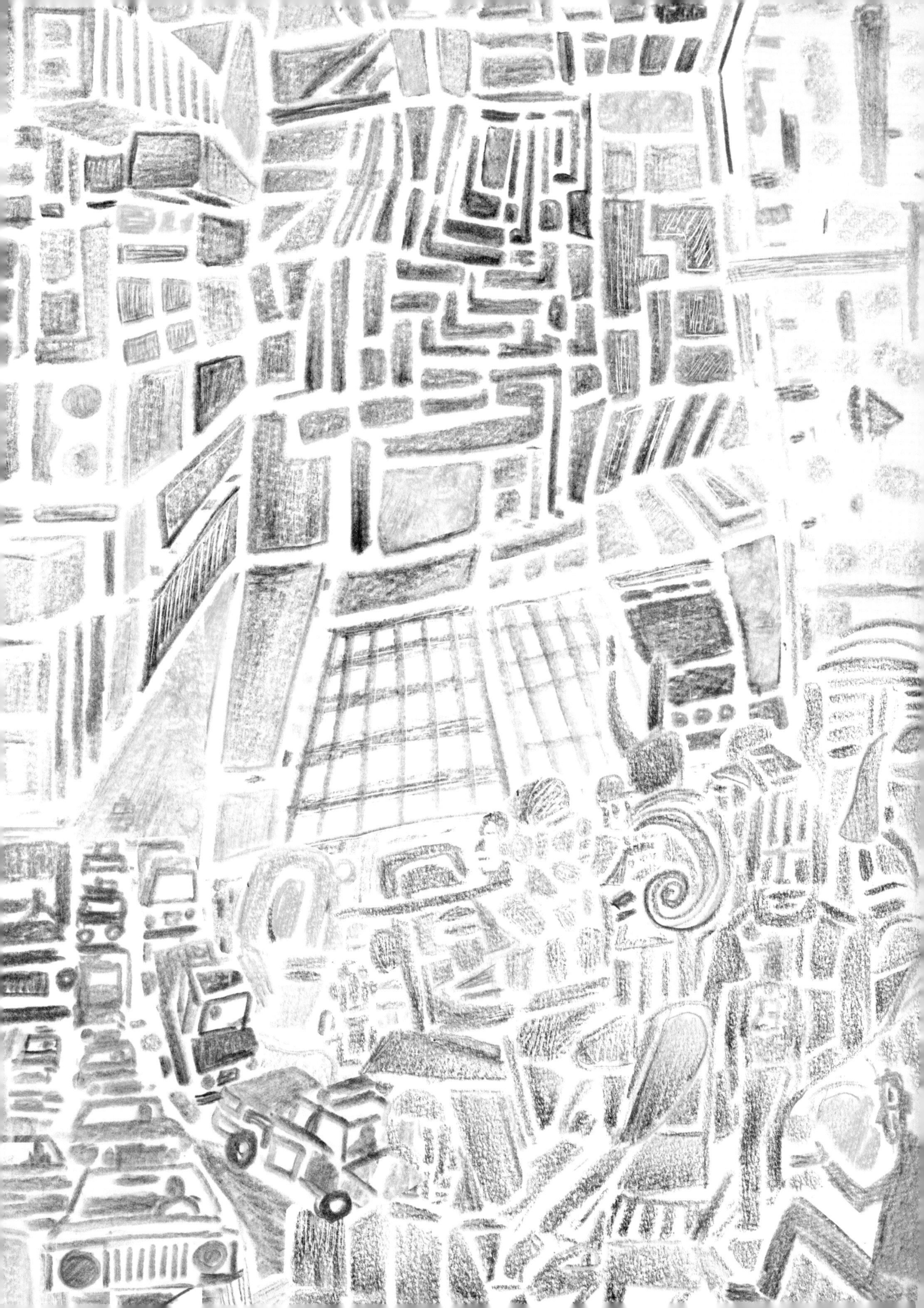

Rooms with a view

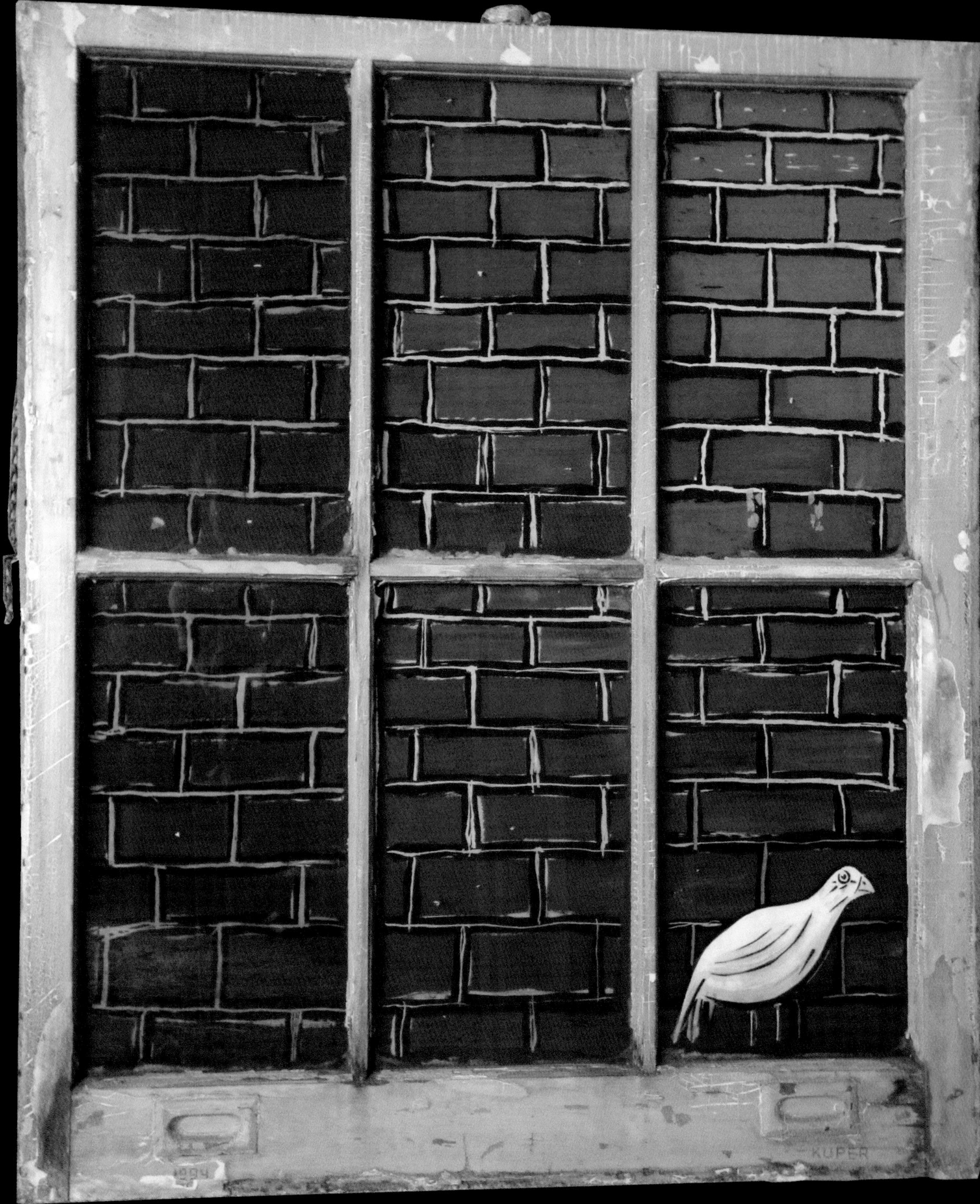

KUPER
1994

One afternoon I was staring out my window when I noticed how the glass panes resembled comic panels. At that time many buildings in my neighborhood were being renovated, so I was able to collect a variety of windows each with its own unique character.

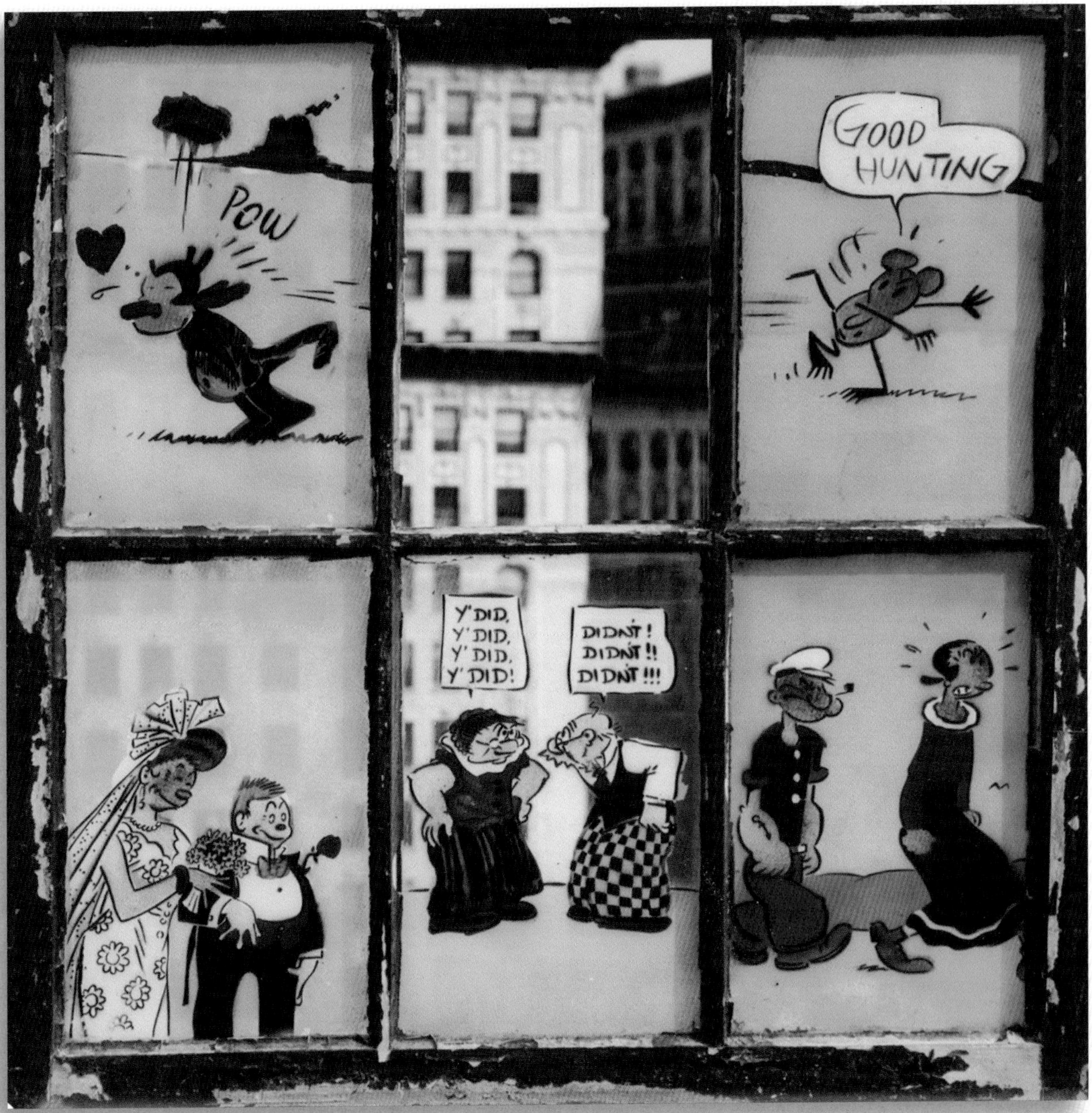
POW
GOOD HUNTING
Y'DID, Y'DID, Y'DID, Y'DID!
DIDN'T! DIDN'T!! DIDN'T!!!

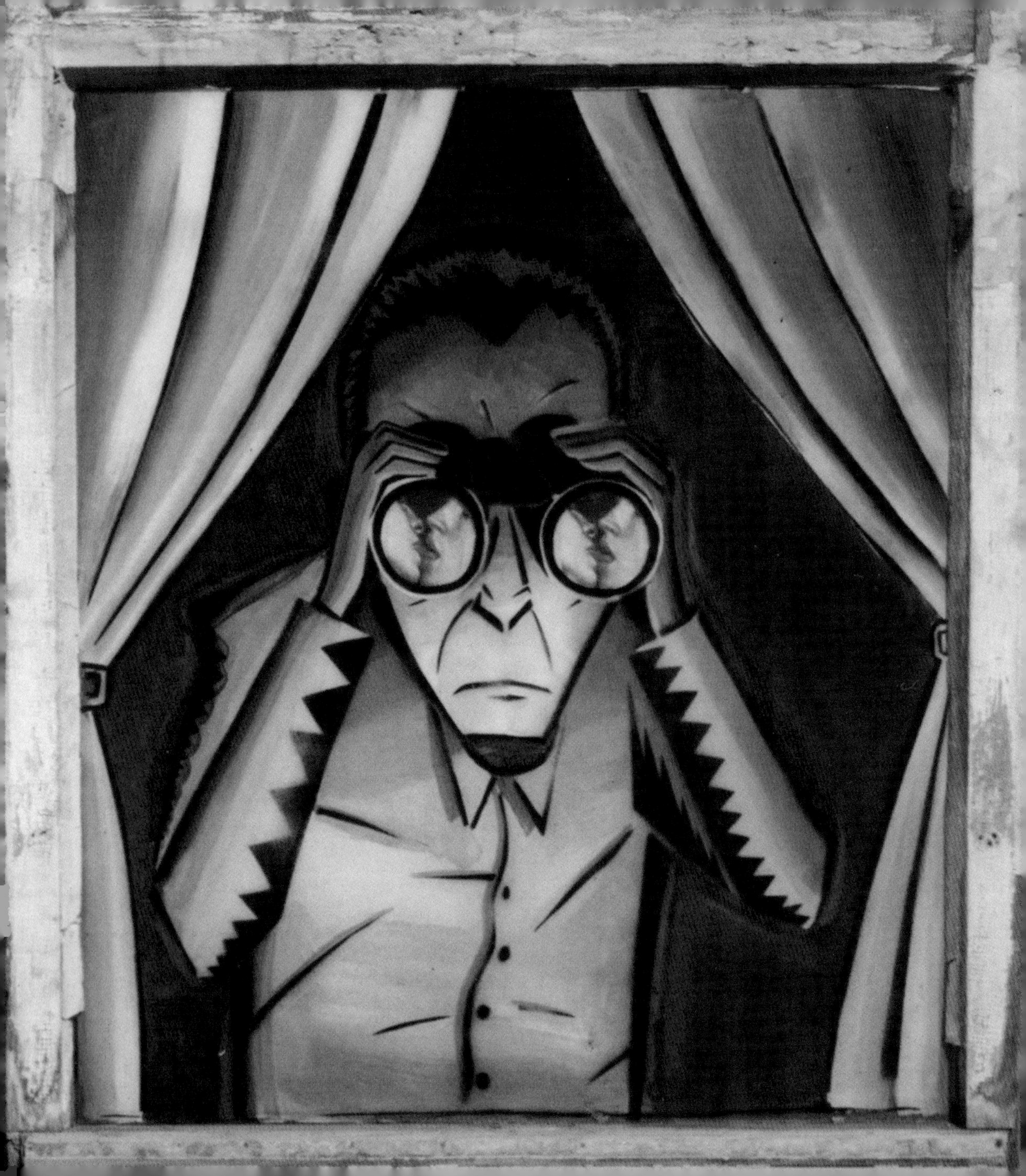

When you look out your window,
you never know who's looking back...

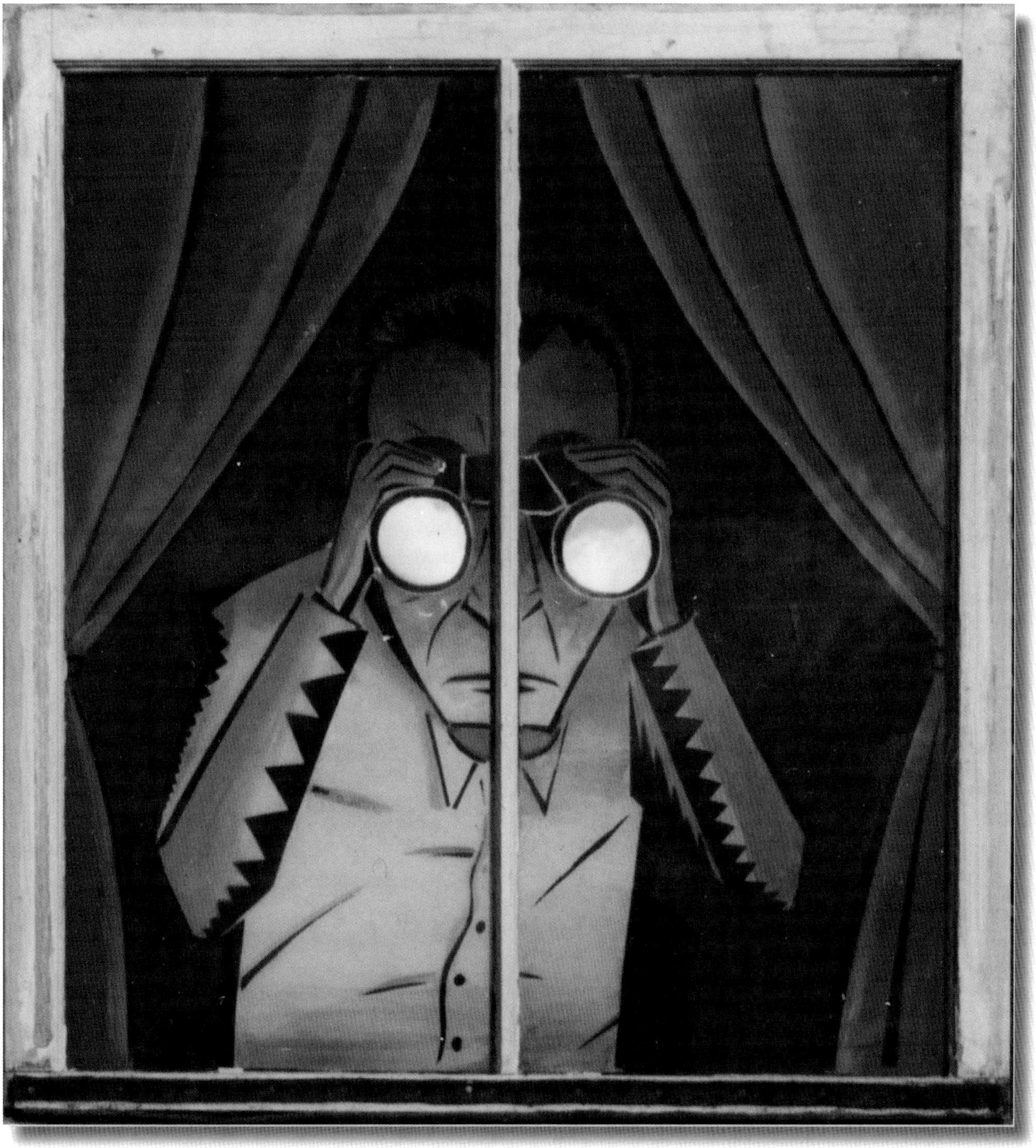

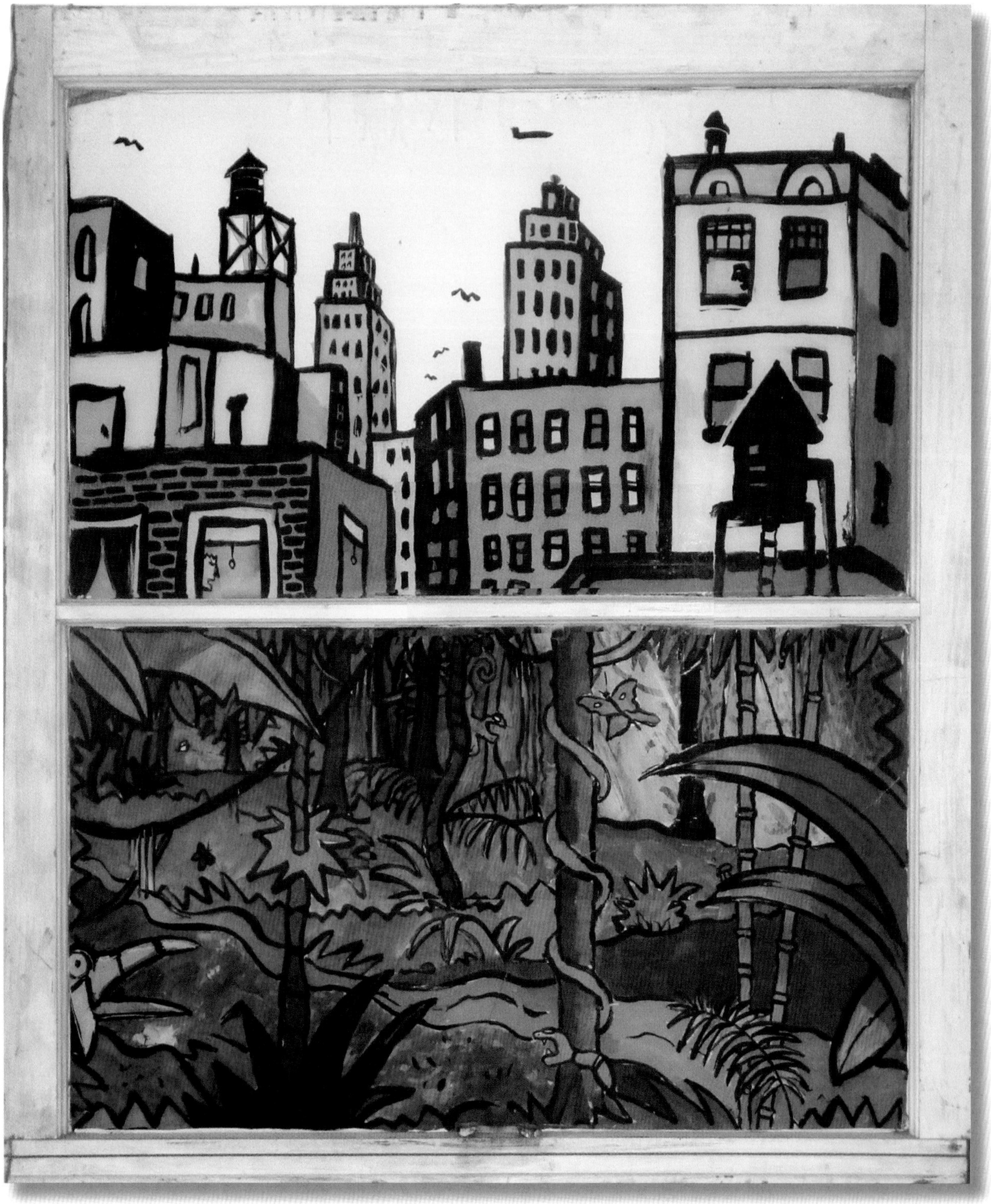

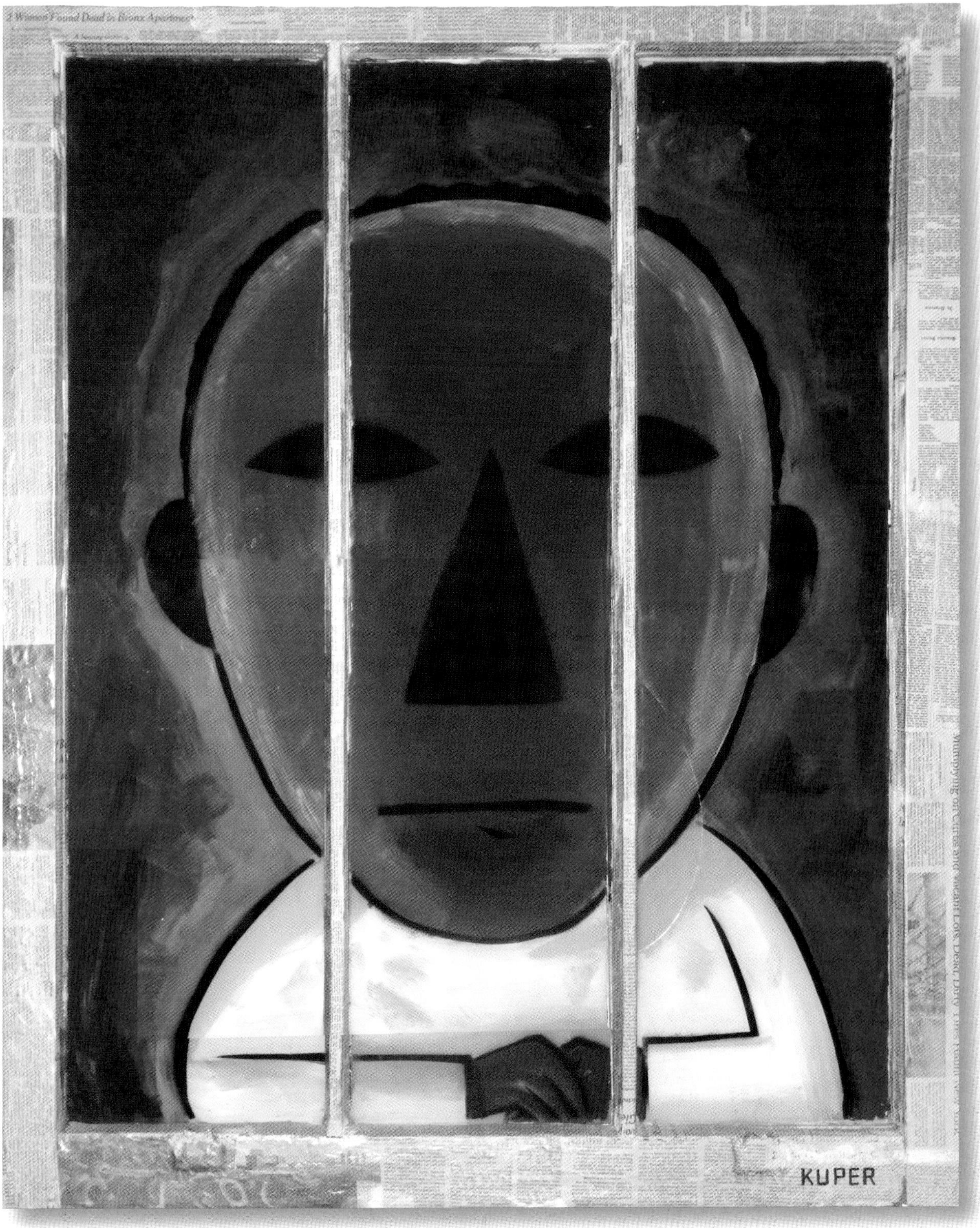
2 Women Found Dead in Bronx Apartment
Multiplying on Curbs and Vacant Lots, Dead, Dirty Flies Haunt New York
KUPER

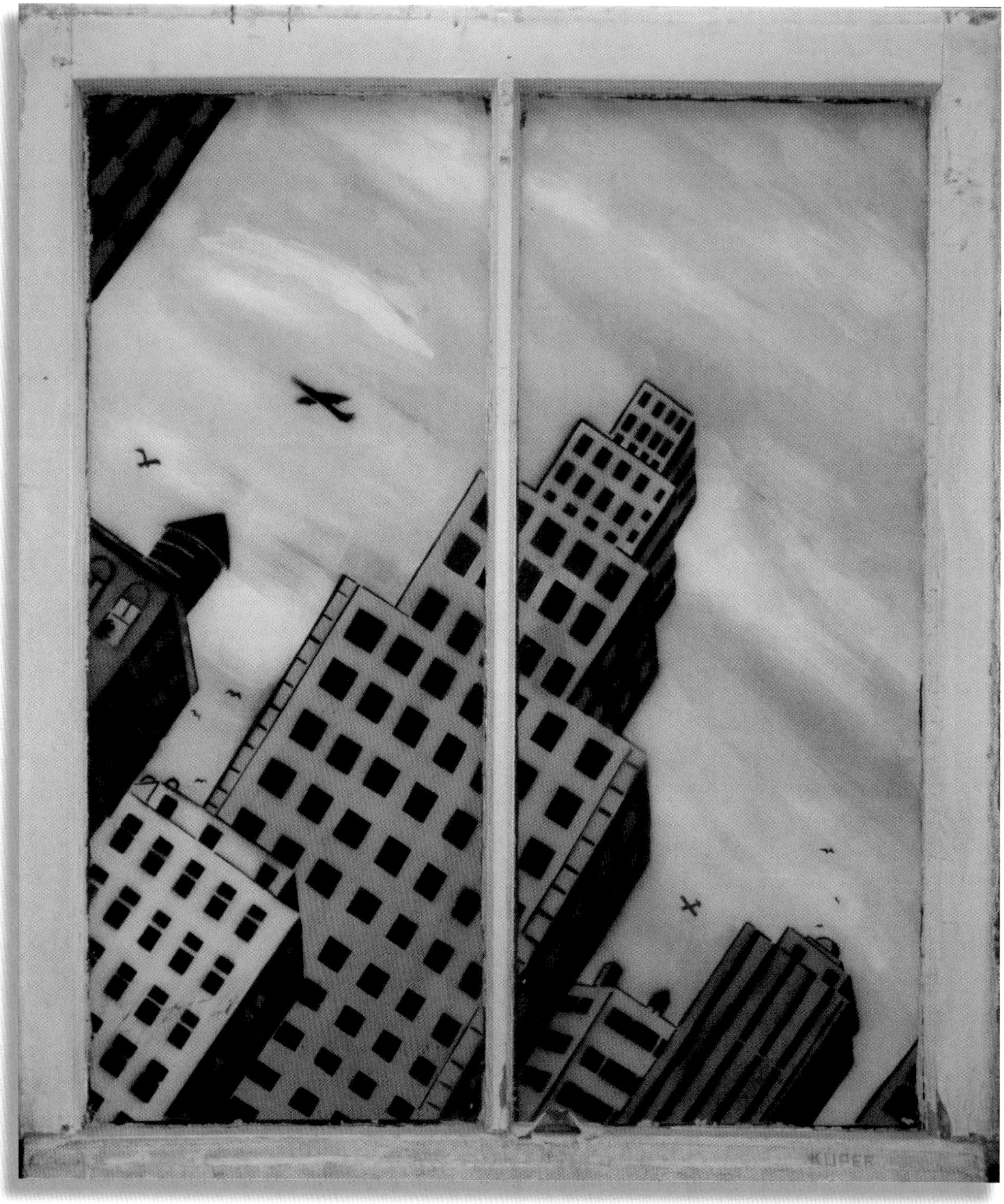
KUPER

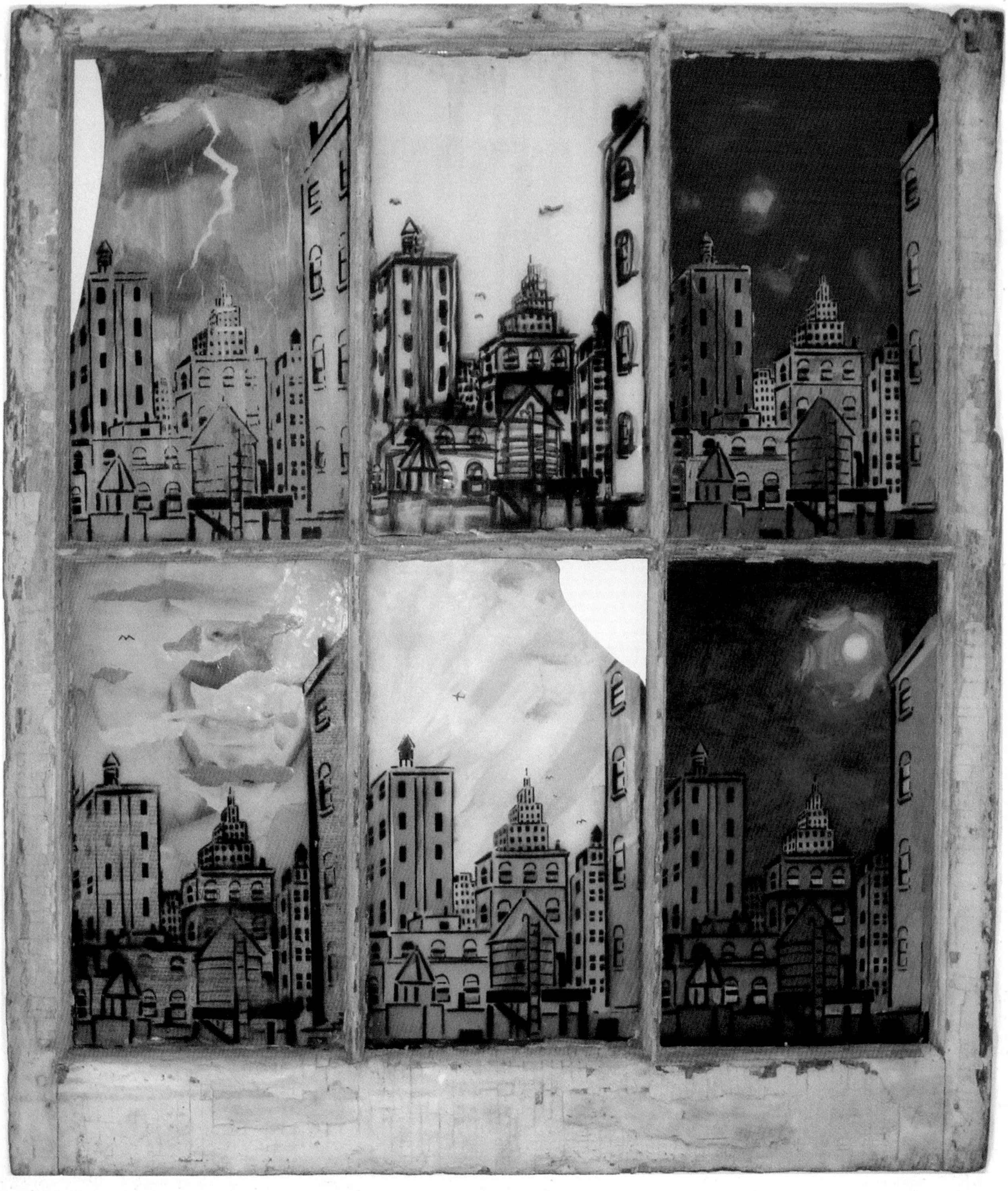

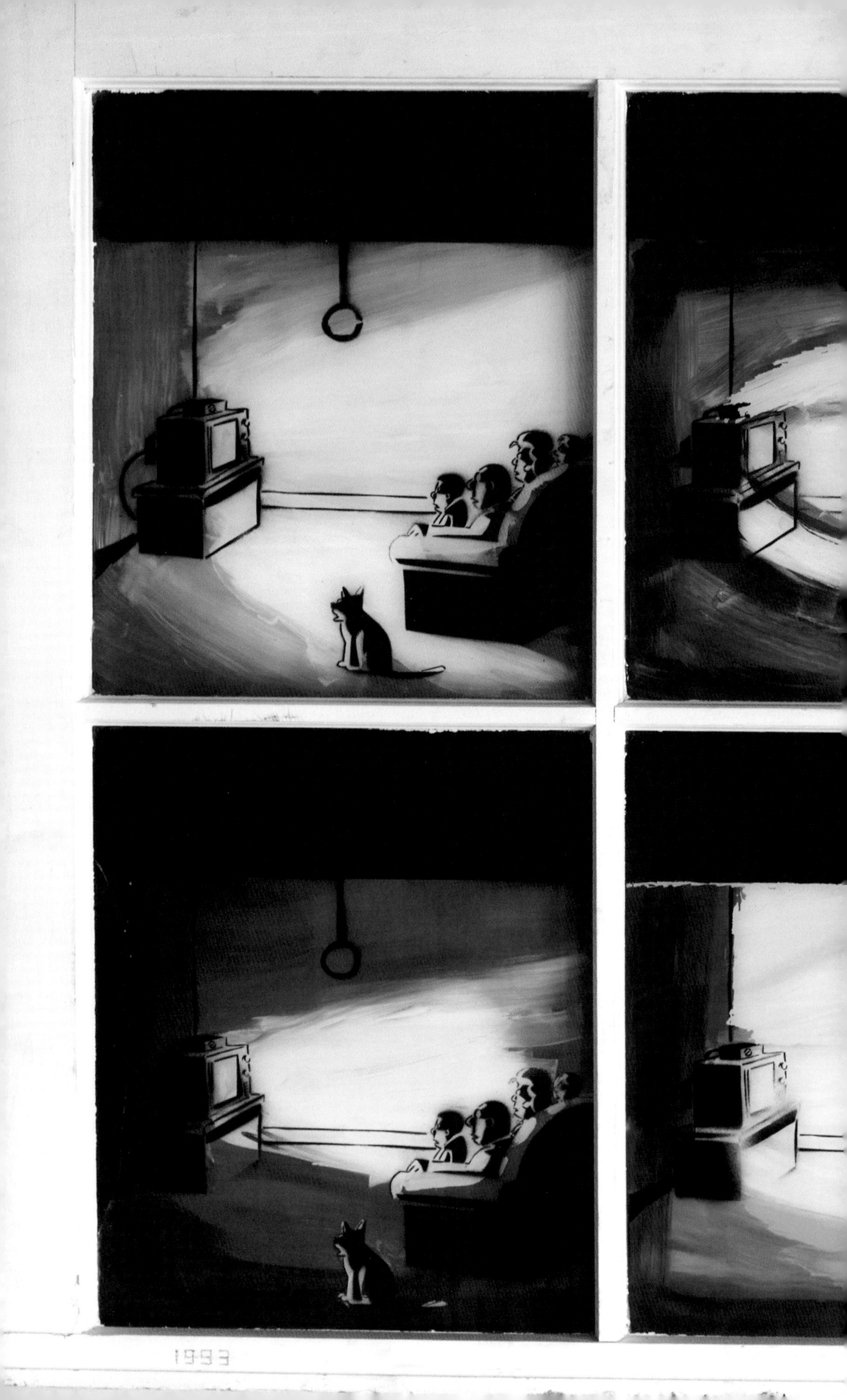
1993

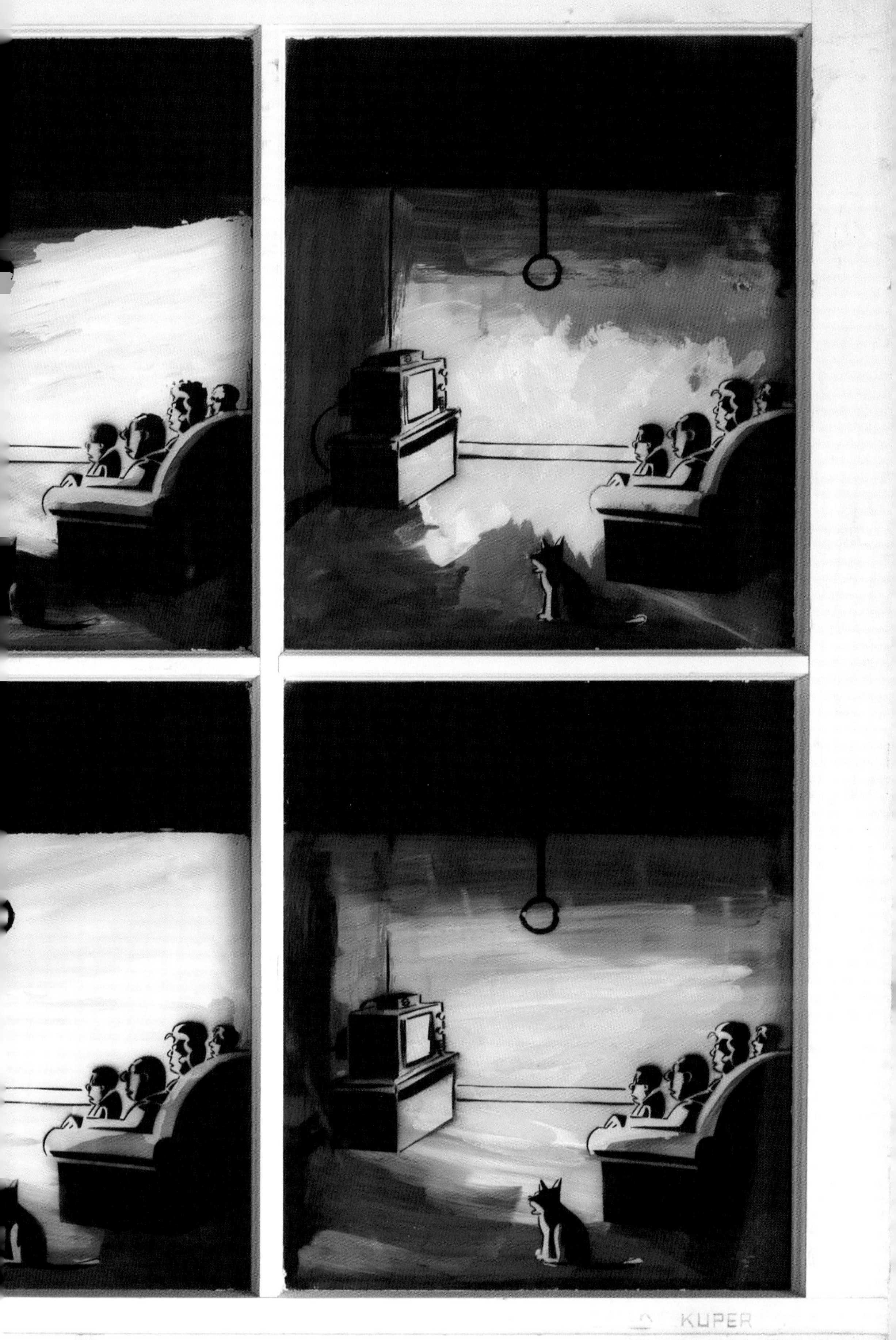
KUPER

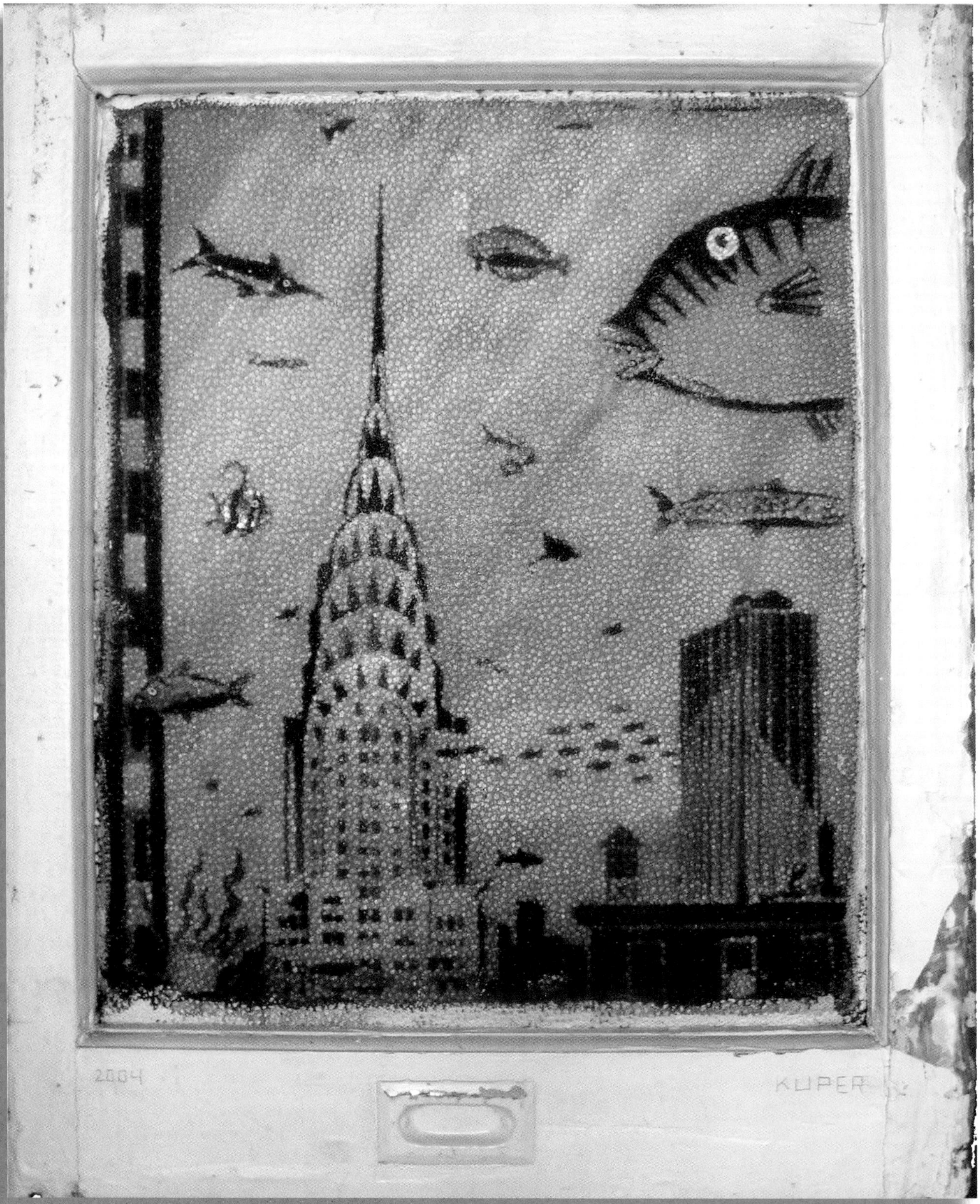
2004
KUPER

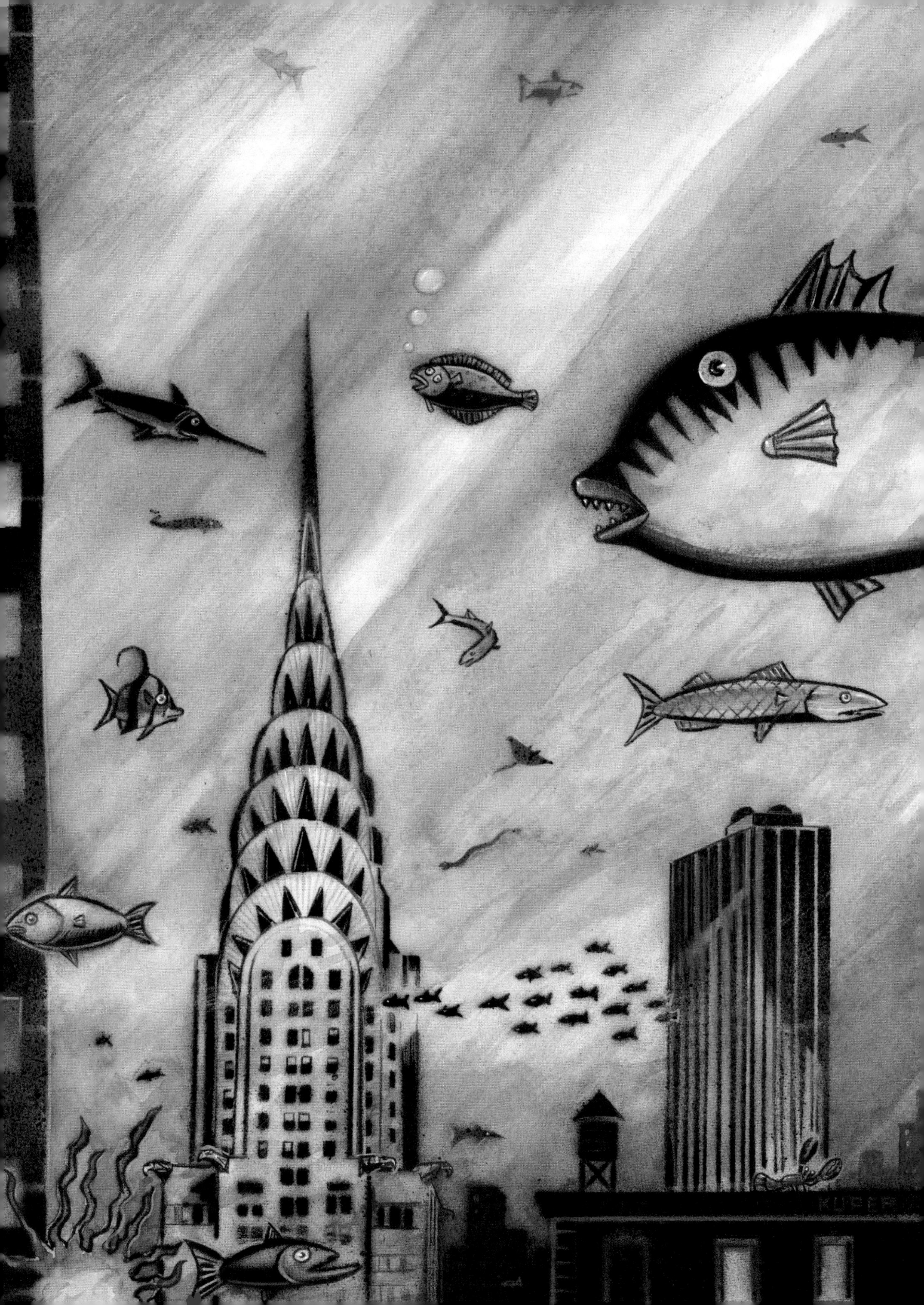
KUPER

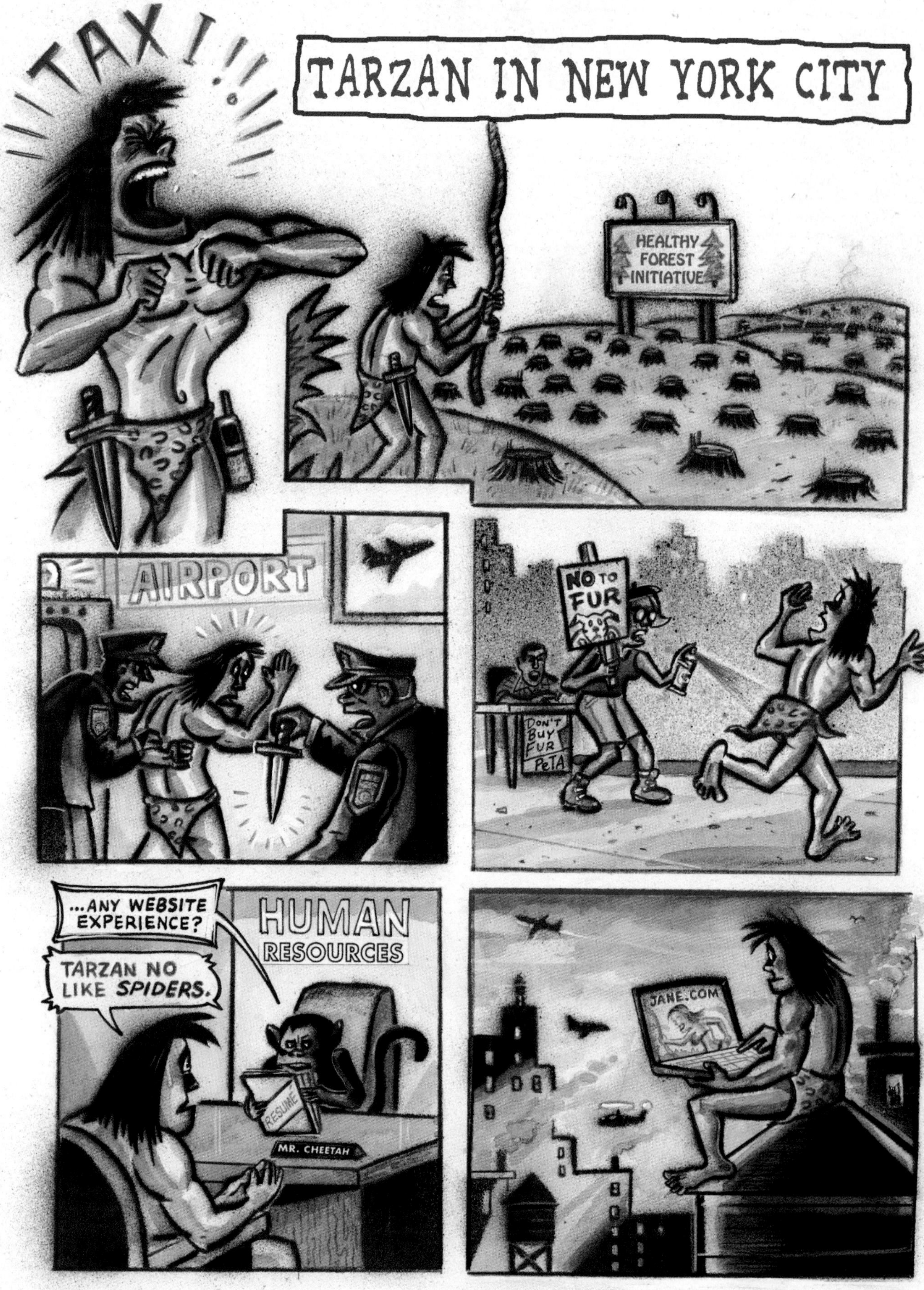
TARZAN IN NEW YORK CITY
TAXI!!!
HEALTHY FOREST INITIATIVE
AIRPORT
NO TO FUR
DON'T BUY FUR PeTA
HUMAN RESOURCES
...ANY WEBSITE EXPERIENCE?
TARZAN NO LIKE SPIDERS.
RESUME
MR. CHEETAH
JANE.COM

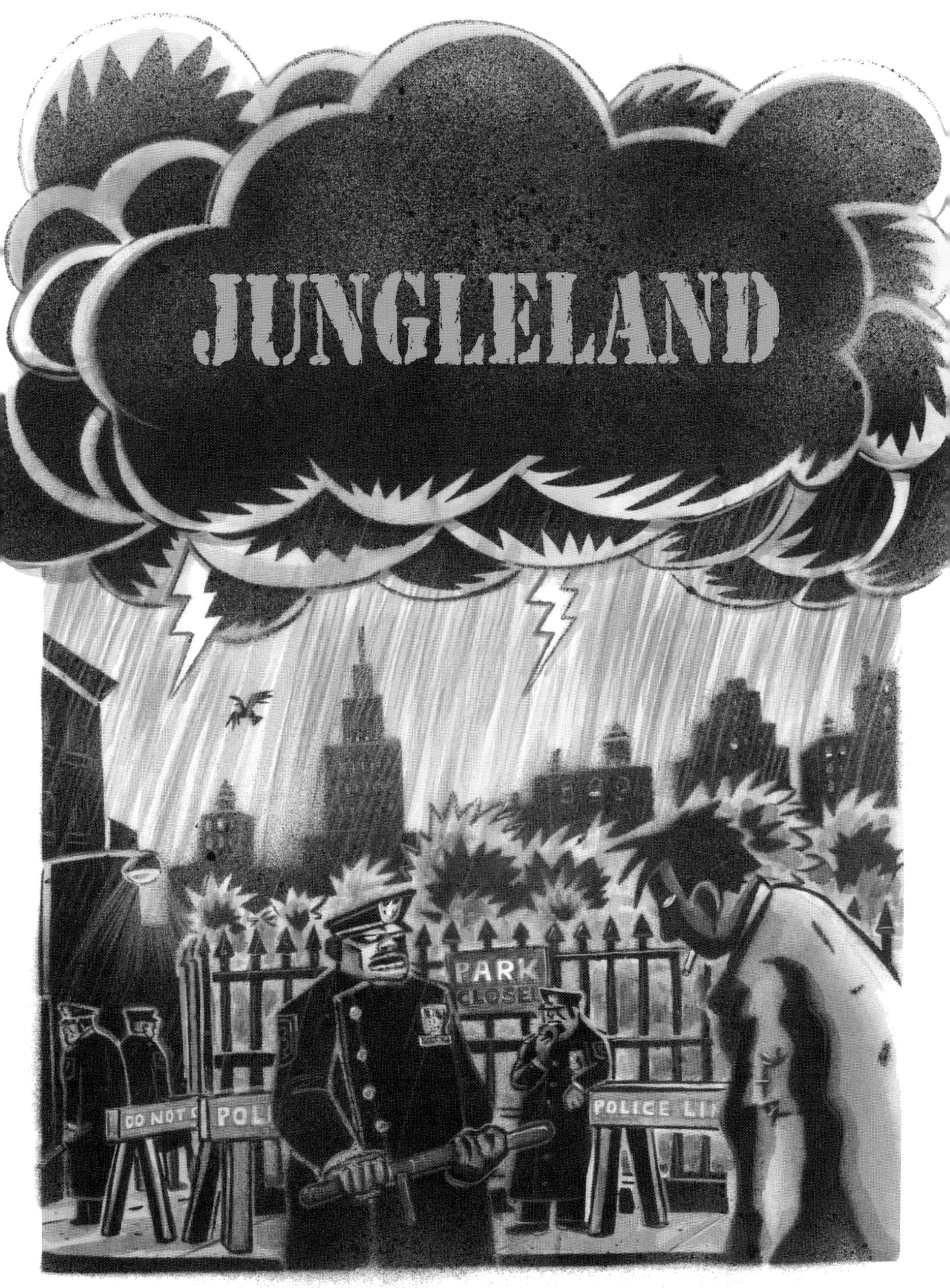
JUNGLELAND
PARK
CLOSE
DO NOT C
POLI
POLICE LI

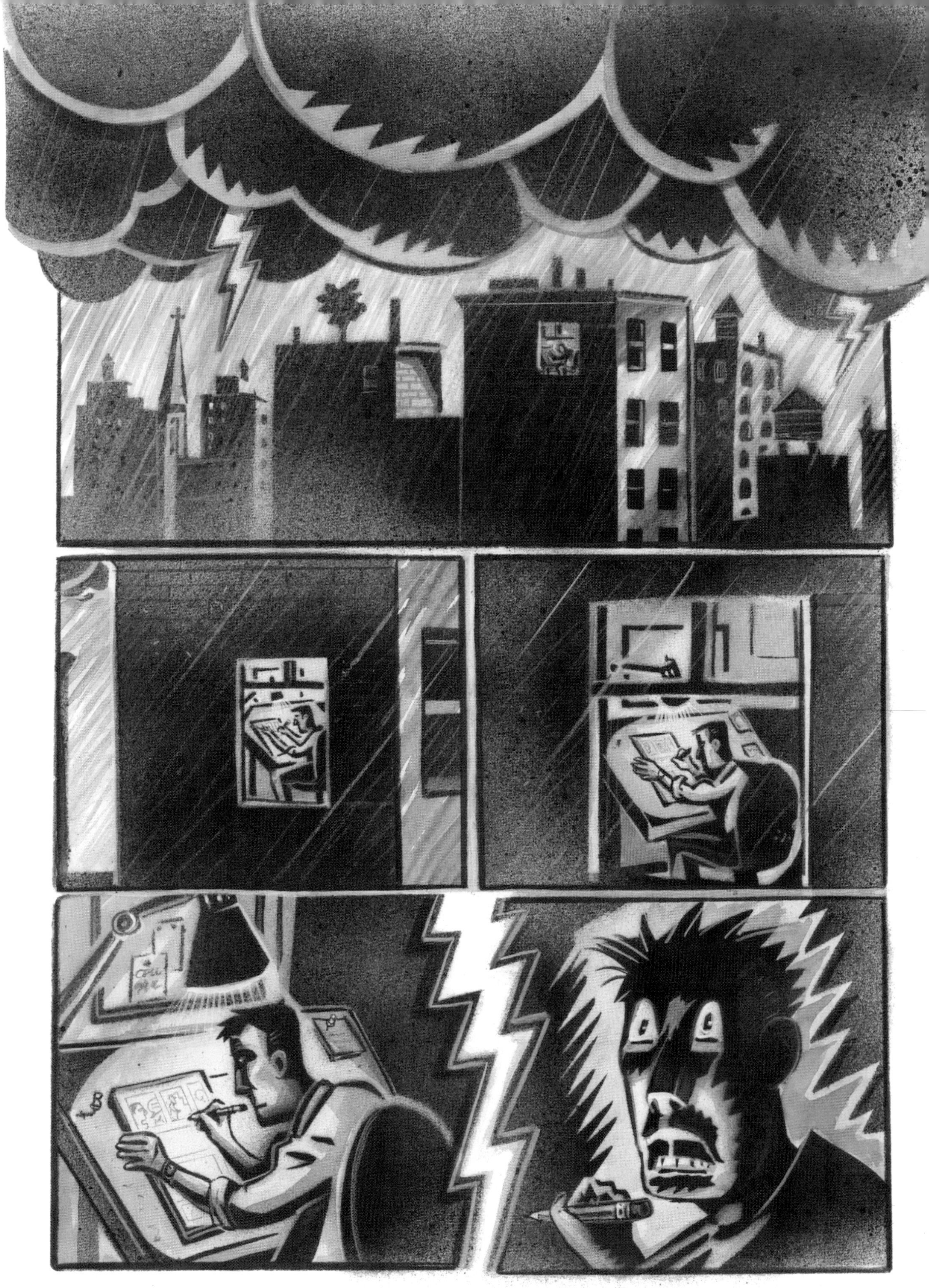

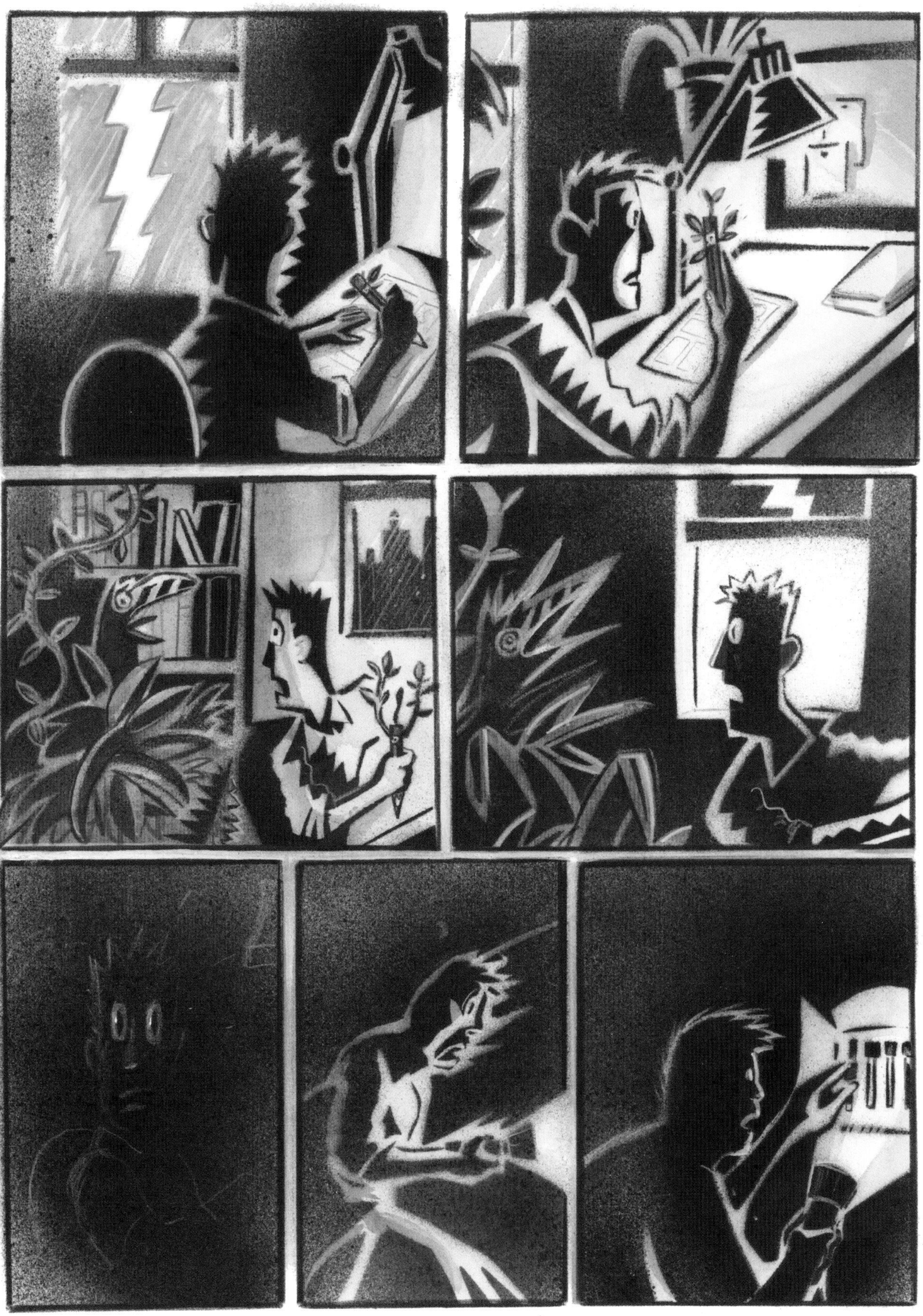

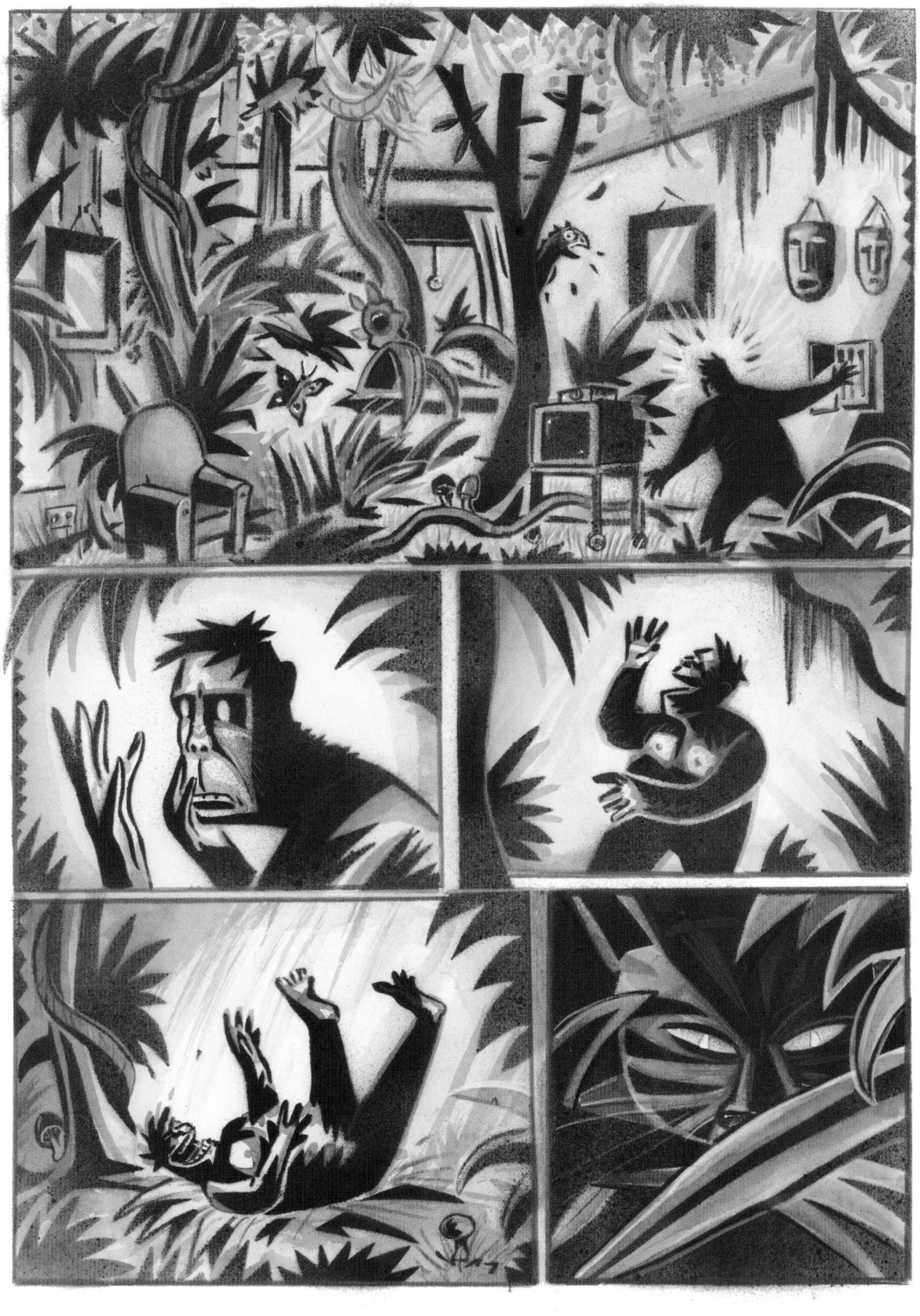

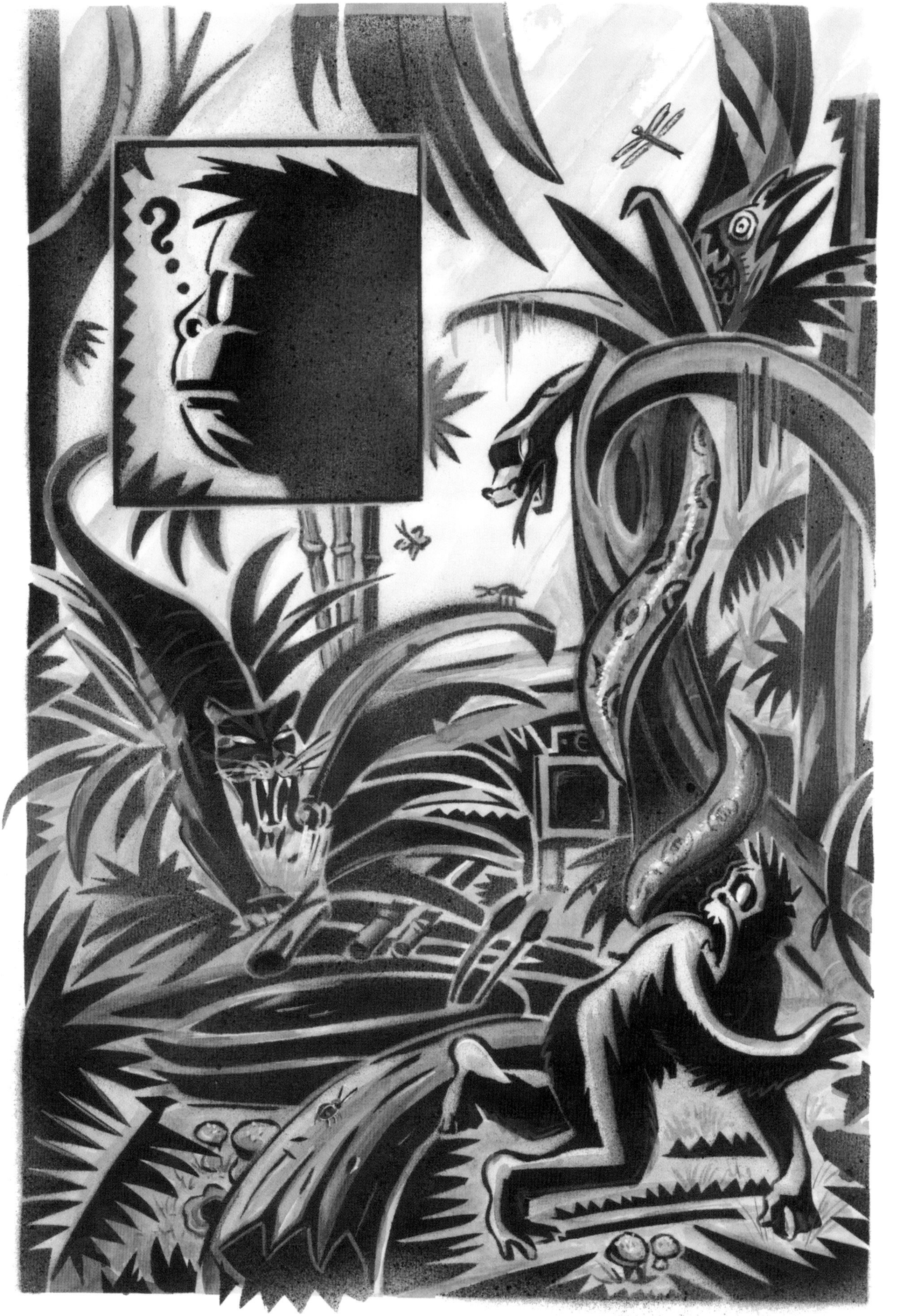
?

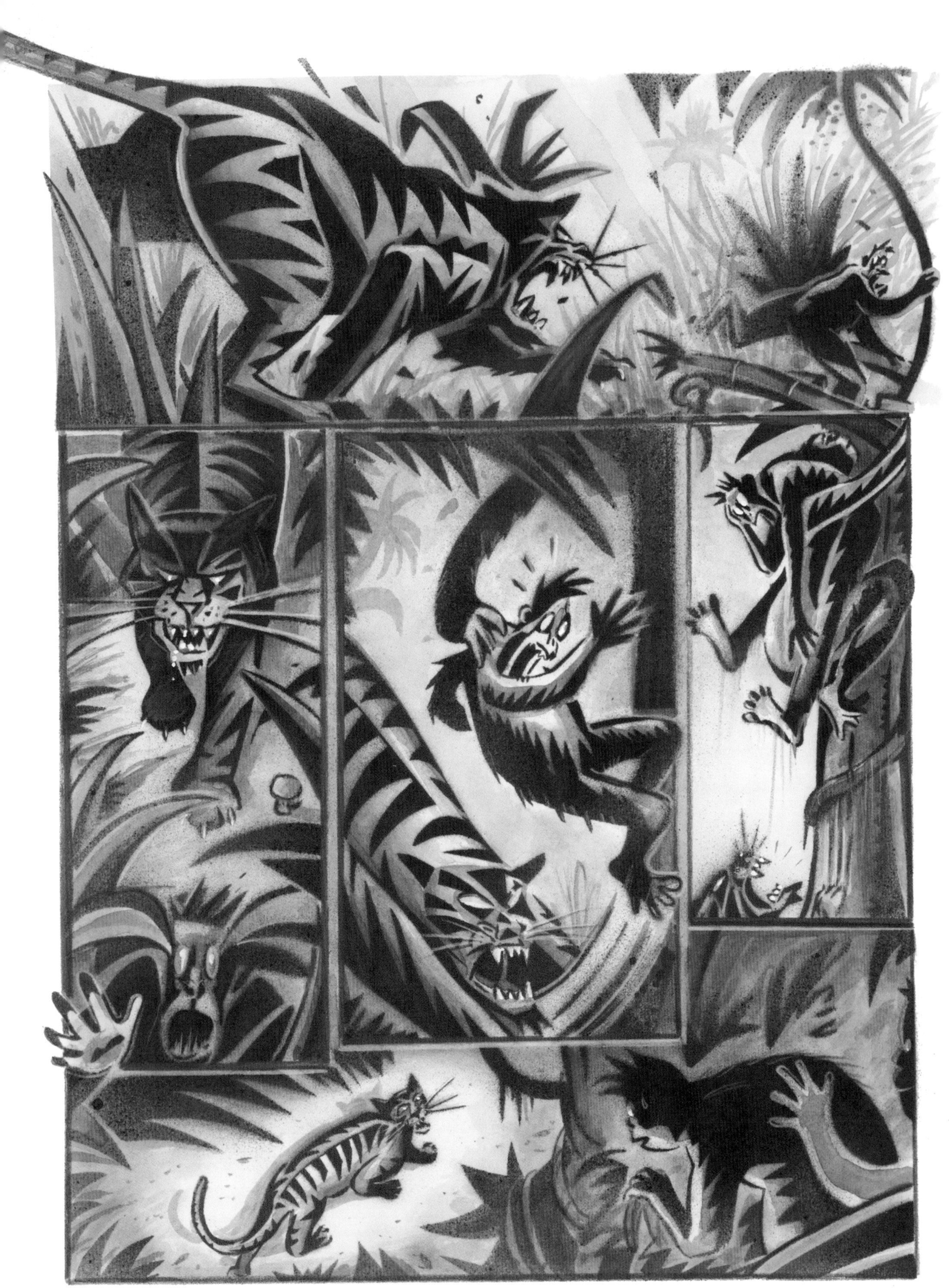

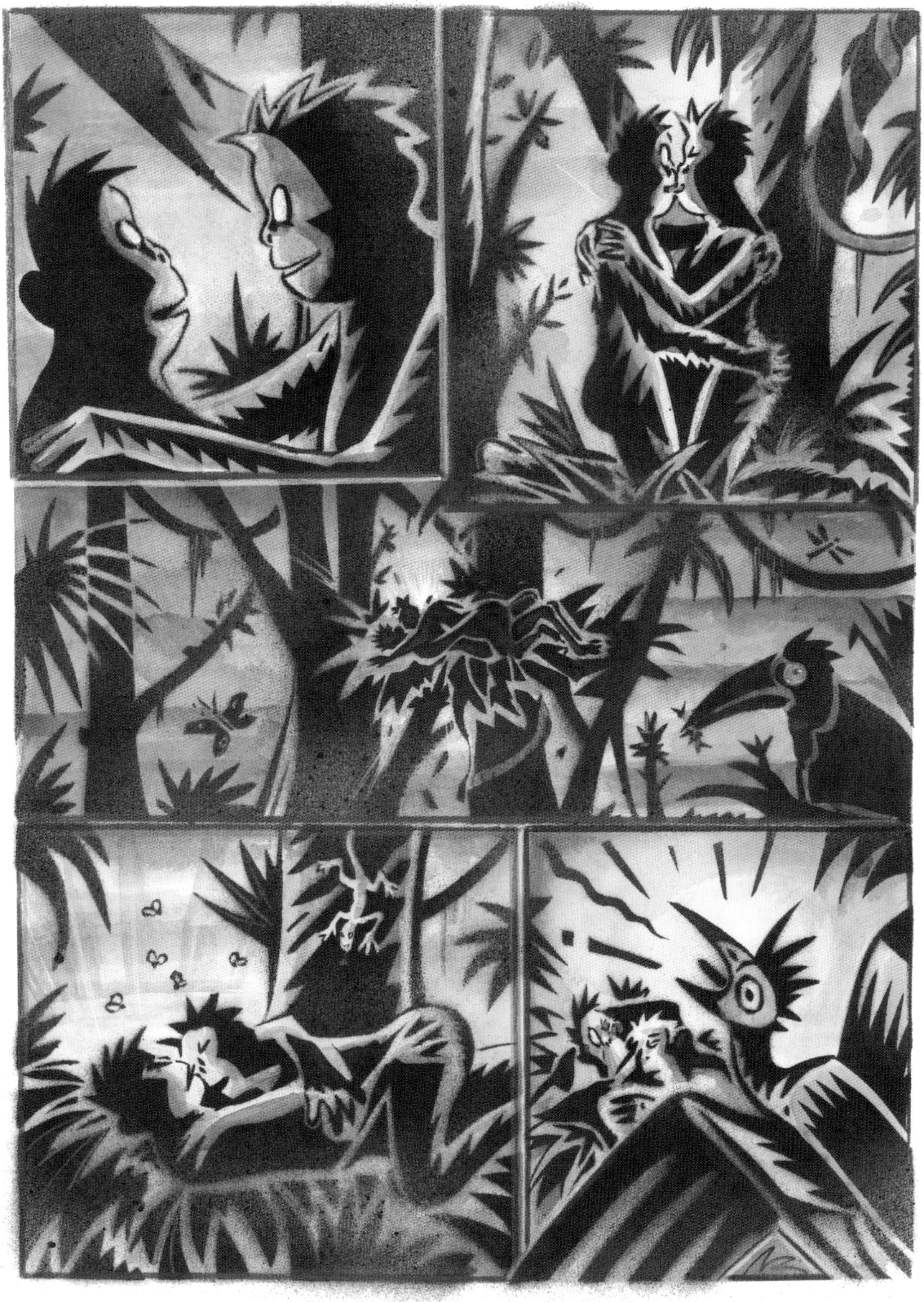

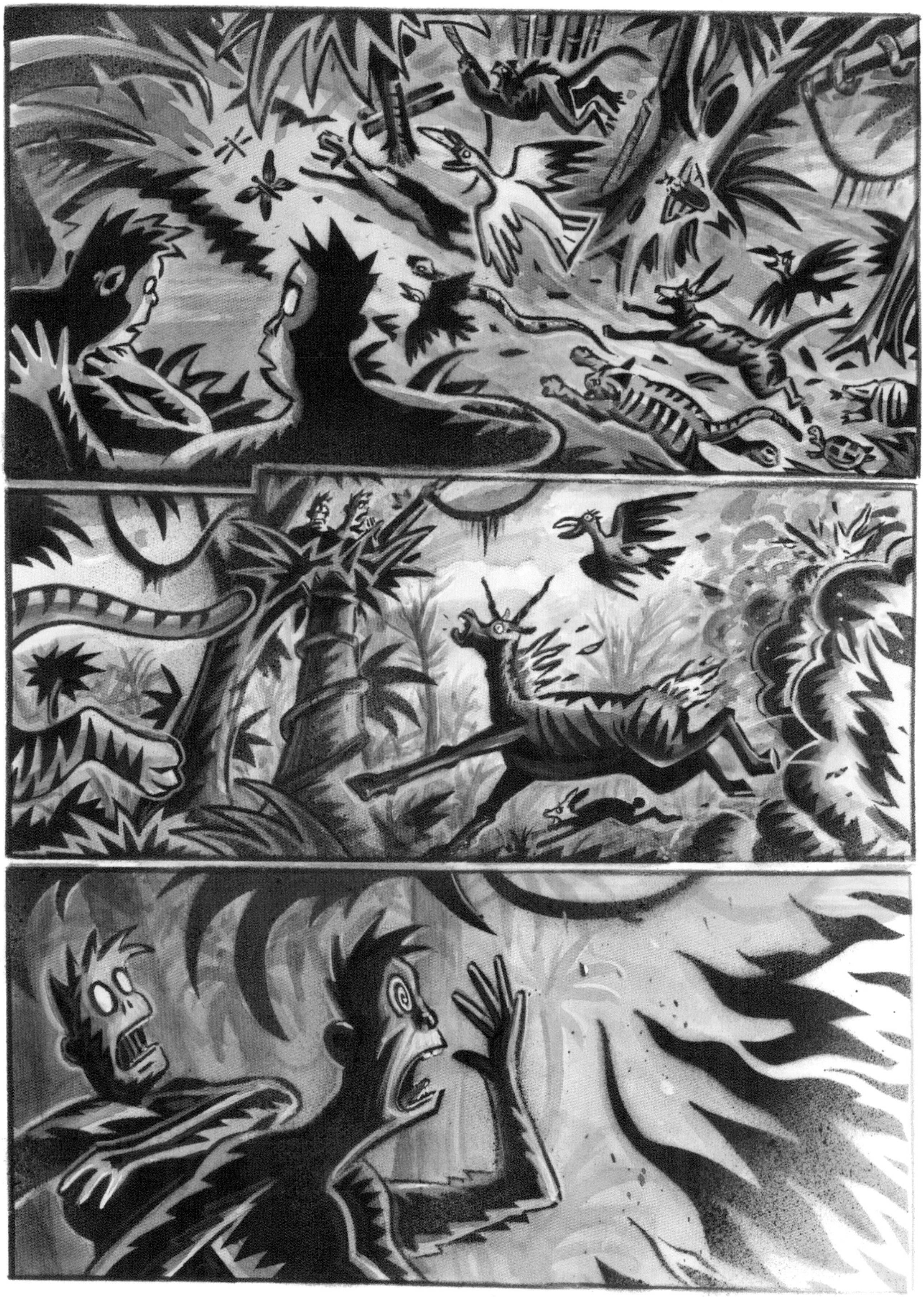

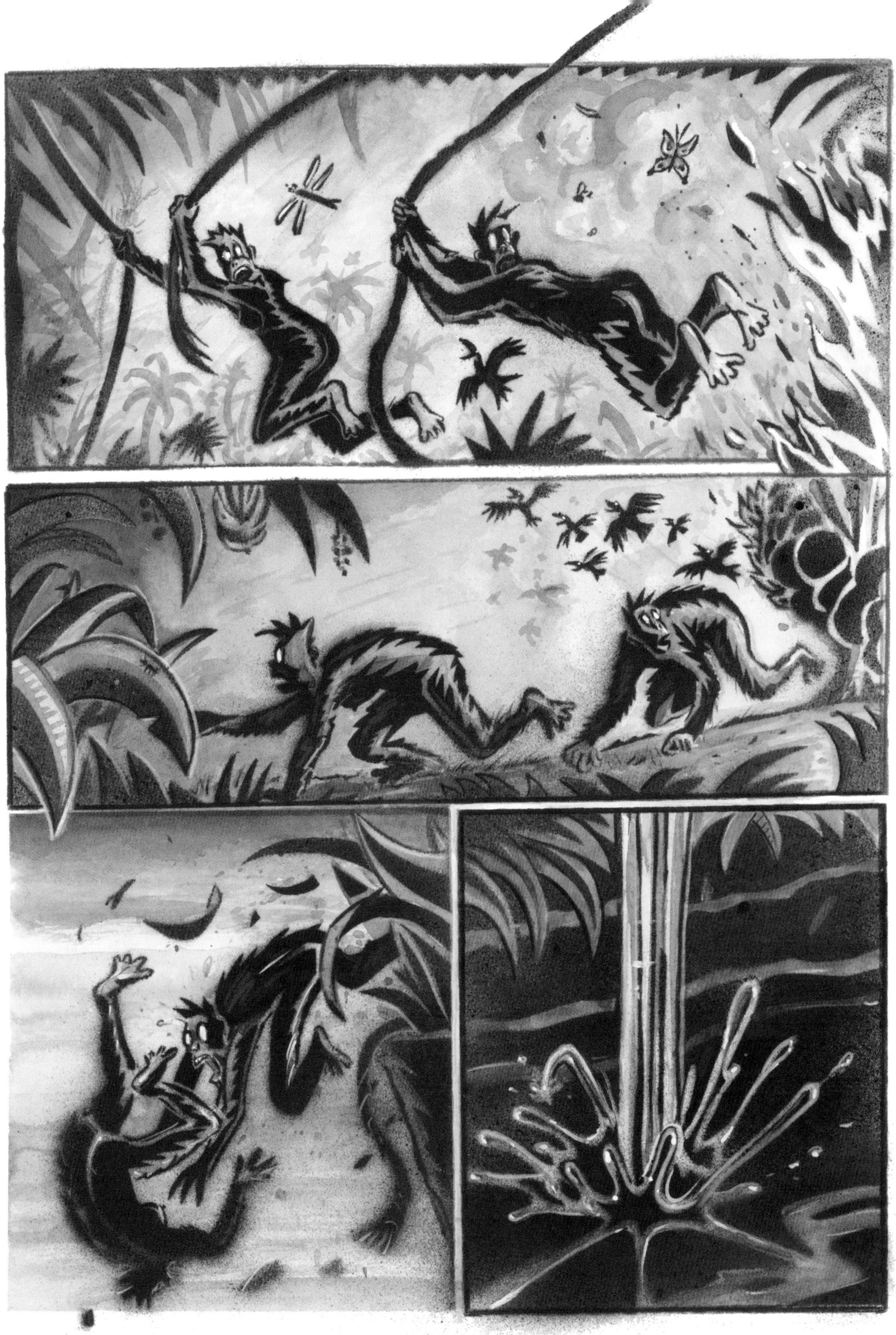

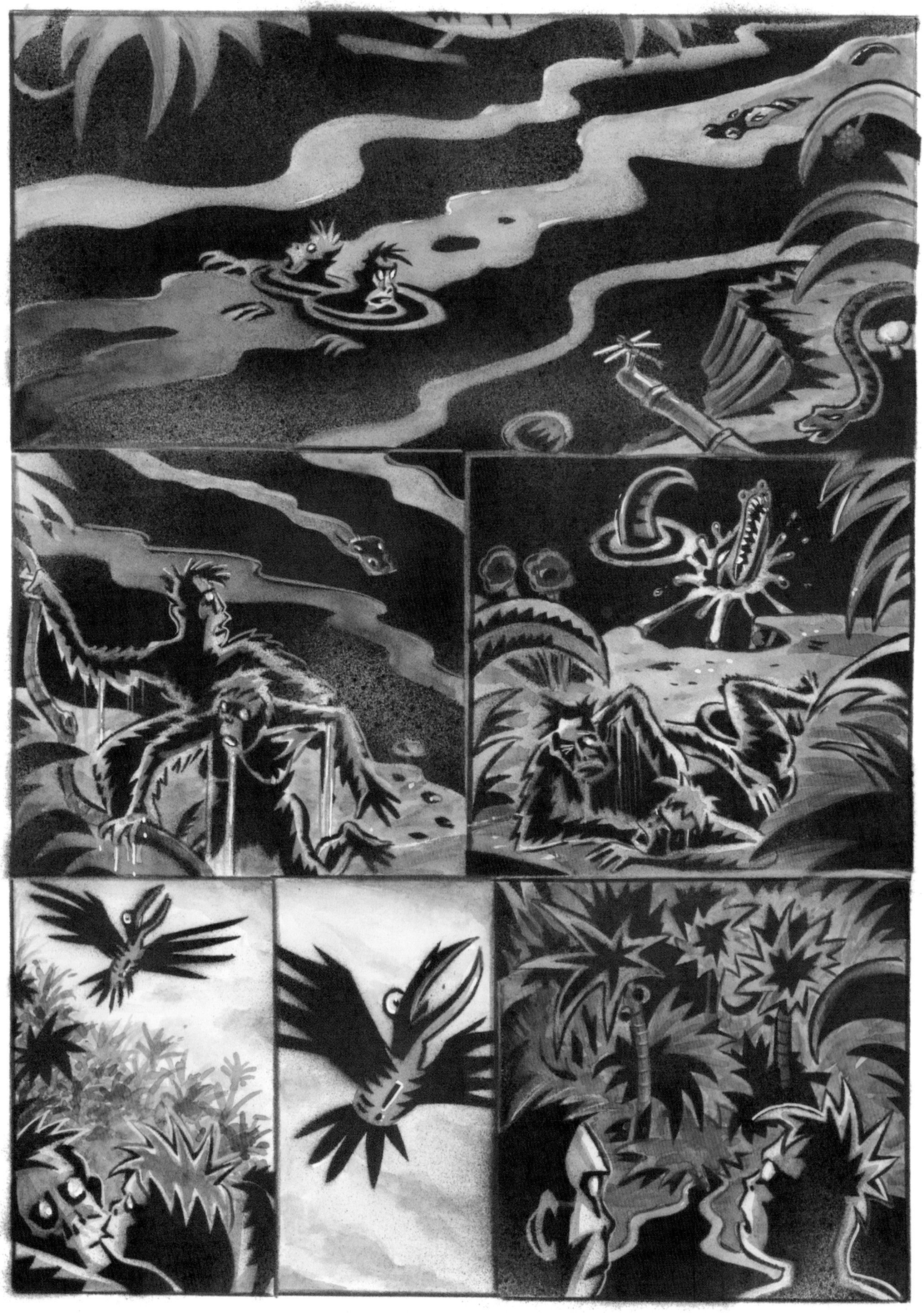

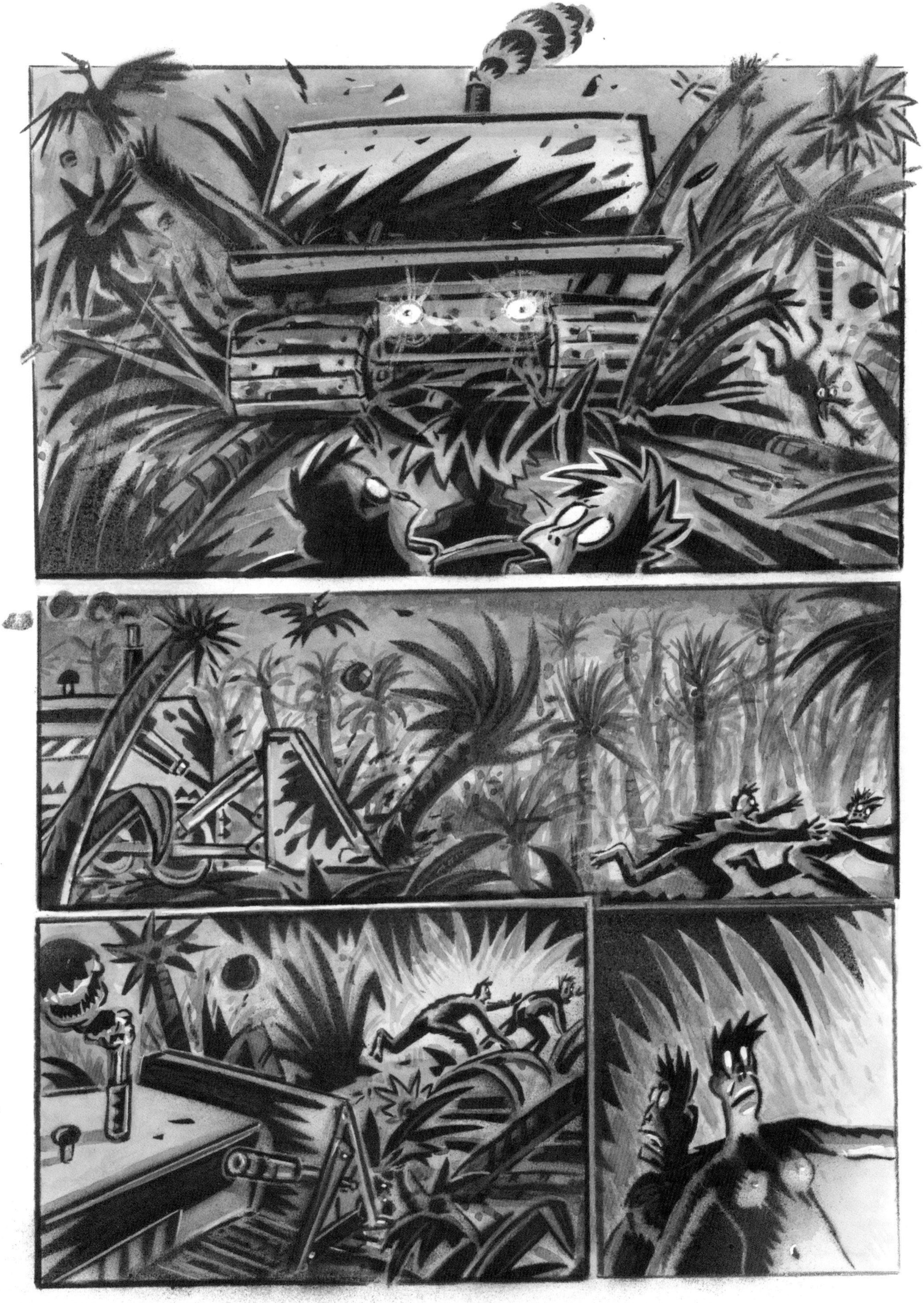

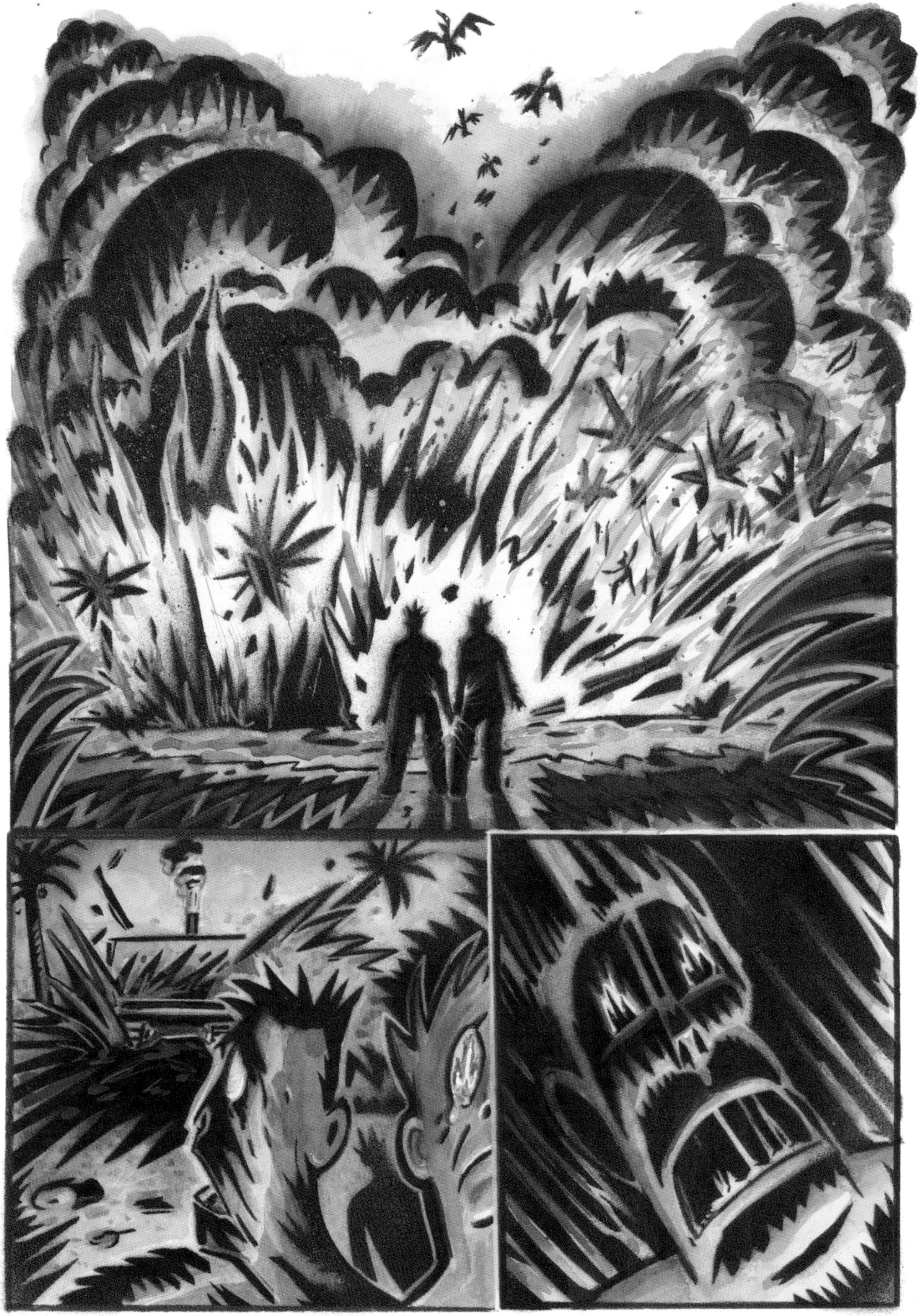

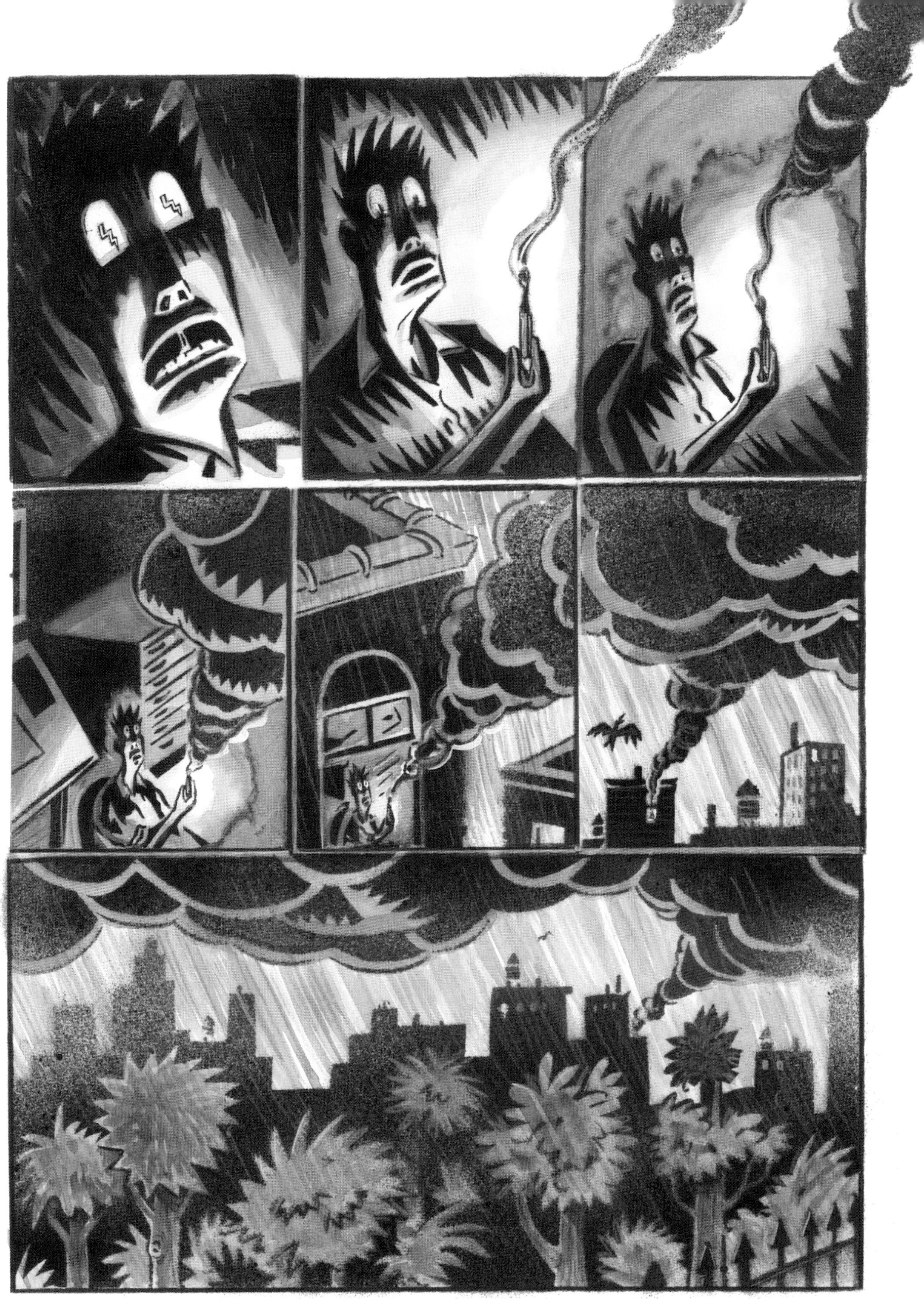

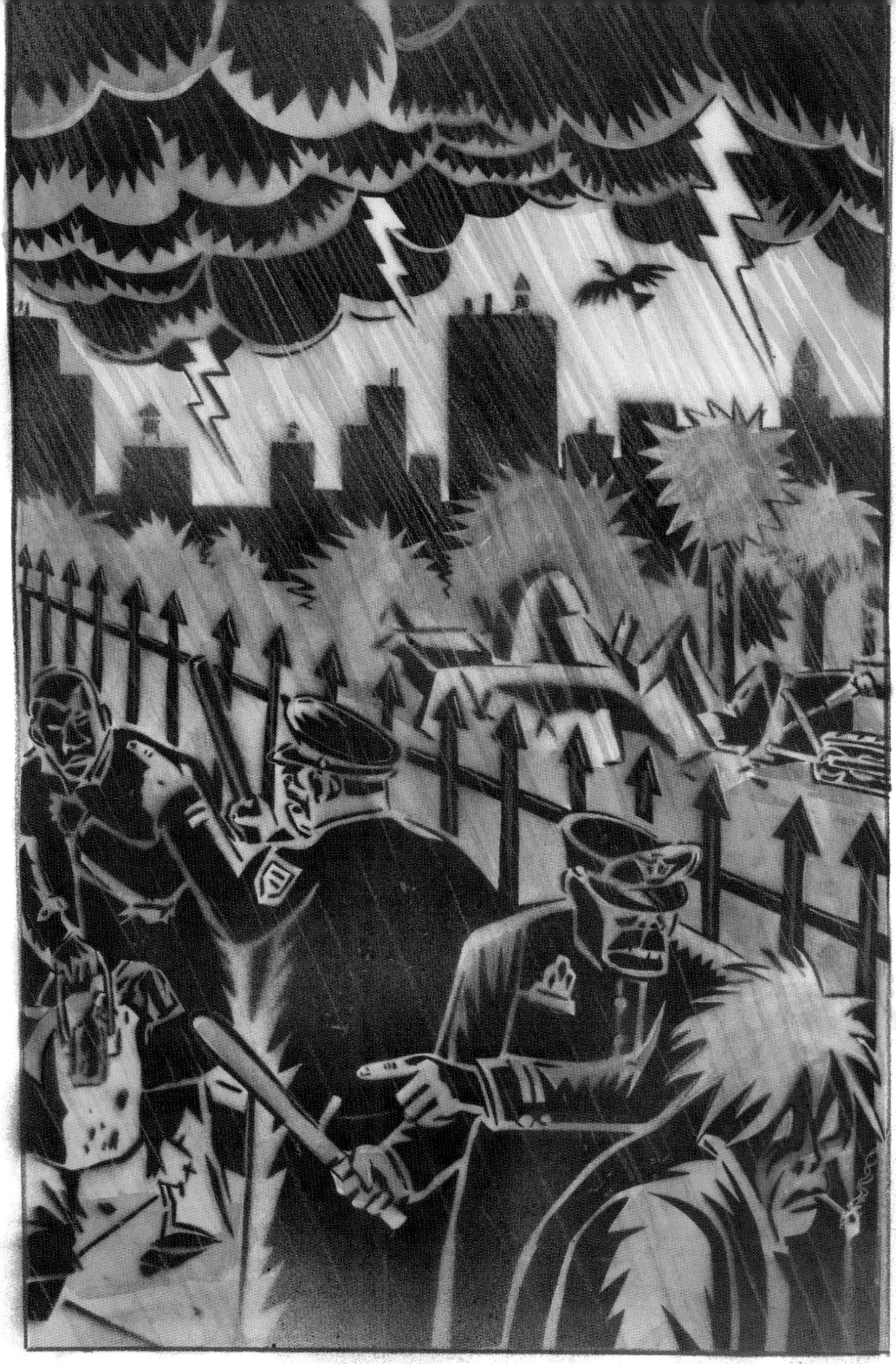

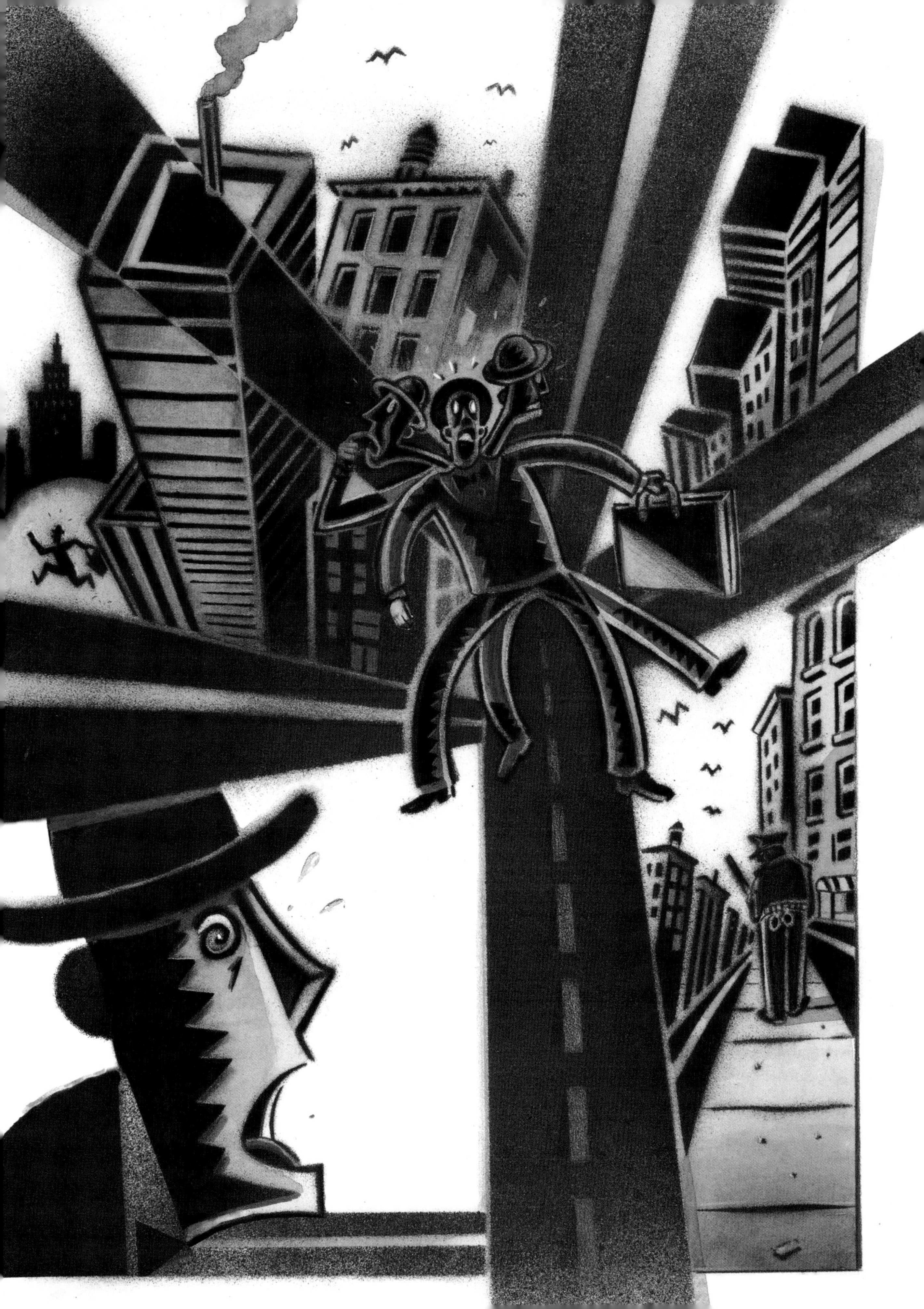

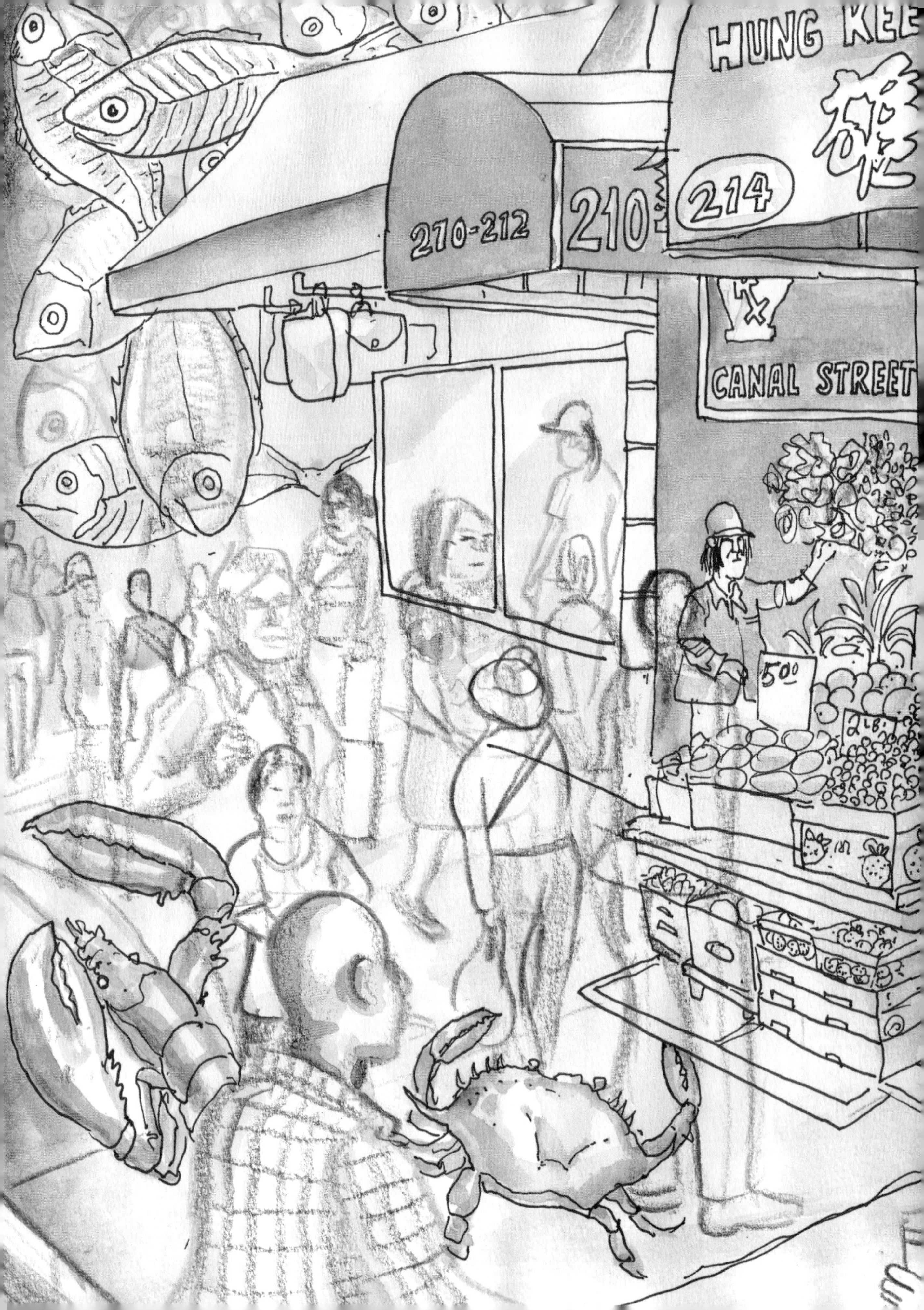
HUNG KE
270-212
210
214
CANAL STREET
500
2LB

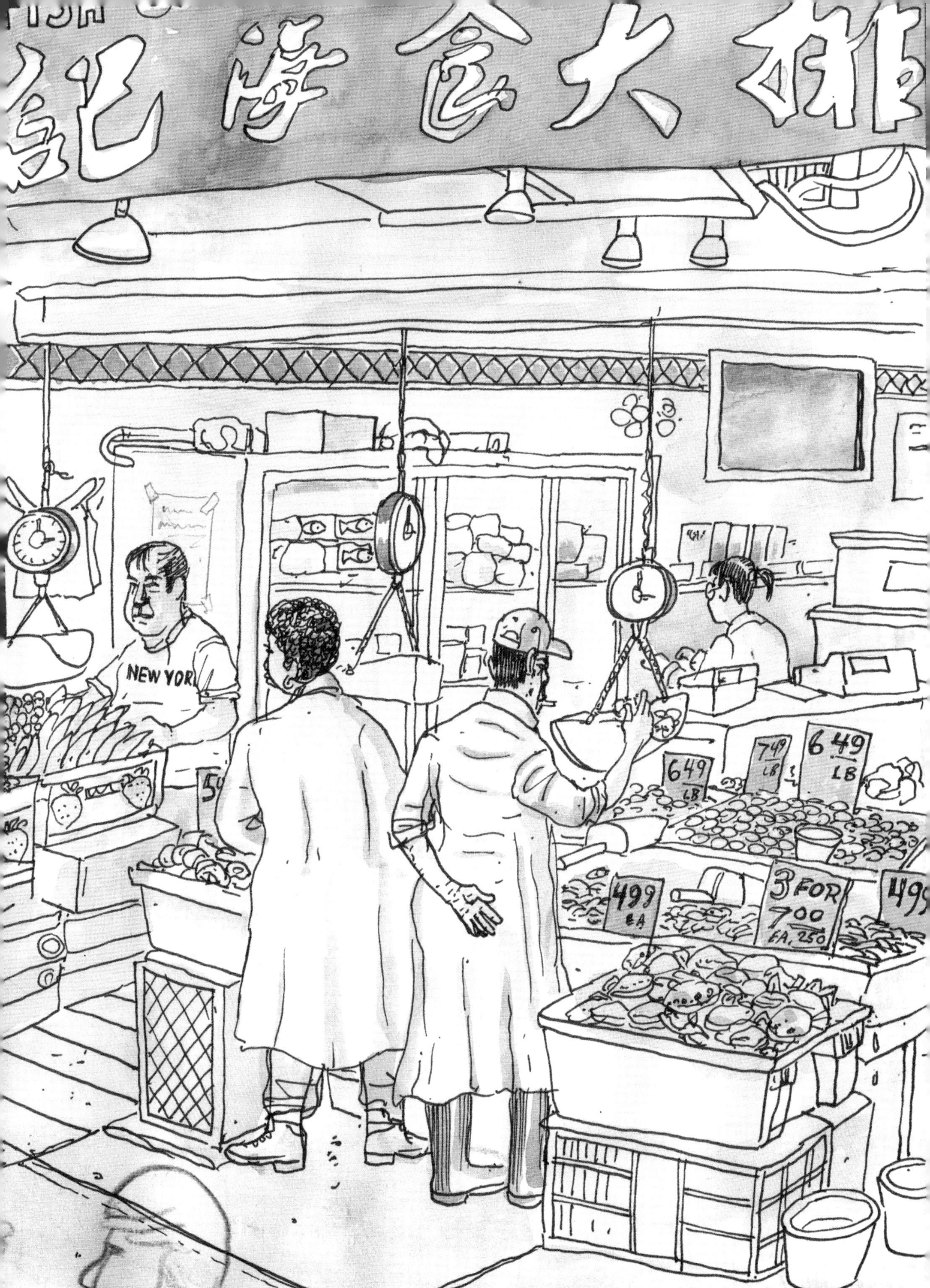
NEW YOR
6 49 LB
7 49 LB
6 49 LB
4 99 EA
3 FOR 7 00 EA. 2 50
4 99

CHINATOWN MAY 27 2010

Odorama

A visual guide to city smells

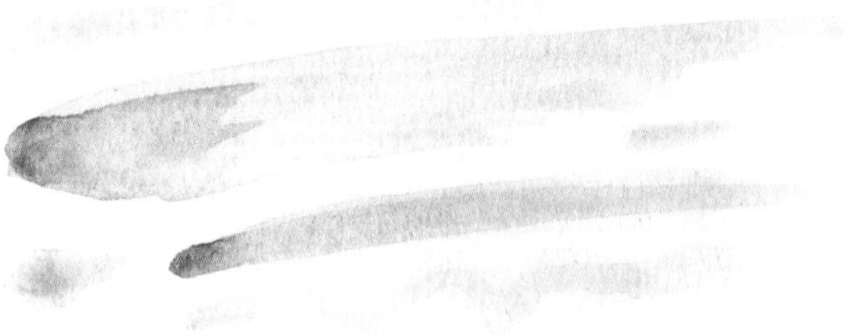

Laundry exhaust
on Amsterdam Ave.

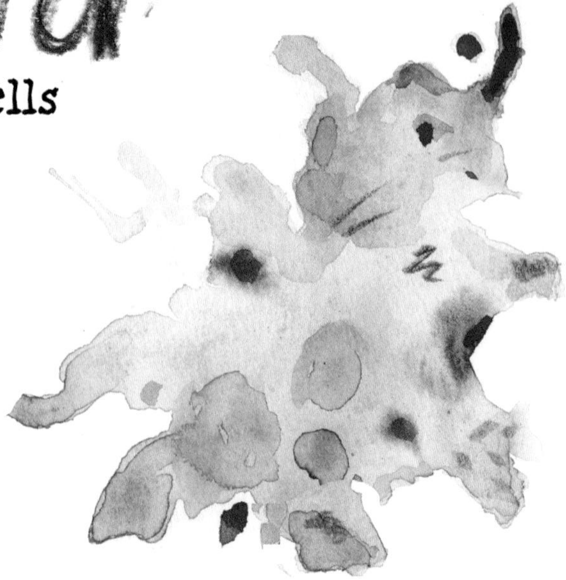

Flower District
Garbage can

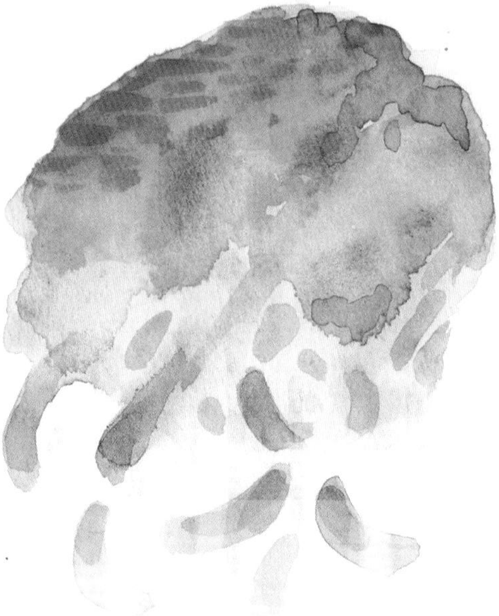

Central Park food-cart

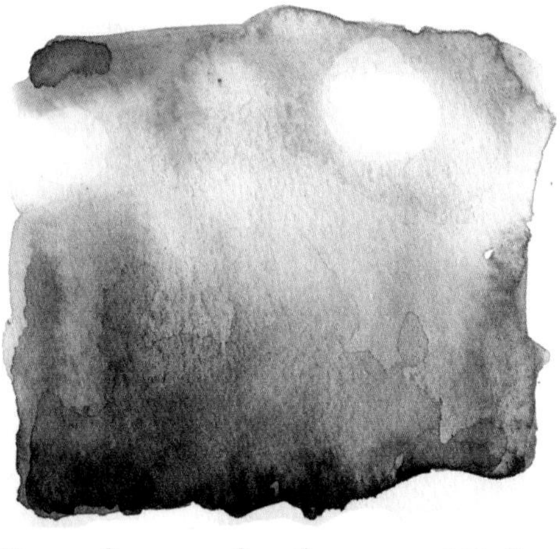

Fresh asphalt on 97th

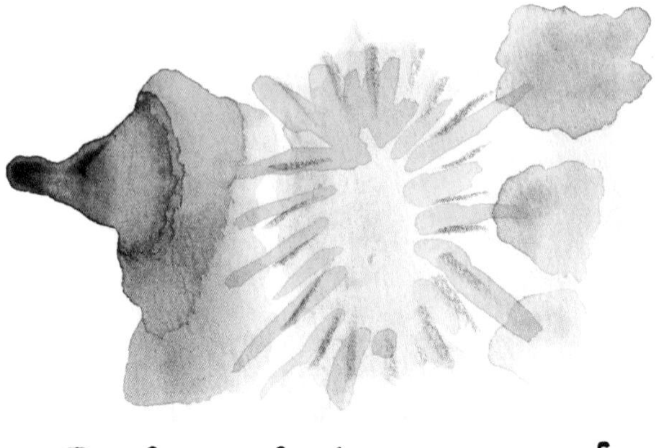

Perfume, hairspray and
cigarettes in front of
Madison Square Garden

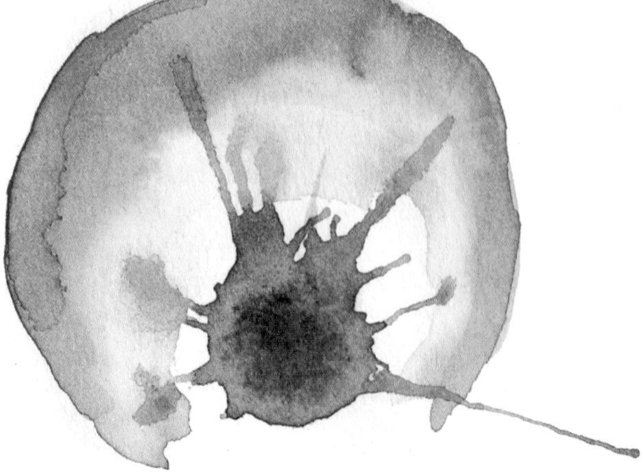

Holland Tunnel

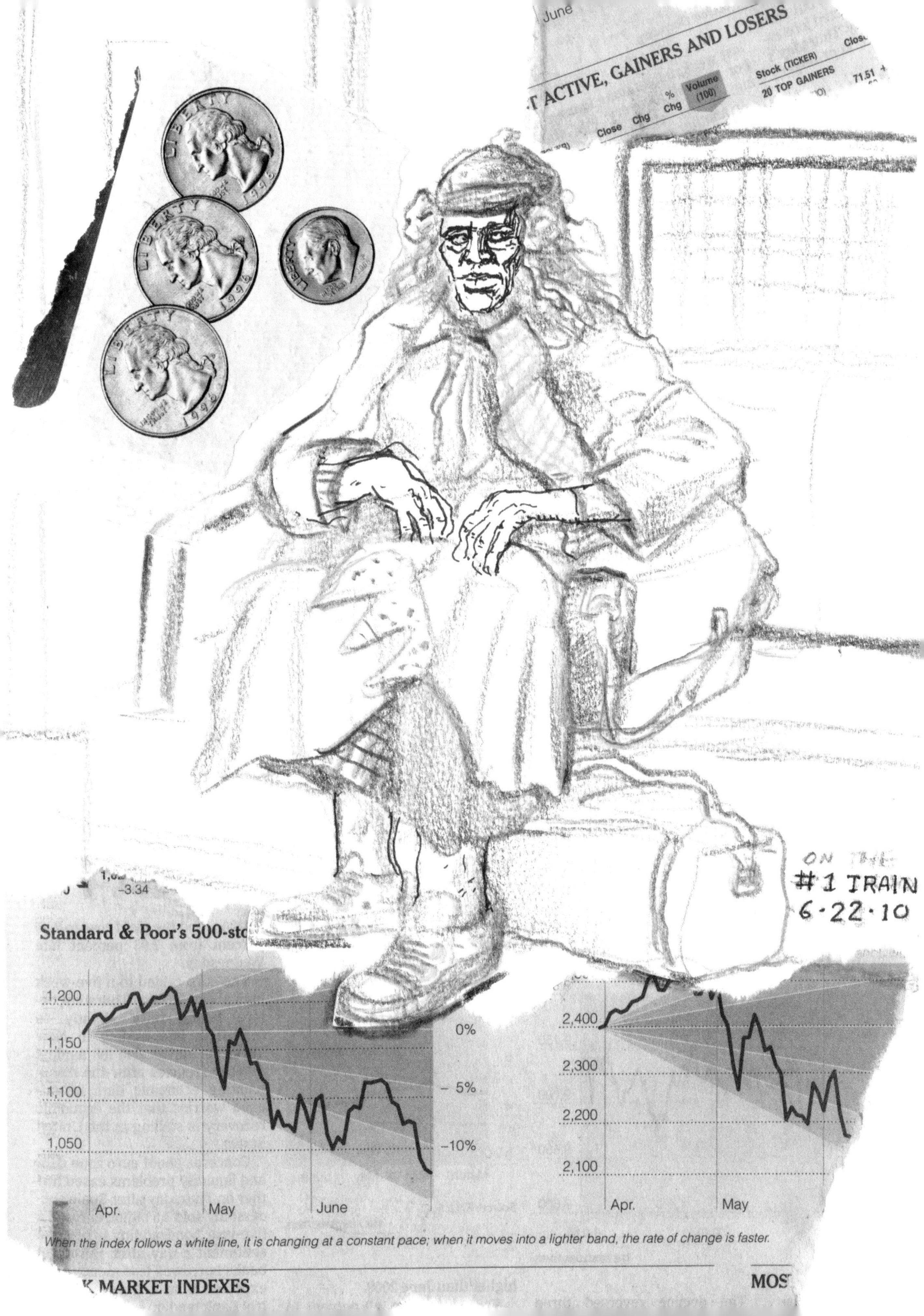
June
T ACTIVE, GAINERS AND LOSERS
Close Chg
% Chg
Volume (100)
Stock (TICKER)
20 TOP GAINERS
Close
71.51
LIBERTY
1996
-3.34
Standard & Poor's 500-sto
1,200
1,150
1,100
1,050
0%
– 5%
–10%
Apr.
May
June
2,400
2,300
2,200
2,100
Apr.
May
ON THE
#1 TRAIN
6·22·10
When the index follows a white line, it is changing at a constant pace; when it moves into a lighter band, the rate of change is faster.
K MARKET INDEXES
MOS

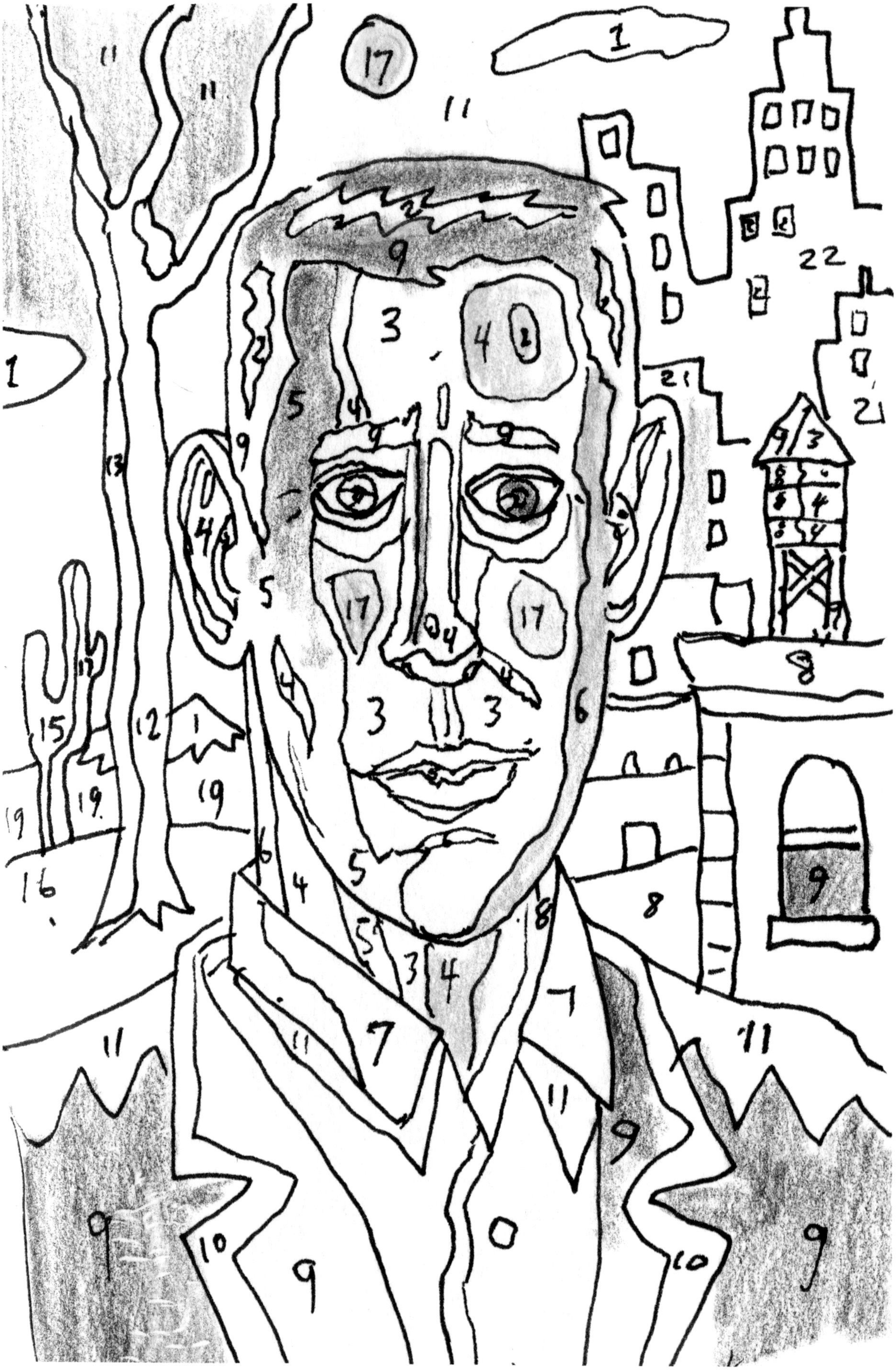

CHAINS

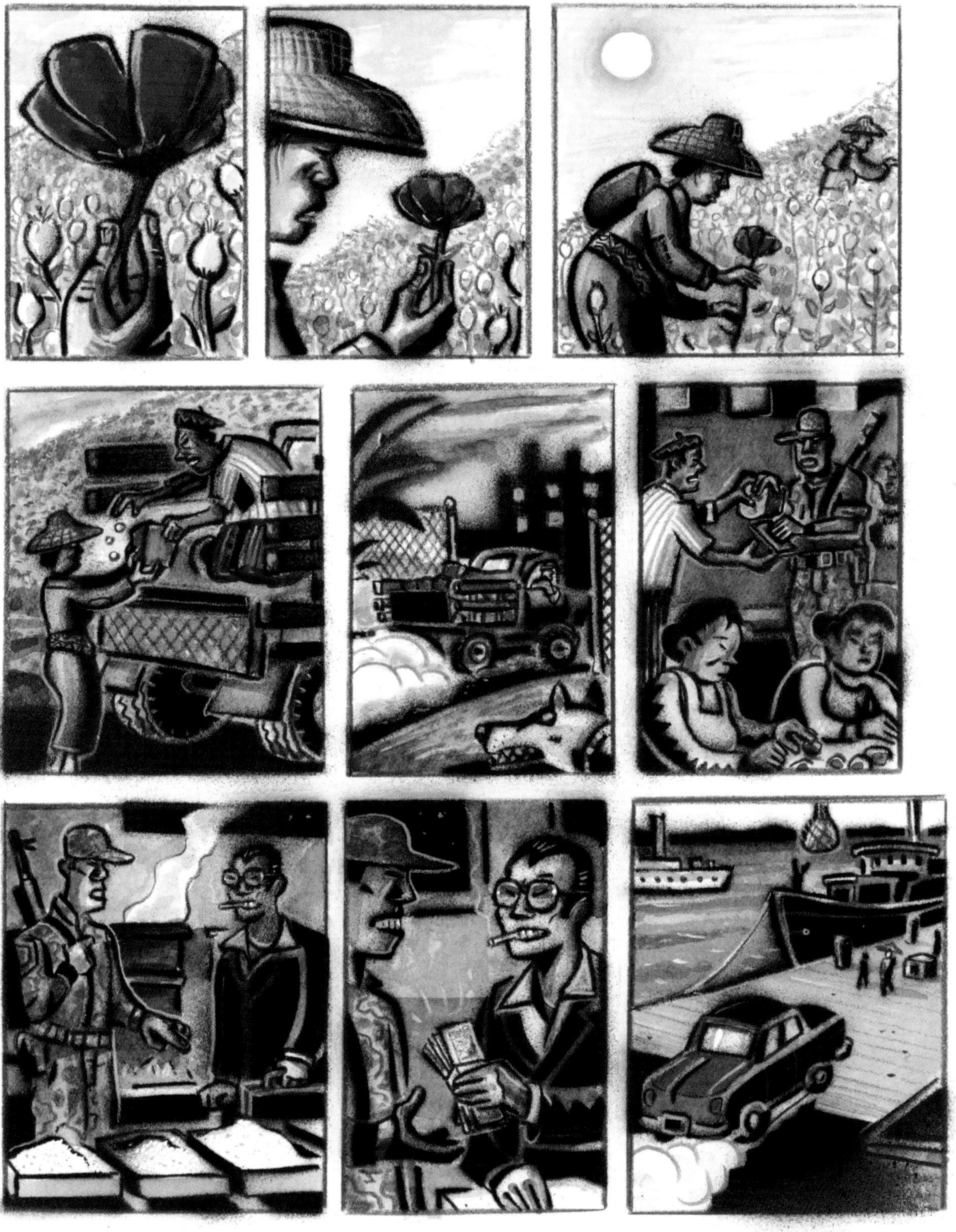

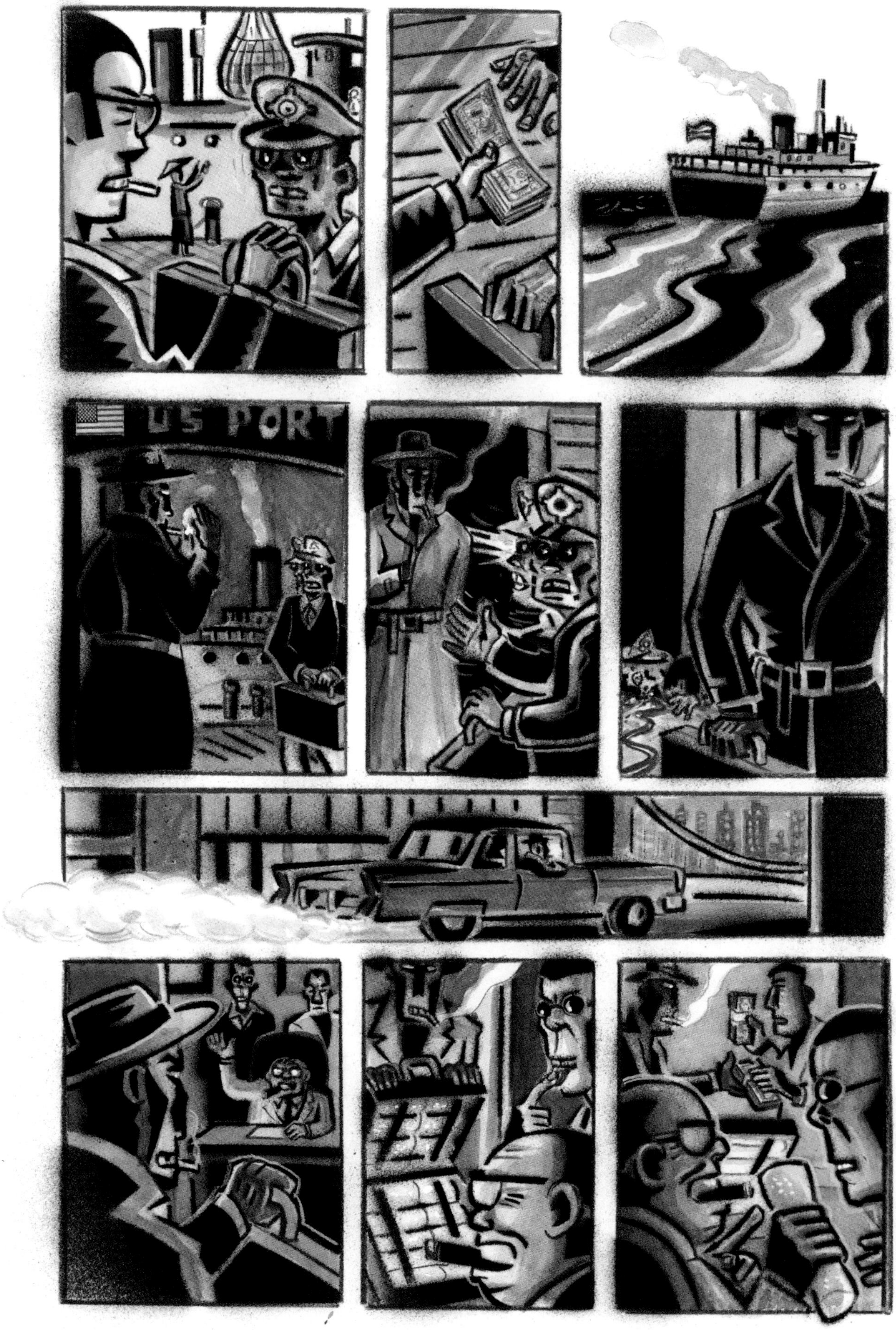
US PORT

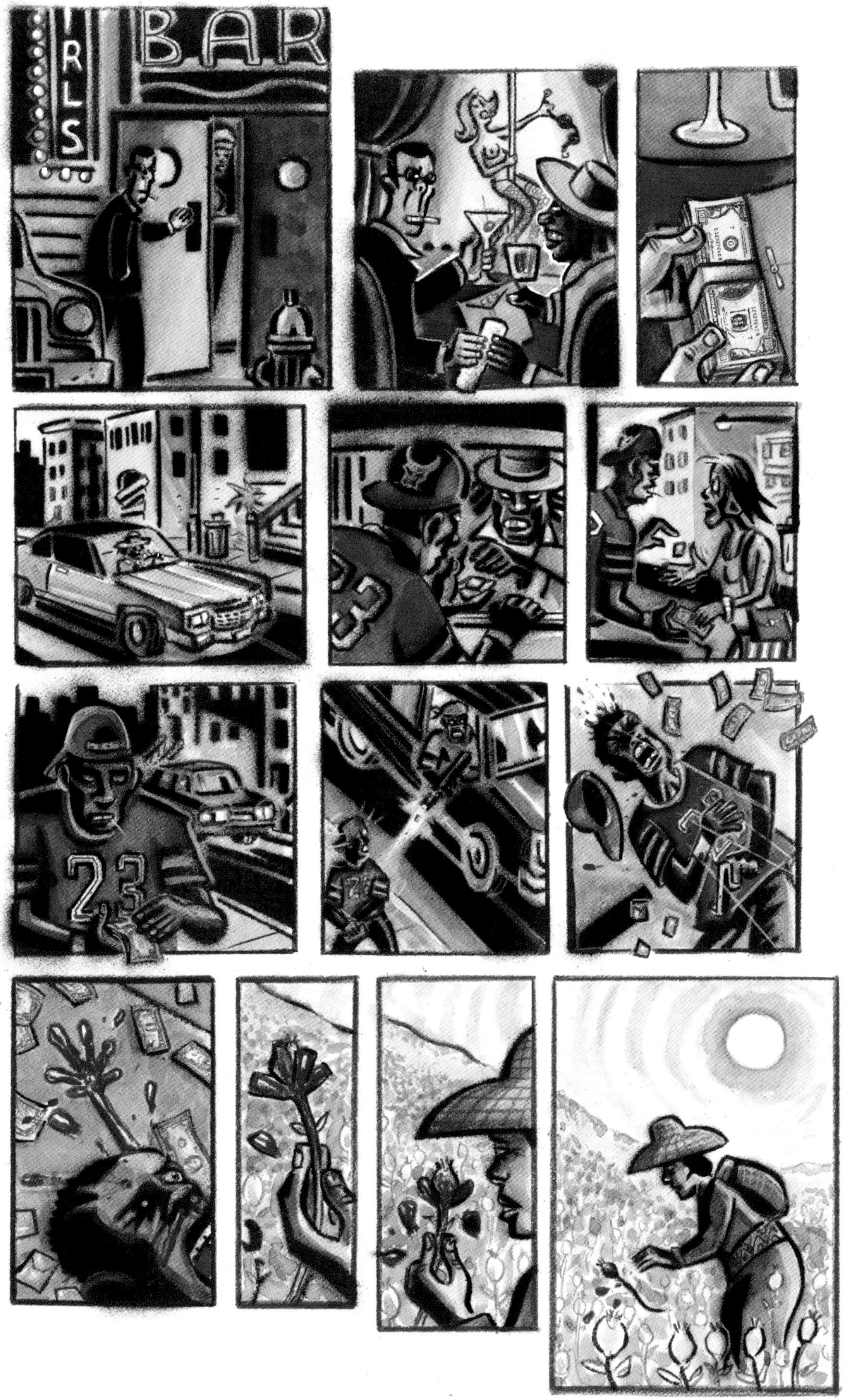
BAR

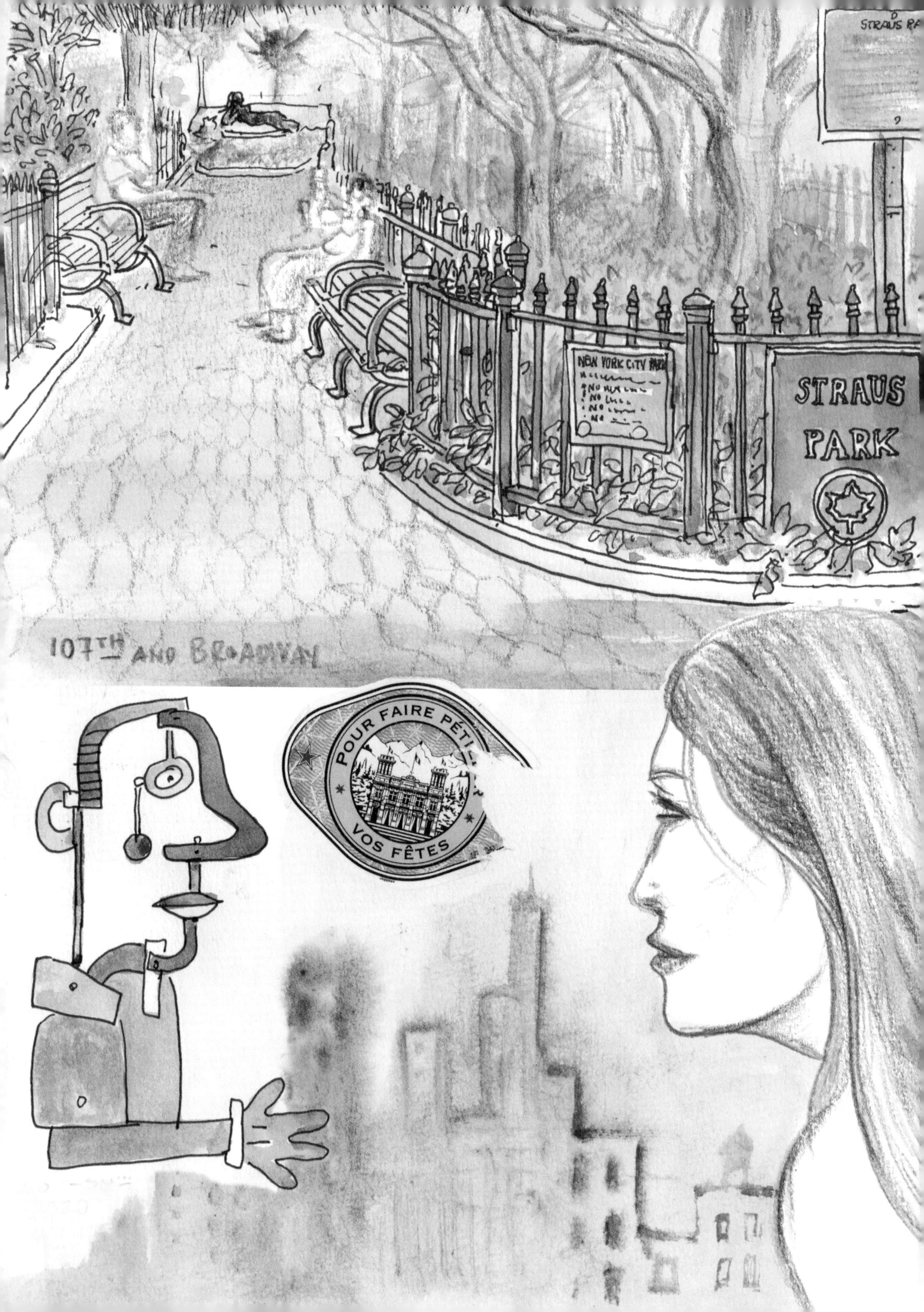
STRAUS PARK
107TH AND BROADWAY
VOS FÊTES

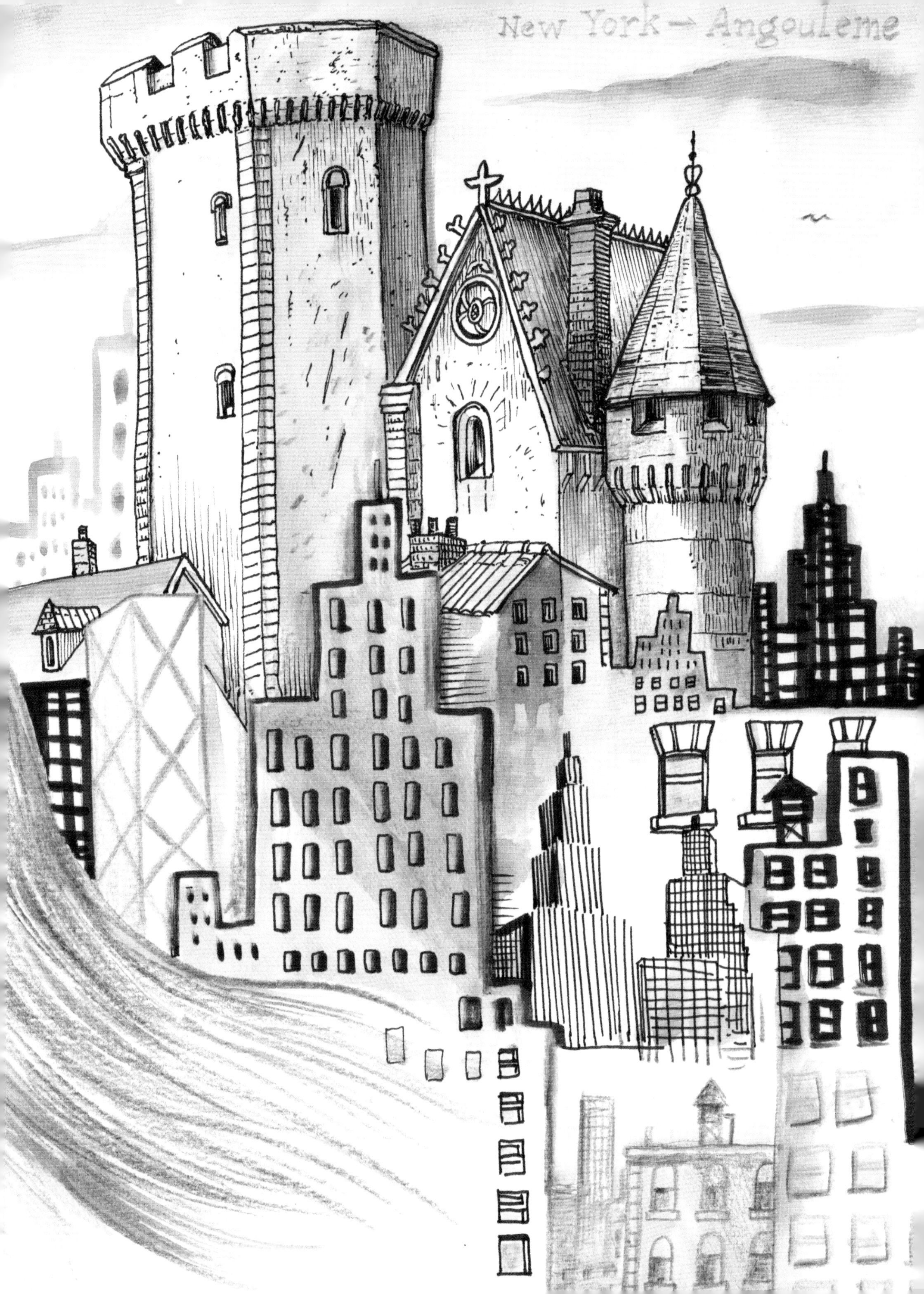
New York → Angouleme

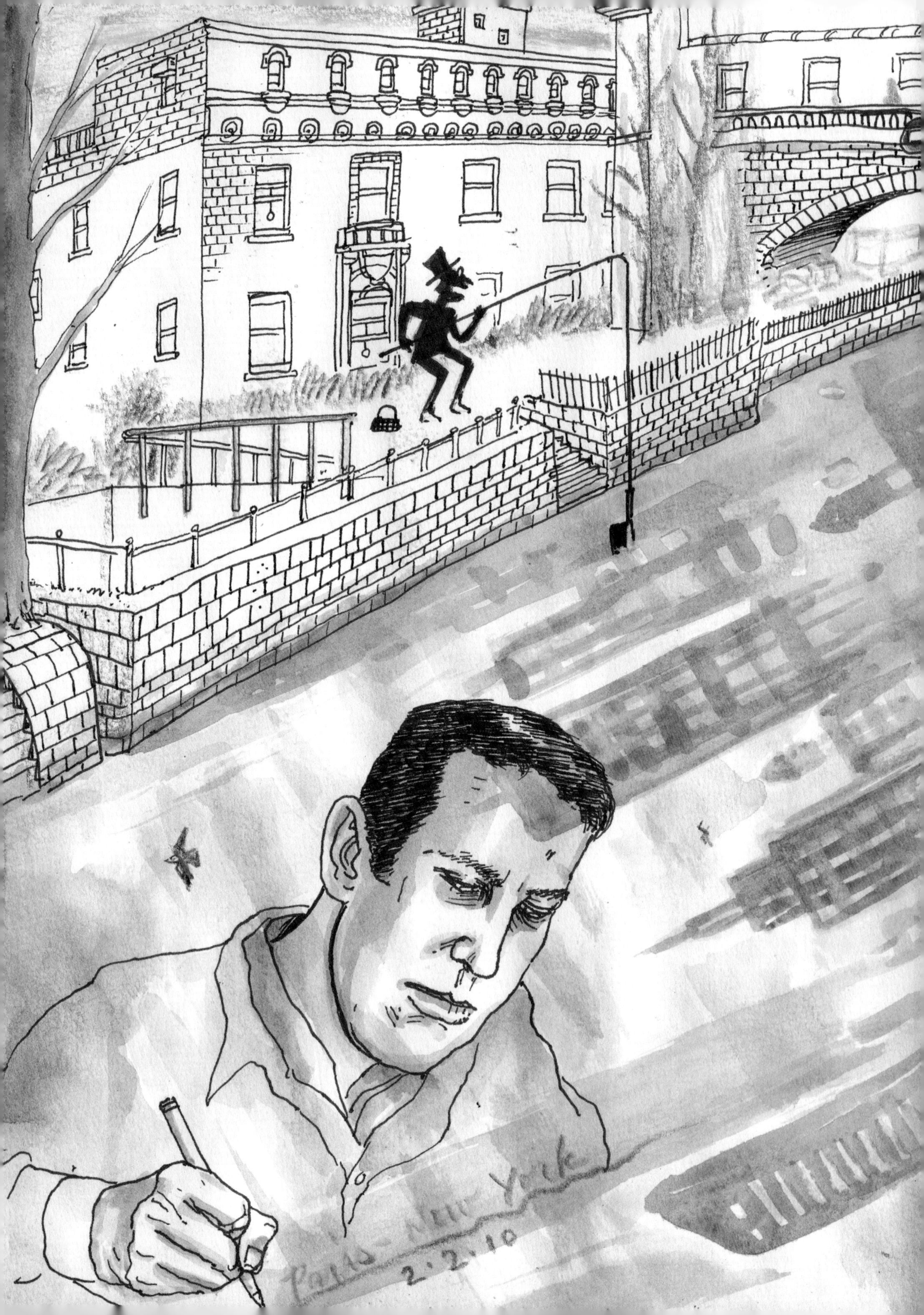
Paris – New York
2.2.10

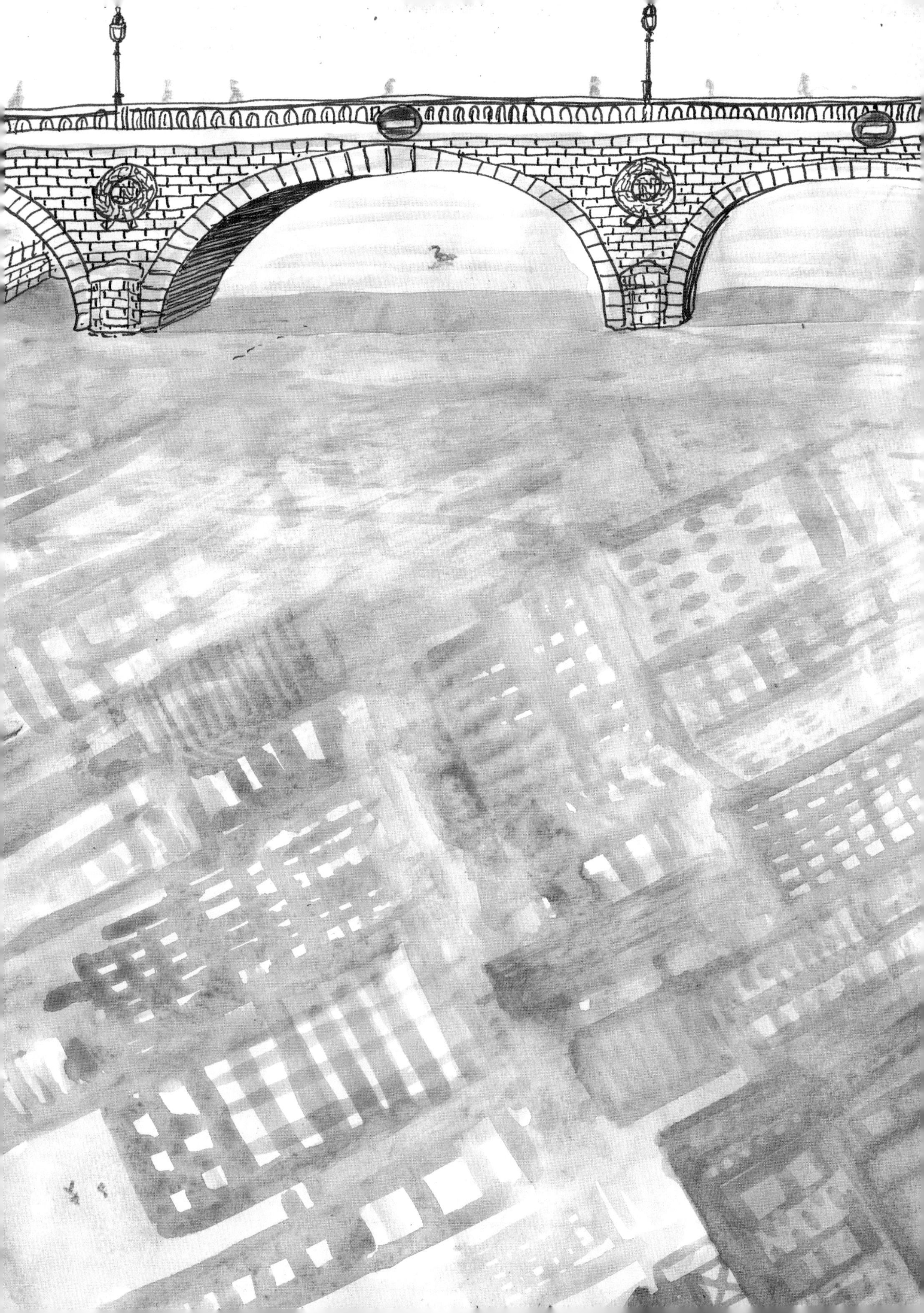

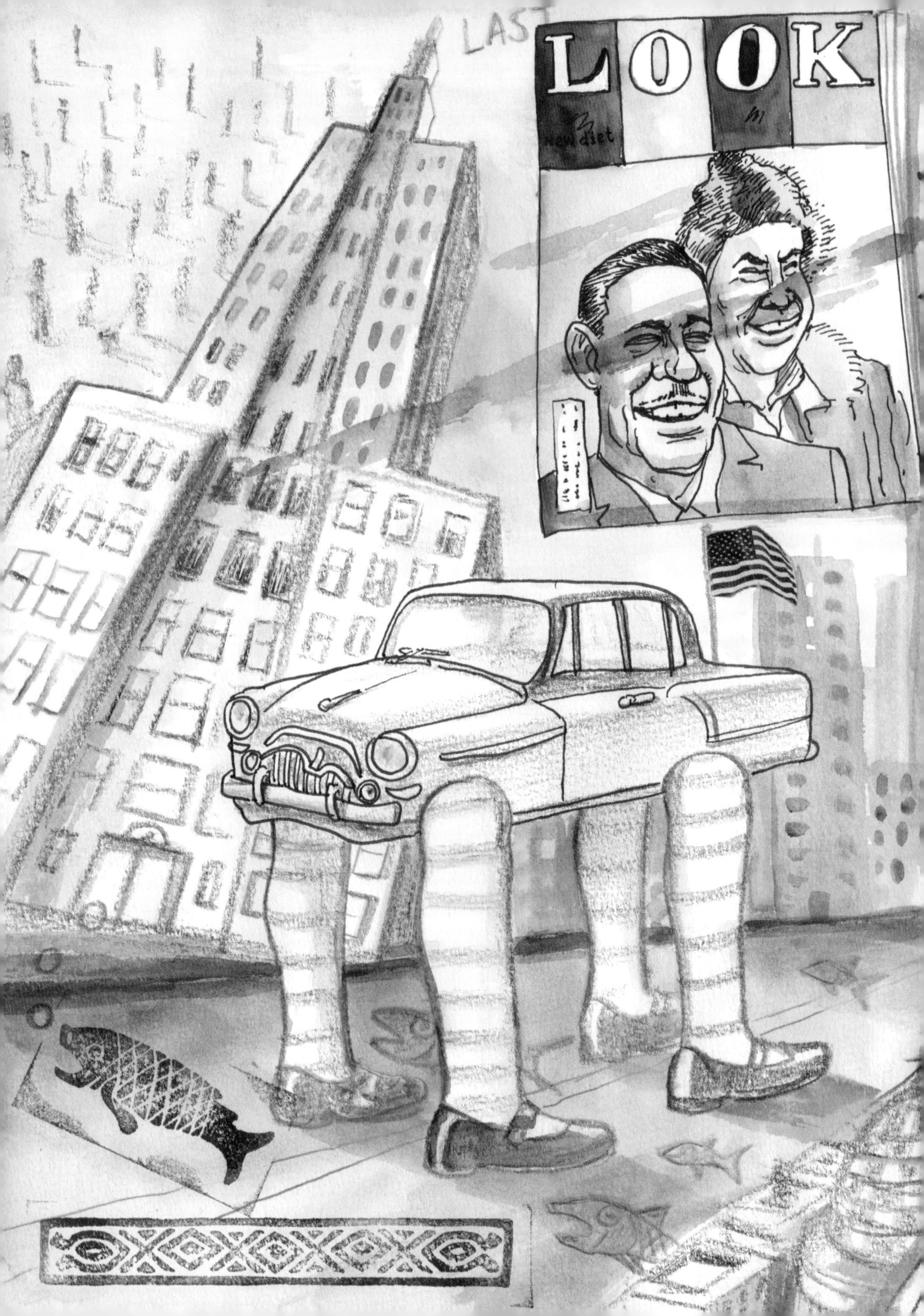
LAST
LOOK
New diet

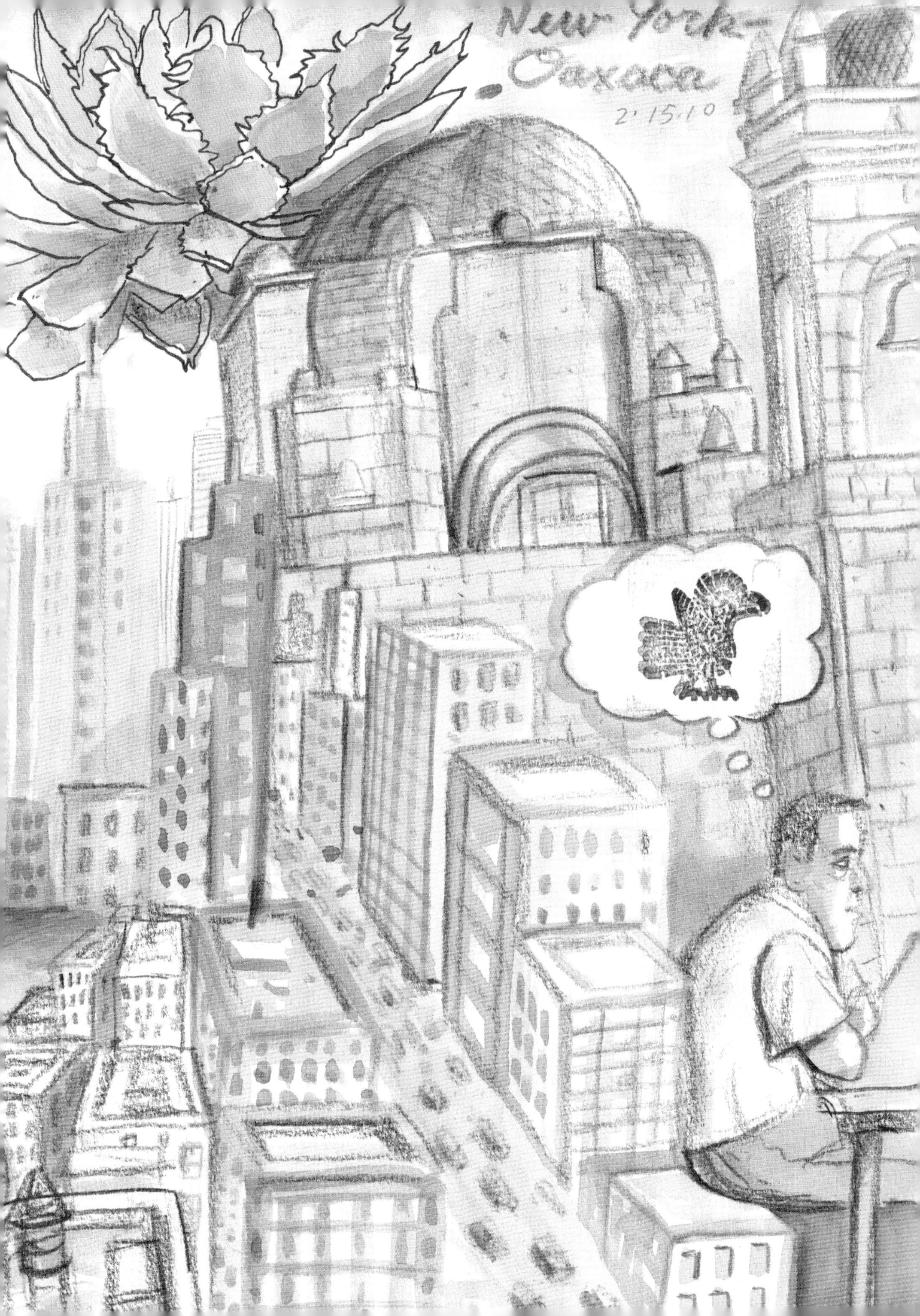
New York-
Oaxaca
2.15.10

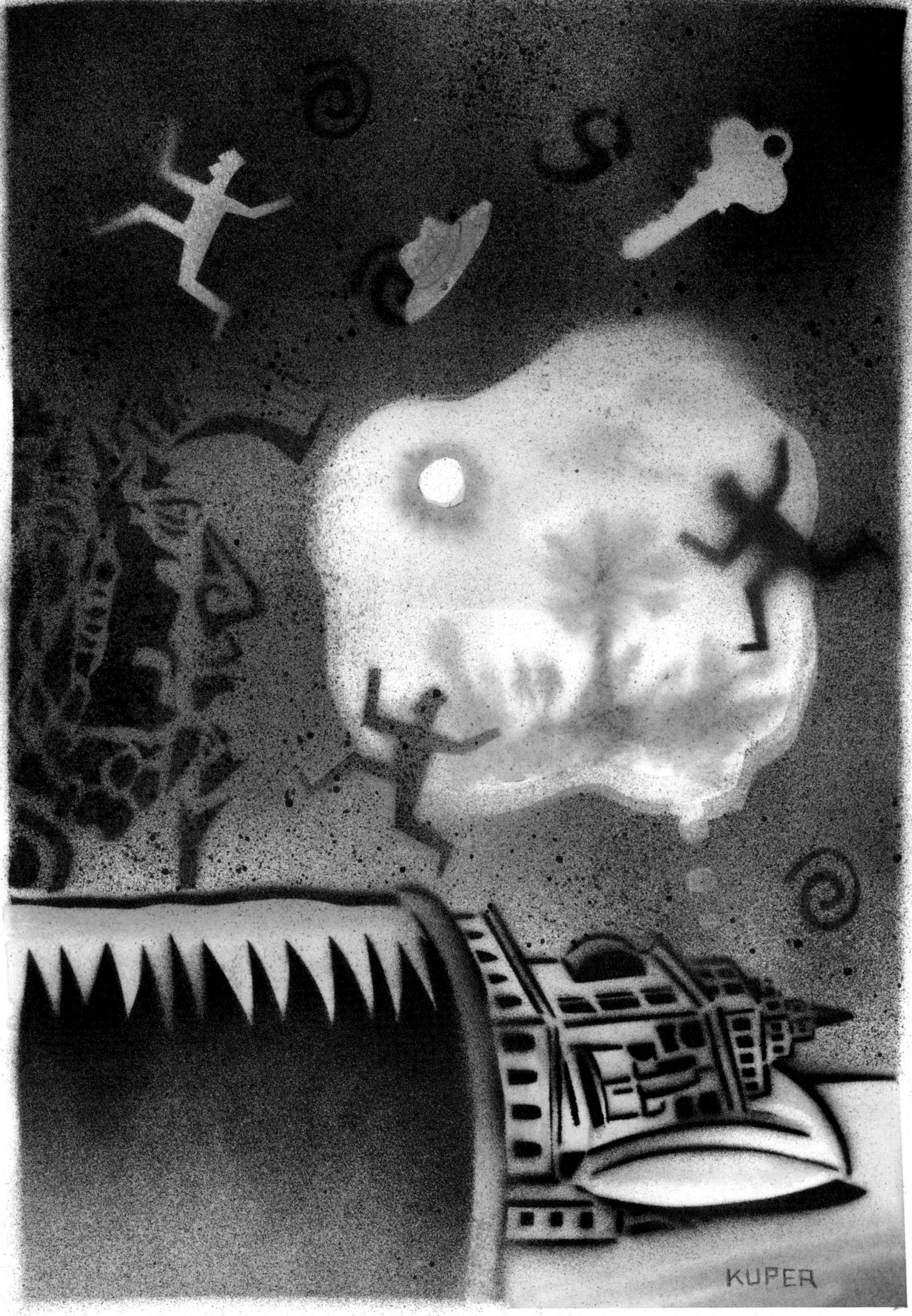
KUPER

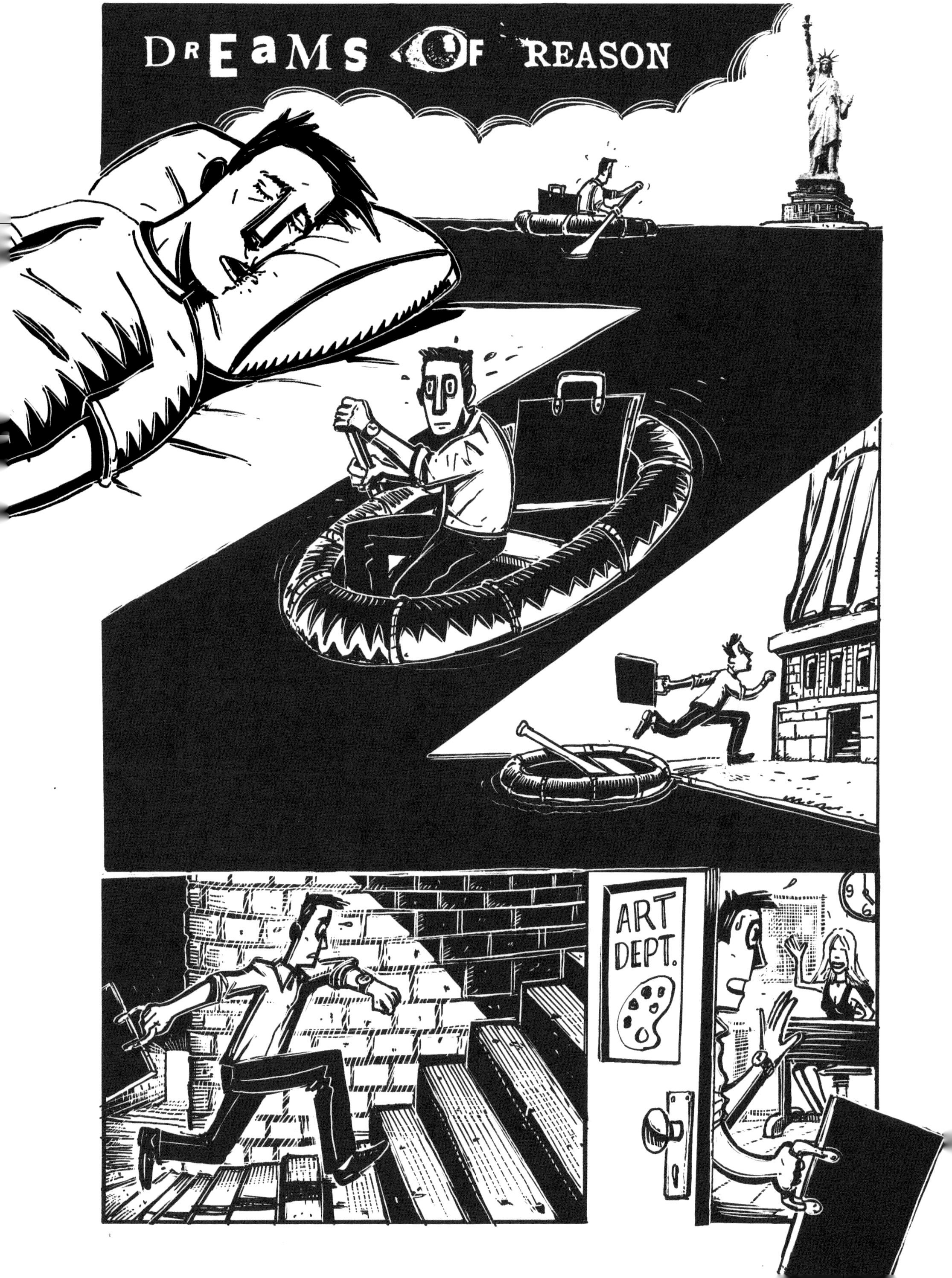
DrEaMs OF REASON
ART DEPT.

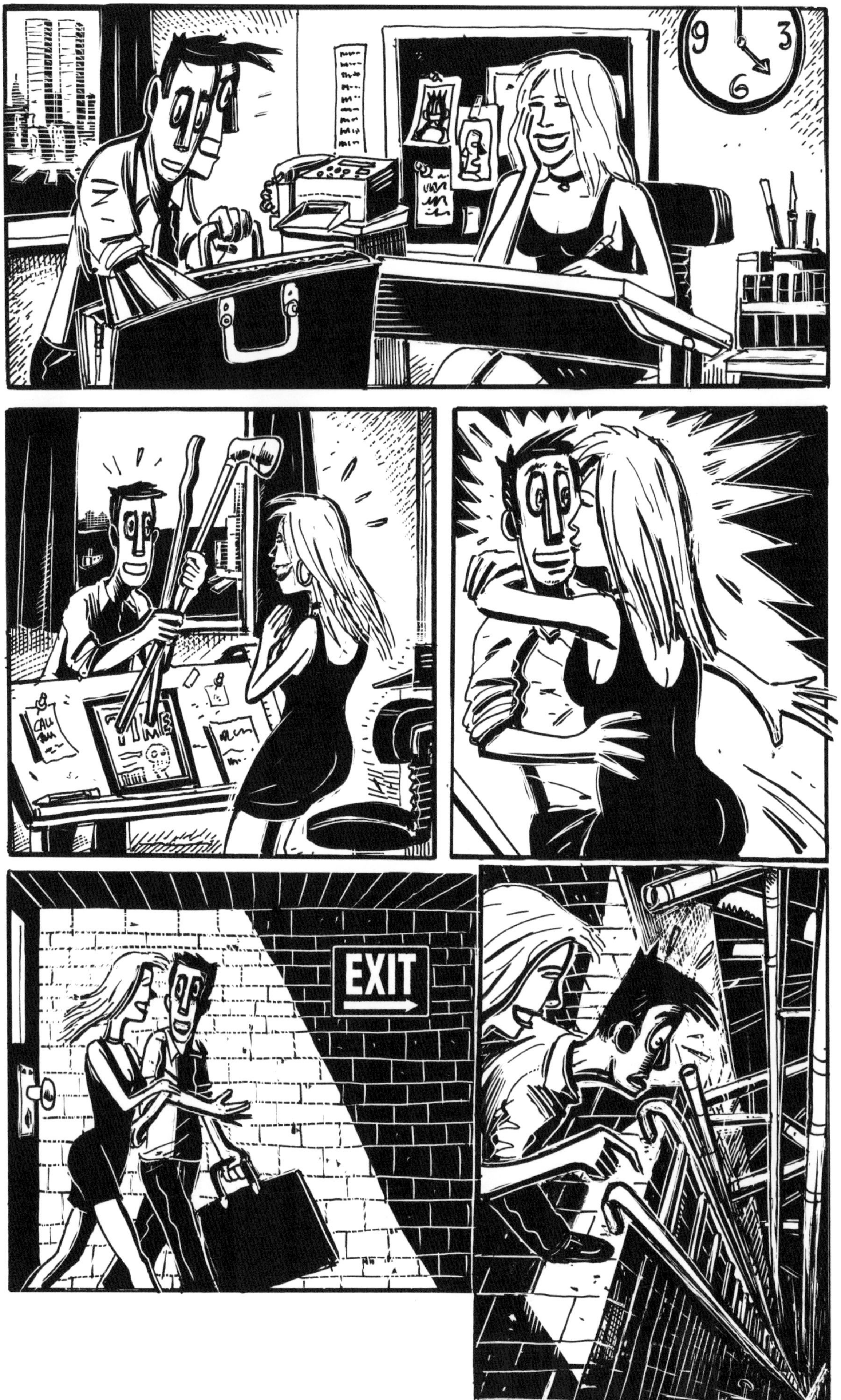
EXIT

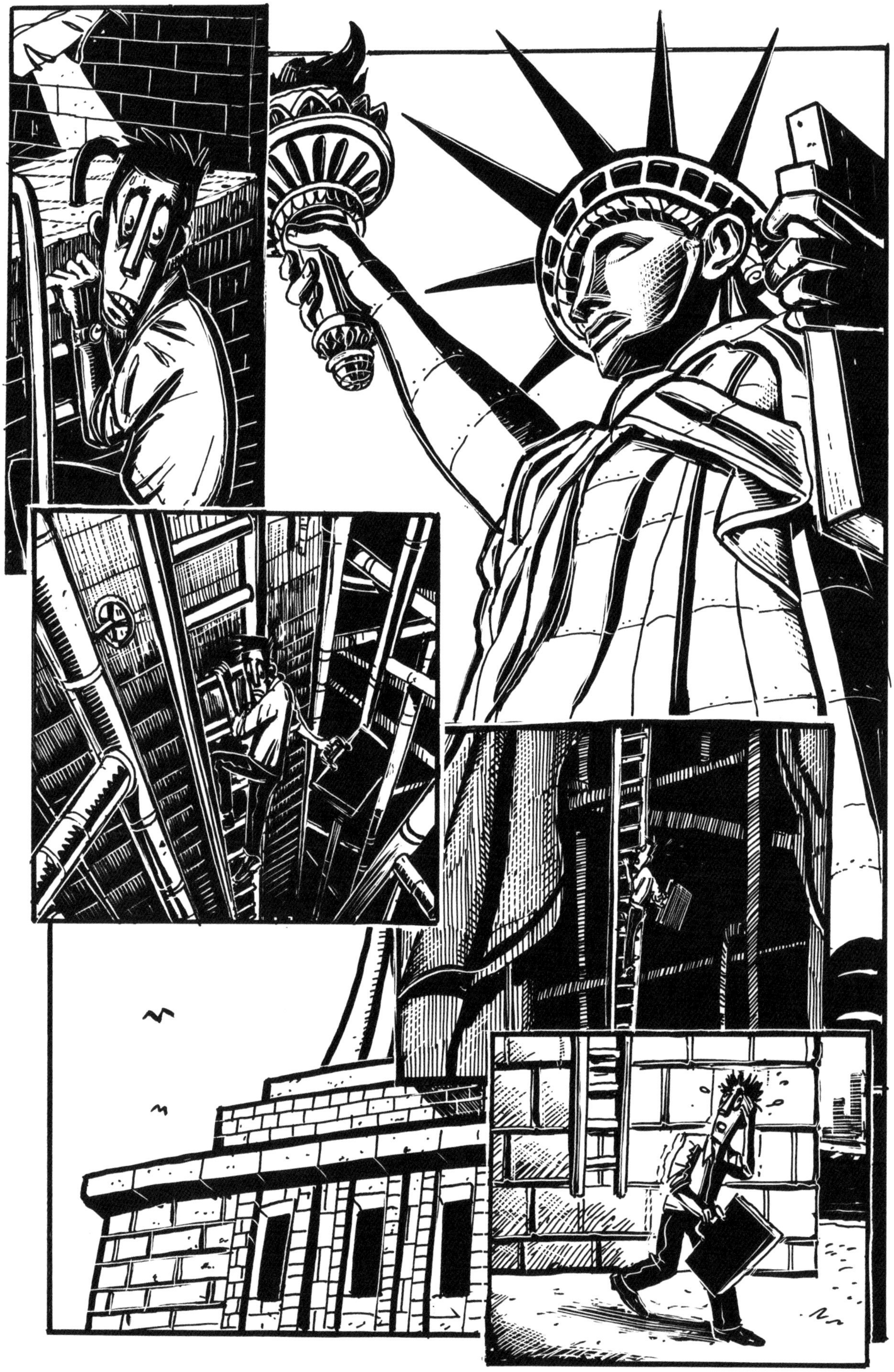

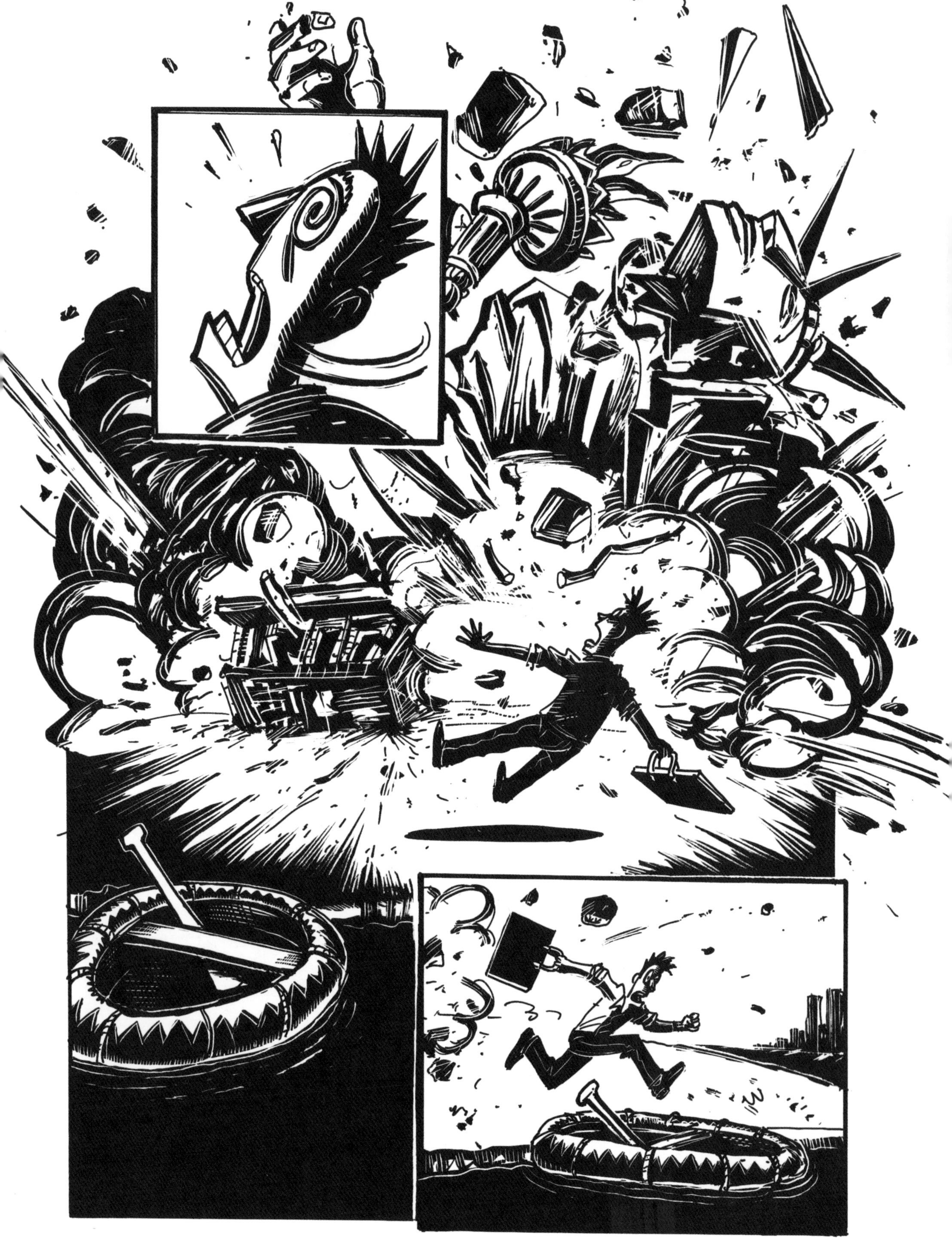

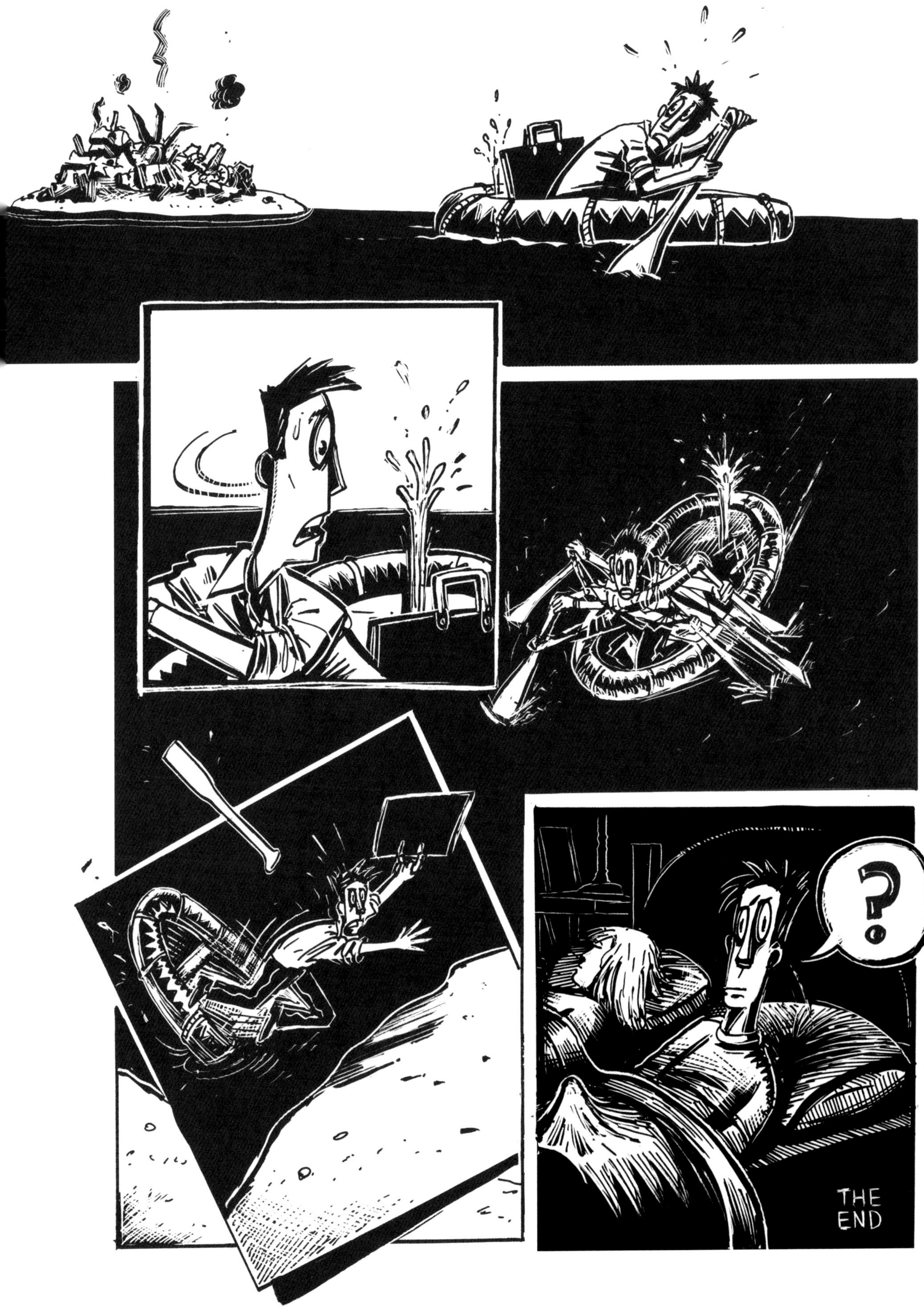
?
THE END

NEW YORK
PRESS

2005 BEST OF
MANHATTAN
READER'S POLL P30

SEPTEMBER 14-20, 2005 ■ VOLUME 18, NUMBER 37 ■ NYPRESS.COM ■ FREE

KUPER

Escape From New Orleans P16
CMJ Rundown P27

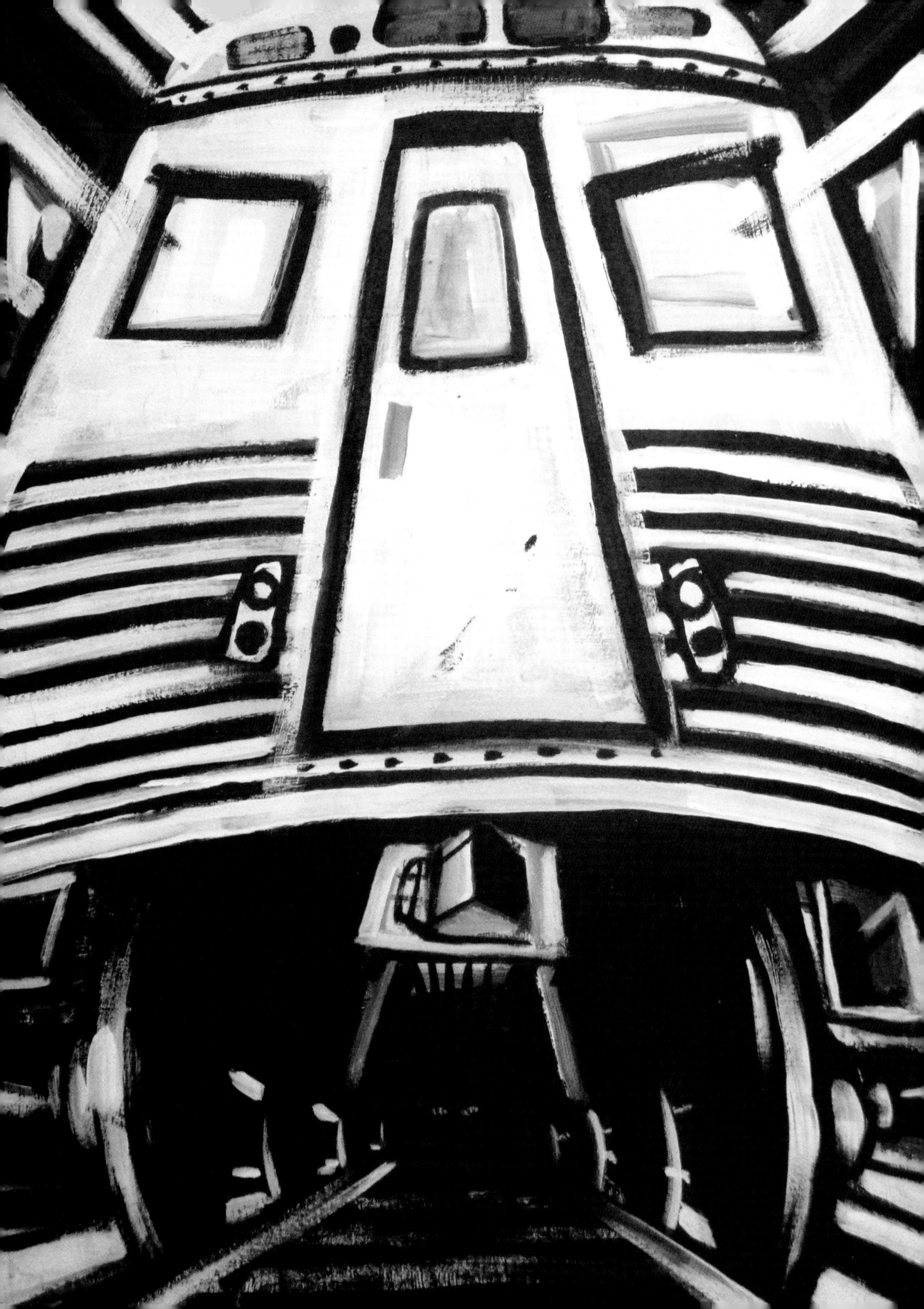

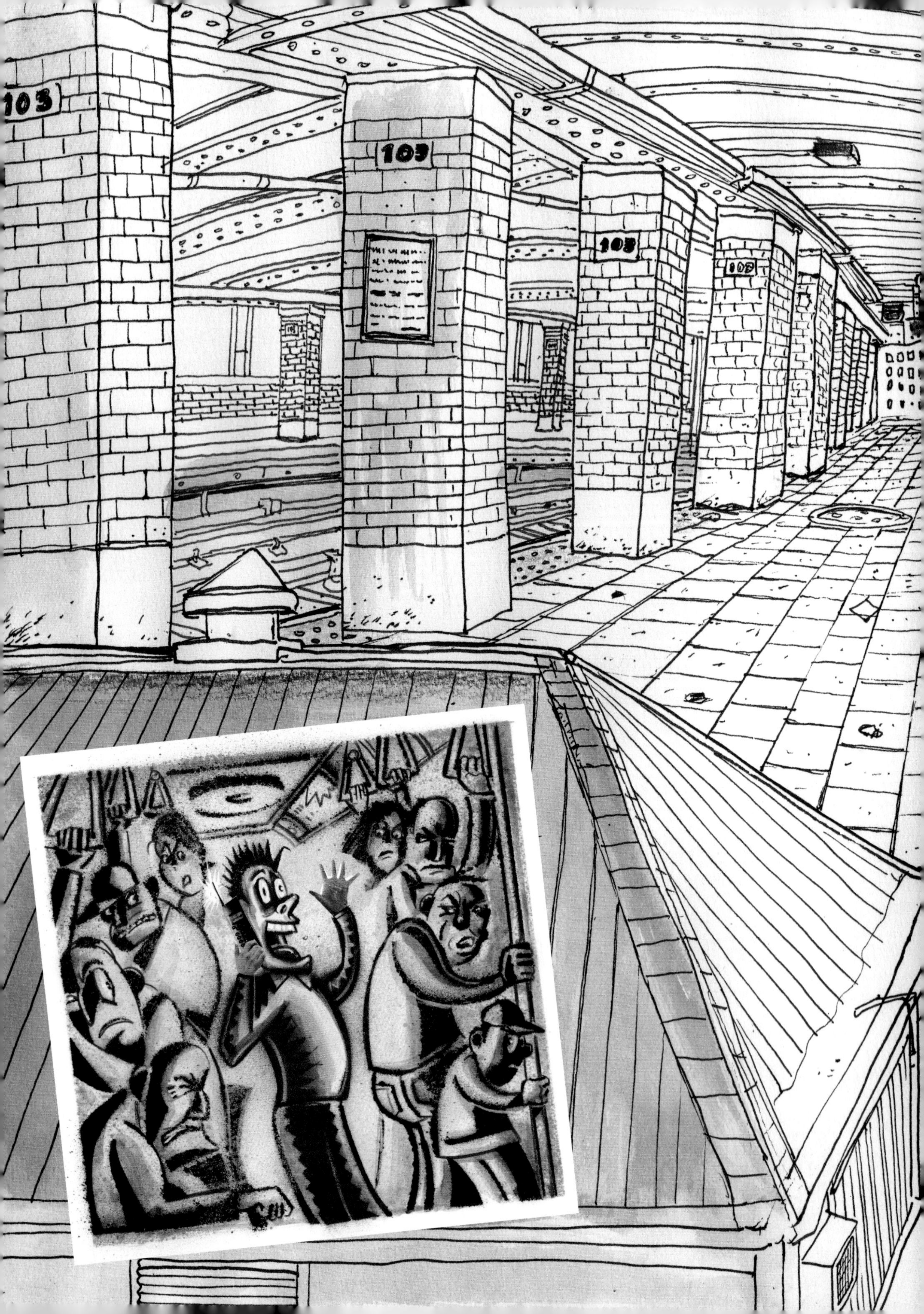
103
103
103
103

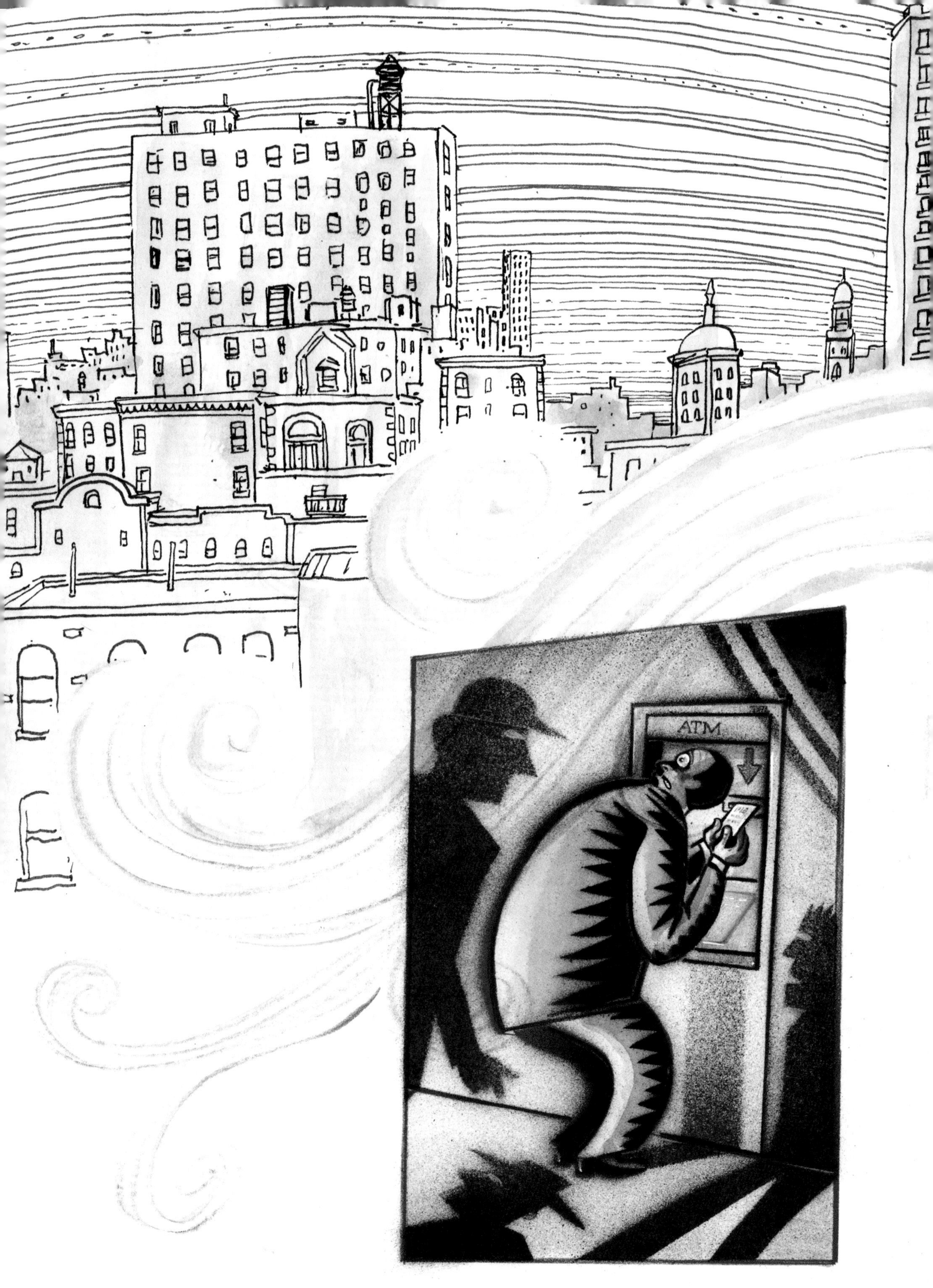
ATM

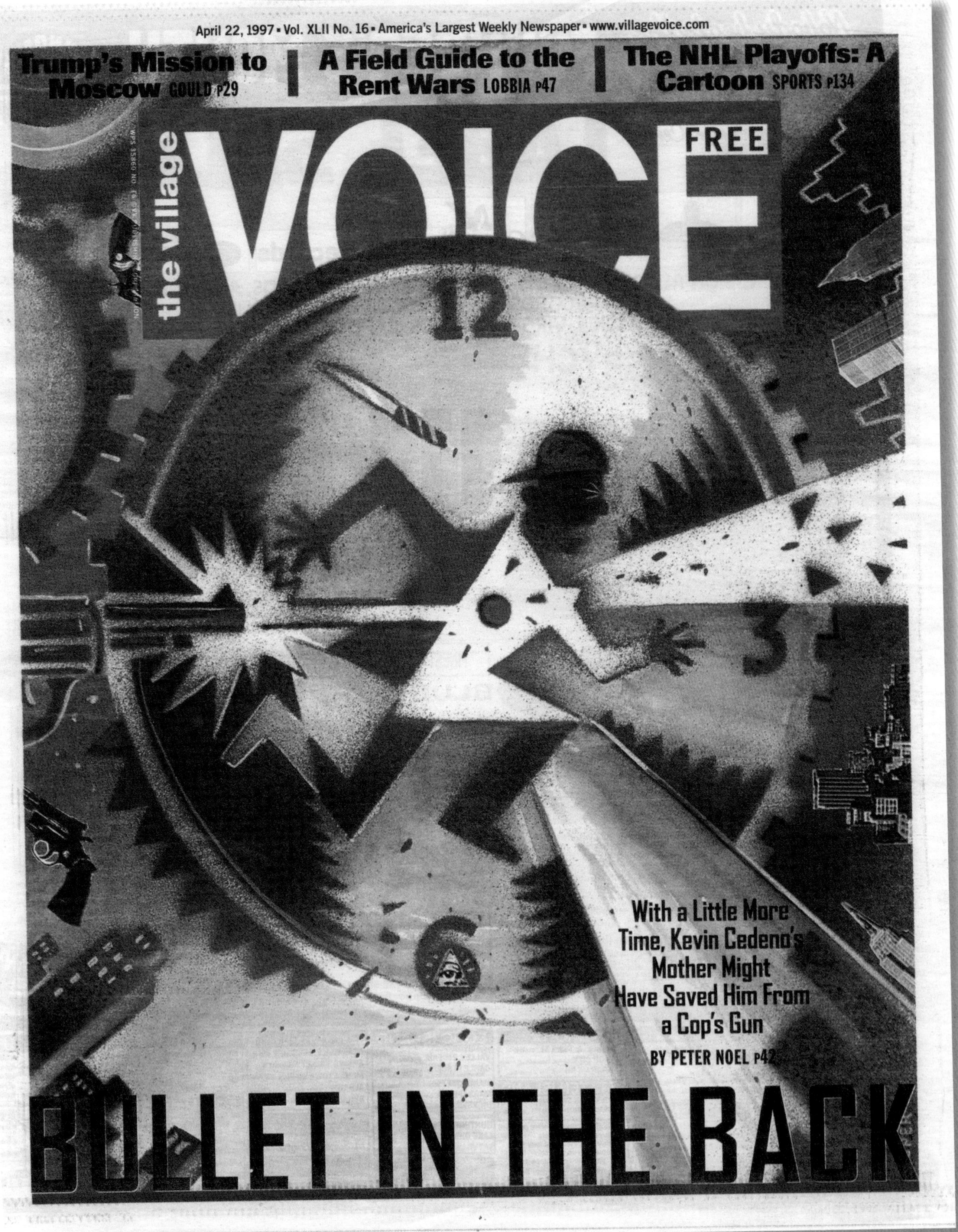
April 22, 1997 ▪ Vol. XLII No. 16 ▪ America's Largest Weekly Newspaper ▪ www.villagevoice.com

Trump's Mission to Moscow GOULD p29 | **A Field Guide to the Rent Wars** LOBBIA p47 | **The NHL Playoffs: A Cartoon** SPORTS p134

the village VOICE

FREE

12

3

6

With a Little More Time, Kevin Cedeno's Mother Might Have Saved Him From a Cop's Gun

BY PETER NOEL p42

BULLET IN THE BACK

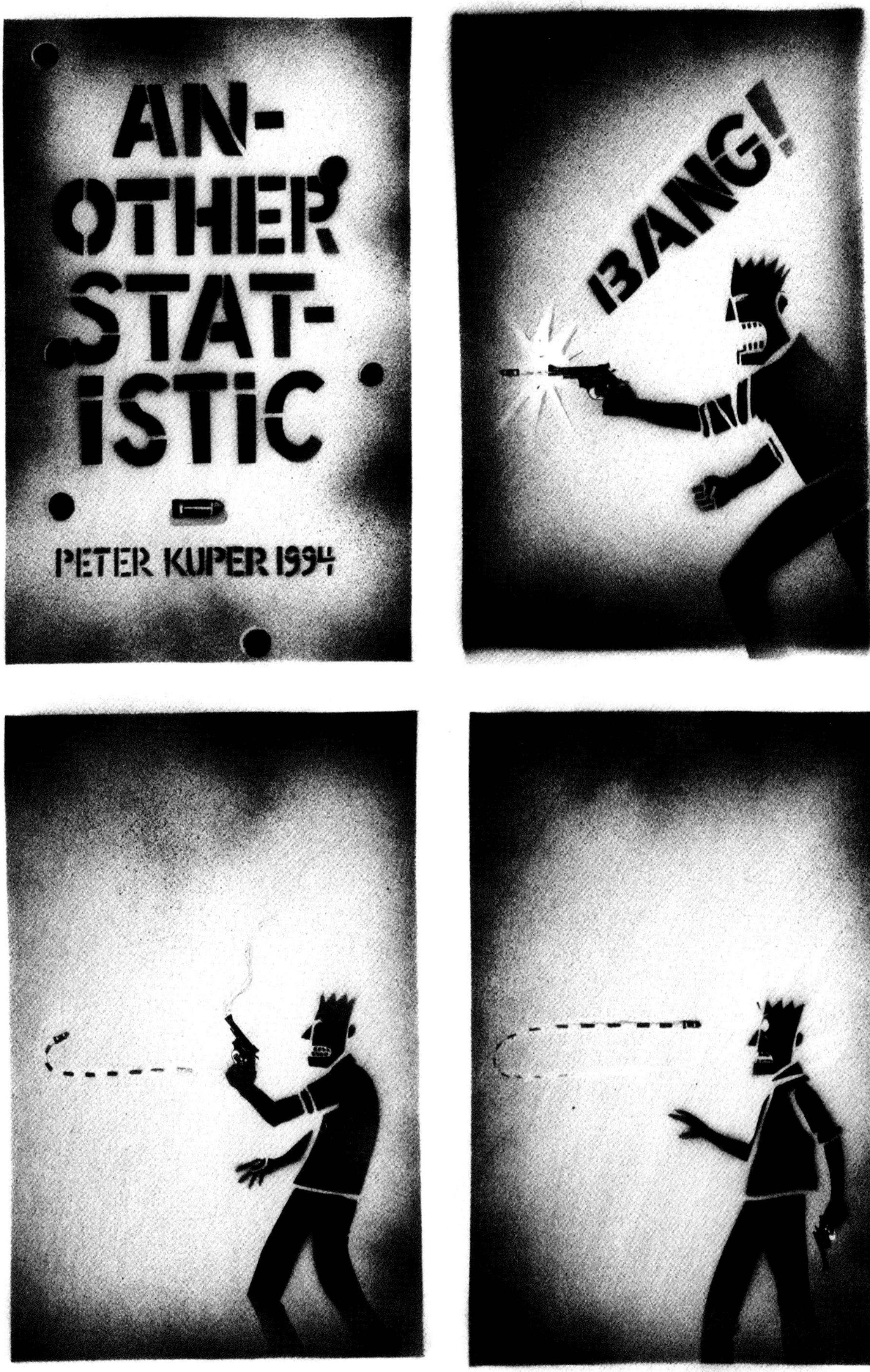

AN-
OTHER
STAT-
ISTIC
PETER KUPER 1994
BANG!

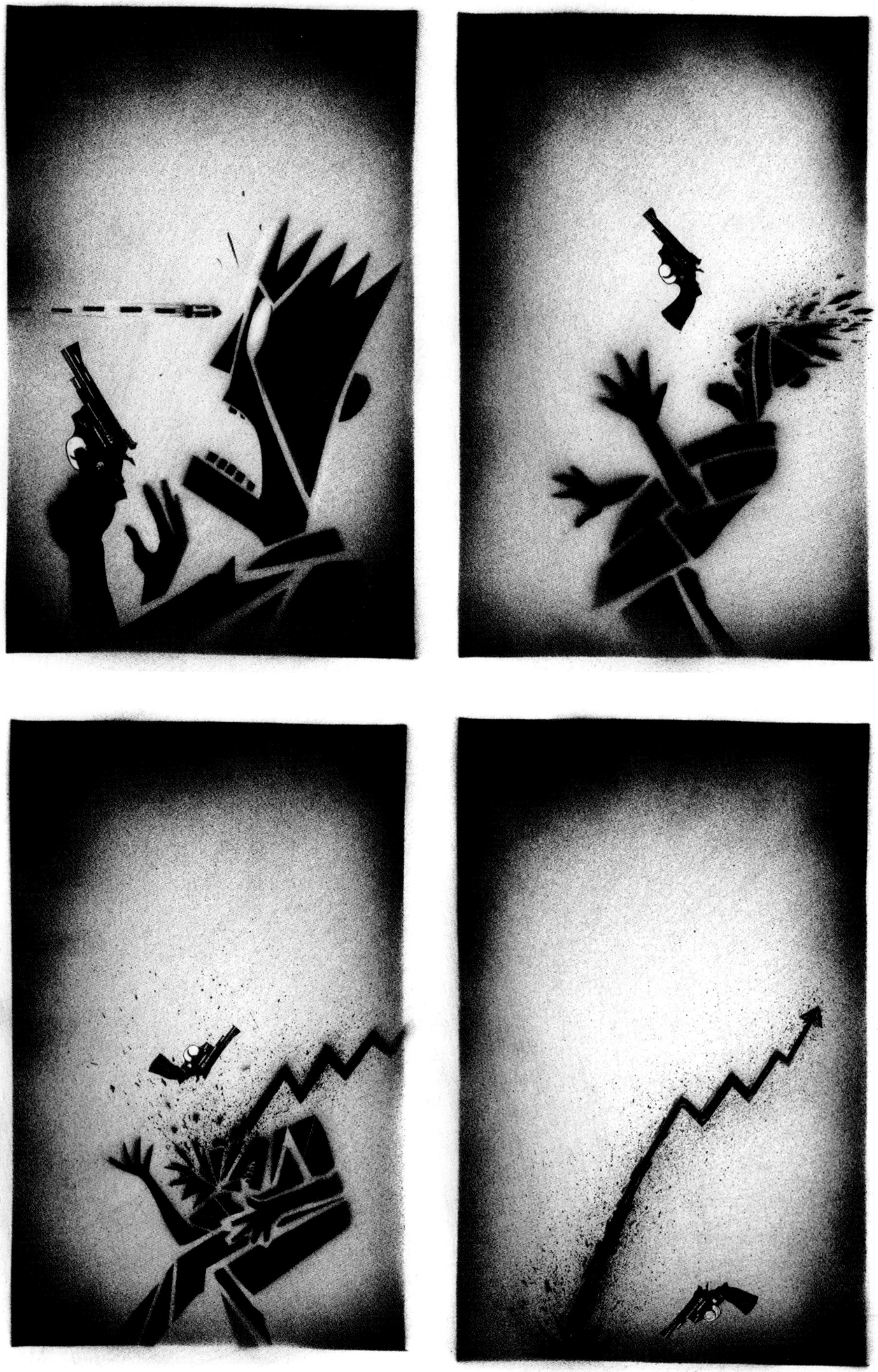

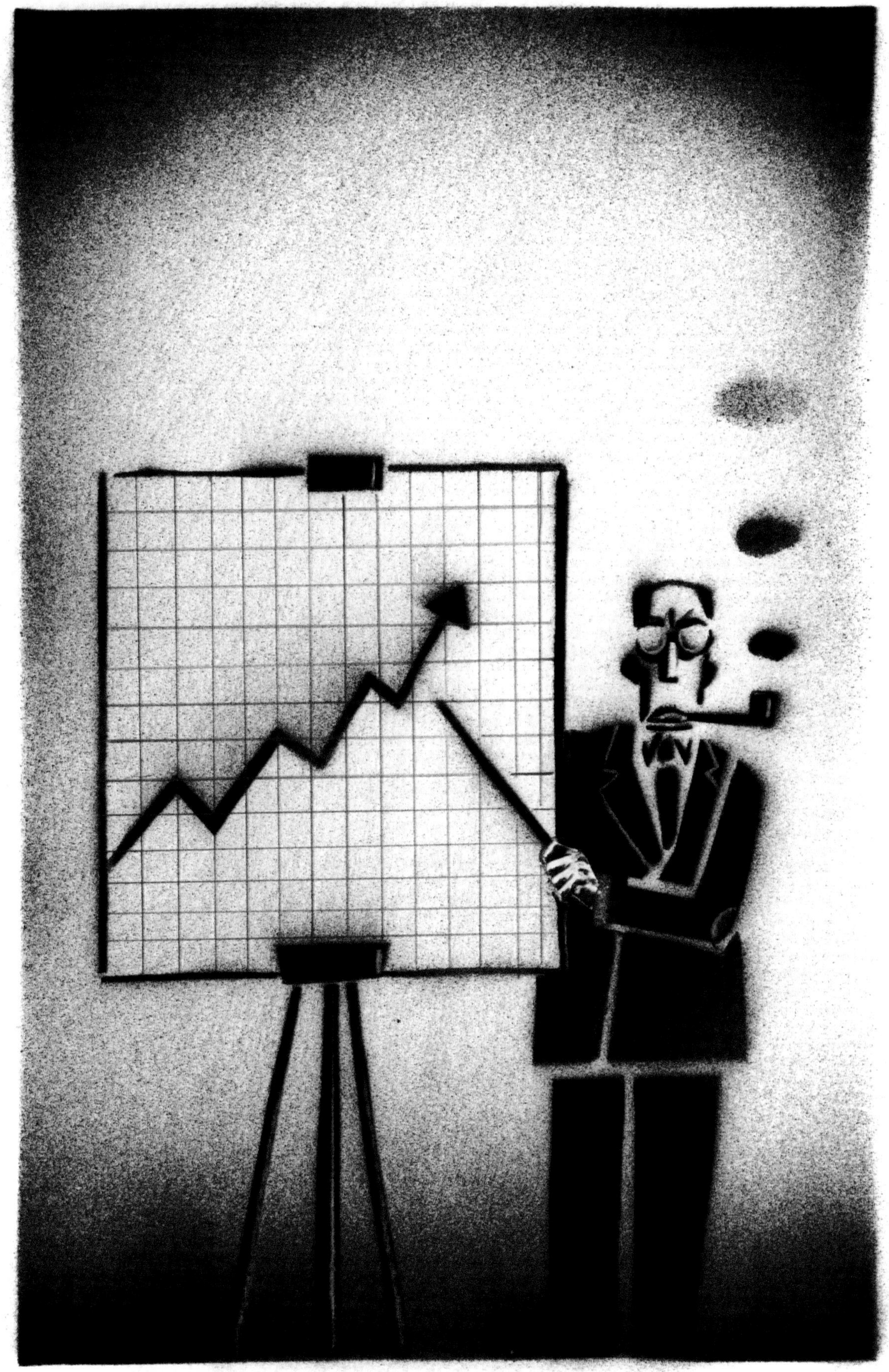

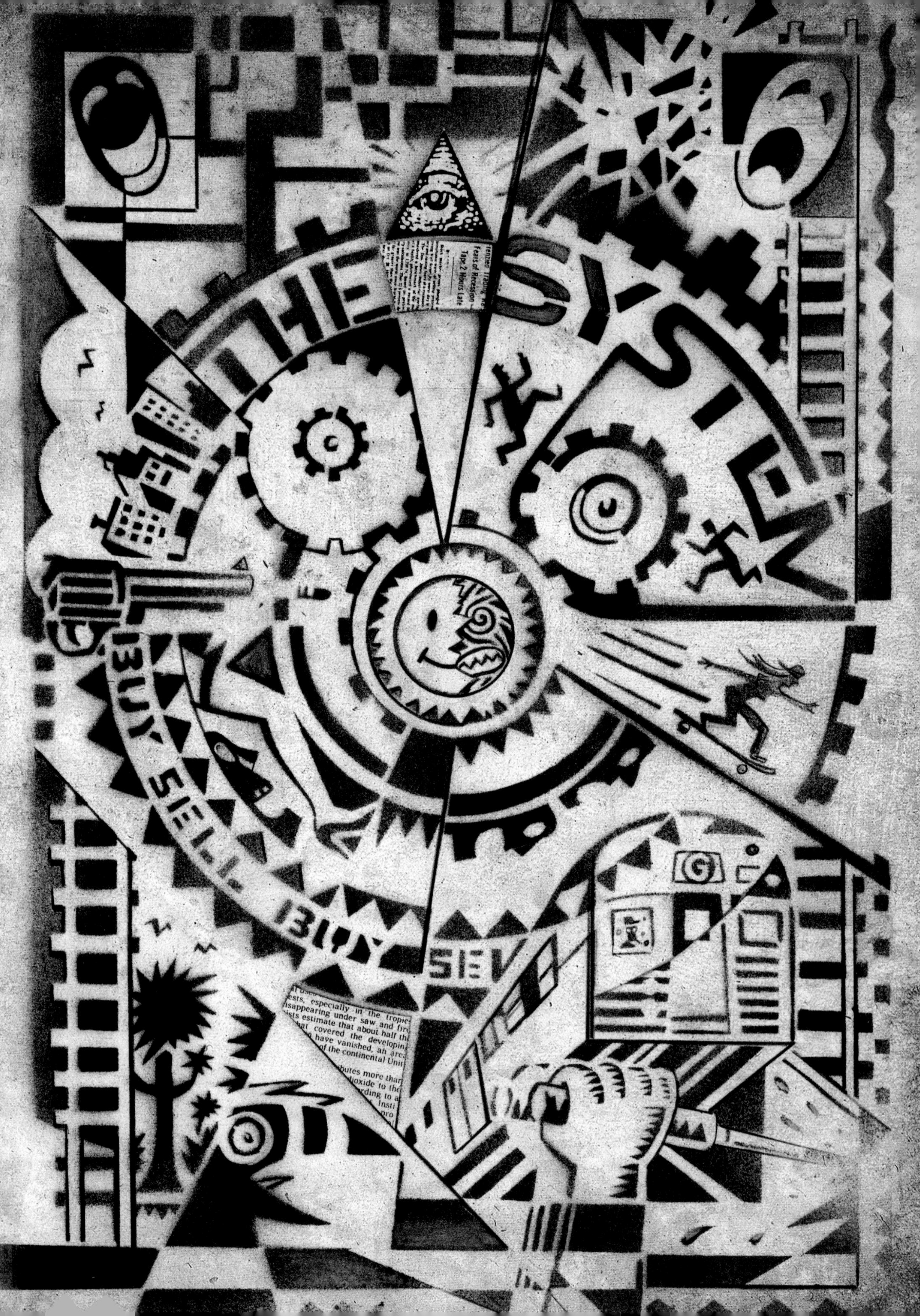
THE SYSTEM
Fears of Recession
Tape 2 Hours Late
BUY SELL BUY SEL
ests, especially in the tropic
disappearing under saw and fire
ists estimate that about half the
that covered the developing
have vanished, an area
of the continental Uni
butes more than
dioxide to the
rding to a
Insti

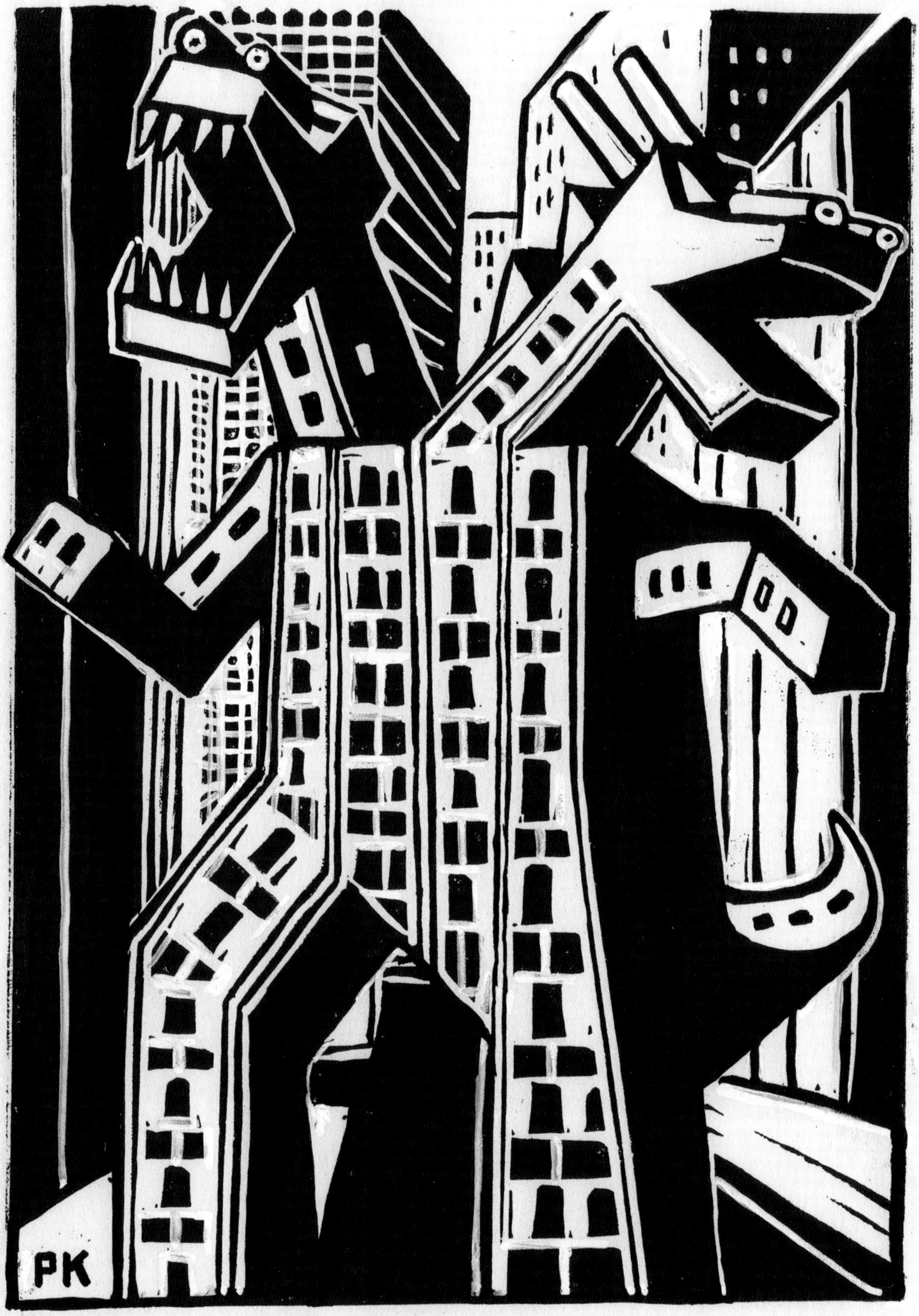
PK

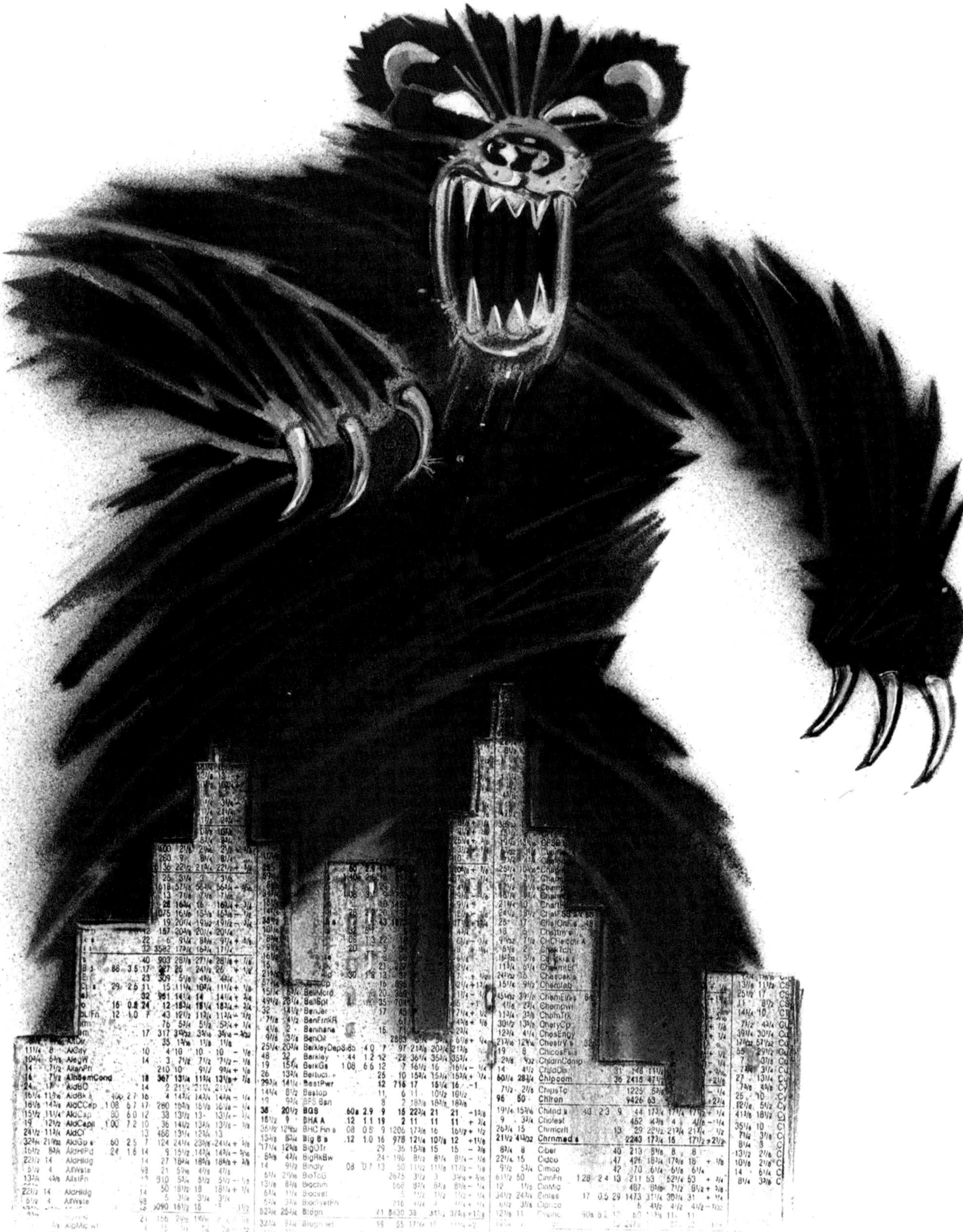

Unstable and Out of Control

In what has become an annual ritual, tenants of many of New York City's 60,000 rent-controlled apartments, their landlords, whose operating costs increased, and state officials, did not come to celebrate either. The hearing provided yet another vivid illustration of how deep problems it hearing provided yet another vivid illustration of how deep problems it city's need to solve.

Virtually every New Yorker has heard stories about the wealthy widow living alone in a spacious apartment with Central Park views for $400 a month. While some of these tales are apocryphal

passed a rule that allows vacated apartments to be phased out of the system once the rent hits $2,000 a month. The change, however, did not affect rent-controlled apartments, a war is on, and to preserve neighborhood diversity and stability, and to ensure that rents do not jump to levels that only the wealthy can afford, forcing lower-income residents to sell; they simply freeze the status quo, so neighborhoods remain only as diverse as they are now, which isn't very diverse at all.

An apartment can only be rent-controlled if it is in a building constructed before 1947 and if its current tenant (or his family) has oc-

vulnerable city residents, 13 percent have incomes greater than $70,000 per year (as do more households with income greater than $75,000 receive twice as much subsidy as households with incomes less than $10,000.

Nor do the laws aid diversity. Contrary to popular belief most of a sharp borhood in Manhattan, where most rent-regulated apartments are. For example, one tract on the Upper East Side is more than 95 percent white, while a tract around West 125th Street is 97 percent black. Rent regulation which rewards people to wh

invest. My own owned more than 1,000 units of residential housing in the Bronx and Manhattan for 80 years, experienced this firsthand. When ownership costs skyrocketed during the 1970's. In addition, for decades there was no incentive to build new units since they would have been subjected to the same system. To this day, these dynamics continue to contribute to the crisis in the availability of moderate income housing.

A better way to create

Pe
about
offici
pledg
say th
of Ira
9/11,
evide
that t
fight
Bu
are be
left-w
where
tive c
the A
I w
who

A

appo
And l
O'Ne
frien
early
was c
Bu
I mis
inval
of the
Ro
Price
inter
plied
admi
sider
— tr
issue
trade
mone
blithe
prove
there
On
Gree

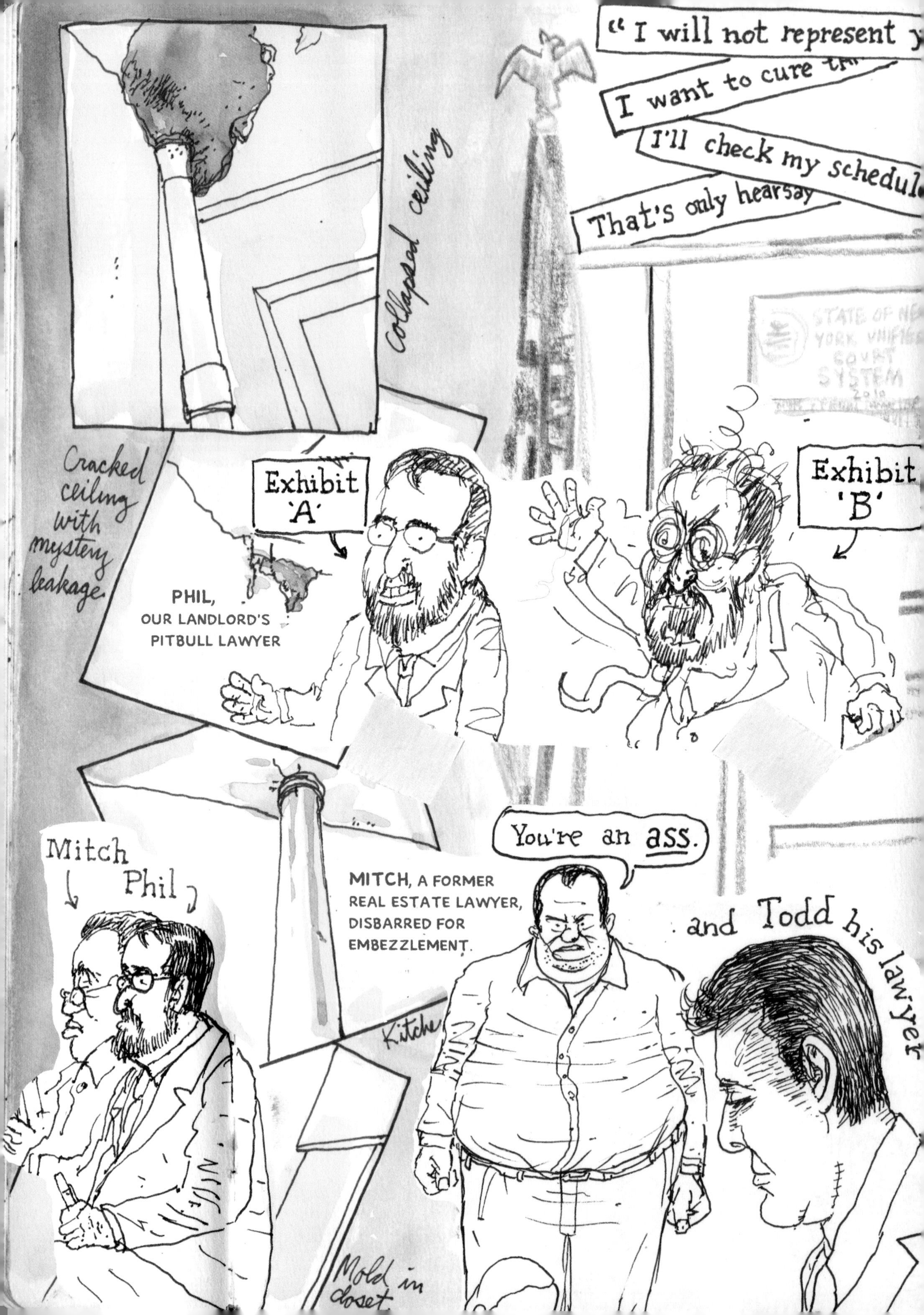

Collapsed ceiling
"I will not represent y
I want to cure th
I'll check my schedule
That's only hearsay
STATE OF NEW YORK UNIFIED COURT SYSTEM
Cracked ceiling with mystery leakage.
Exhibit 'A'
PHIL, OUR LANDLORD'S PITBULL LAWYER
Exhibit 'B'
Mitch
Phil
MITCH, A FORMER REAL ESTATE LAWYER, DISBARRED FOR EMBEZZLEMENT.
You're an ass.
and Todd his lawyer
Kitche
Mold in closet

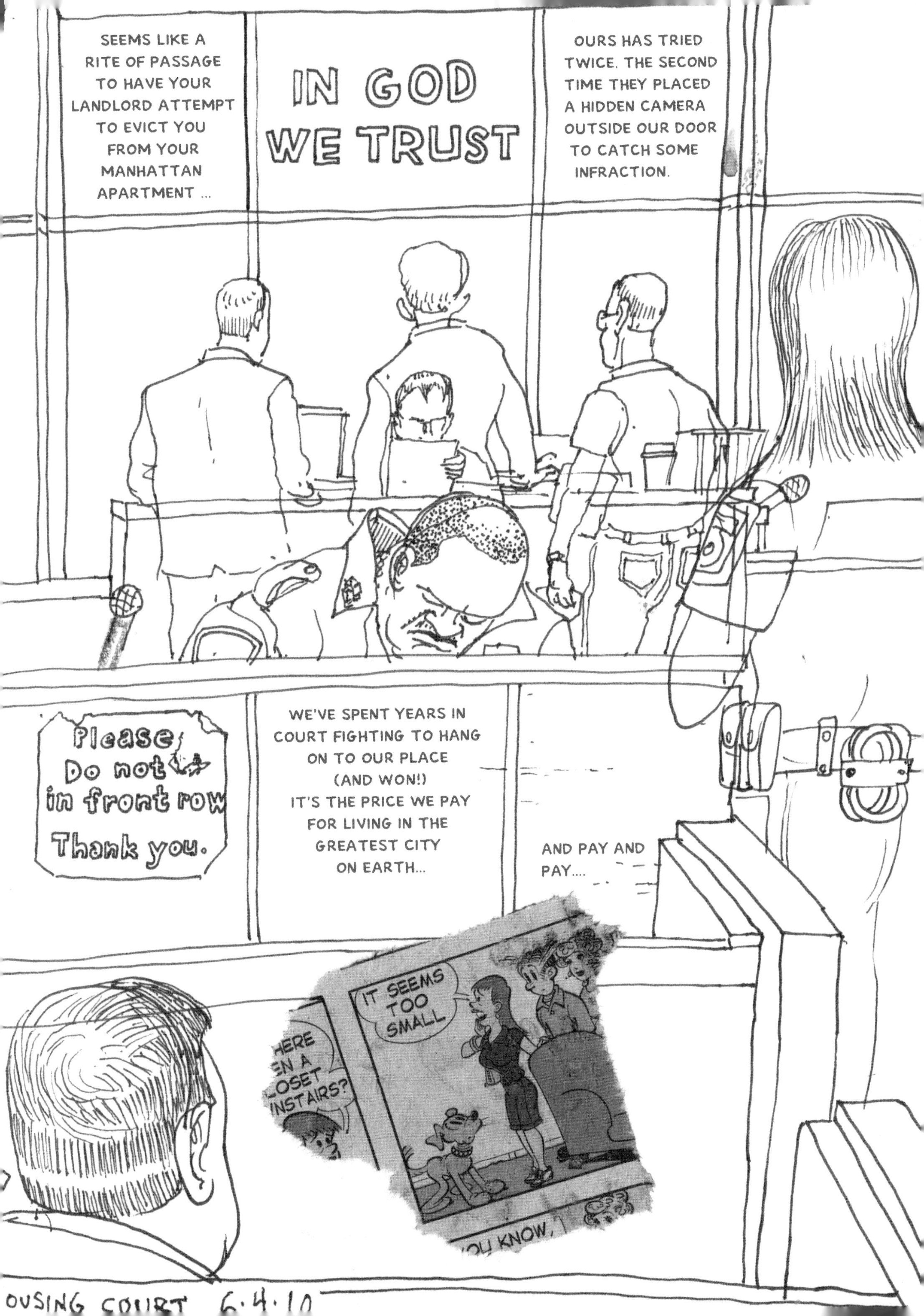
SEEMS LIKE A RITE OF PASSAGE TO HAVE YOUR LANDLORD ATTEMPT TO EVICT YOU FROM YOUR MANHATTAN APARTMENT ...
IN GOD WE TRUST
OURS HAS TRIED TWICE. THE SECOND TIME THEY PLACED A HIDDEN CAMERA OUTSIDE OUR DOOR TO CATCH SOME INFRACTION.
Please Do not in front row Thank you.
WE'VE SPENT YEARS IN COURT FIGHTING TO HANG ON TO OUR PLACE (AND WON!) IT'S THE PRICE WE PAY FOR LIVING IN THE GREATEST CITY ON EARTH...
AND PAY AND PAY....
IT SEEMS TOO SMALL
OUSING COURT 6.4.10

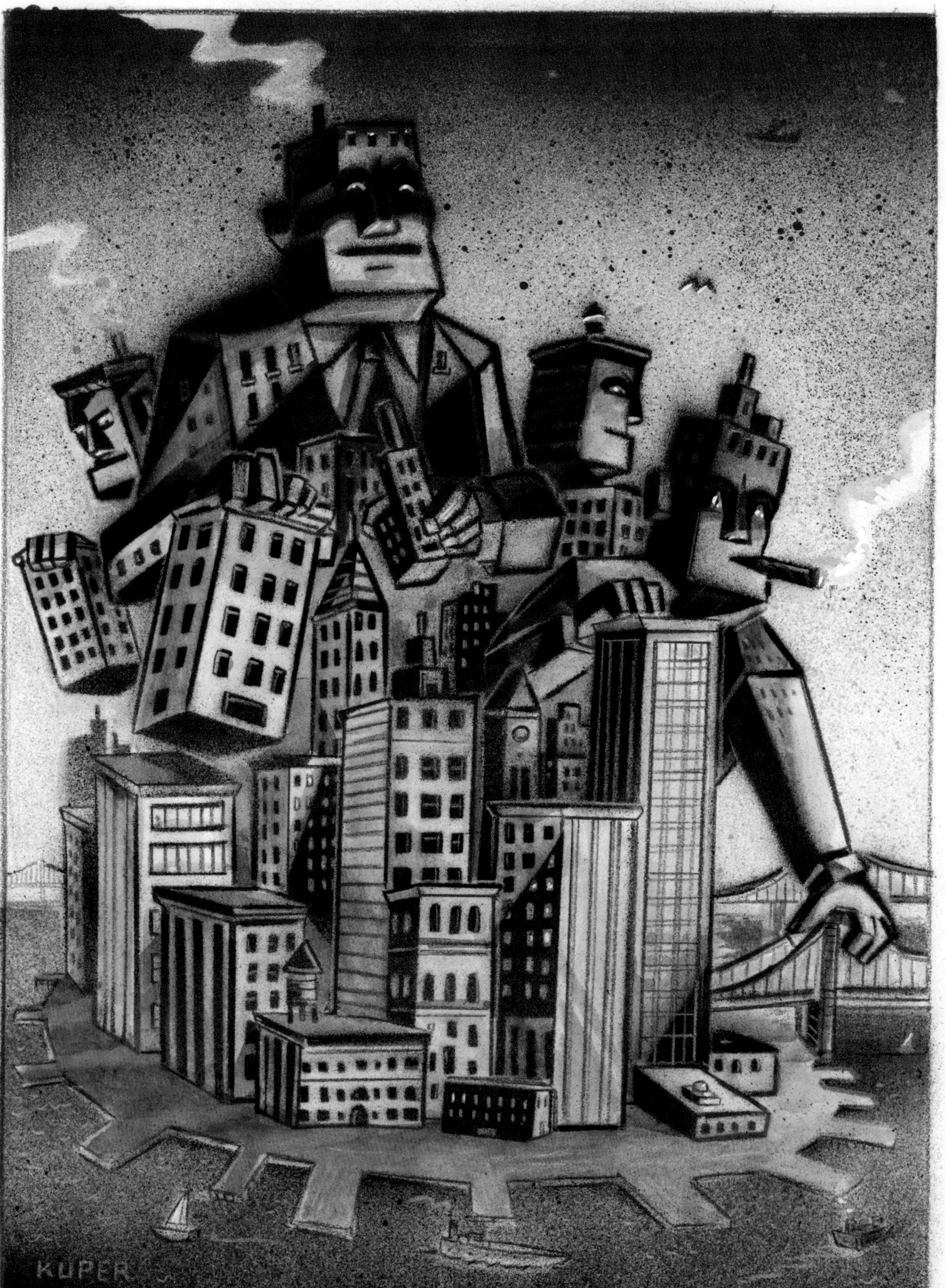
KUPER

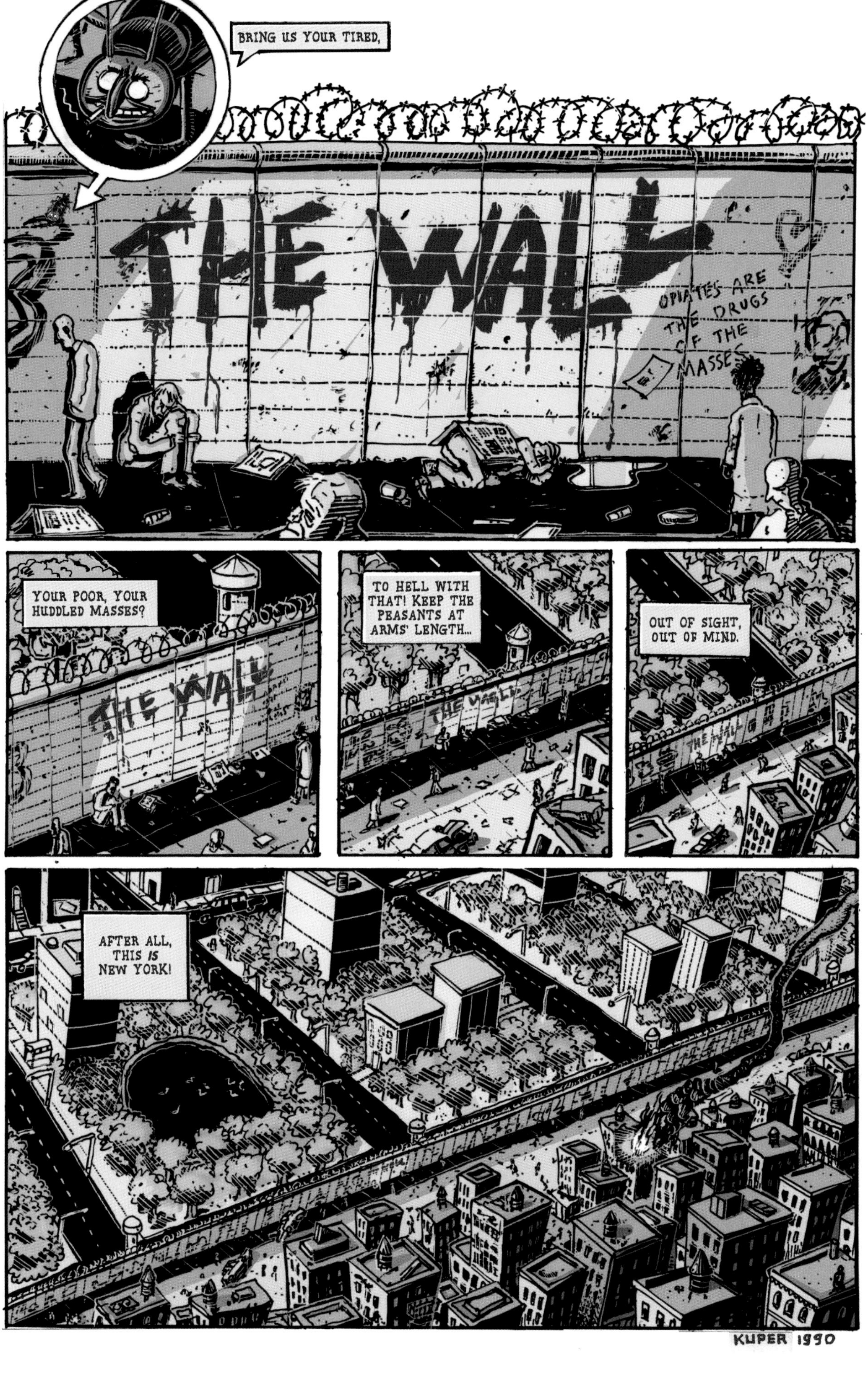
BRING US YOUR TIRED,
THE WALL
OPIATES ARE THE DRUGS OF THE MASSES
YOUR POOR, YOUR HUDDLED MASSES?
THE WALL
TO HELL WITH THAT! KEEP THE PEASANTS AT ARMS' LENGTH...
OUT OF SIGHT, OUT OF MIND.
AFTER ALL, THIS *IS* NEW YORK!
KUPER 1990

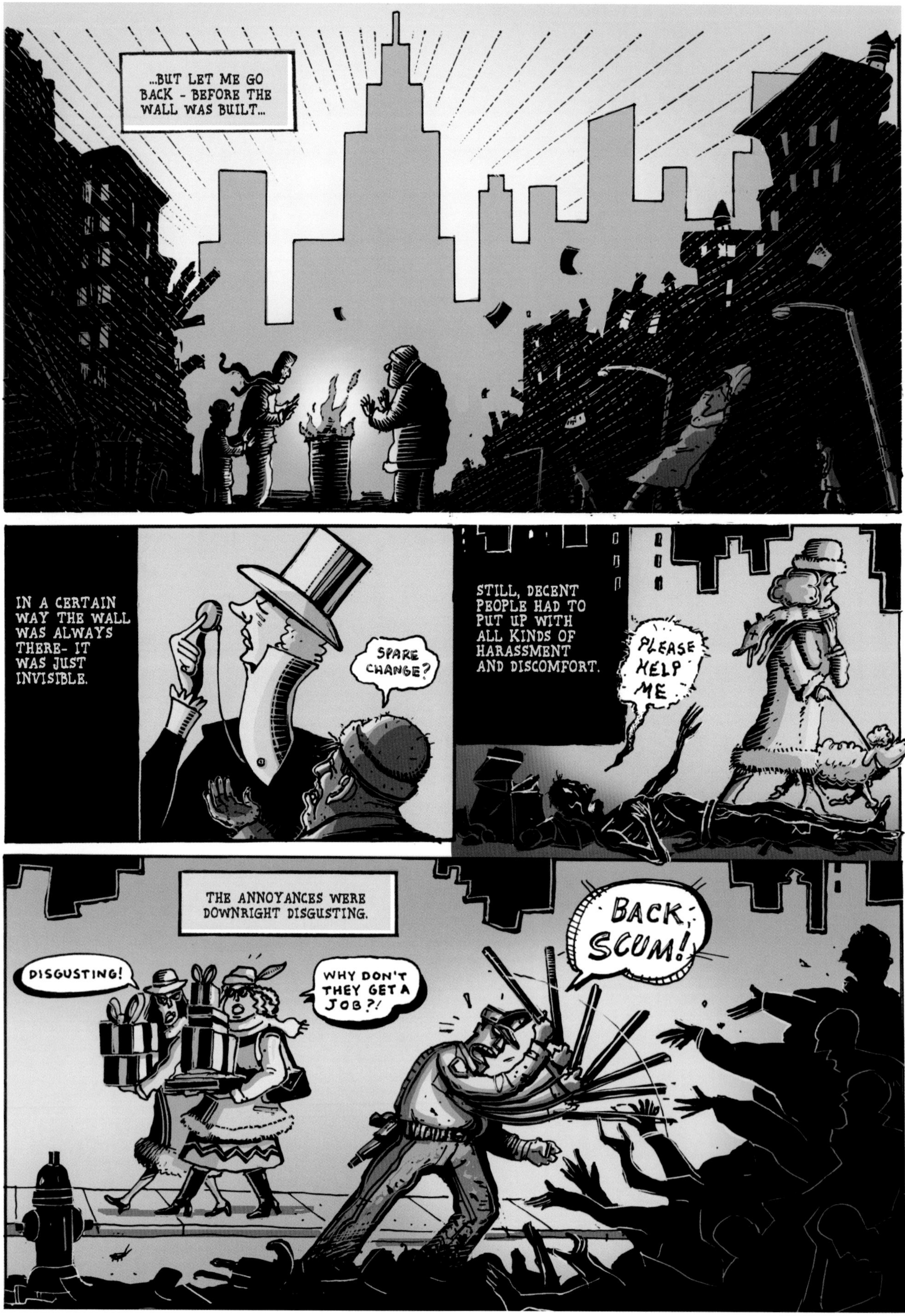

...BUT LET ME GO BACK - BEFORE THE WALL WAS BUILT...
IN A CERTAIN WAY THE WALL WAS ALWAYS THERE- IT WAS JUST INVISIBLE.
SPARE CHANGE?
STILL, DECENT PEOPLE HAD TO PUT UP WITH ALL KINDS OF HARASSMENT AND DISCOMFORT.
PLEASE HELP ME
THE ANNOYANCES WERE DOWNRIGHT DISGUSTING.
DISGUSTING!
WHY DON'T THEY GET A JOB?!
BACK, SCUM!

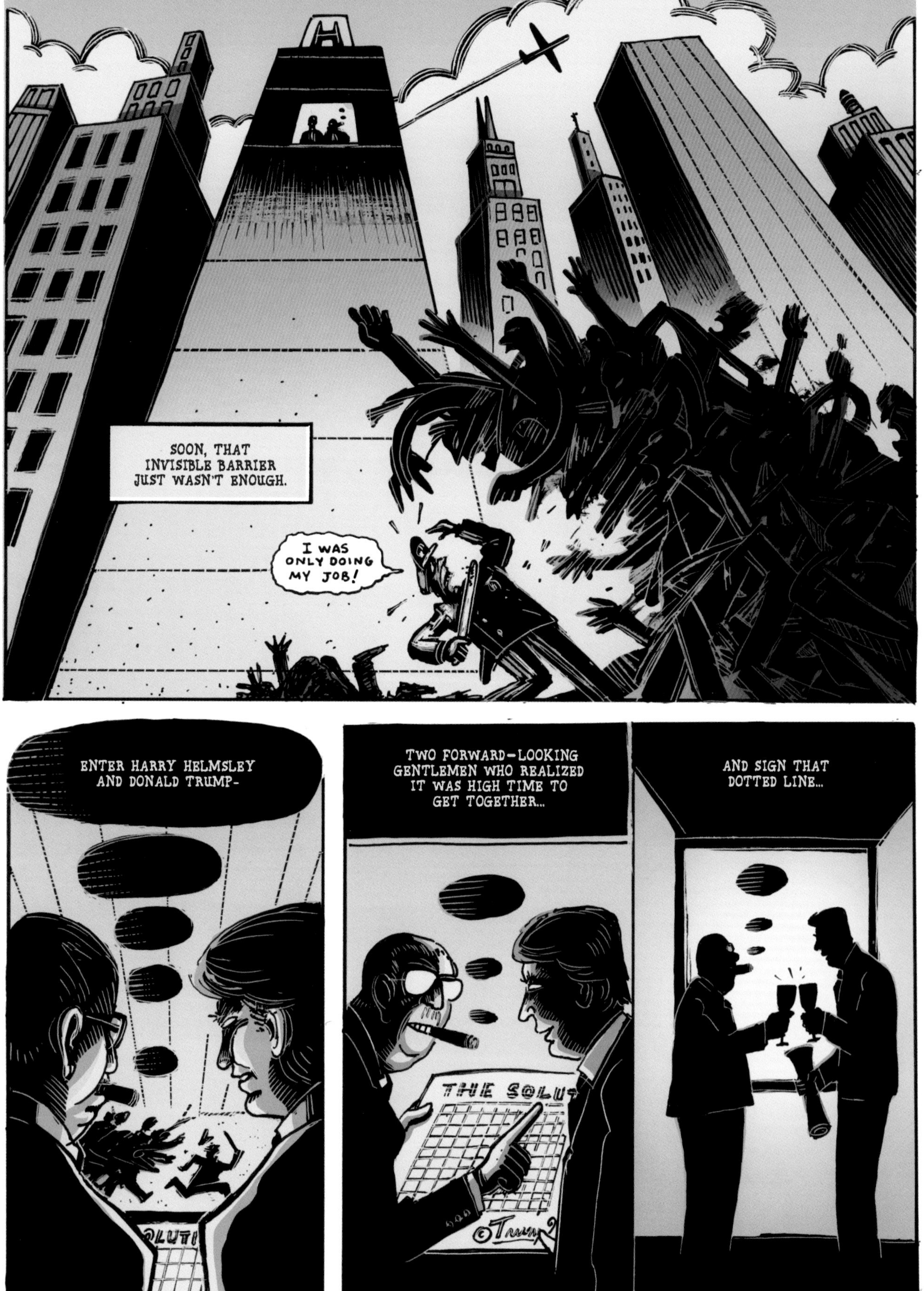
SOON, THAT INVISIBLE BARRIER JUST WASN'T ENOUGH.
I WAS ONLY DOING MY JOB!
ENTER HARRY HELMSLEY AND DONALD TRUMP-
TWO FORWARD-LOOKING GENTLEMEN WHO REALIZED IT WAS HIGH TIME TO GET TOGETHER...
THE SOLU
©Trump
AND SIGN THAT DOTTED LINE...

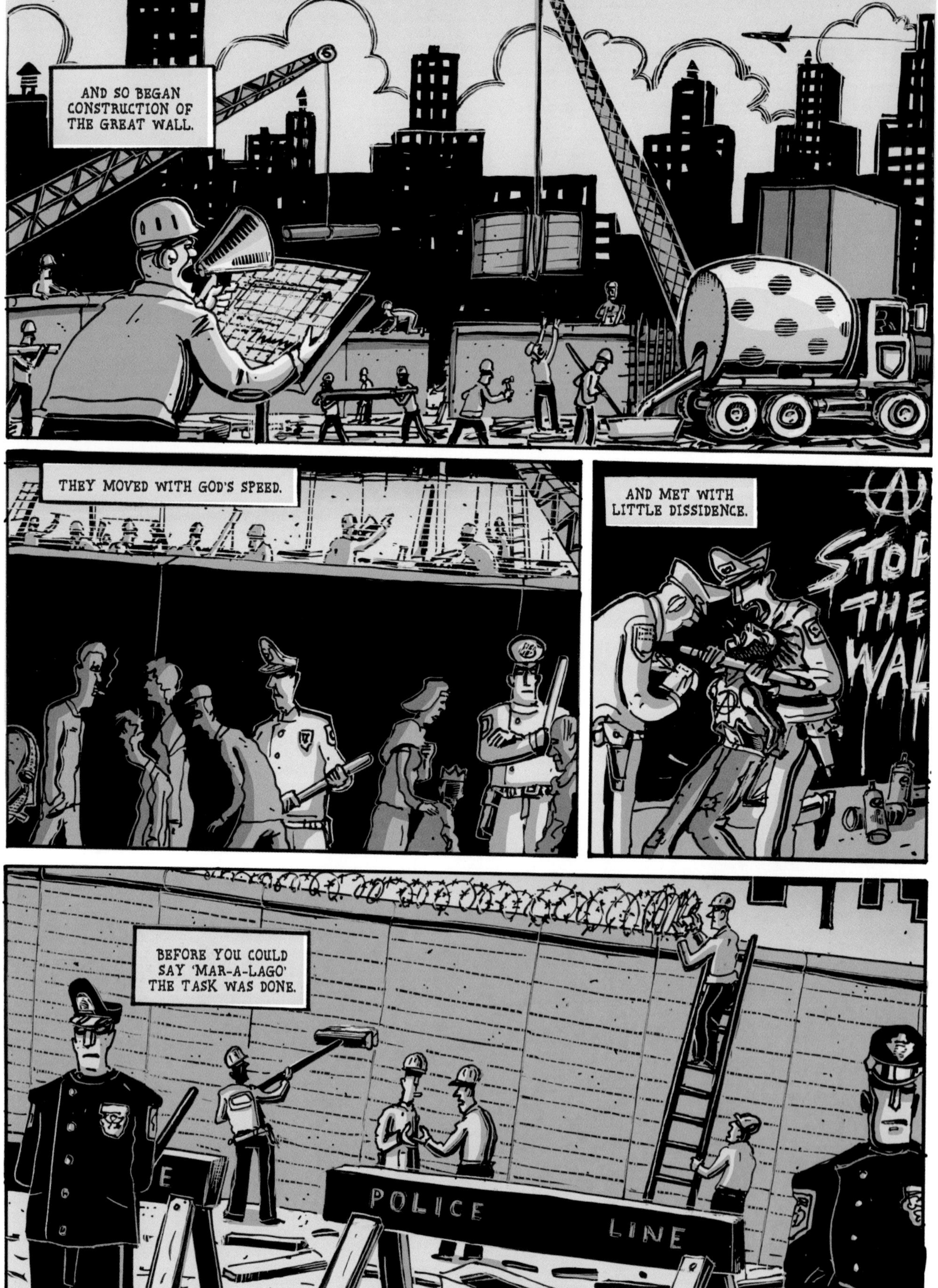
AND SO BEGAN CONSTRUCTION OF THE GREAT WALL.
THEY MOVED WITH GOD'S SPEED.
AND MET WITH LITTLE DISSIDENCE.
BEFORE YOU COULD SAY 'MAR-A-LAGO' THE TASK WAS DONE.
POLICE
LINE

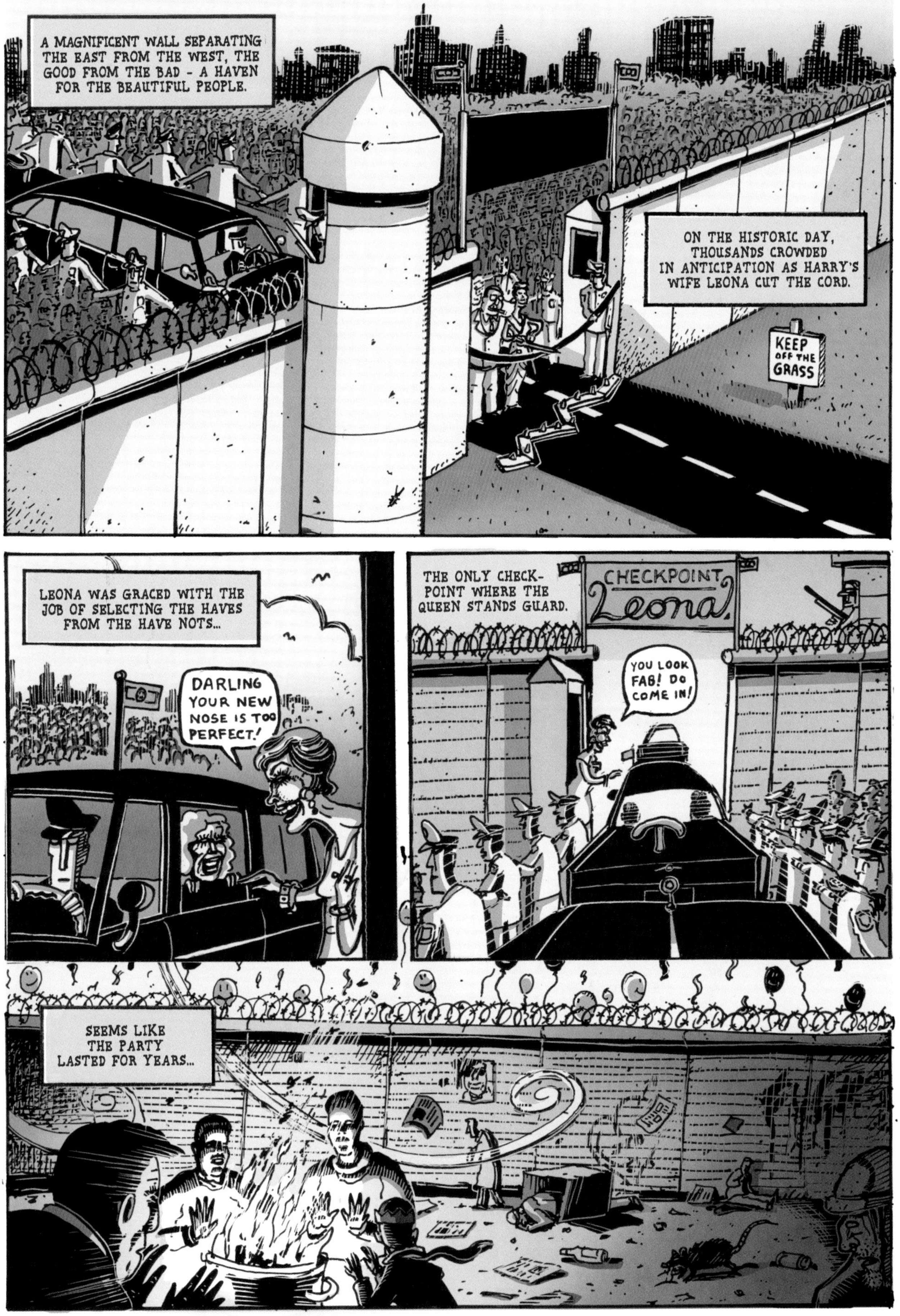
A MAGNIFICENT WALL SEPARATING THE EAST FROM THE WEST, THE GOOD FROM THE BAD - A HAVEN FOR THE BEAUTIFUL PEOPLE.
ON THE HISTORIC DAY, THOUSANDS CROWDED IN ANTICIPATION AS HARRY'S WIFE LEONA CUT THE CORD.
KEEP OFF THE GRASS
LEONA WAS GRACED WITH THE JOB OF SELECTING THE HAVES FROM THE HAVE NOTS...
DARLING YOUR NEW NOSE IS TOO PERFECT!
THE ONLY CHECK-POINT WHERE THE QUEEN STANDS GUARD.
CHECKPOINT Leona
YOU LOOK FAB! DO COME IN!
SEEMS LIKE THE PARTY LASTED FOR YEARS...

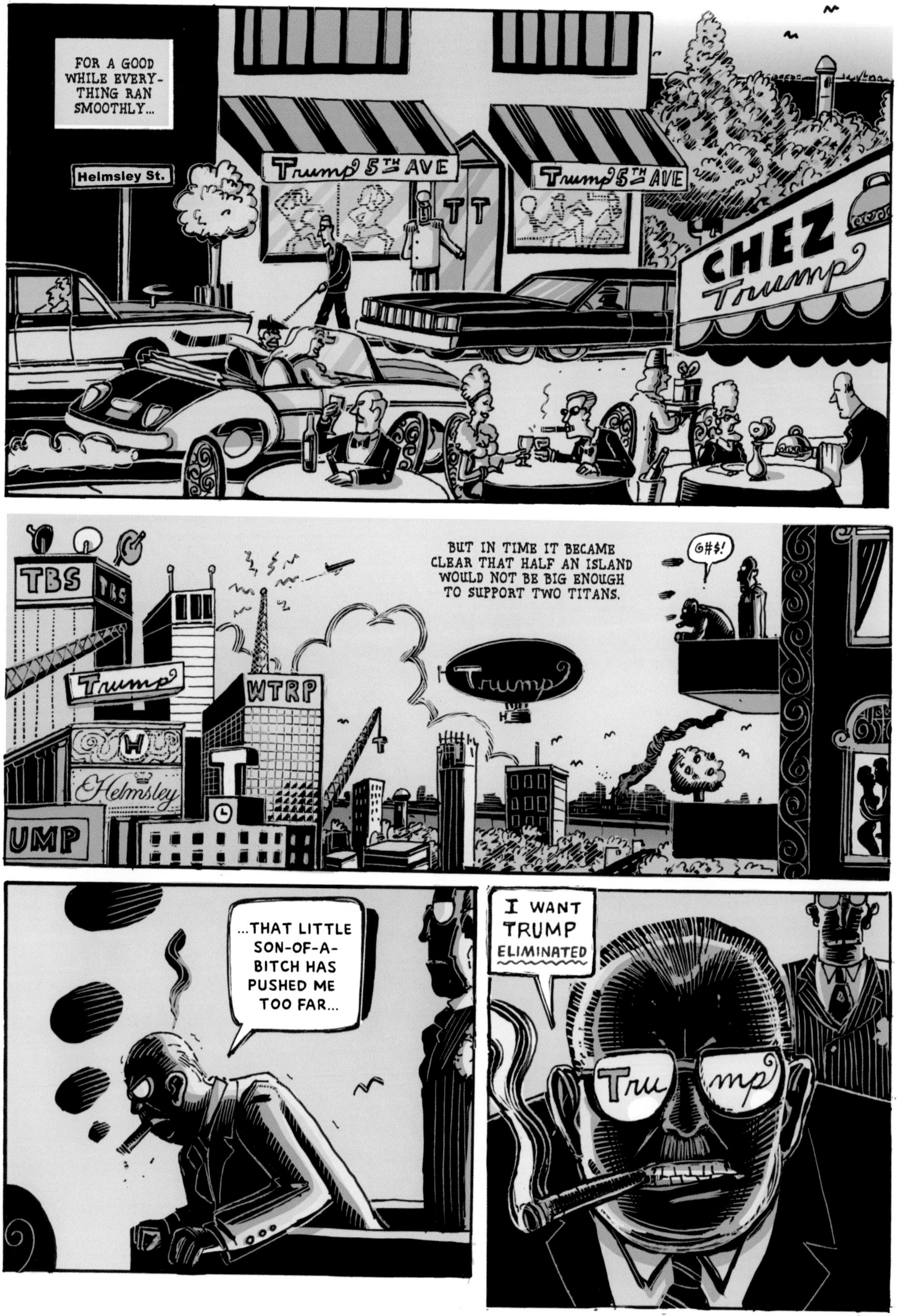
FOR A GOOD WHILE EVERY-THING RAN SMOOTHLY...
Helmsley St.
Trump 5TH AVE
TT
Trump 5TH AVE
CHEZ Trump
TBS
TBS
Trump
WTRP
Helmsley
UMP
BUT IN TIME IT BECAME CLEAR THAT HALF AN ISLAND WOULD NOT BE BIG ENOUGH TO SUPPORT TWO TITANS.
G#$!
Trump
...THAT LITTLE SON-OF-A-BITCH HAS PUSHED ME TOO FAR...
I WANT TRUMP ELIMINATED
Tru mp

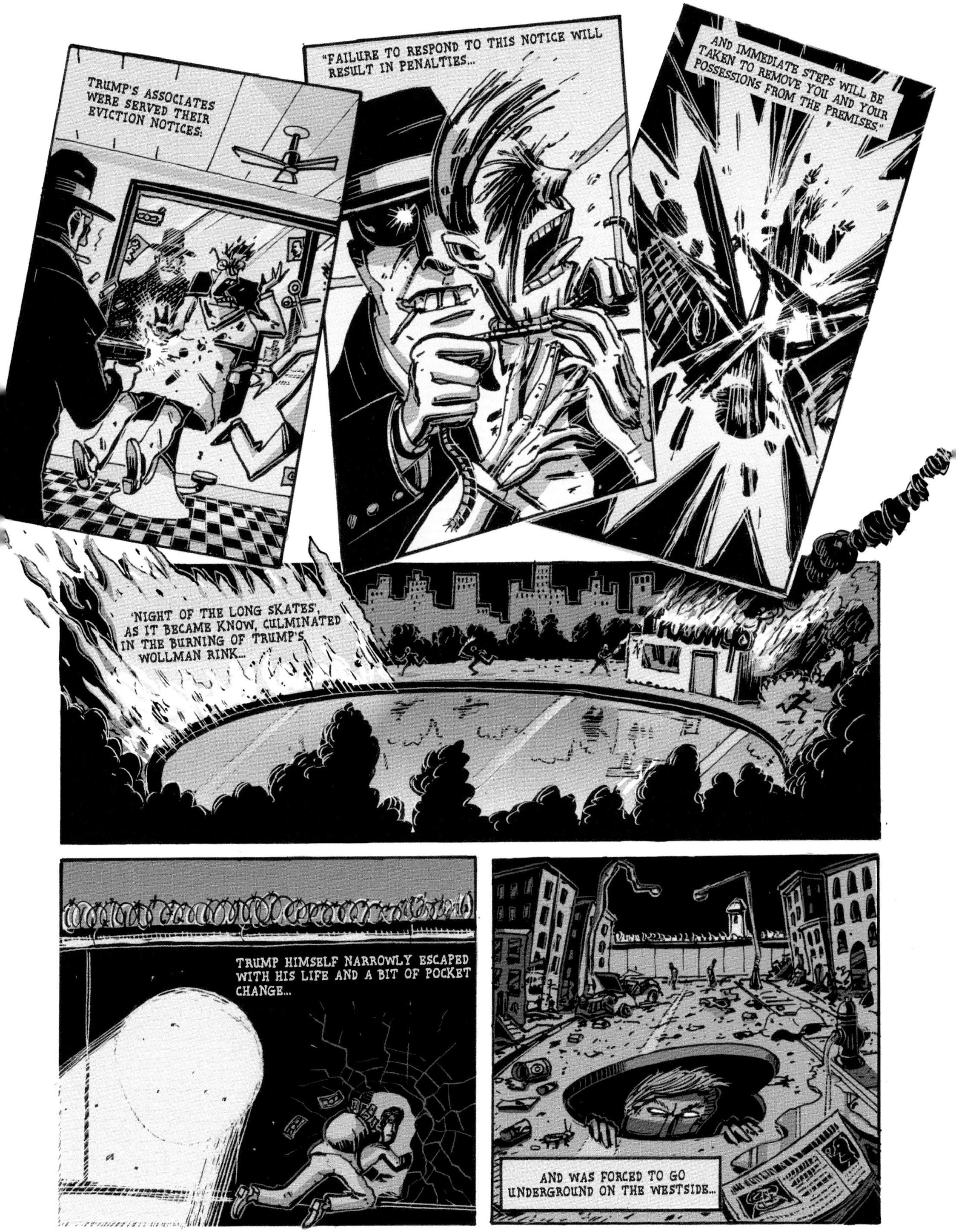
TRUMP'S ASSOCIATES WERE SERVED THEIR EVICTION NOTICES:
"FAILURE TO RESPOND TO THIS NOTICE WILL RESULT IN PENALTIES...
AND IMMEDIATE STEPS WILL BE TAKEN TO REMOVE YOU AND YOUR POSSESSIONS FROM THE PREMISES."
'NIGHT OF THE LONG SKATES', AS IT BECAME KNOW, CULMINATED IN THE BURNING OF TRUMP'S WOLLMAN RINK...
TRUMP HIMSELF NARROWLY ESCAPED WITH HIS LIFE AND A BIT OF POCKET CHANGE...
AND WAS FORCED TO GO UNDERGROUND ON THE WESTSIDE...

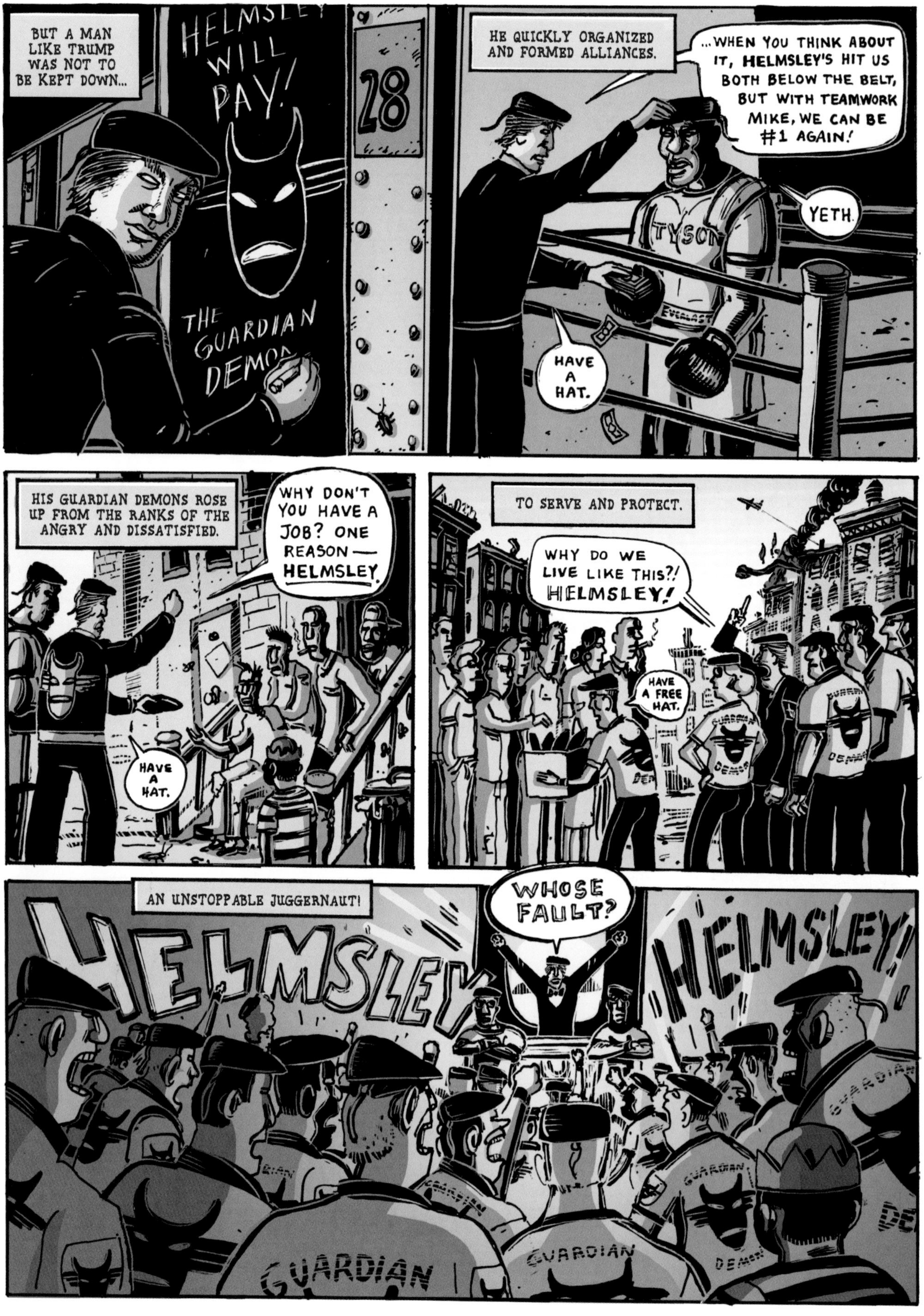
BUT A MAN LIKE TRUMP WAS NOT TO BE KEPT DOWN...
HELMSLEY WILL PAY!
THE GUARDIAN DEMON
28
HE QUICKLY ORGANIZED AND FORMED ALLIANCES.
...WHEN YOU THINK ABOUT IT, HELMSLEY'S HIT US BOTH BELOW THE BELT, BUT WITH TEAMWORK MIKE, WE CAN BE #1 AGAIN!
YETH.
TYSON
HAVE A HAT.
HIS GUARDIAN DEMONS ROSE UP FROM THE RANKS OF THE ANGRY AND DISSATISFIED.
WHY DON'T YOU HAVE A JOB? ONE REASON— HELMSLEY.
HAVE A HAT.
TO SERVE AND PROTECT.
WHY DO WE LIVE LIKE THIS?! HELMSLEY!
HAVE A FREE HAT.
AN UNSTOPPABLE JUGGERNAUT!
WHOSE FAULT?
HELMSLEY
HELMSLEY!
GUARDIAN
GUARDIAN

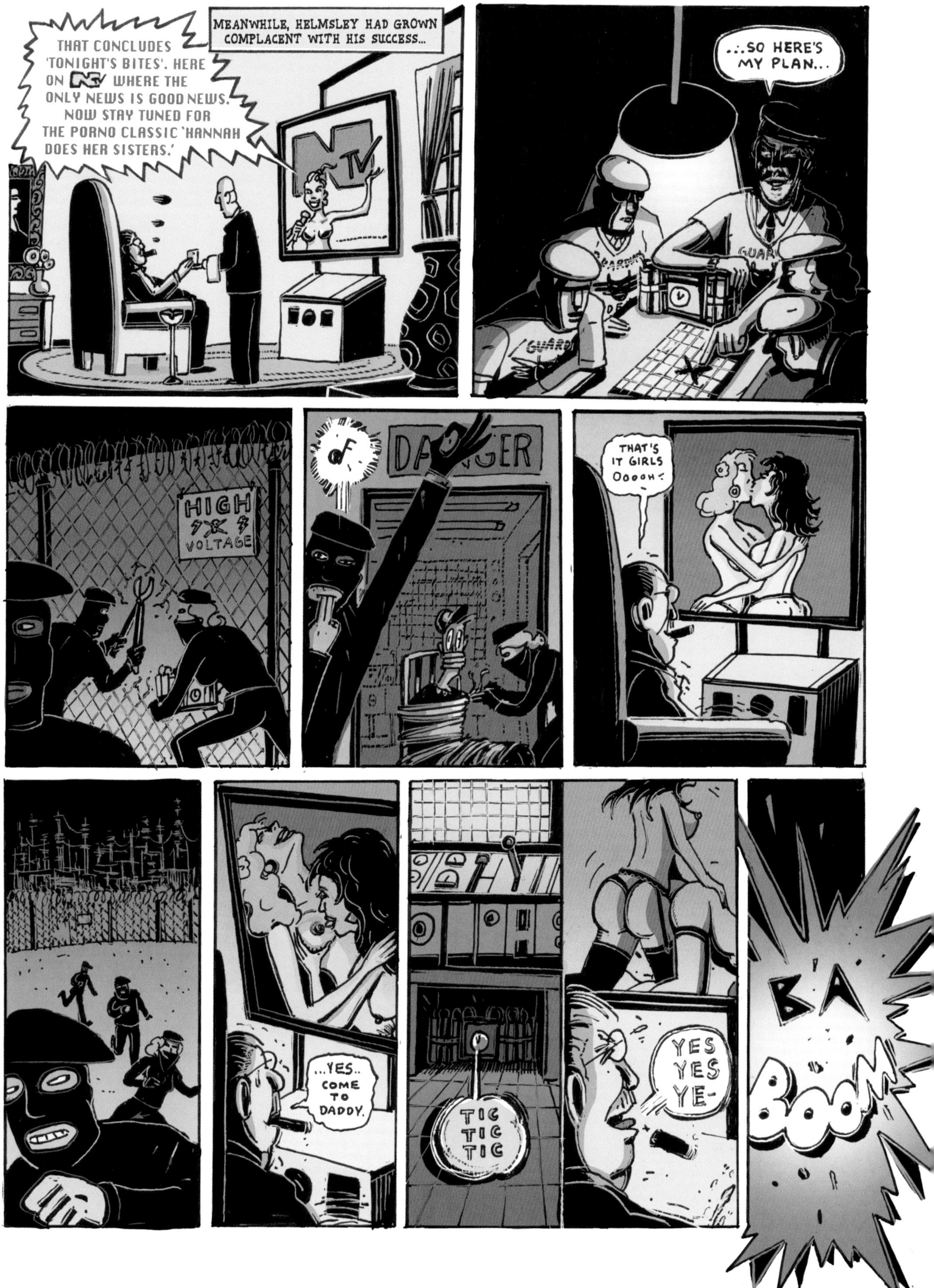
THAT CONCLUDES 'TONIGHT'S BITES'. HERE ON NTV WHERE THE ONLY NEWS IS GOOD NEWS. NOW STAY TUNED FOR THE PORNO CLASSIC 'HANNAH DOES HER SISTERS.'
MEANWHILE, HELMSLEY HAD GROWN COMPLACENT WITH HIS SUCCESS...
...SO HERE'S MY PLAN...
HIGH VOLTAGE
DANGER
THAT'S IT GIRLS OOOOH
...YES.. COME TO DADDY.
TIC TIC TIC
YES YES YE-
BA BOOM

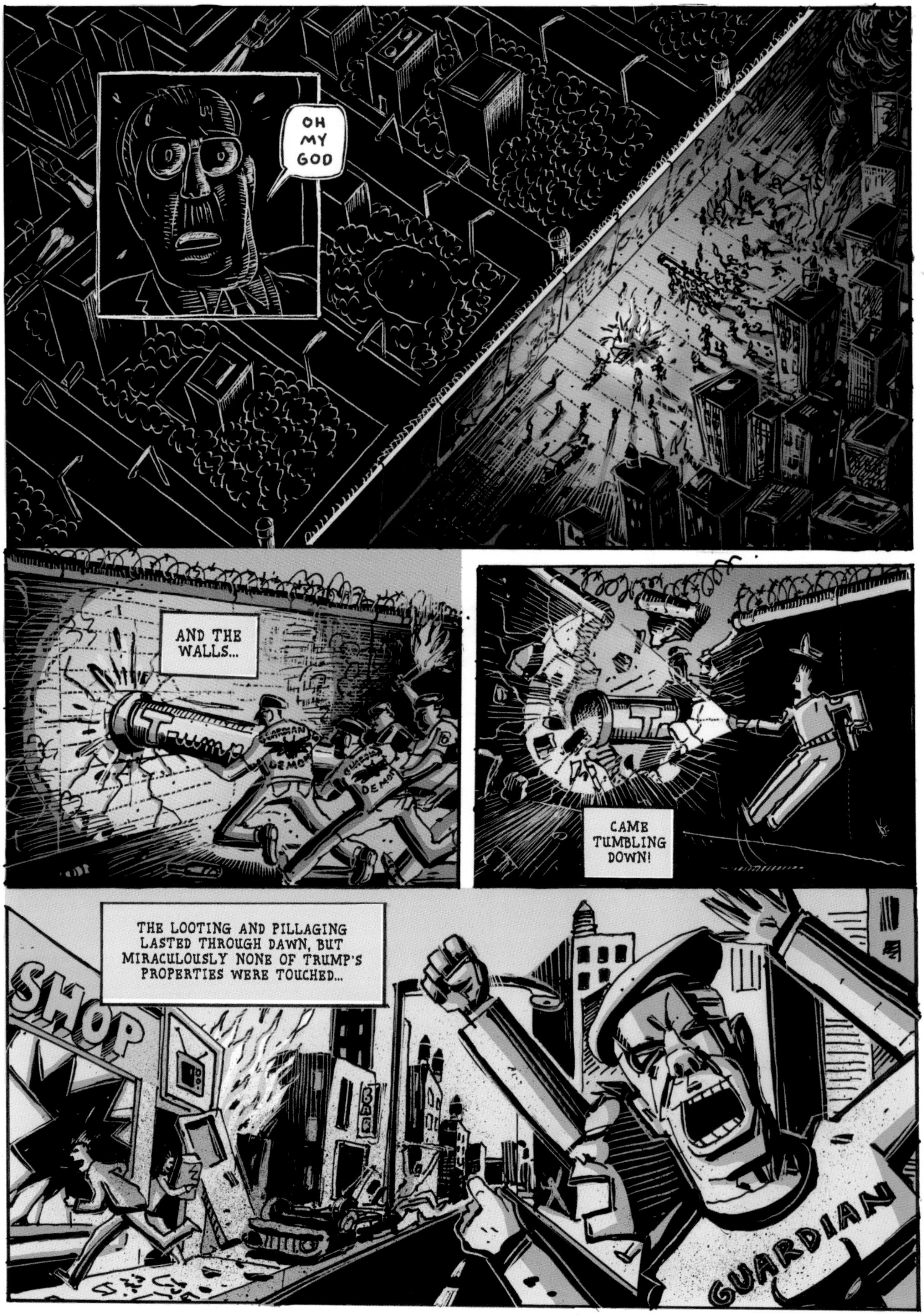
OH MY GOD
AND THE WALLS...
CAME TUMBLING DOWN!
THE LOOTING AND PILLAGING LASTED THROUGH DAWN, BUT MIRACULOUSLY NONE OF TRUMP'S PROPERTIES WERE TOUCHED...
SHOP
BAR
GUARDIAN

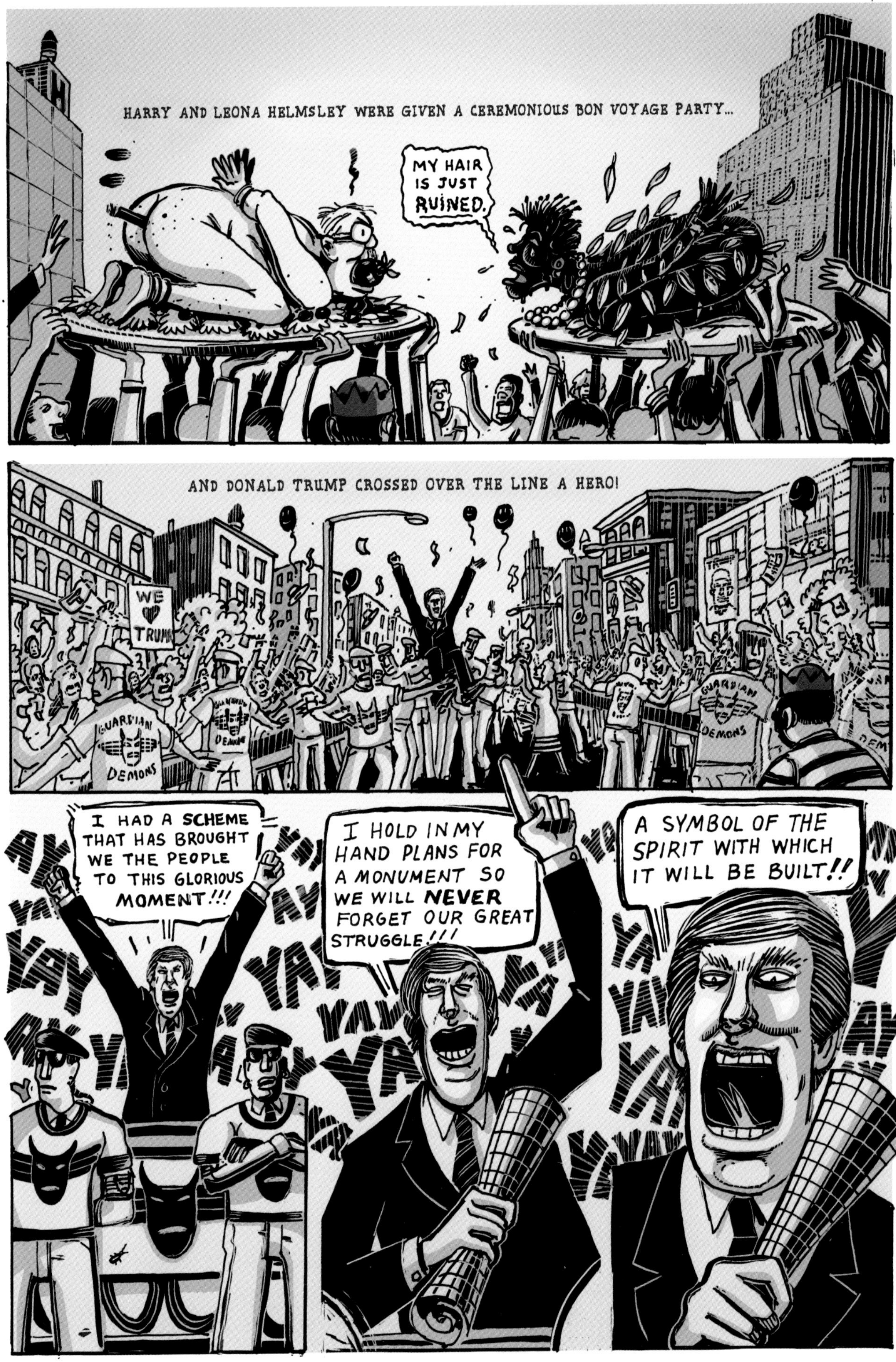
HARRY AND LEONA HELMSLEY WERE GIVEN A CEREMONIOUS BON VOYAGE PARTY...
MY HAIR IS JUST RUINED.
AND DONALD TRUMP CROSSED OVER THE LINE A HERO!
WE ♥ TRUMP
GUARDIAN DEMONS
I HAD A SCHEME THAT HAS BROUGHT WE THE PEOPLE TO THIS GLORIOUS MOMENT!!!
I HOLD IN MY HAND PLANS FOR A MONUMENT SO WE WILL NEVER FORGET OUR GREAT STRUGGLE!!!
A SYMBOL OF THE SPIRIT WITH WHICH IT WILL BE BUILT!!
YAY

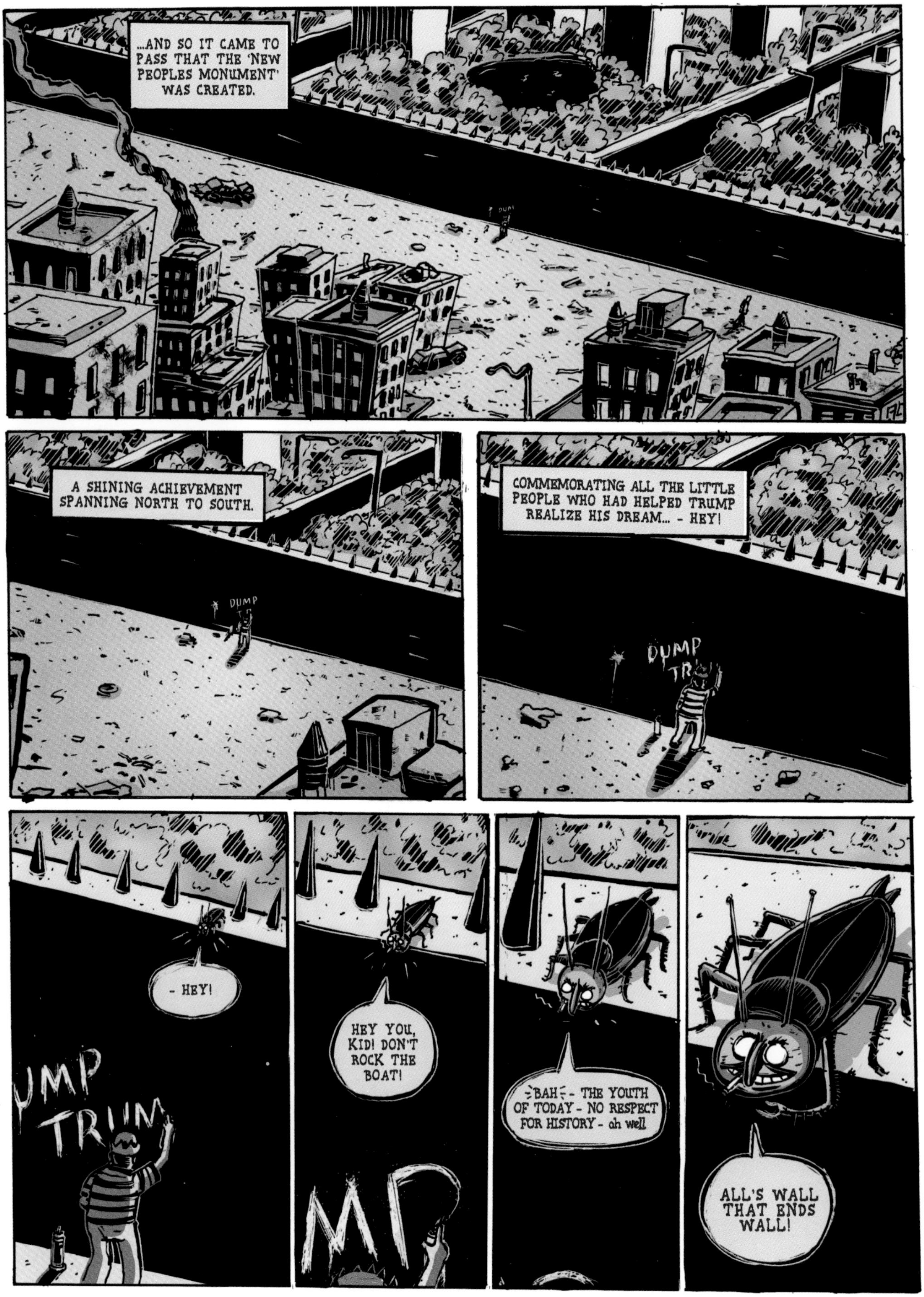
...AND SO IT CAME TO PASS THAT THE 'NEW PEOPLES MONUMENT' WAS CREATED.
A SHINING ACHIEVEMENT SPANNING NORTH TO SOUTH.
DUMP
COMMEMORATING ALL THE LITTLE PEOPLE WHO HAD HELPED TRUMP REALIZE HIS DREAM... - HEY!
DUMP TR
- HEY!
UMP TRUM
HEY YOU, KID! DON'T ROCK THE BOAT!
BAH - THE YOUTH OF TODAY - NO RESPECT FOR HISTORY - oh well
ALL'S WALL THAT ENDS WALL!

DREAMS OF REASON
(ALL STORIES GUARANTEED DREAMED) ®

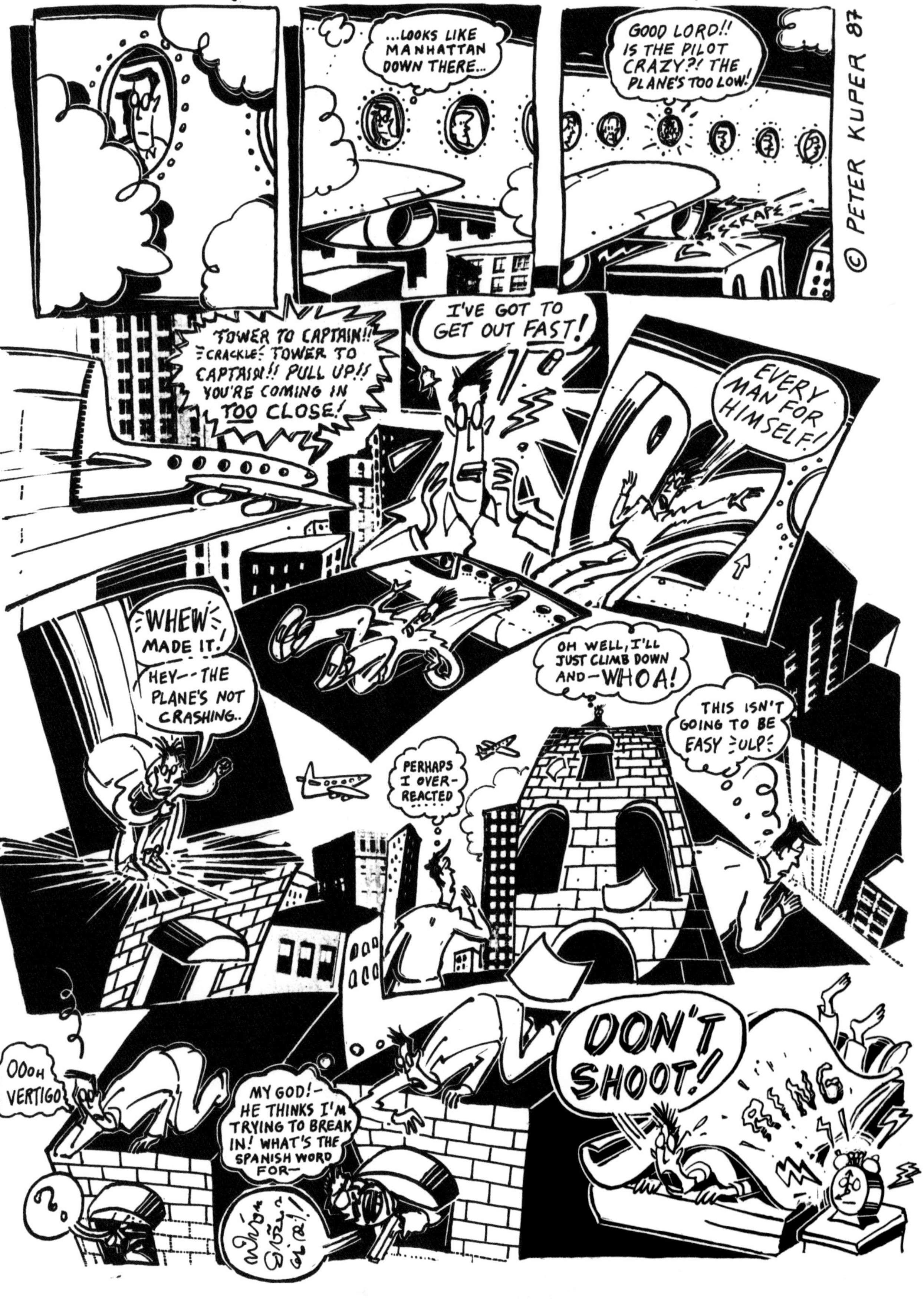

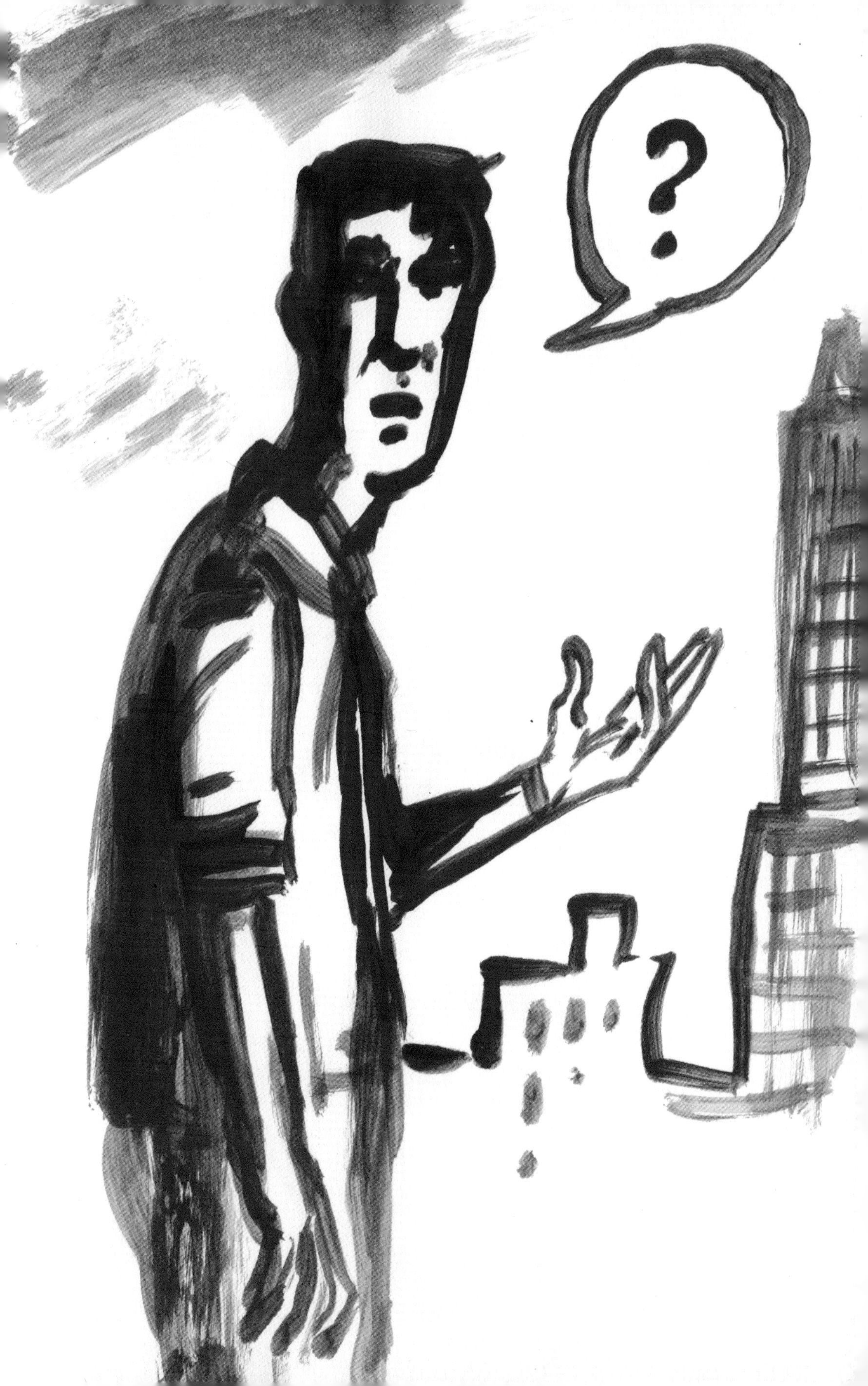
?

A NEW YORKER

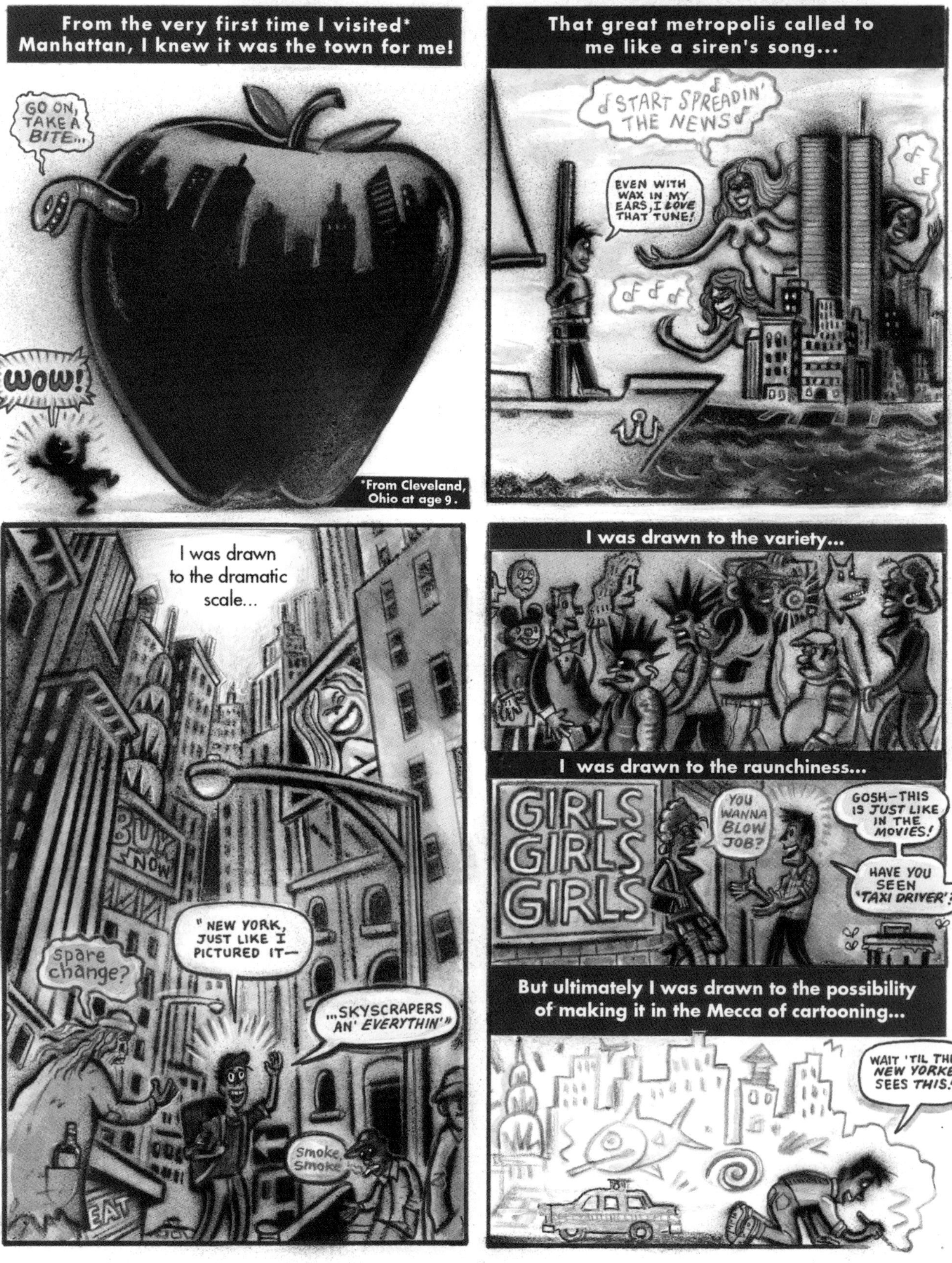
From the very first time I visited* Manhattan, I knew it was the town for me!
GO ON, TAKE A BITE...
WOW!
*From Cleveland, Ohio at age 9.
That great metropolis called to me like a siren's song...
START SPREADIN' THE NEWS
EVEN WITH WAX IN MY EARS, I LOVE THAT TUNE!
I was drawn to the dramatic scale...
BUY NOW
"NEW YORK, JUST LIKE I PICTURED IT—
spare change?
...SKYSCRAPERS AN' EVERYTHIN'"
Smoke, Smoke
EAT
I was drawn to the variety...
I was drawn to the raunchiness...
GIRLS GIRLS GIRLS
YOU WANNA BLOW JOB?
GOSH—THIS IS JUST LIKE IN THE MOVIES!
HAVE YOU SEEN 'TAXI DRIVER'?
But ultimately I was drawn to the possibility of making it in the Mecca of cartooning...
WAIT 'TIL THE NEW YORKER SEES THIS!

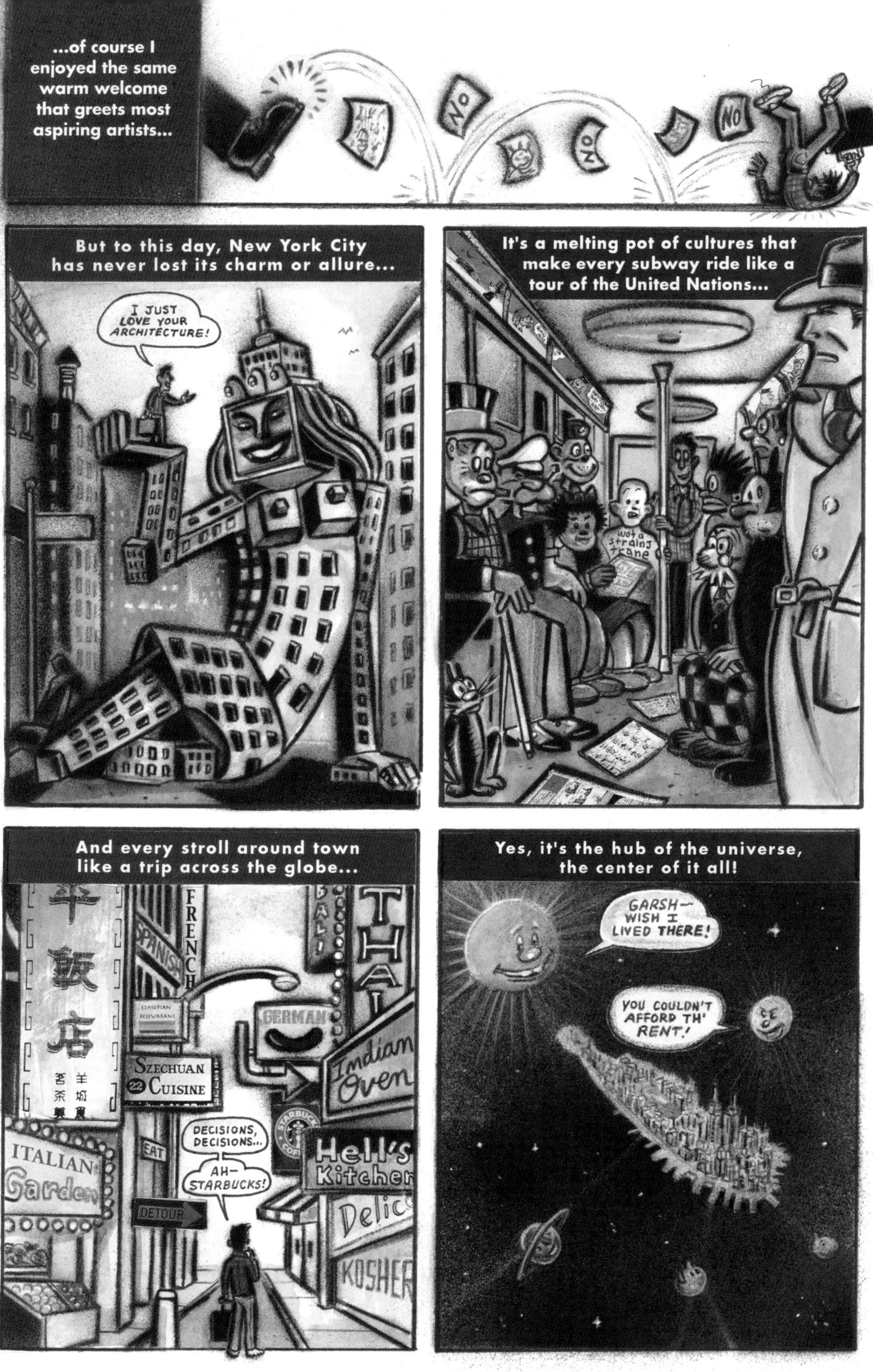

...of course I enjoyed the same warm welcome that greets most aspiring artists...
NO
NO
NO
But to this day, New York City has never lost its charm or allure...
I JUST LOVE YOUR ARCHITECTURE!
It's a melting pot of cultures that make every subway ride like a tour of the United Nations...
wot a strainj trane
And every stroll around town like a trip across the globe...
SPANISH
FRENCH
GERMAN
THAI
SZECHUAN 22 CUISINE
Indian Oven
ITALIAN Garden
EAT
DECISIONS, DECISIONS...
AH— STARBUCKS!
Hell's Kitchen
DETOUR
Delic
KOSHER
Yes, it's the hub of the universe, the center of it all!
GARSH— WISH I LIVED THERE!
YOU COULDN'T AFFORD TH' RENT!

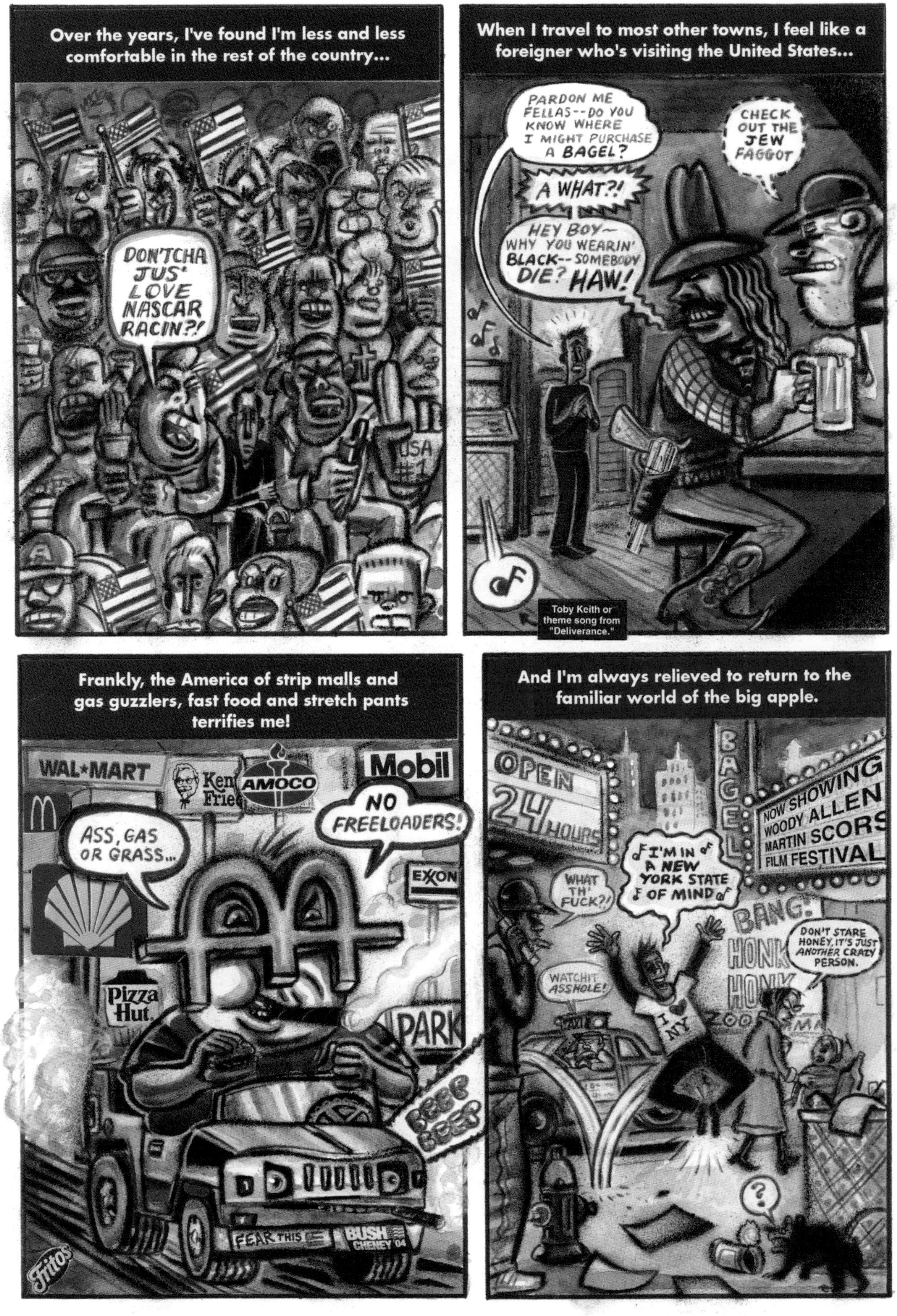
Over the years, I've found I'm less and less comfortable in the rest of the country...
DON'TCHA JUS' LOVE NASCAR RACIN?!
When I travel to most other towns, I feel like a foreigner who's visiting the United States...
PARDON ME FELLAS--DO YOU KNOW WHERE I MIGHT PURCHASE A BAGEL?
A WHAT?!
CHECK OUT THE JEW FAGGOT
HEY BOY~ WHY YOU WEARIN' BLACK--SOMEBODY DIE? HAW!
Toby Keith or theme song from "Deliverance."
Frankly, the America of strip malls and gas guzzlers, fast food and stretch pants terrifies me!
WAL★MART
AMOCO
Mobil
ASS, GAS OR GRASS...
NO FREELOADERS!
EXXON
Pizza Hut
PARK
BEEP BEEP
FEAR THIS
BUSH CHENEY '04
Fritos
And I'm always relieved to return to the familiar world of the big apple.
OPEN 24 HOURS
BAGEL
NOW SHOWING WOODY ALLEN MARTIN SCORS FILM FESTIVAL
WHAT TH' FUCK?!
I'M IN A NEW YORK STATE OF MIND
BANG!
HONK HONK
DON'T STARE HONEY, IT'S JUST ANOTHER CRAZY PERSON.
WATCHIT ASSHOLE!
TAXI
I ♥ NY
?

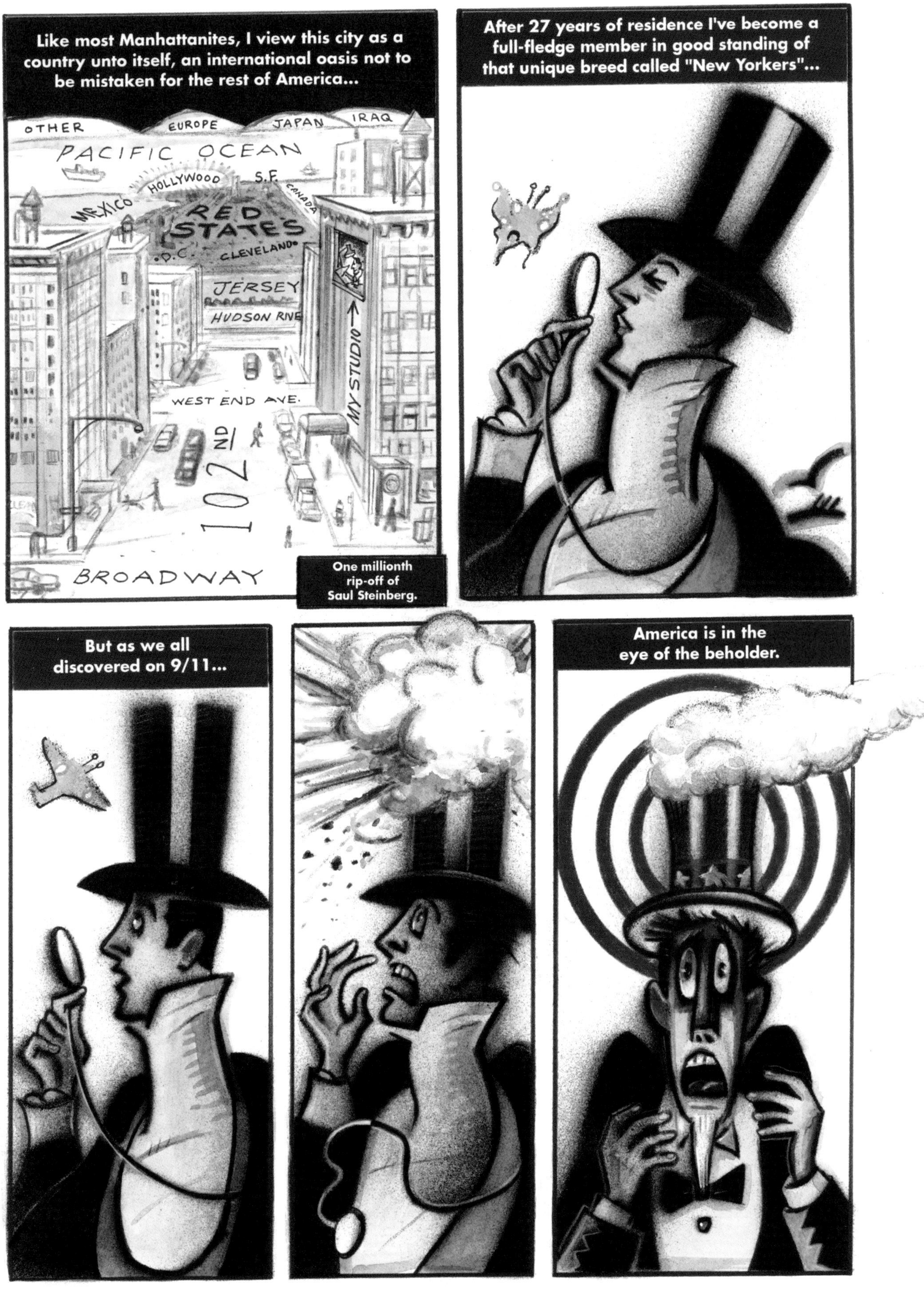
Like most Manhattanites, I view this city as a country unto itself, an international oasis not to be mistaken for the rest of America...
OTHER
EUROPE
JAPAN
IRAQ
PACIFIC OCEAN
HOLLYWOOD
S.F.
CANADA
MEXICO
RED STATES
D.C.
CLEVELAND
JERSEY
HUDSON RIVE
MY STUDIO
WEST END AVE.
102 ND
BROADWAY
One millionth rip-off of Saul Steinberg.
After 27 years of residence I've become a full-fledge member in good standing of that unique breed called "New Yorkers"...
But as we all discovered on 9/11...
America is in the eye of the beholder.

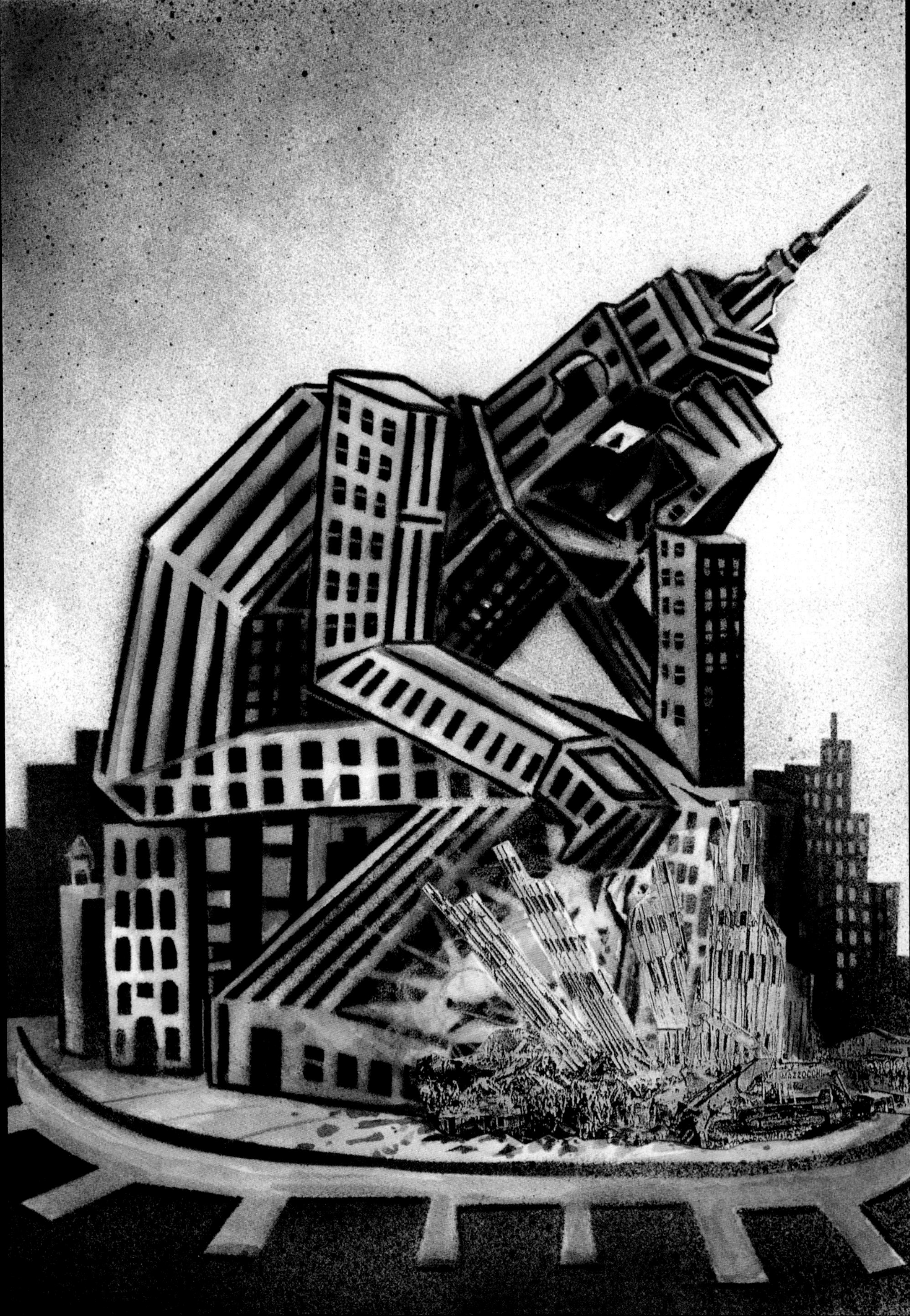

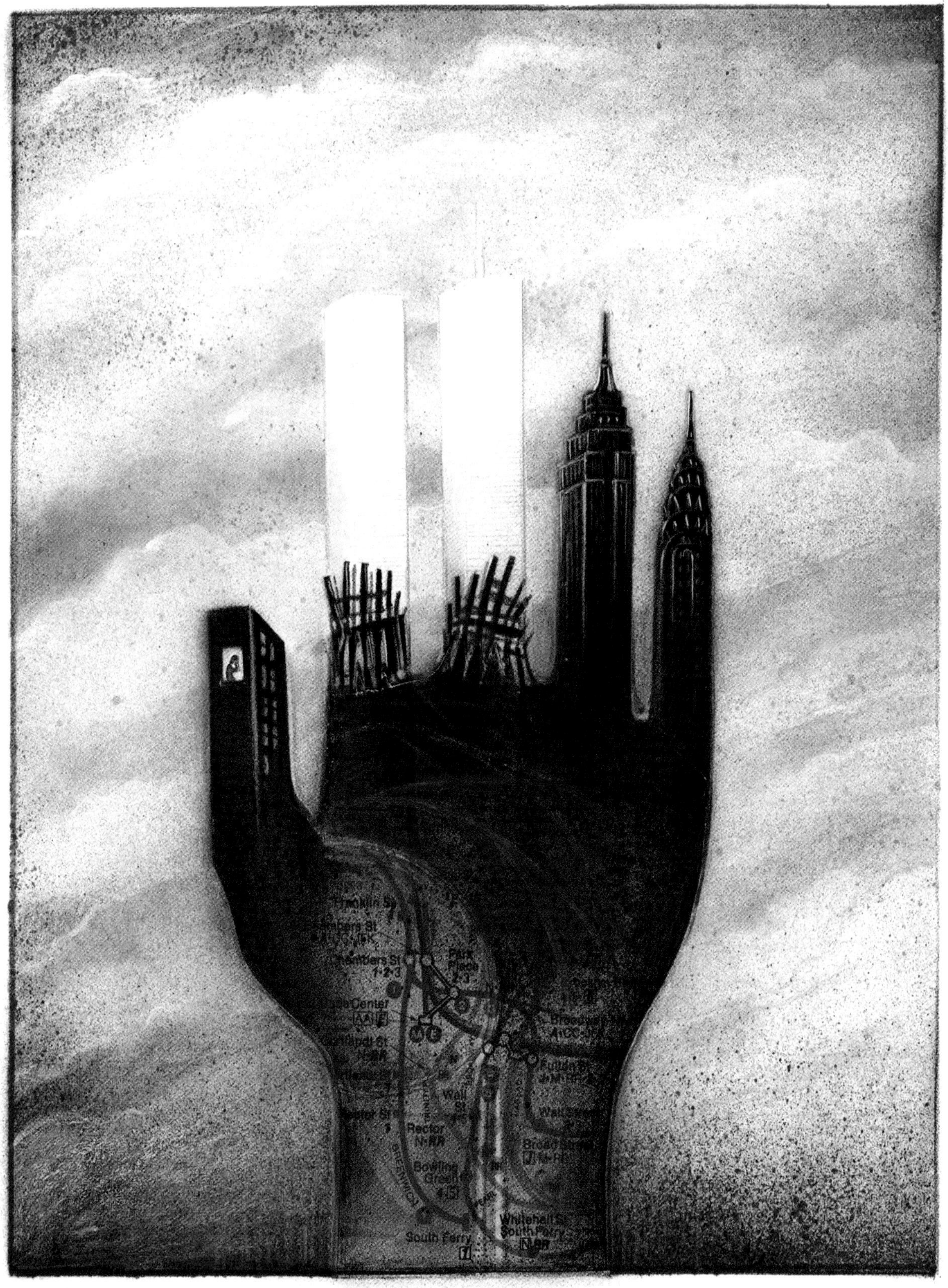
Franklin St
Chambers St
Park Place
Wall St
Rector
Bowling Green
South Ferry
Whitehall St
South Ferry

WAR OF THE WORLDS

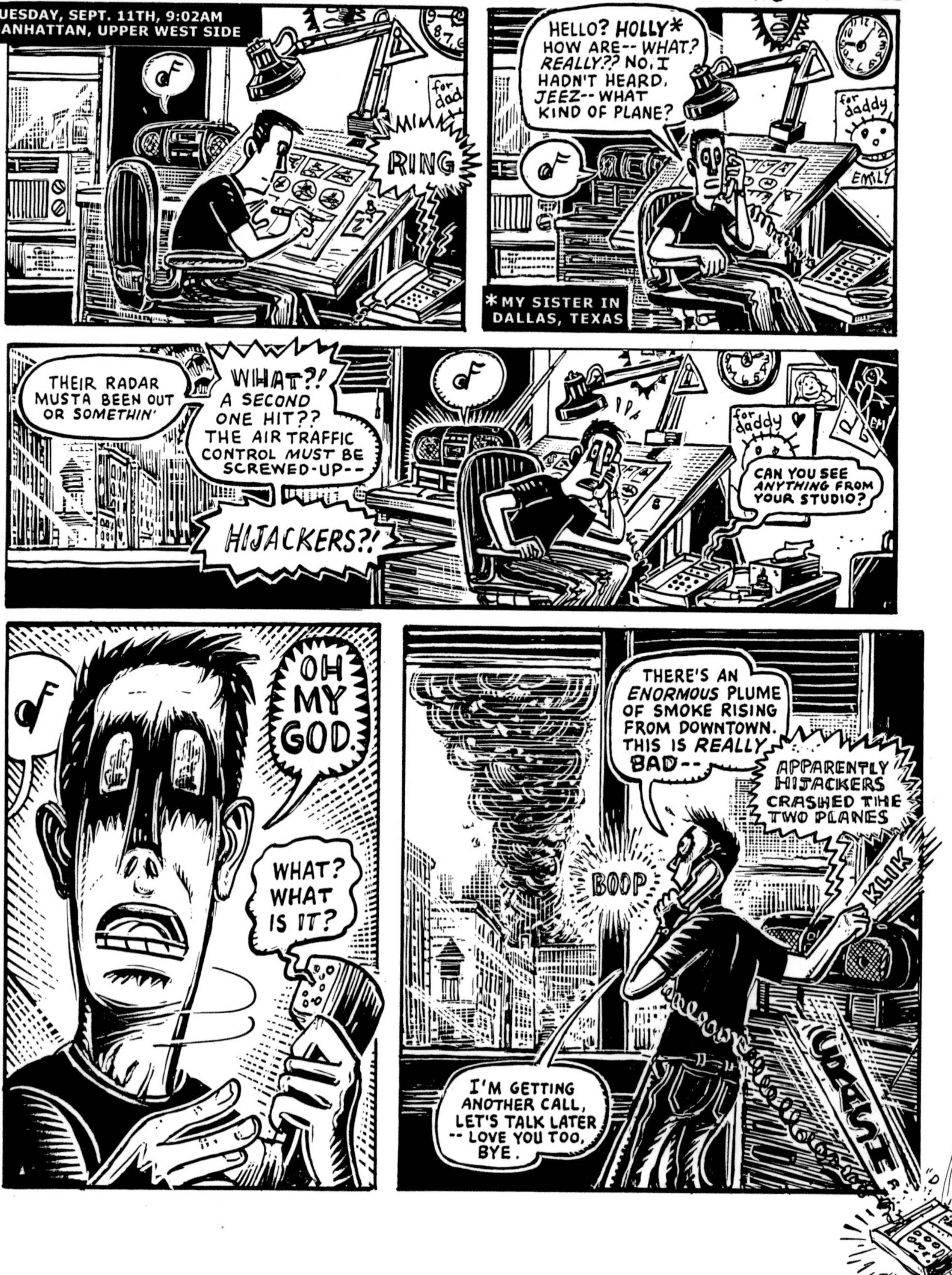

TUESDAY, SEPT. 11TH, 9:02AM
MANHATTAN, UPPER WEST SIDE
for dad
RING
HELLO? HOLLY* HOW ARE-- WHAT? REALLY?? NO, I HADN'T HEARD, JEEZ-- WHAT KIND OF PLANE?
for daddy
EMILY
*MY SISTER IN DALLAS, TEXAS
THEIR RADAR MUSTA BEEN OUT OR SOMETHIN'
WHAT?! A SECOND ONE HIT?? THE AIR TRAFFIC CONTROL MUST BE SCREWED-UP--
HIJACKERS?!
for daddy
CAN YOU SEE ANYTHING FROM YOUR STUDIO?
OH MY GOD
WHAT? WHAT IS IT?
THERE'S AN ENORMOUS PLUME OF SMOKE RISING FROM DOWNTOWN. THIS IS REALLY BAD--
APPARENTLY HIJACKERS CRASHED THE TWO PLANES
BOOP
KLIK
I'M GETTING ANOTHER CALL, LET'S TALK LATER -- LOVE YOU TOO, BYE.
CRASH

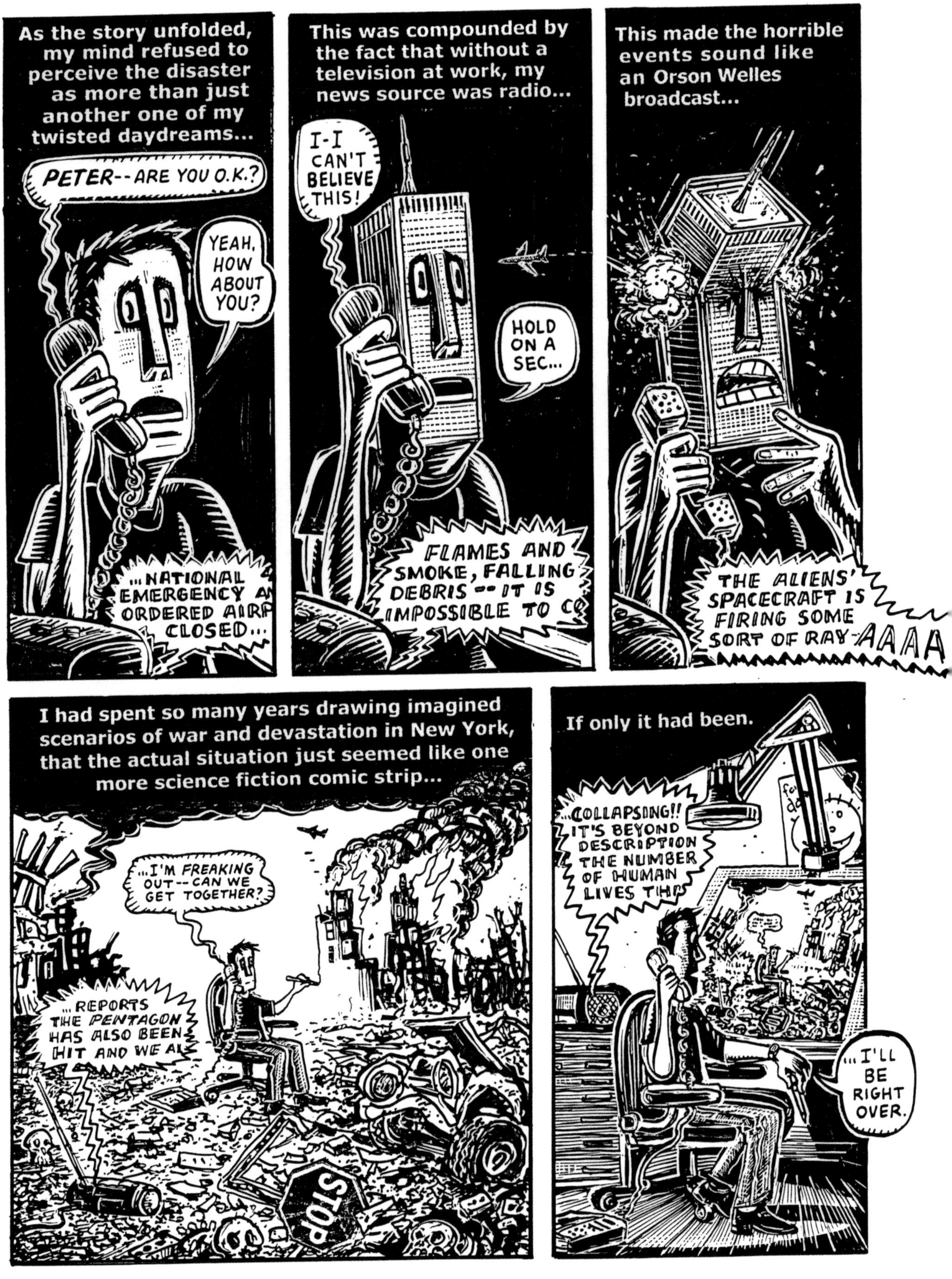
As the story unfolded, my mind refused to perceive the disaster as more than just another one of my twisted daydreams...
PETER--ARE YOU O.K.?
YEAH, HOW ABOUT YOU?
...NATIONAL EMERGENCY AN ORDERED AIRP CLOSED...
This was compounded by the fact that without a television at work, my news source was radio...
I-I CAN'T BELIEVE THIS!
HOLD ON A SEC...
FLAMES AND SMOKE, FALLING DEBRIS--IT IS IMPOSSIBLE TO CO
This made the horrible events sound like an Orson Welles broadcast...
THE ALIENS' SPACECRAFT IS FIRING SOME SORT OF RAY-AAAA
I had spent so many years drawing imagined scenarios of war and devastation in New York, that the actual situation just seemed like one more science fiction comic strip...
...I'M FREAKING OUT--CAN WE GET TOGETHER?
...REPORTS THE PENTAGON HAS ALSO BEEN HIT AND WE AI
STOP
If only it had been.
...COLLAPSING!! IT'S BEYOND DESCRIPTION THE NUMBER OF HUMAN LIVES THA
...I'LL BE RIGHT OVER.

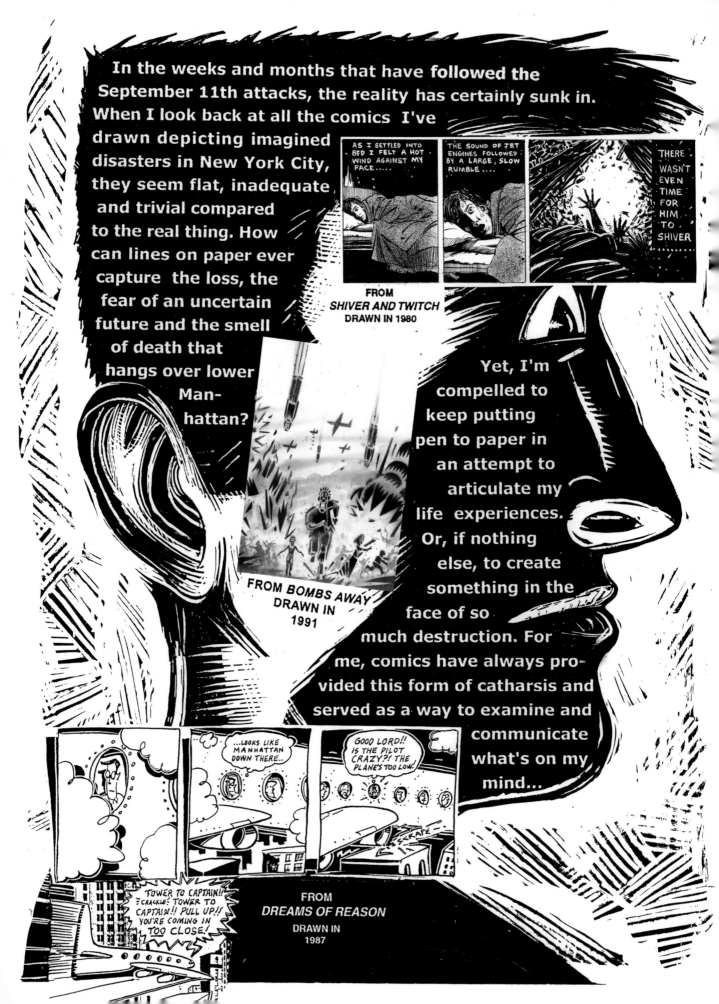

In the weeks and months that have followed the September 11th attacks, the reality has certainly sunk in. When I look back at all the comics I've drawn depicting imagined disasters in New York City, they seem flat, inadequate and trivial compared to the real thing. How can lines on paper ever capture the loss, the fear of an uncertain future and the smell of death that hangs over lower Manhattan?

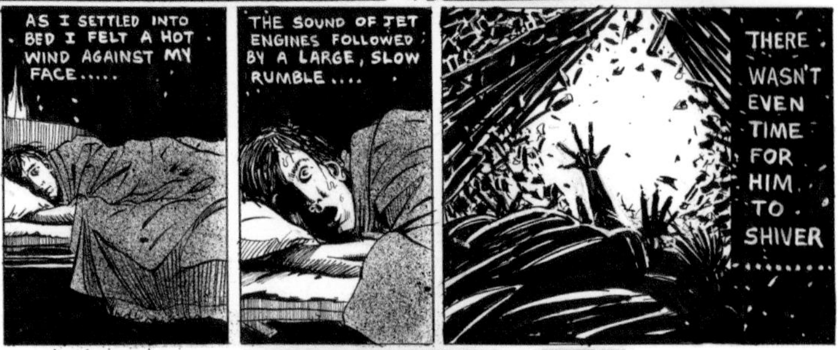

AS I SETTLED INTO BED I FELT A HOT WIND AGAINST MY FACE.....
THE SOUND OF JET ENGINES FOLLOWED BY A LARGE, SLOW RUMBLE....
THERE WASN'T EVEN TIME FOR HIM TO SHIVER

FROM *SHIVER AND TWITCH* DRAWN IN 1980

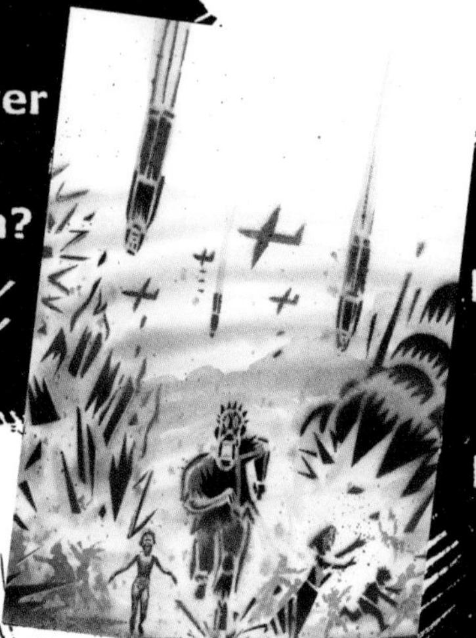

FROM *BOMBS AWAY* DRAWN IN 1991

Yet, I'm compelled to keep putting pen to paper in an attempt to articulate my life experiences. Or, if nothing else, to create something in the face of so much destruction. For me, comics have always provided this form of catharsis and served as a way to examine and communicate what's on my mind...

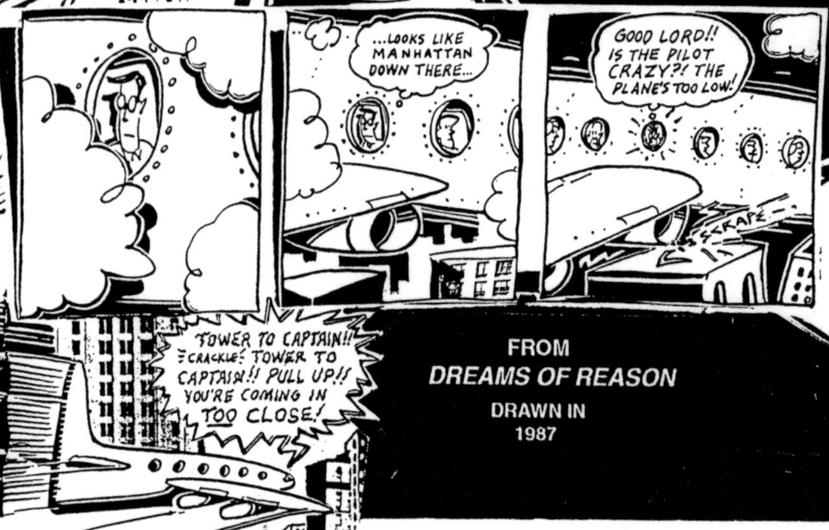

...LOOKS LIKE MANHATTAN DOWN THERE...
GOOD LORD!! IS THE PILOT CRAZY?! THE PLANE'S TOO LOW!
SCRAPE
TOWER TO CAPTAIN!! CRACKLE TOWER TO CAPTAIN!! PULL UP!! YOU'RE COMING IN TOO CLOSE!

FROM *DREAMS OF REASON* DRAWN IN 1987

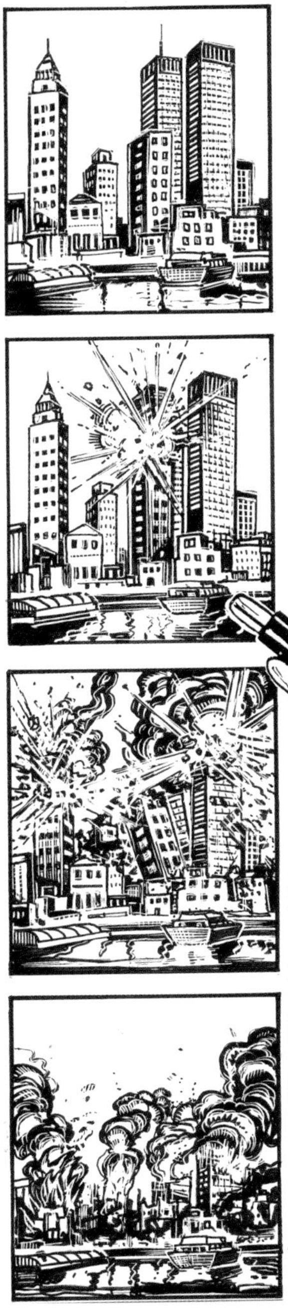

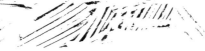

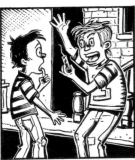

FROM
EYE OF THE BEHOLDER
DRAWN IN
1997

But here in this new world, in post 9-11 America, I feel like putting my thoughts down on paper and drawing these kind comics will soon be viewed as an act of sedition.

These days patriotism has become quantifiable, measured by a willingness to blindly follow Presidential policies. To fight a war on terrorism, apparently, we must suspend our justice system, censor our media and watch our tongues.

FROM *OBSESSION* DRAWN IN 1982

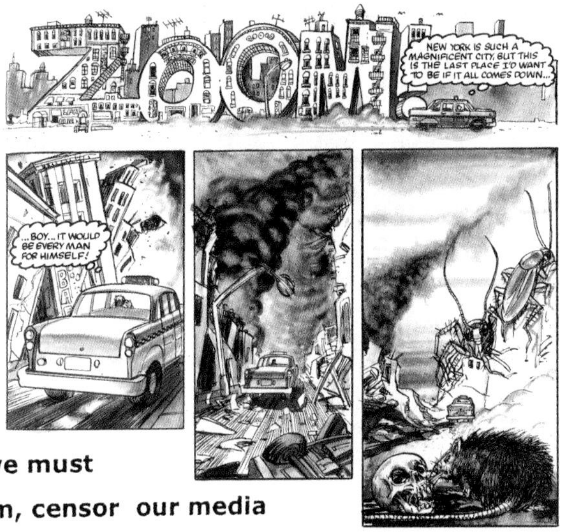

NEW YORK IS SUCH A MAGNIFICENT CITY, BUT THIS IS THE LAST PLACE I'D WANT TO BE IF IT ALL COMES DOWN...
...BOY... IT WOULD BE EVERY MAN FOR HIMSELF!

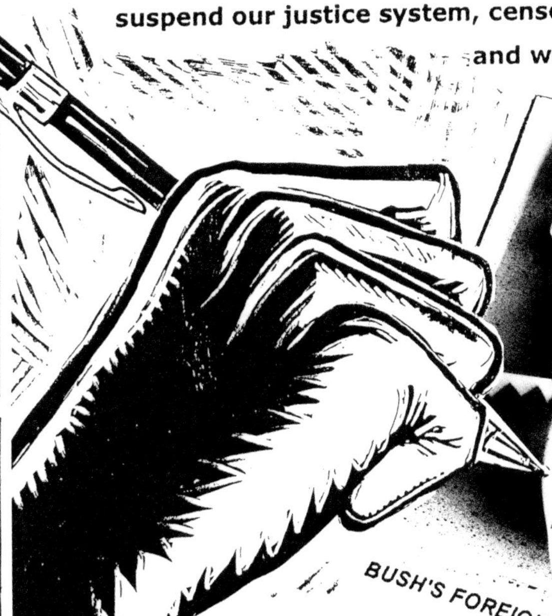

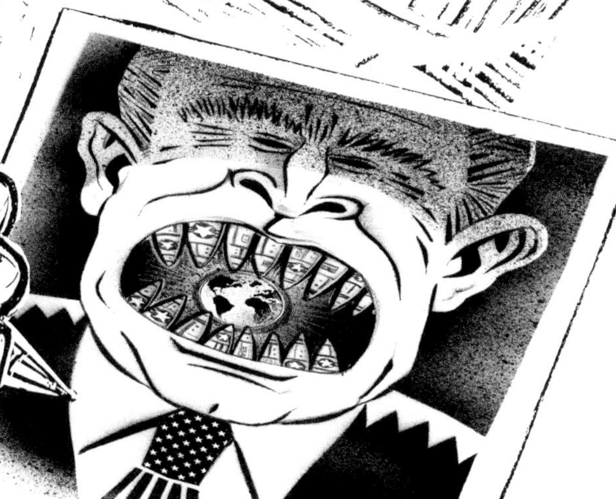

KUPER

BUSH'S FOREIGN POLICY DRAWN IN APRIL, 2001

In the name of national security, will we allow ourselves to be told how we express opinions, discuss ideas and debate the very decisions that affect our lives and our children's future? Though I'm as uncertain and frightened as the next guy by what new acts of terrorism may be in store, the threat I *am* certain of is the one posed by politicians who are cynically taking advantage of our fear to manipulate and--

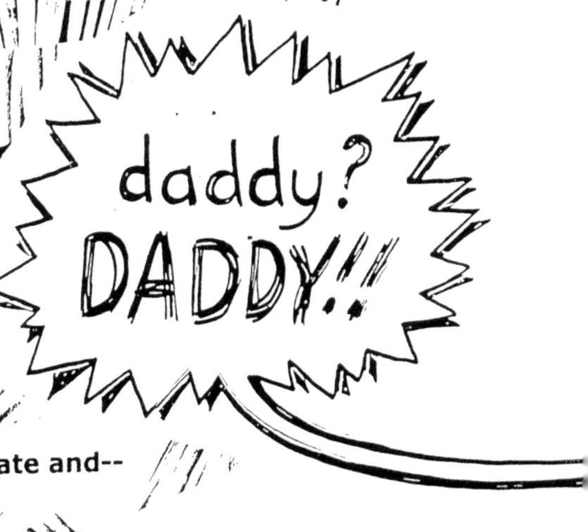

daddy?
DADDY!!

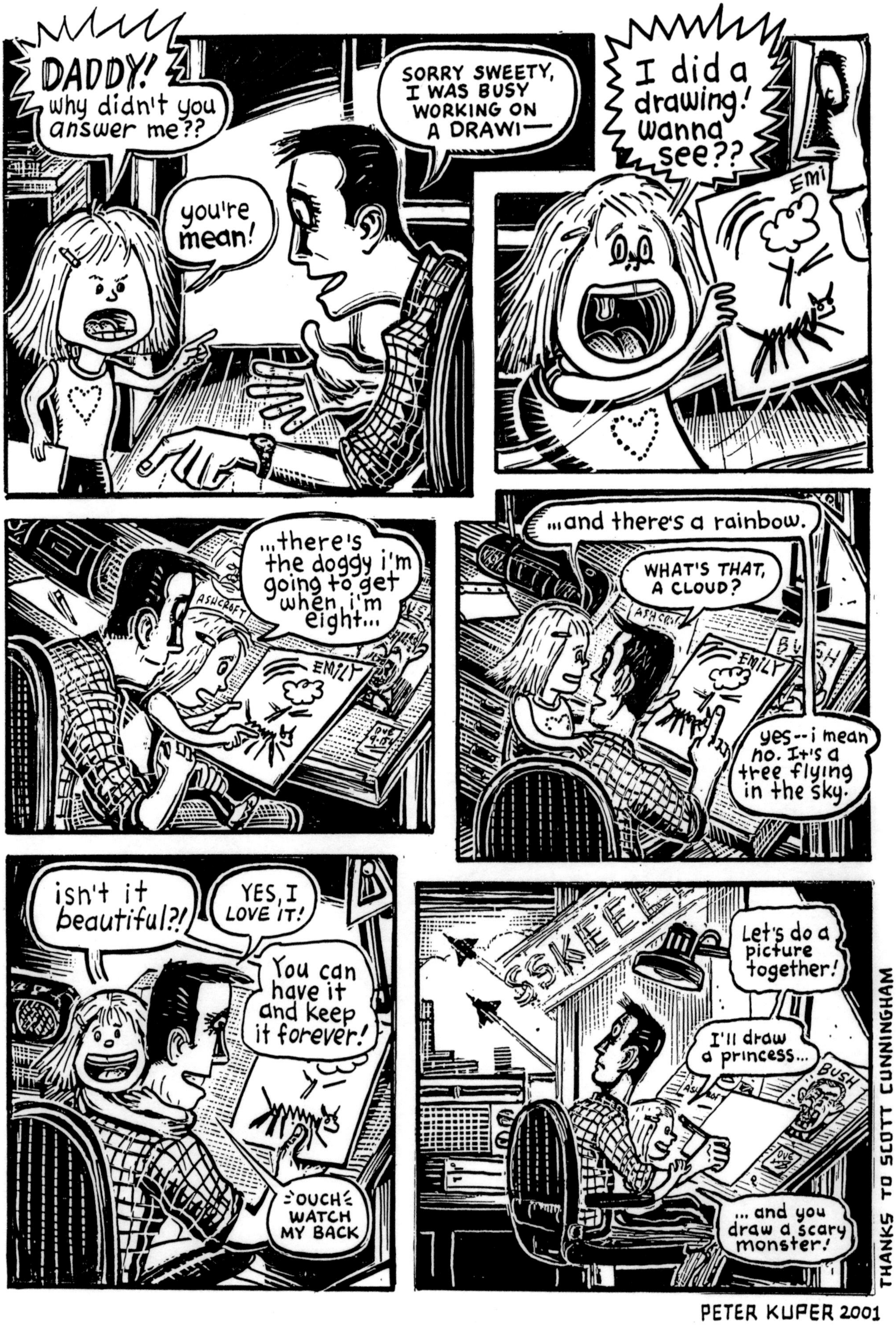
DADDY! why didn't you answer me??
SORRY SWEETY, I WAS BUSY WORKING ON A DRAWI—
you're mean!
I did a drawing! wanna see??
EMI
...there's the doggy i'm going to get when i'm eight...
ASHCROFT
EMILY
...and there's a rainbow.
WHAT'S THAT, A CLOUD?
EMILY
yes--i mean no. It's a tree flying in the sky.
isn't it beautiful?!
YES, I LOVE IT!
You can have it and keep it forever!
OUCH WATCH MY BACK
SKEEE
Let's do a picture together!
I'll draw a princess...
BUSH
...and you draw a scary monster!
THANKS TO SCOTT CUNNINGHAM
PETER KUPER 2001

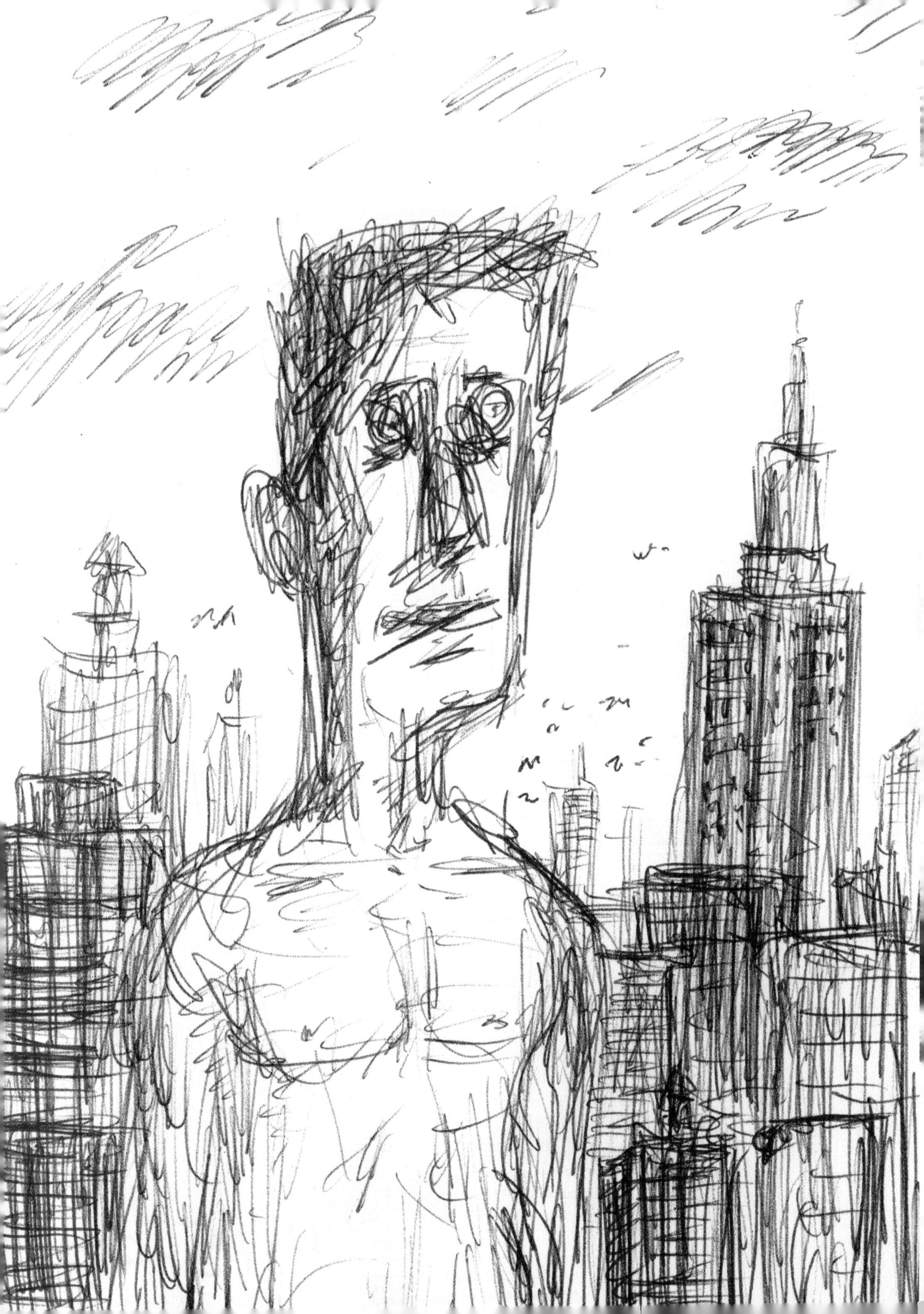

STRIPES AND STARS

© 2002

Peter Kuper

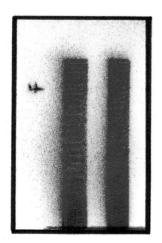

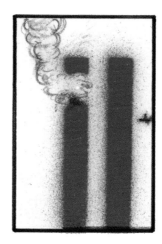
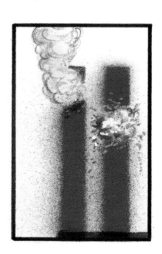

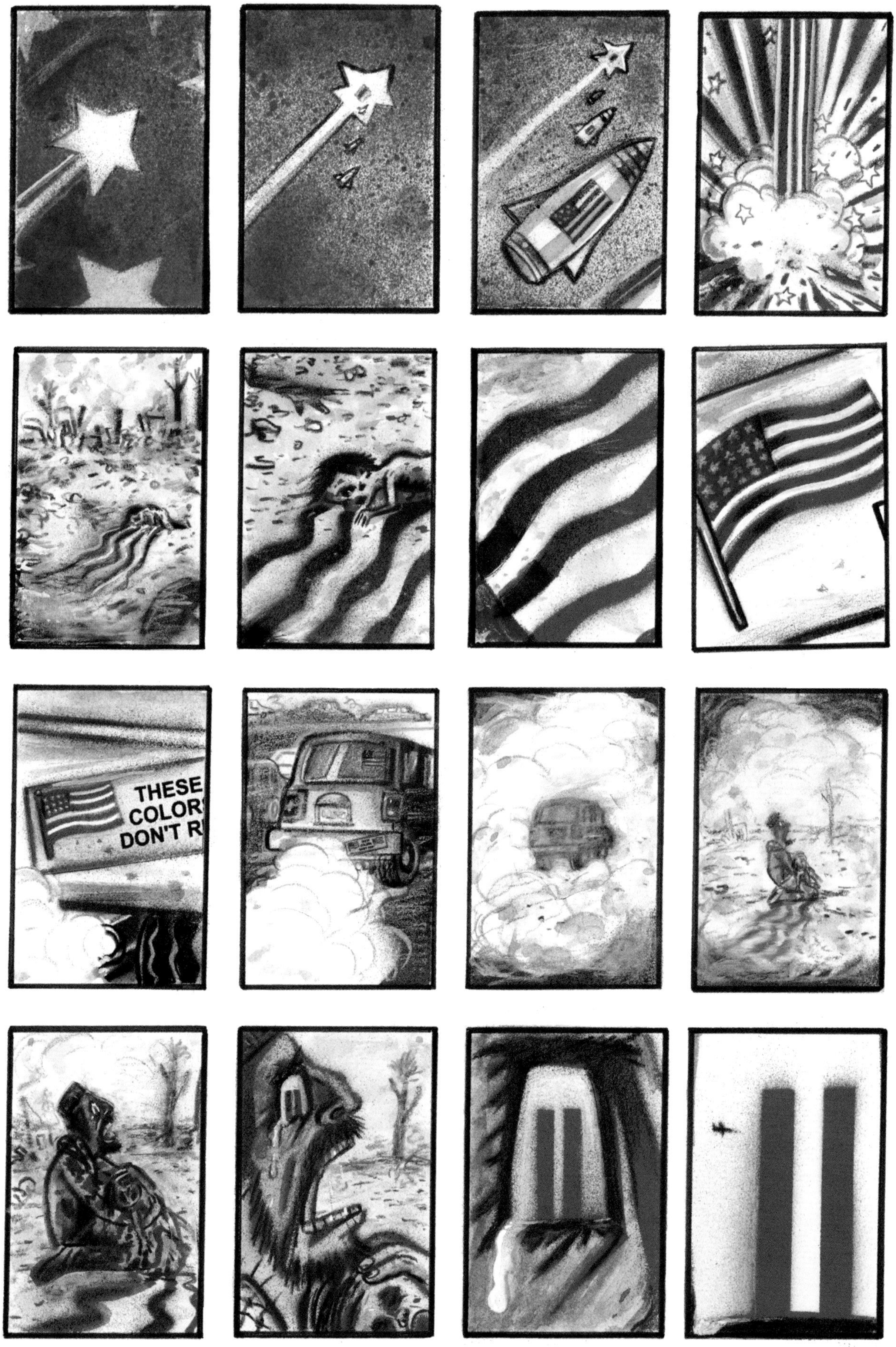
THESE
COLORS
DON'T R

INDOMITABLE HUMAN SPIRIT

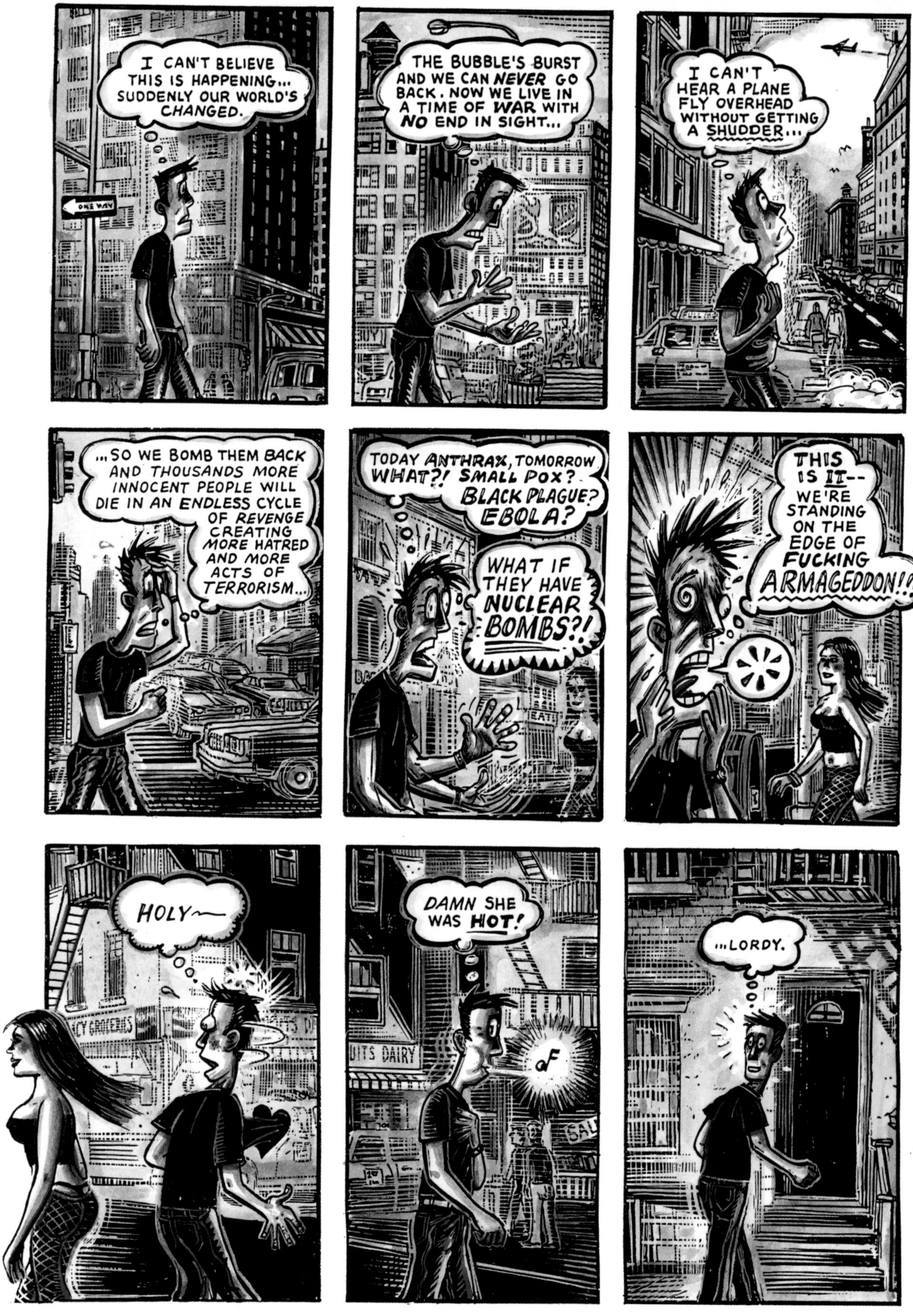
I CAN'T BELIEVE THIS IS HAPPENING... SUDDENLY OUR WORLD'S CHANGED.
ONE WAY
THE BUBBLE'S BURST AND WE CAN NEVER GO BACK. NOW WE LIVE IN A TIME OF WAR WITH NO END IN SIGHT...
I CAN'T HEAR A PLANE FLY OVERHEAD WITHOUT GETTING A SHUDDER...
...SO WE BOMB THEM BACK AND THOUSANDS MORE INNOCENT PEOPLE WILL DIE IN AN ENDLESS CYCLE OF REVENGE CREATING MORE HATRED AND MORE ACTS OF TERRORISM...
TODAY ANTHRAX, TOMORROW WHAT?! SMALL POX? BLACK PLAGUE? EBOLA?
WHAT IF THEY HAVE NUCLEAR BOMBS?!
THIS IS IT-- WE'RE STANDING ON THE EDGE OF FUCKING ARMAGEDDON!?!
HOLY—
DAMN SHE WAS HOT!
...LORDY.

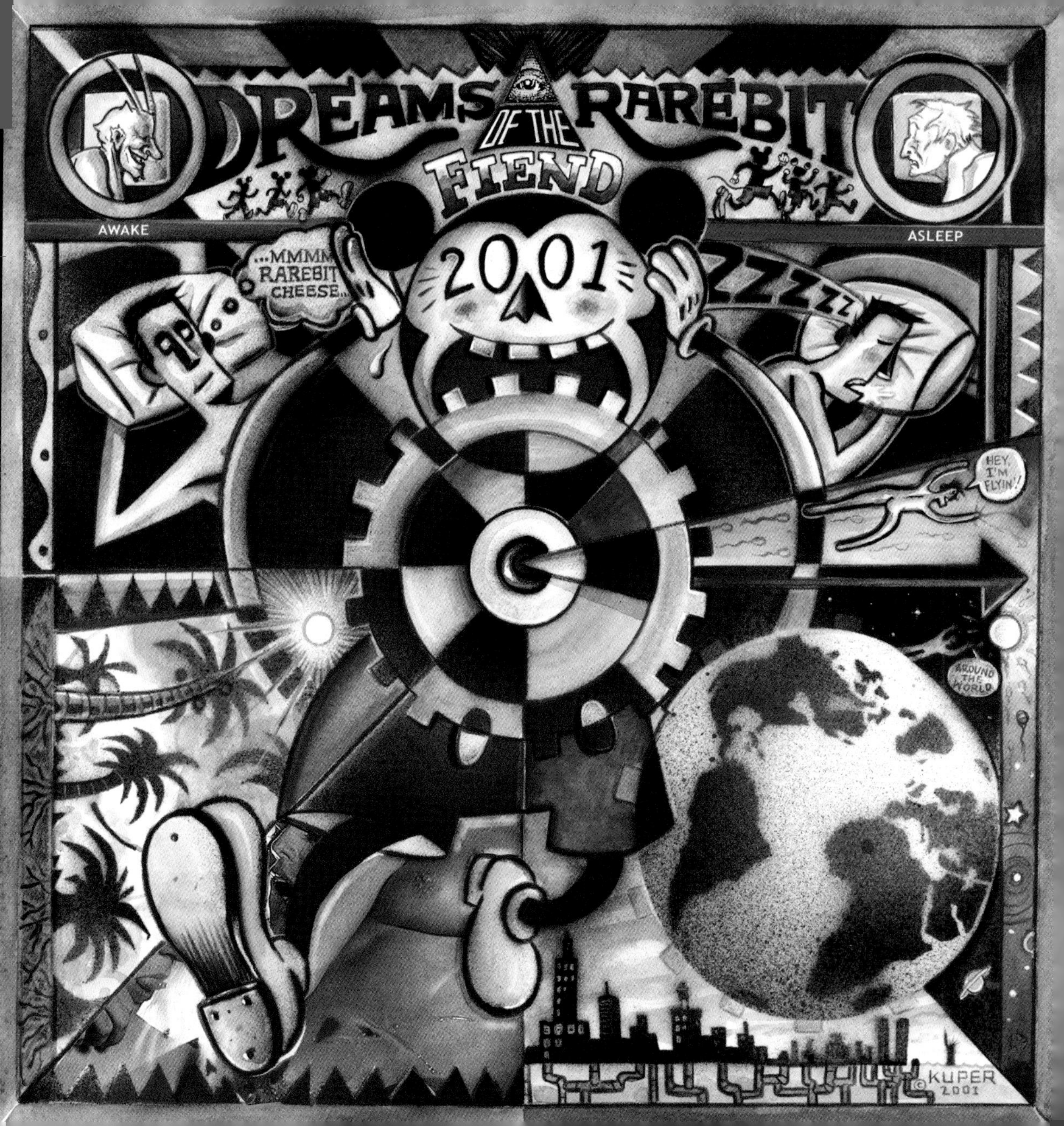
DREAMS OF THE RAREBIT FIEND
2001
AWAKE
ASLEEP
...MMMM RAREBIT CHEESE...
ZZZZZzz
HEY, I'M FLYIN'!
AROUND THE WORLD
© KUPER 2001

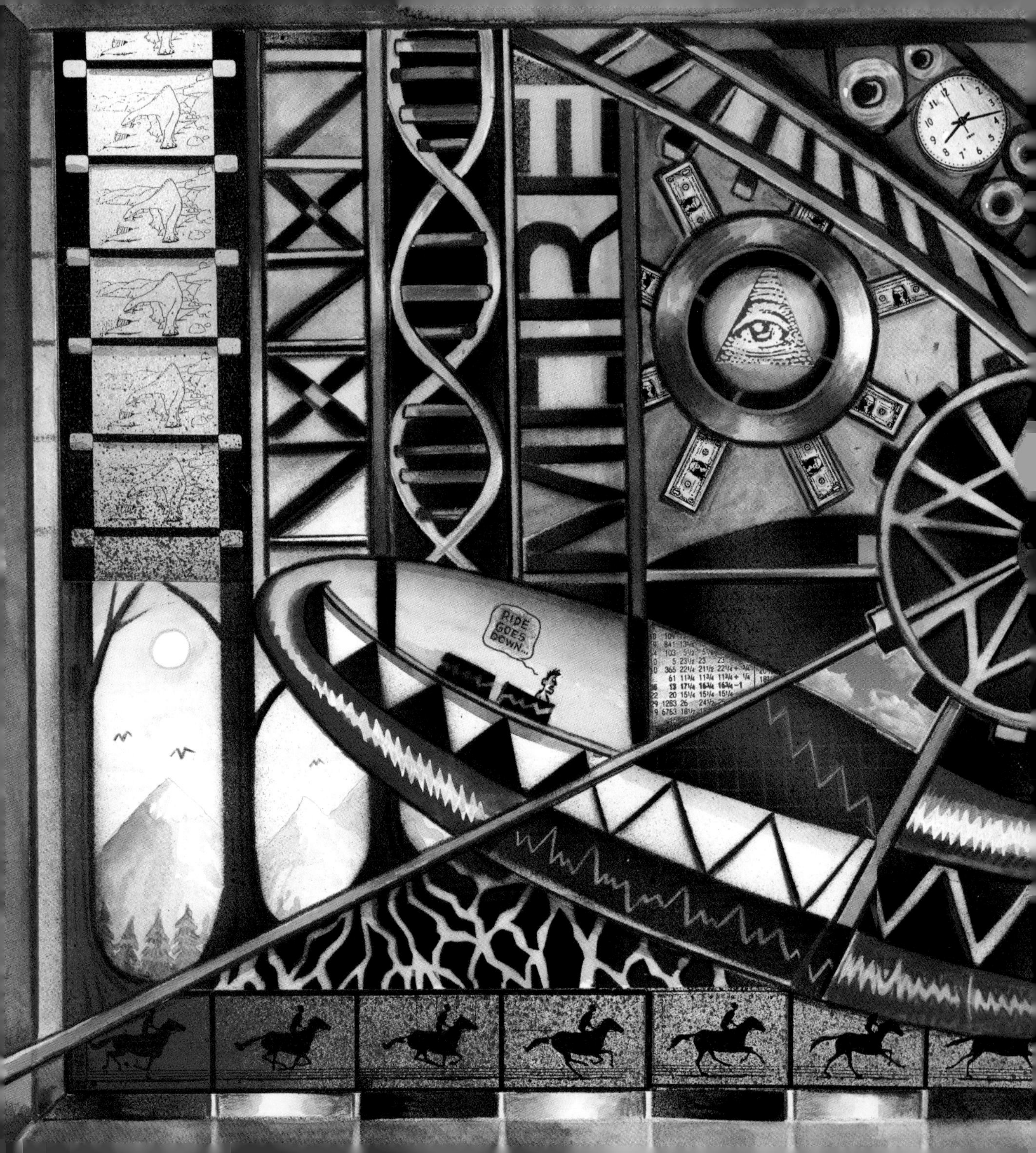
RIDE GOES DOWN...

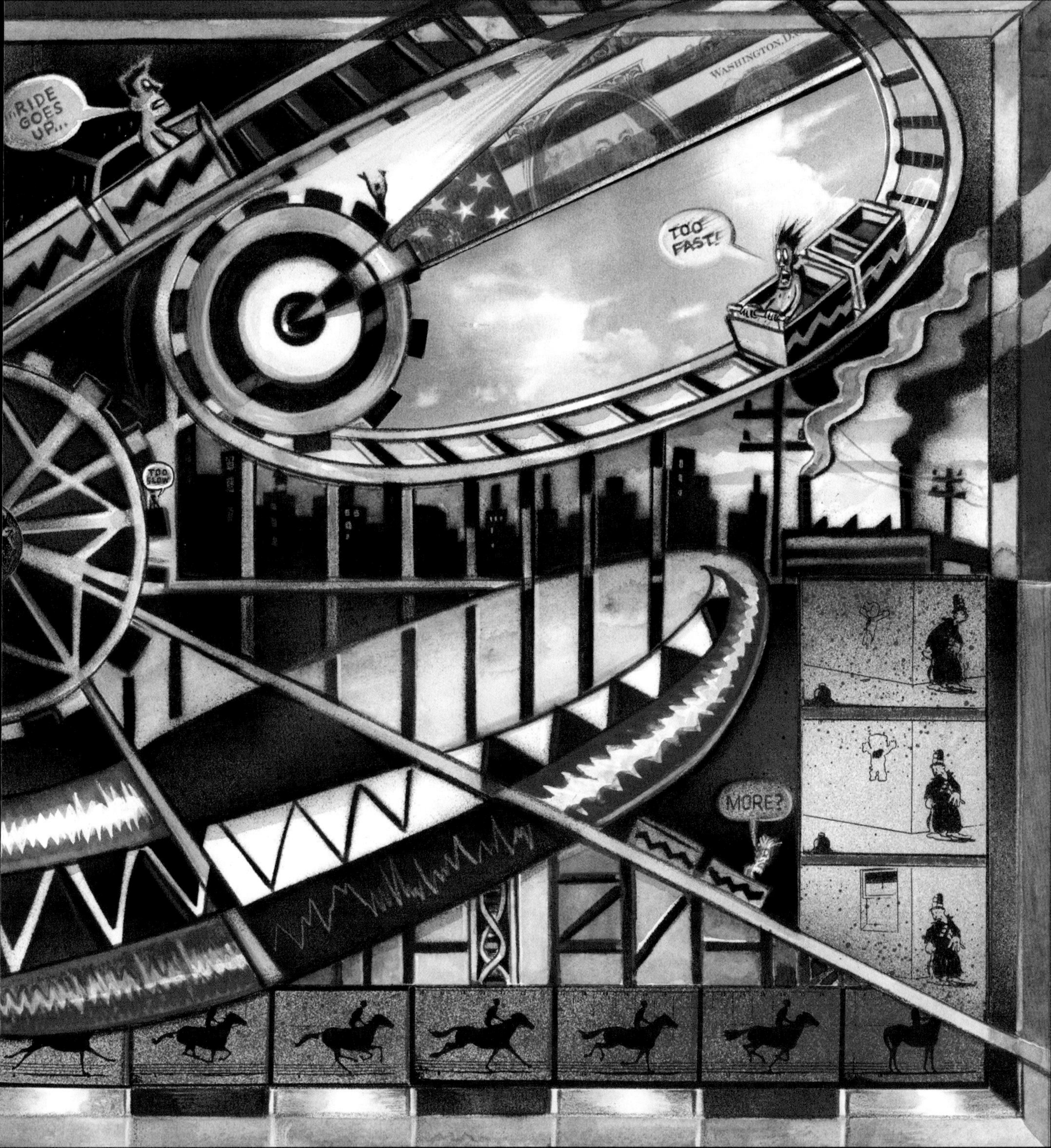
...RIDE GOES UP...
TOO FAST!
TOO SLOW
MORE?

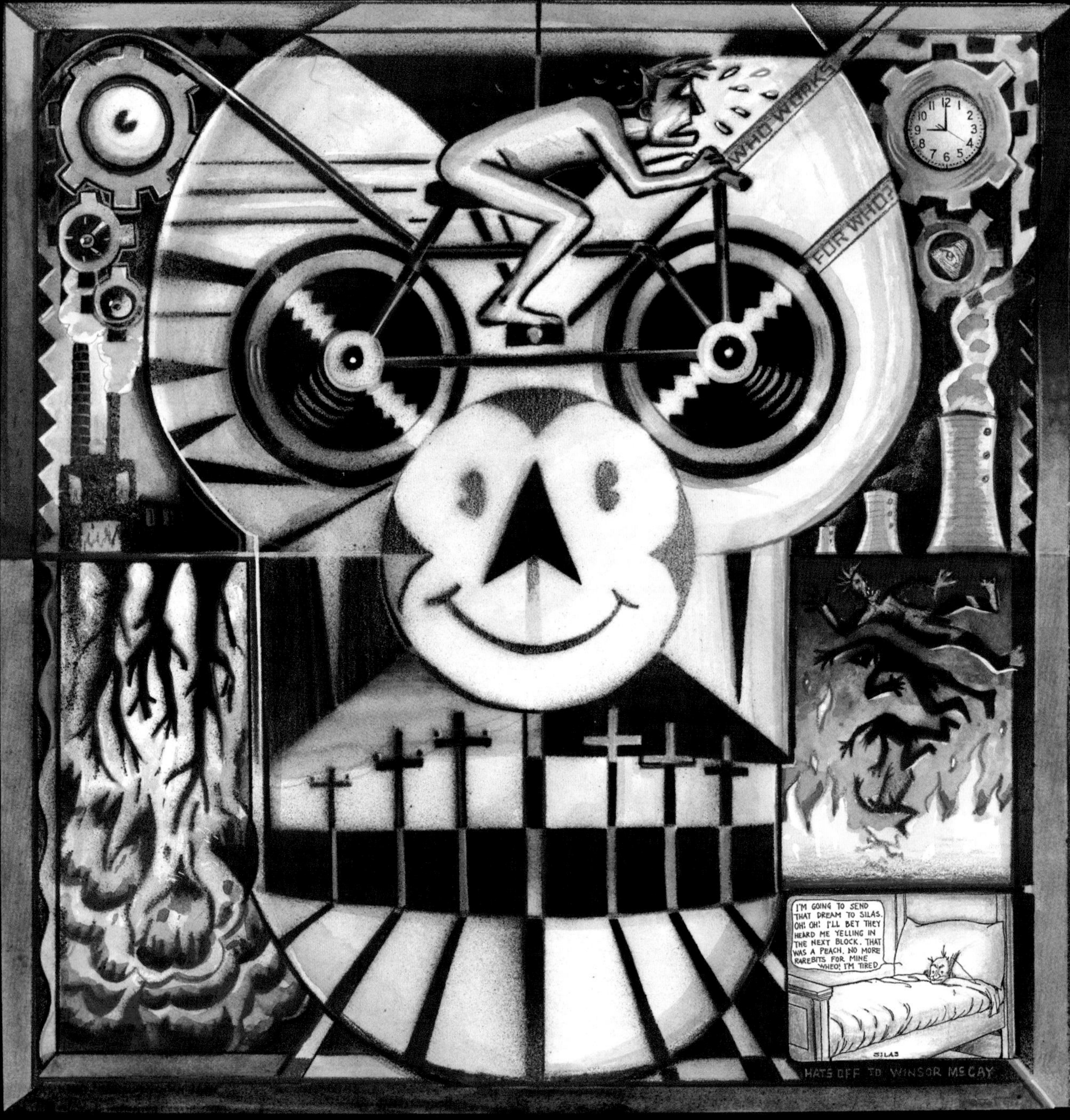
WHO WORKS
FOR WHO?
I'M GOING TO SEND THAT DREAM TO SILAS. OH! OH! I'LL BET THEY HEARD ME YELLING IN THE NEXT BLOCK. THAT WAS A PEACH. NO MORE RAREBITS FOR MINE WHEO! I'M TIRED
SILAS
HATS OFF TO WINSOR McCAY

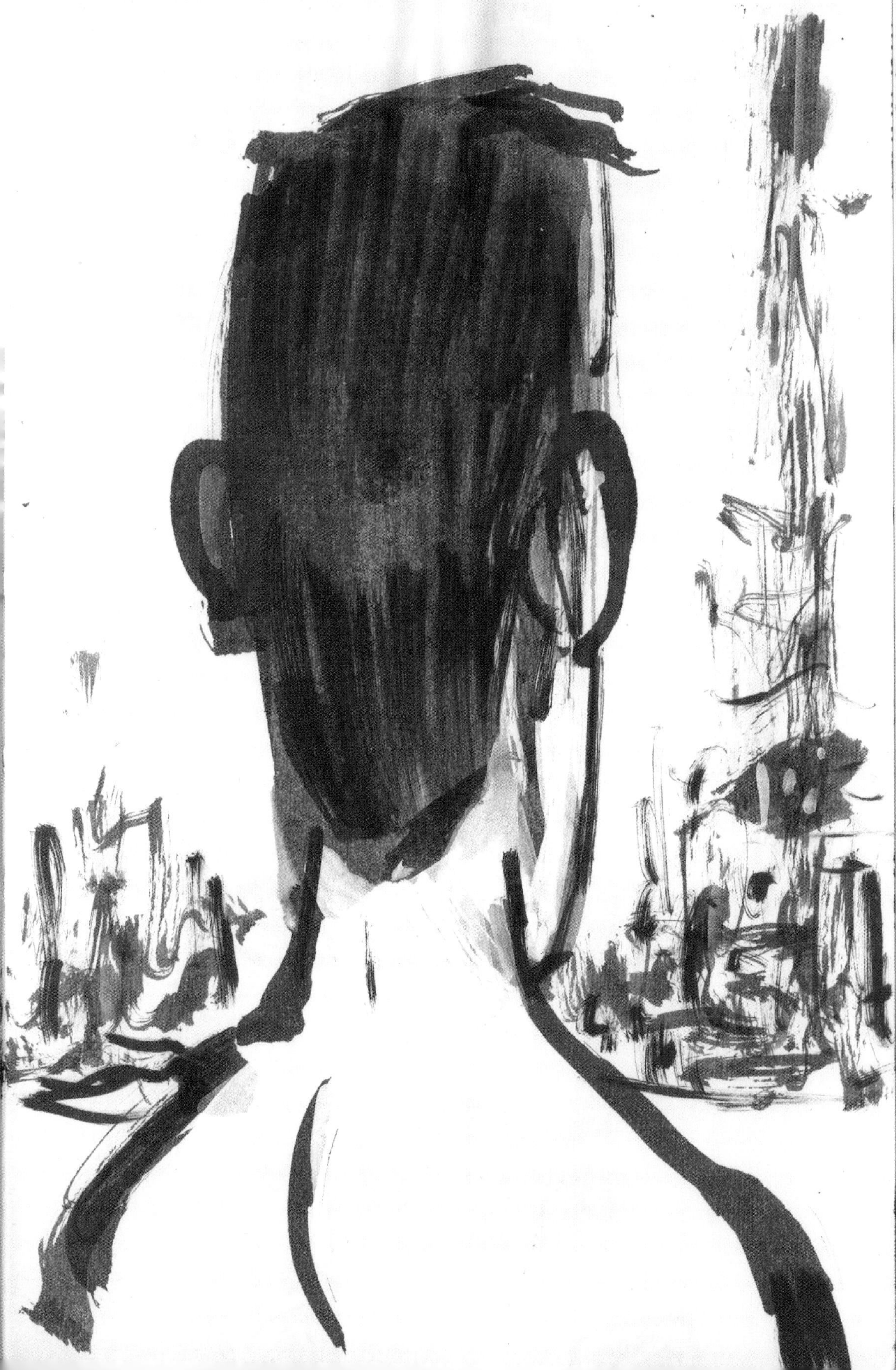

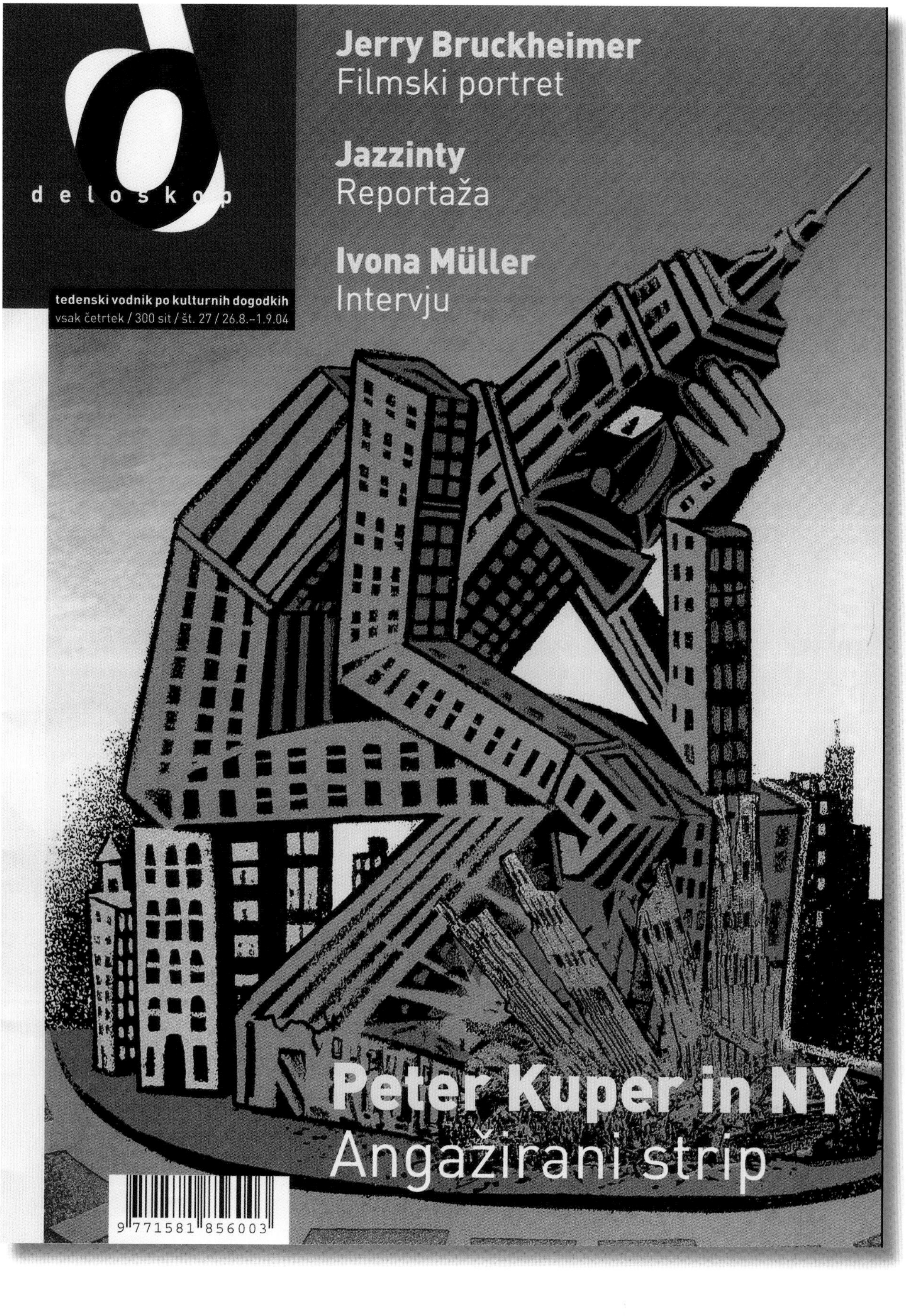
deloskop
tedenski vodnik po kulturnih dogodkih
vsak četrtek / 300 sit / št. 27 / 26.8.–1.9.04
Jerry Bruckheimer
Filmski portret
Jazzinty
Reportaža
Ivona Müller
Intervju
Peter Kuper in NY
Angažirani strip
9 771581 856003

REVIEW
Campo Santo
by W.G. Sebald
C30

TALKING WITH
Michael Rips
An ear for the eccentric
C28

The key to the city

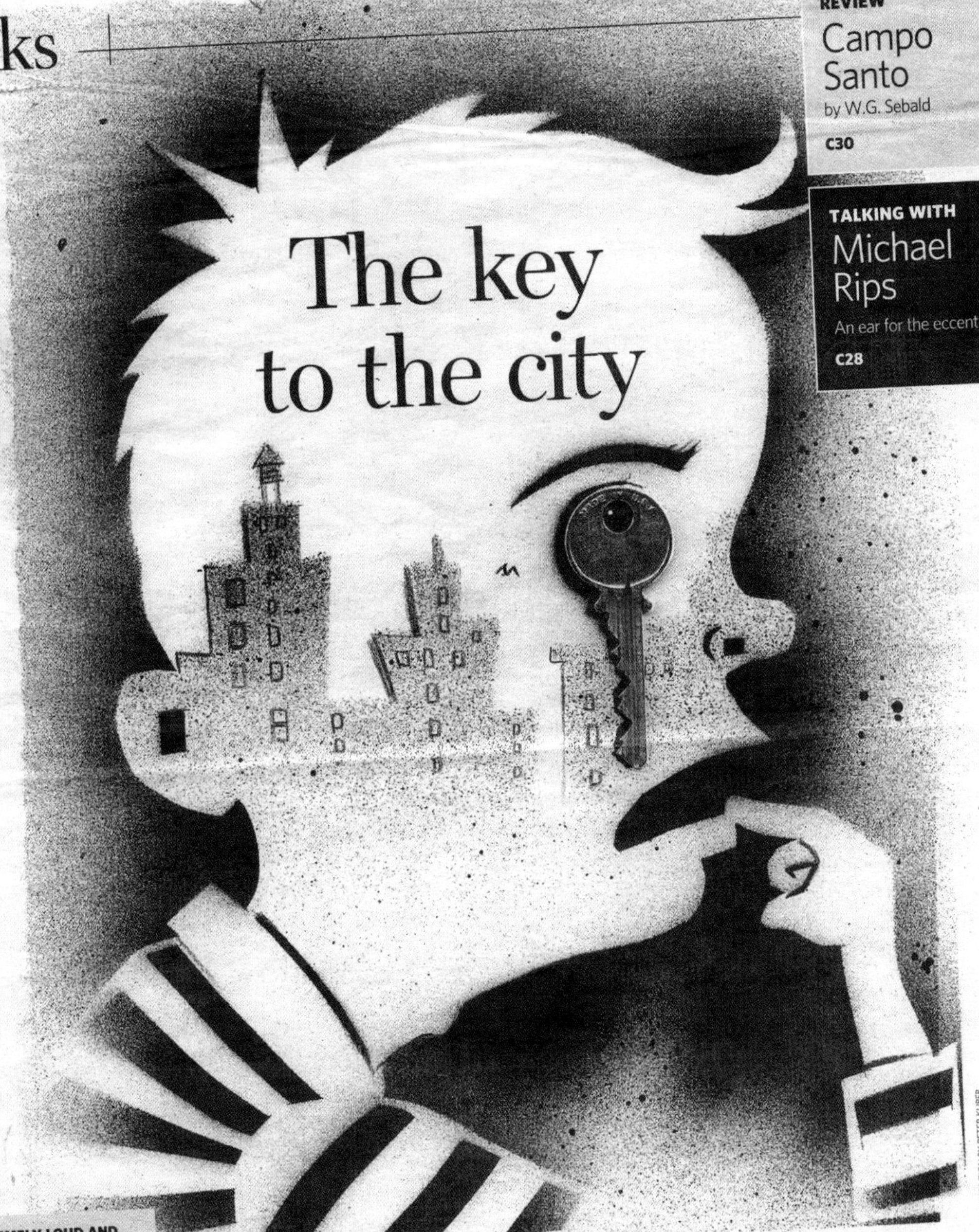

ILLUSTRATION BY PETER KUPER

EXTREMELY LOUD AND INCREDIBLY CLOSE, by Jonathan Safran Foer. Houghton Mifflin, 355 pages, $24.95.

In Jonathan Safran Foer's much anticipated new novel, a precocious 9-year-old searches the five boroughs for a memory of his father, a victim of 9/11

'Humorous is the only truthful way to tell a sad story," Jonathan Safran Foer wrote in his debut novel, "Everything Is Illuminated," whose success blessed and cursed him with fame before

Foer and his journey into the lost heartland of Eastern European Jewry, accompanied by an exuberantly English-fracturing translator from Odessa, "Everything Is Illuminated"

one part magical realism (if the paintings of Marc Chagall may be described by that label) and one part "Adventures of Huckleberry Finn" (if Huck may be

next, a large and demanding audience would be waiting to judge.

He has not shrunk from

the biggest, saddest story he could think of. It's the tale of 9-year-old

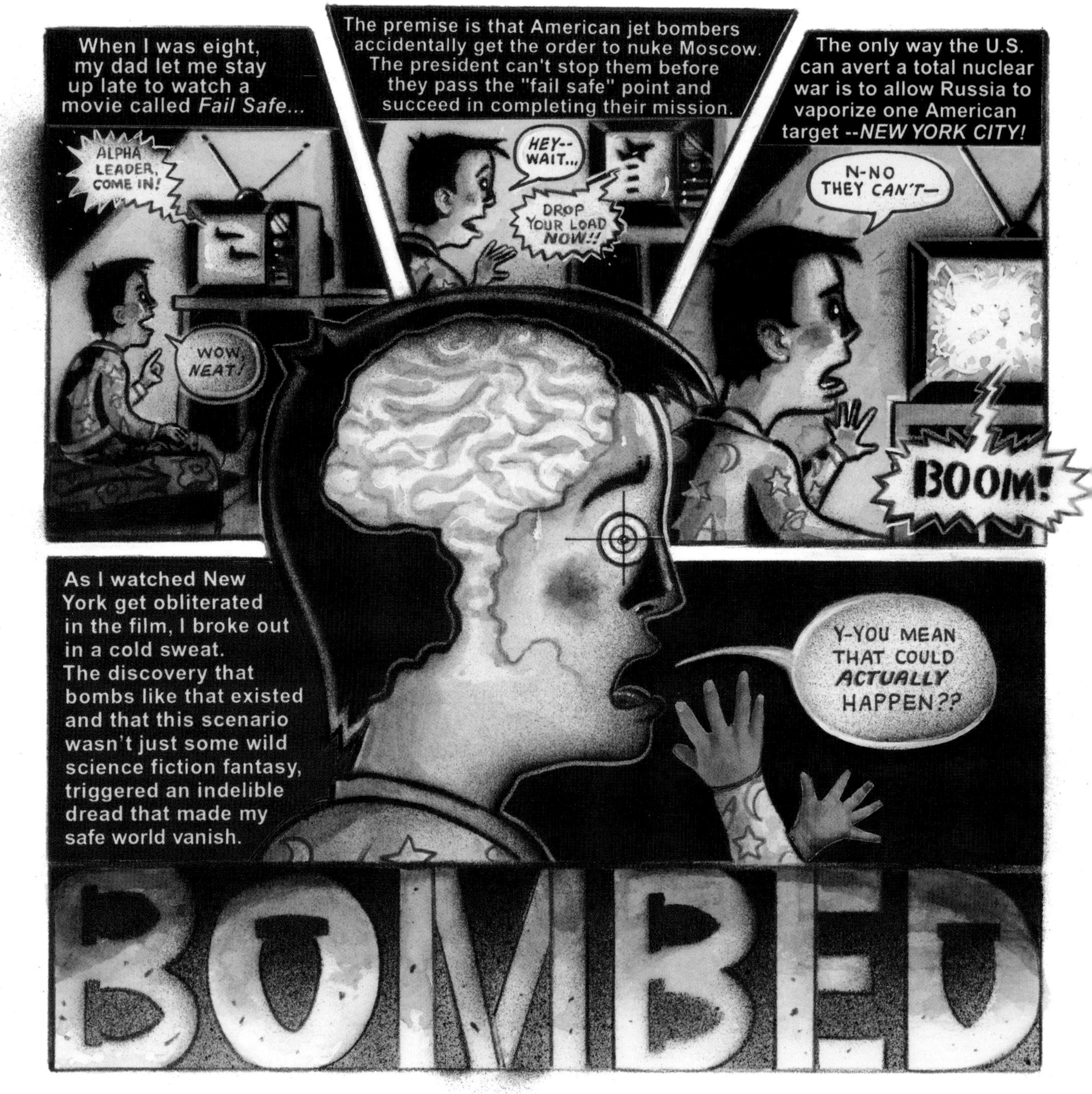
When I was eight, my dad let me stay up late to watch a movie called *Fail Safe*...
ALPHA LEADER, COME IN!
WOW, NEAT!
The premise is that American jet bombers accidentally get the order to nuke Moscow. The president can't stop them before they pass the "fail safe" point and succeed in completing their mission.
HEY--WAIT...
DROP YOUR LOAD NOW!!
The only way the U.S. can avert a total nuclear war is to allow Russia to vaporize one American target --*NEW YORK CITY!*
N-NO THEY CAN'T—
BOOM!
As I watched New York get obliterated in the film, I broke out in a cold sweat. The discovery that bombs like that existed and that this scenario wasn't just some wild science fiction fantasy, triggered an indelible dread that made my safe world vanish.
Y-YOU MEAN THAT COULD *ACTUALLY* HAPPEN??
BOMBED

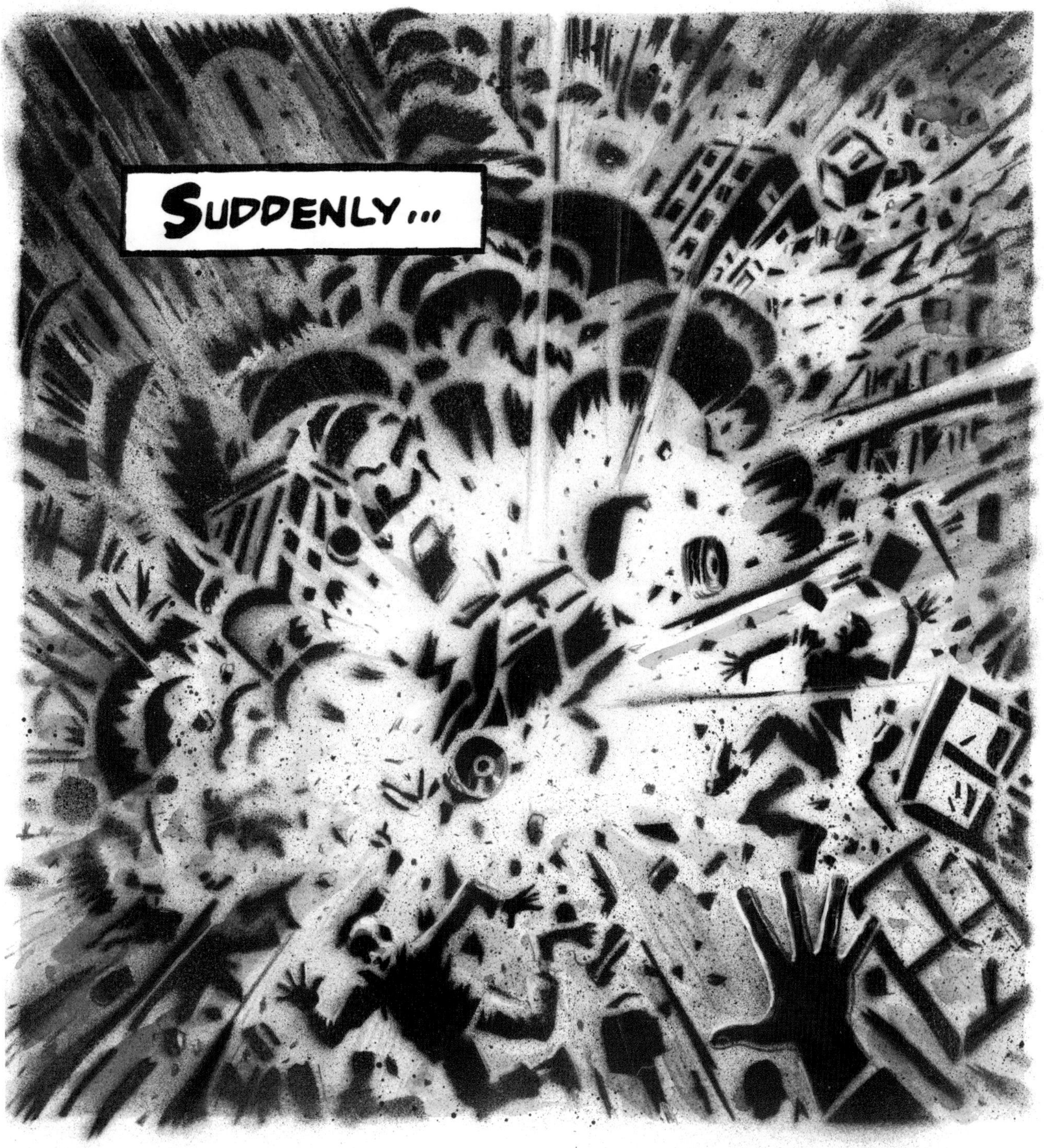
SUDDENLY...

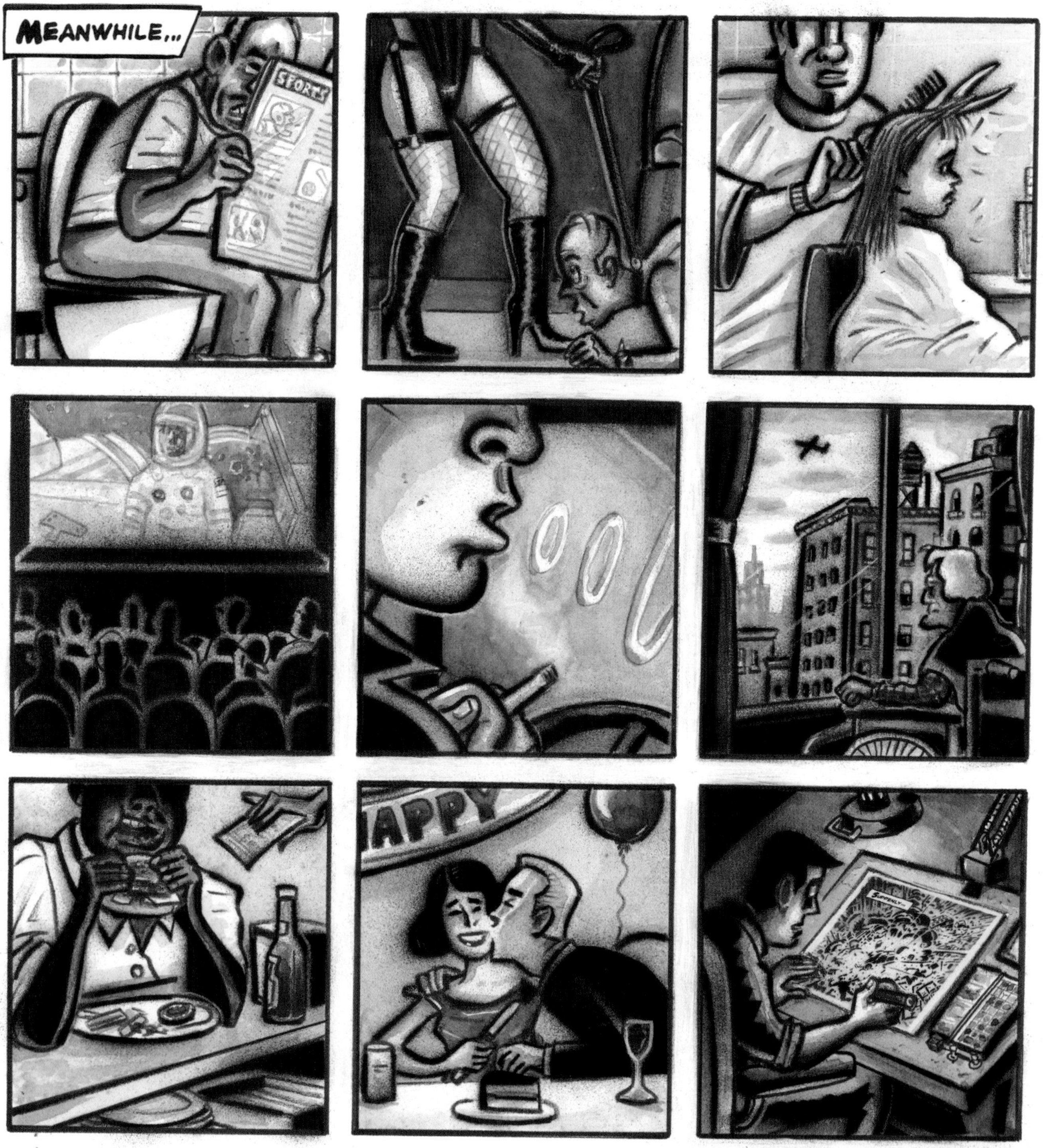
MEANWHILE...
SPORTS

MIGHTIER

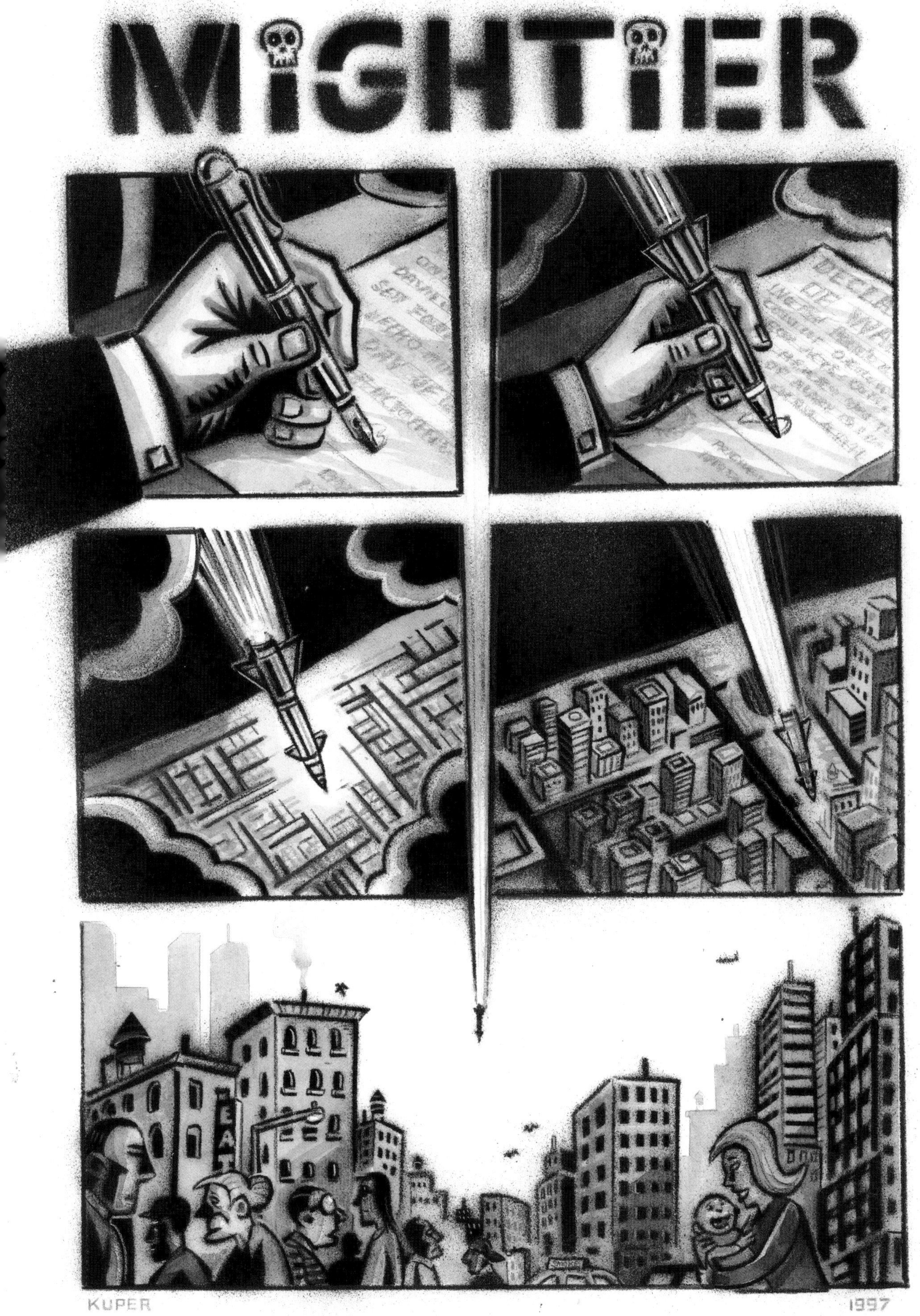
EAT

KUPER 1997

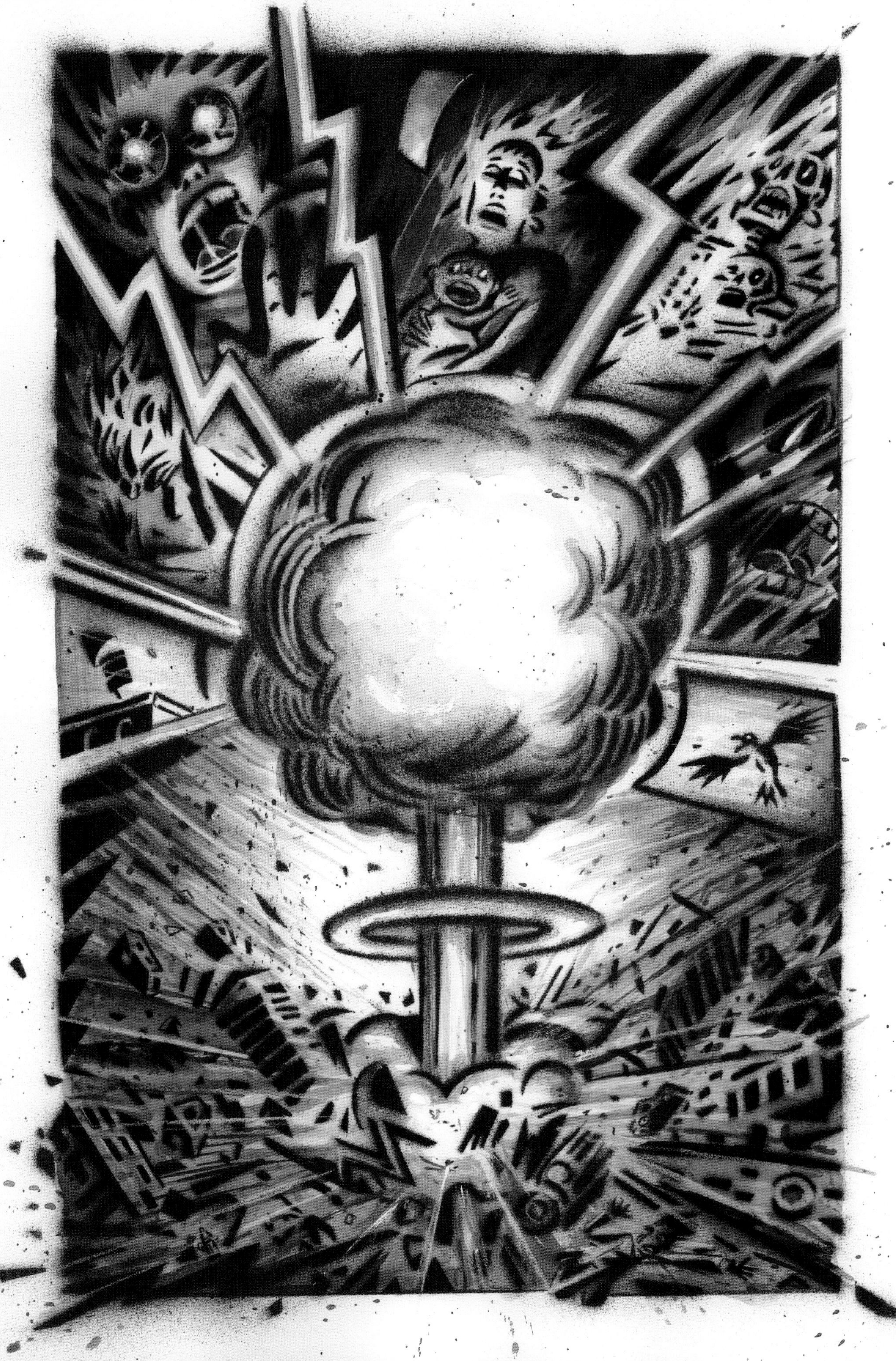

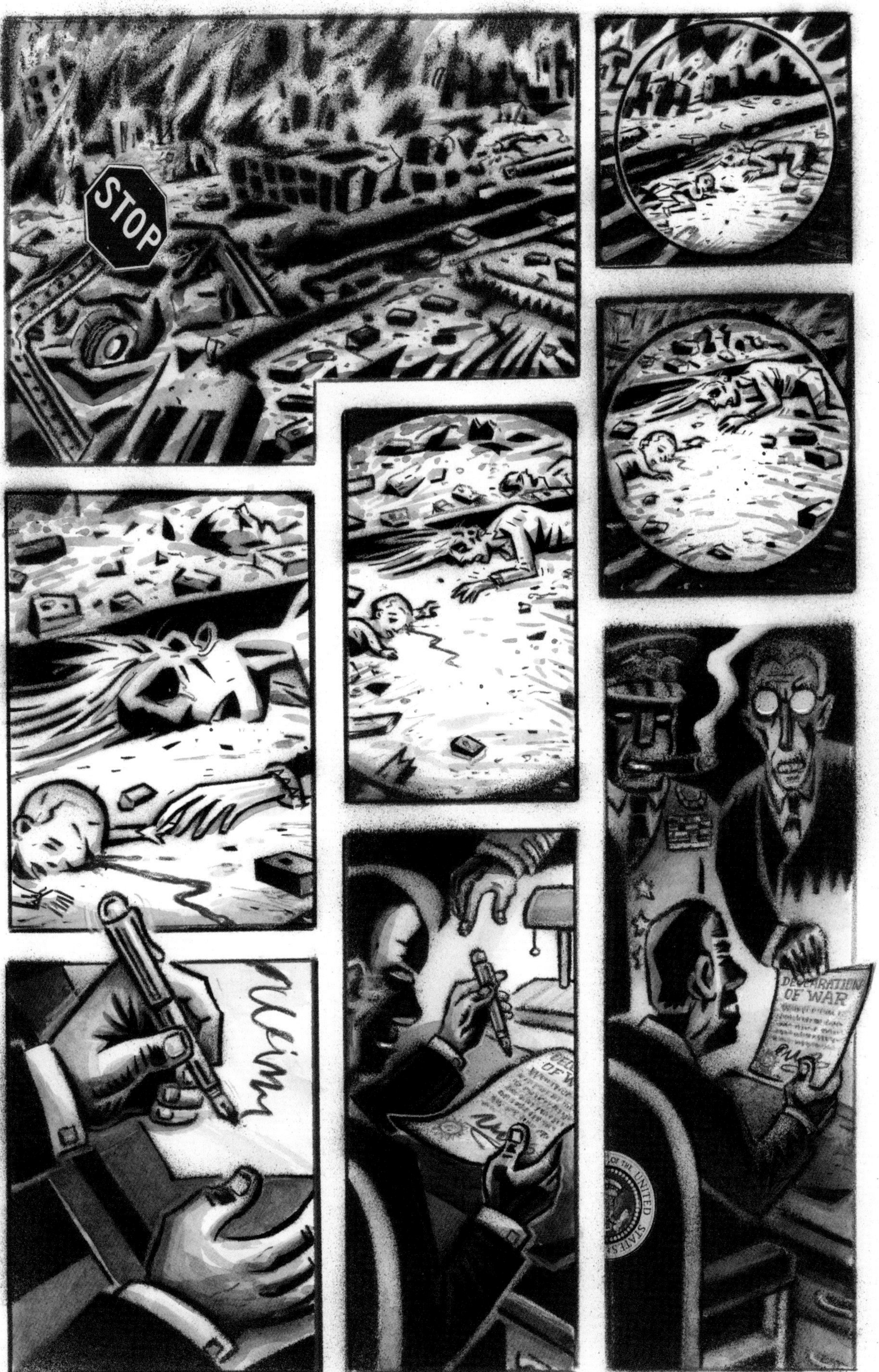
STOP
DECLARATION OF WAR

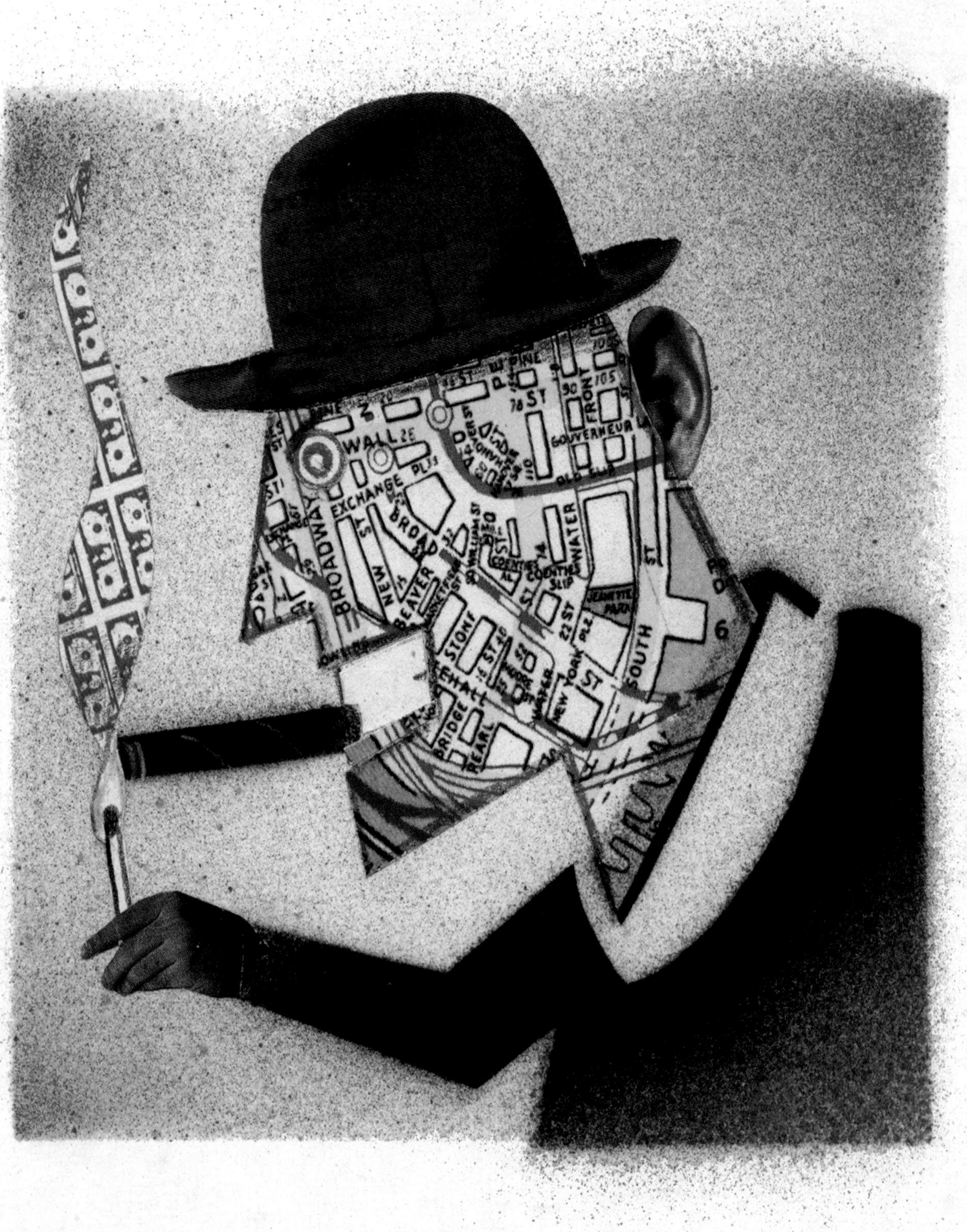

WALL
EXCHANGE PL
BROADWAY
NEW
BROAD
BEAVER
STONE
PEARL
BRIDGE
WATER
FRONT
SOUTH
GOUVERNEUR
COENTIES SLIP
NEW YORK PLZ

ONE DOLLAR

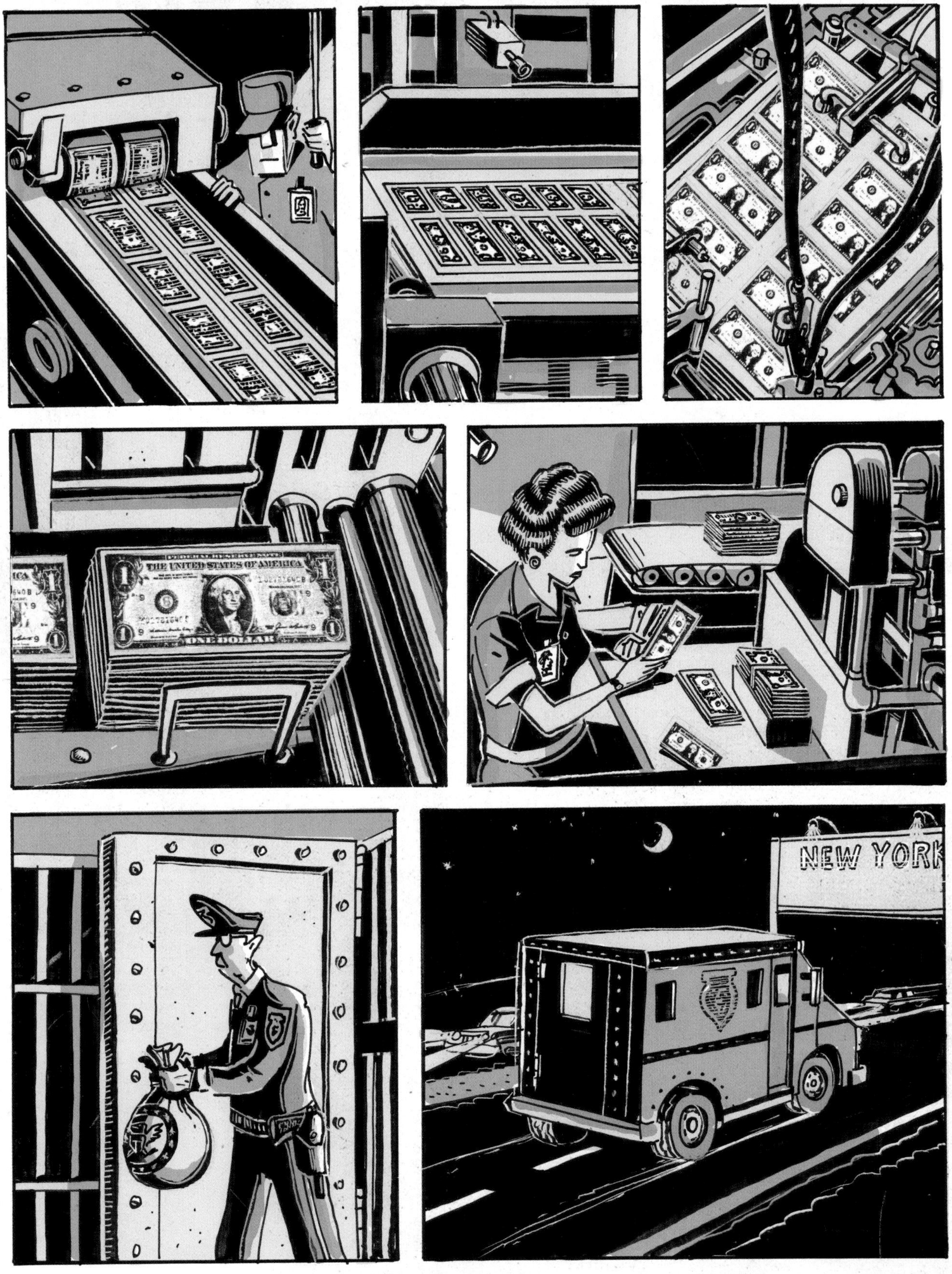

THE UNITED STATES OF AMERICA
ONE DOLLAR
NEW YORK

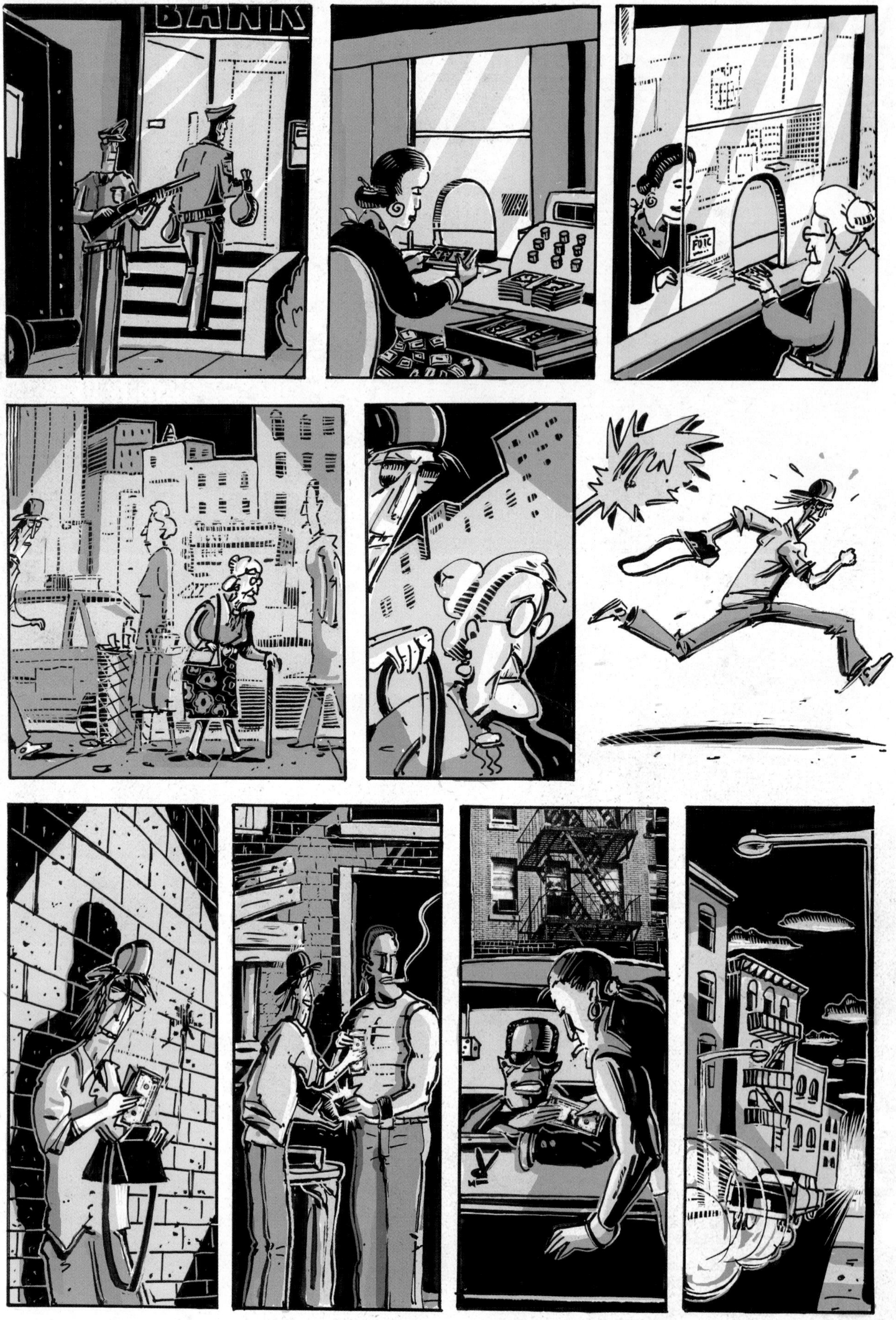
BANK
FDIC

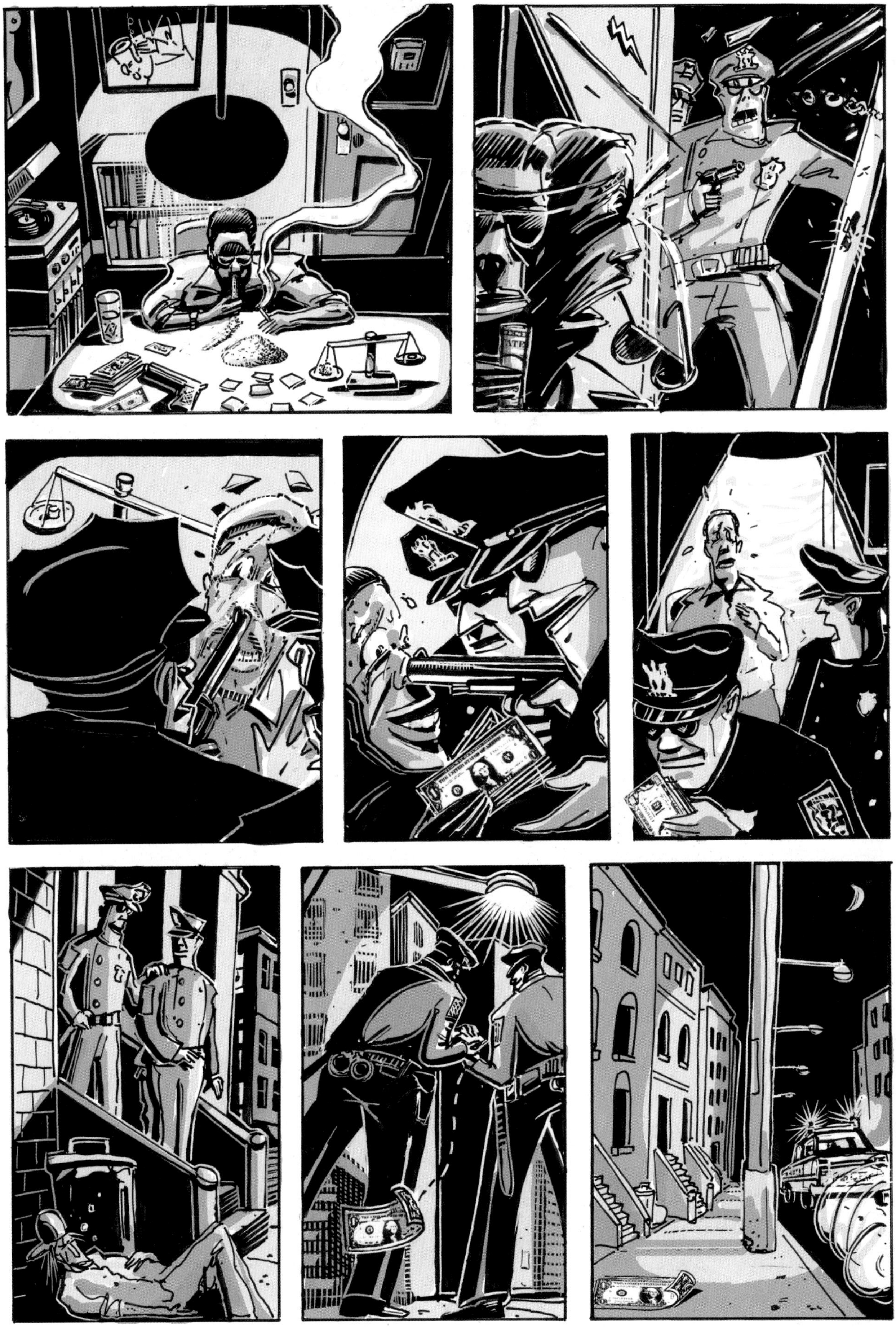

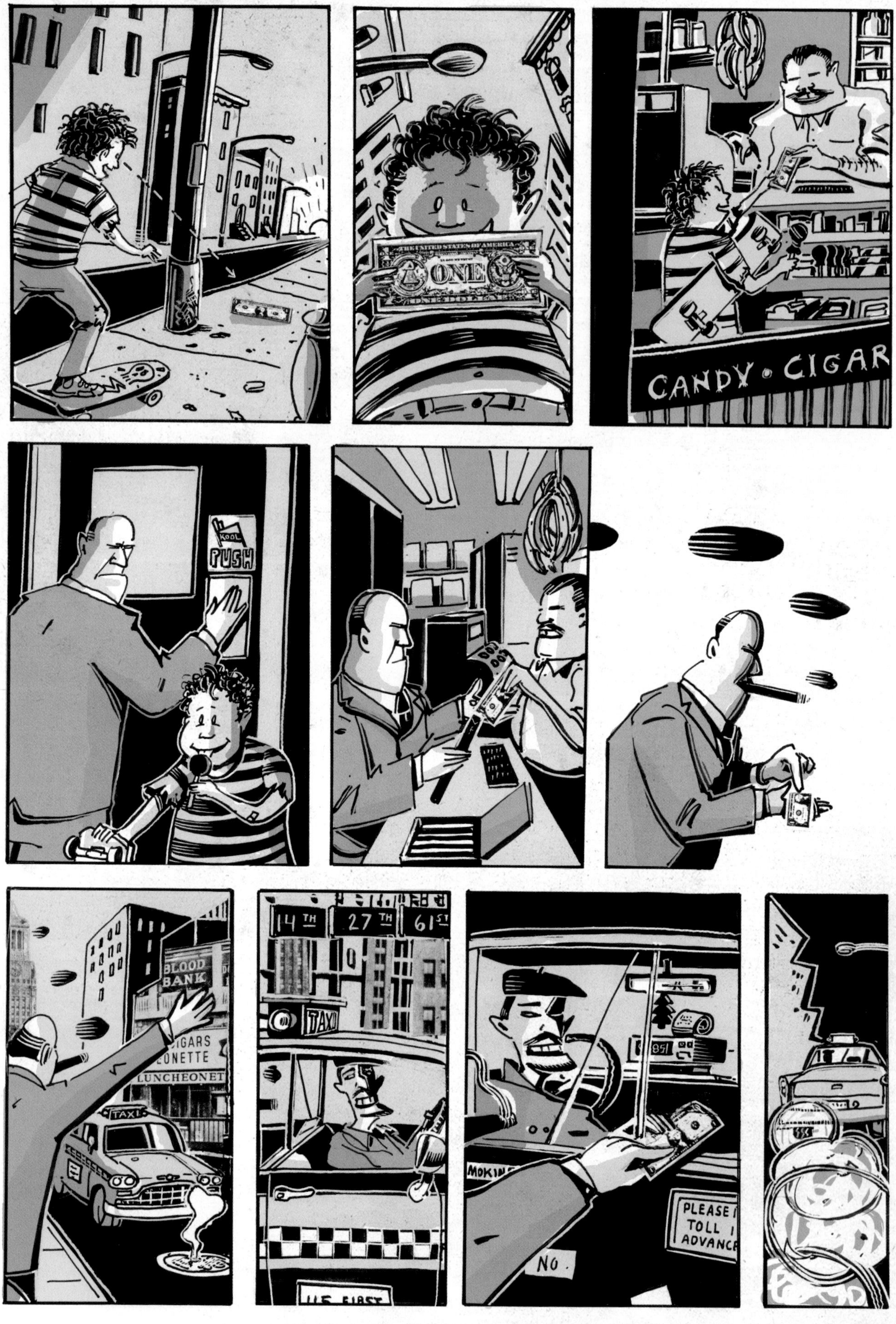
THE UNITED STATES OF AMERICA
ONE
CANDY • CIGAR
KOOL
PUSH
BLOOD BANK
CIGARS
LONETTE
LUNCHEONET
TAXI
14TH
27TH
61ST
TAXI
PLEASE
TOLL
ADVANCE
NO.

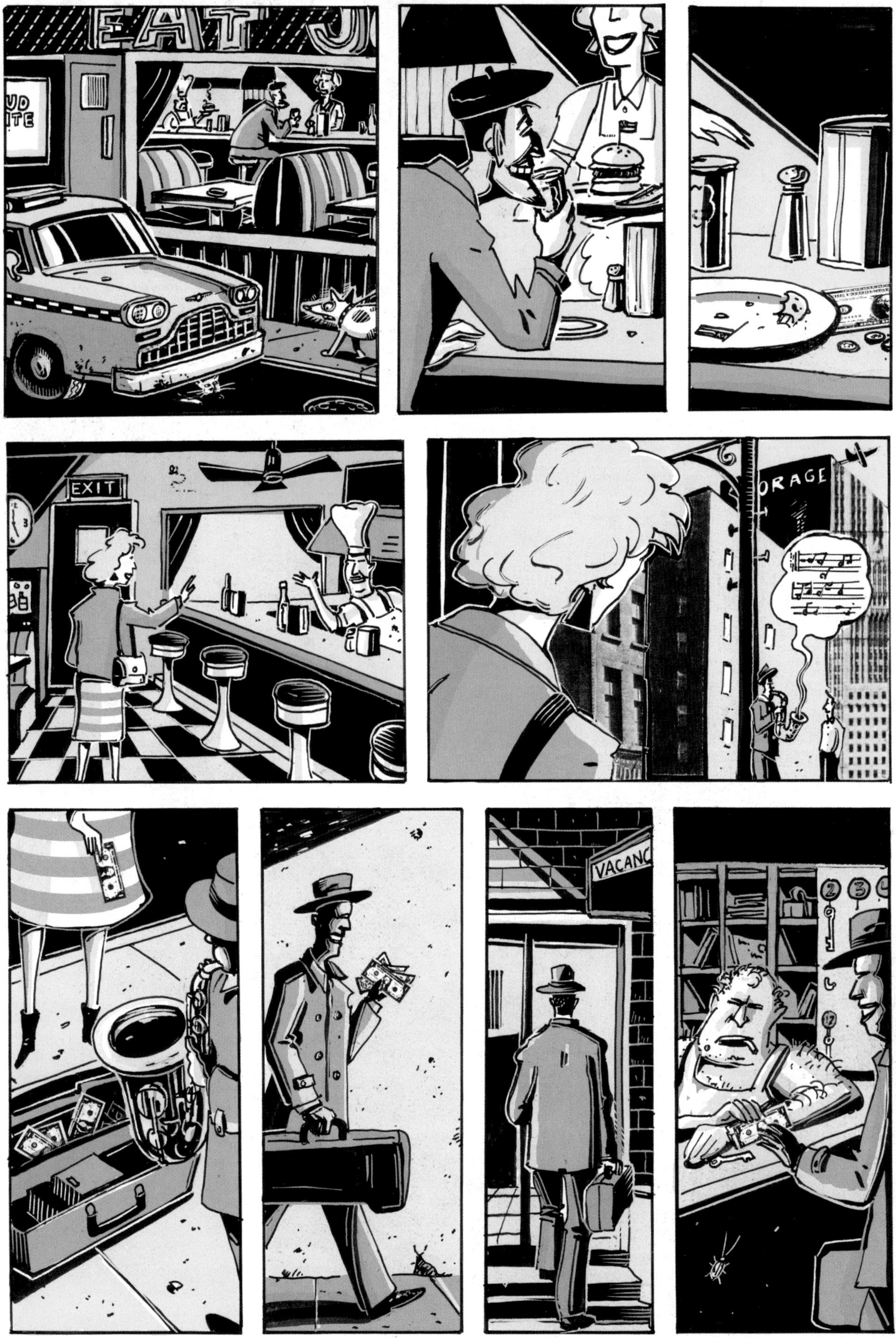
EAT
EXIT
ORAGE
VAÇANC

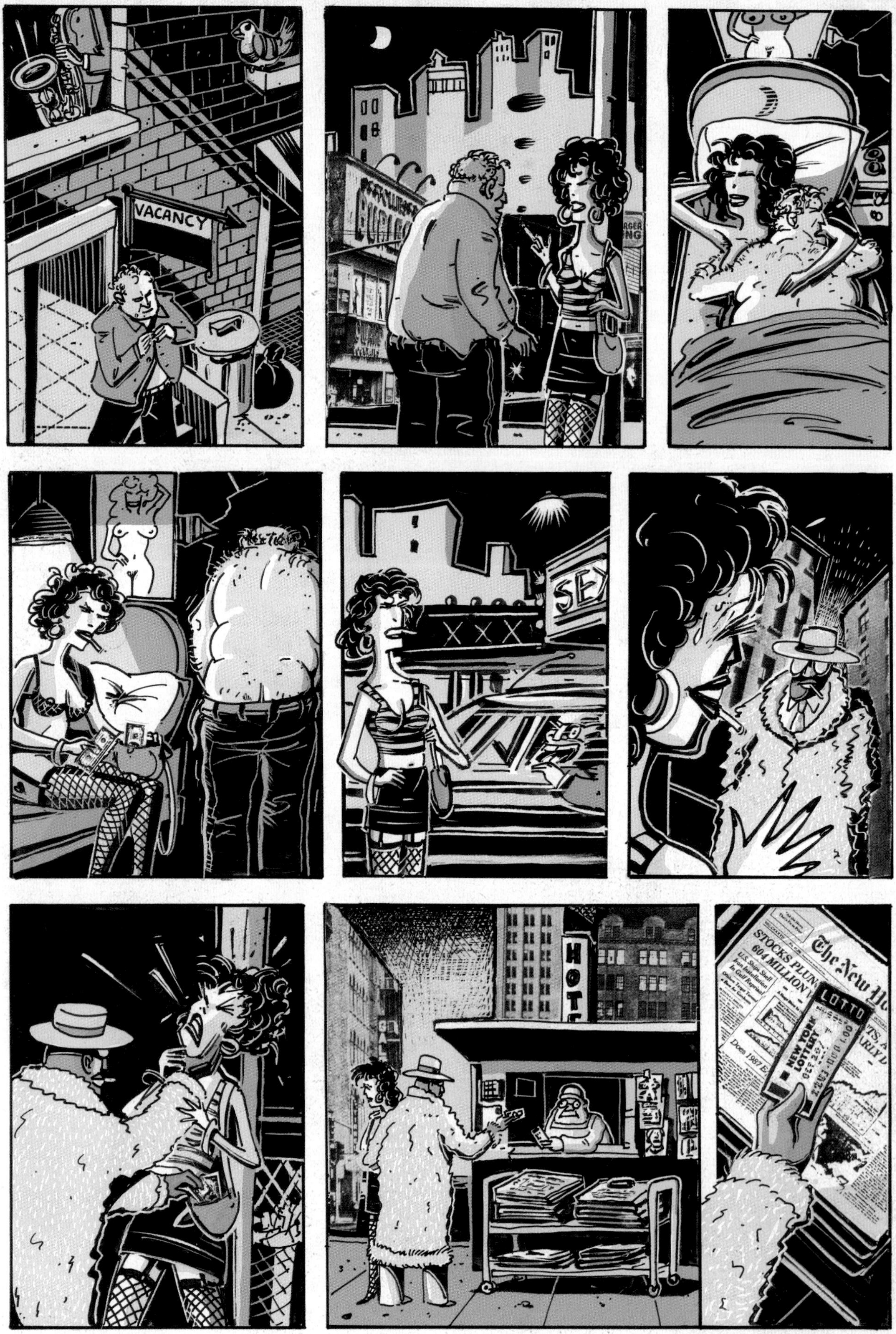
VACANCY
SEX
X X X
LOTTO
NEW YORK LOTTERY

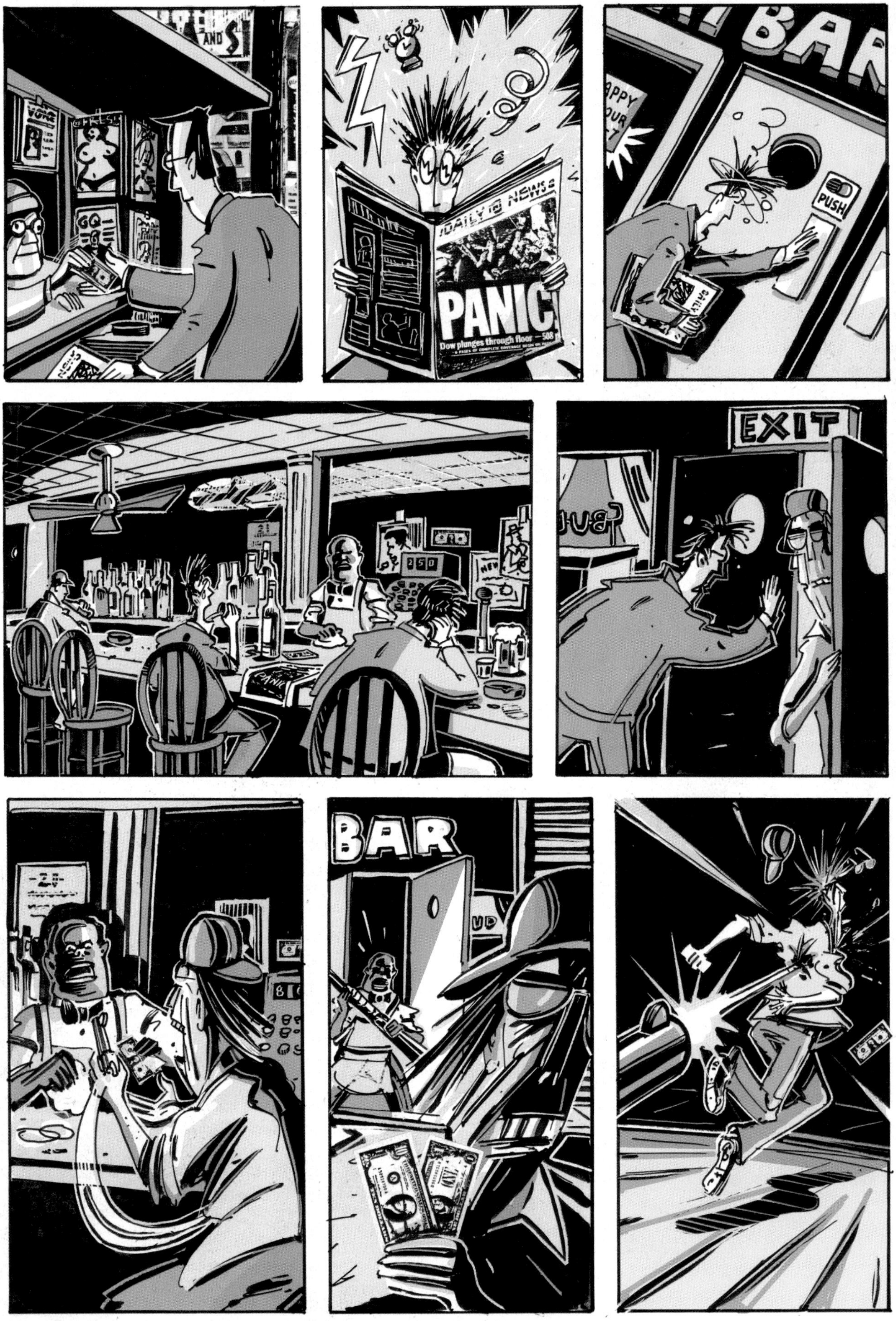
DAILY NEWS
PANIC
Dow plunges through floor — 508
PUSH
EXIT
BAR

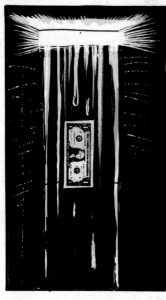

END

BULK RATE
U. S. POSTAGE
PAID
New York, N. Y.
Permit No. 7442
FEDERAL RESERVE NOTE
THE UNITED STATES OF AMERICA
THIS NOTE IS LEGAL TENDER FOR ALL DEBTS, PUBLIC AND PRIVATE
G57210205E
WASHINGTON, D.C.
ONE DOLLAR
TAXI

IN GOD WE TRUST

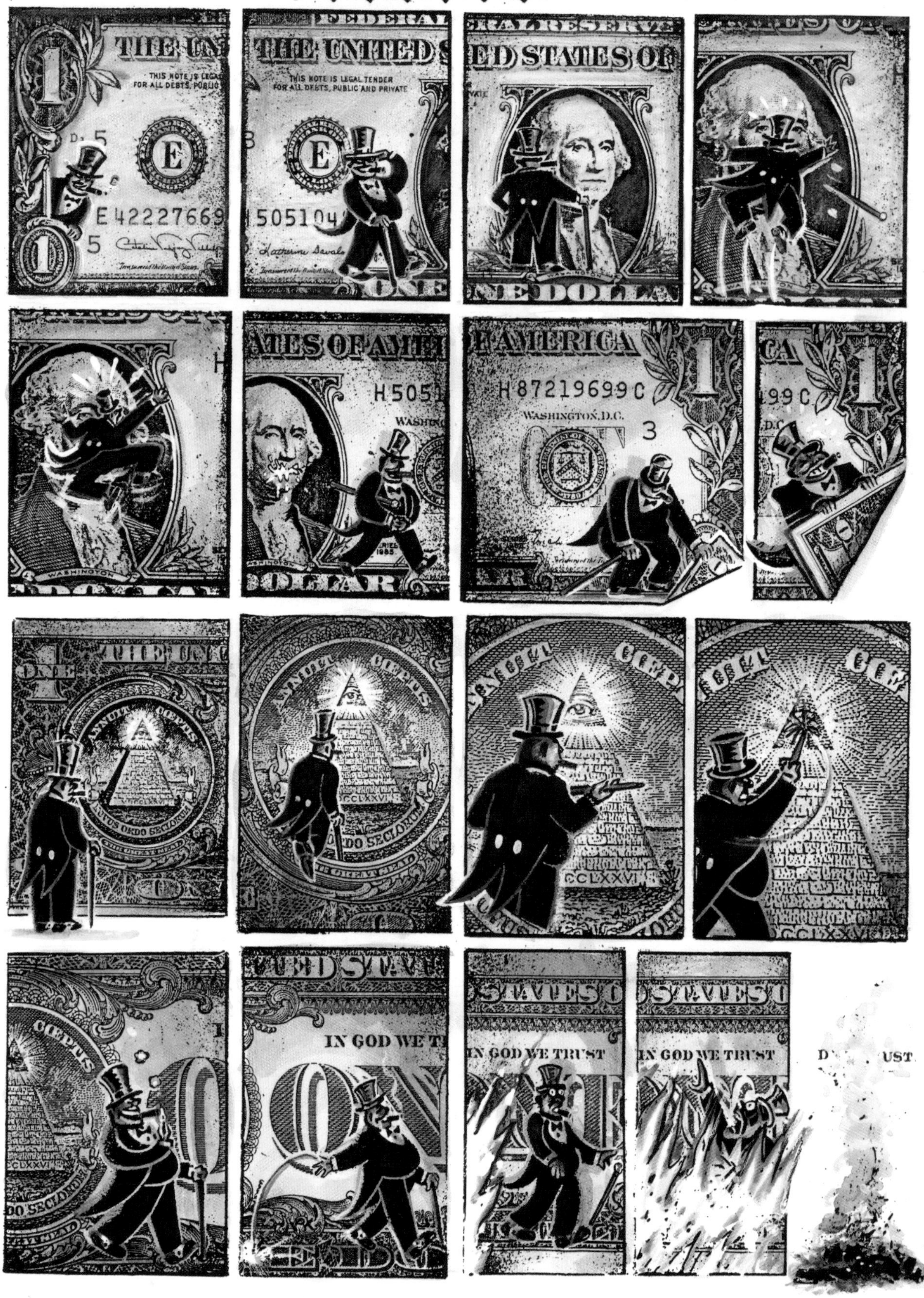

THE UN
THIS NOTE IS LEGAL
FOR ALL DEBTS, PUBLIC
E42227669
THE UNITED S
THIS NOTE IS LEGAL TENDER
FOR ALL DEBTS, PUBLIC AND PRIVATE
I505104
ED STATES OF
ATES OF AME
H505
F AMERICA
H87219699C
WASHINGTON, D.C.
IN GOD WE T
IN GOD WE TRUST
IN GOD WE TRUST
D UST

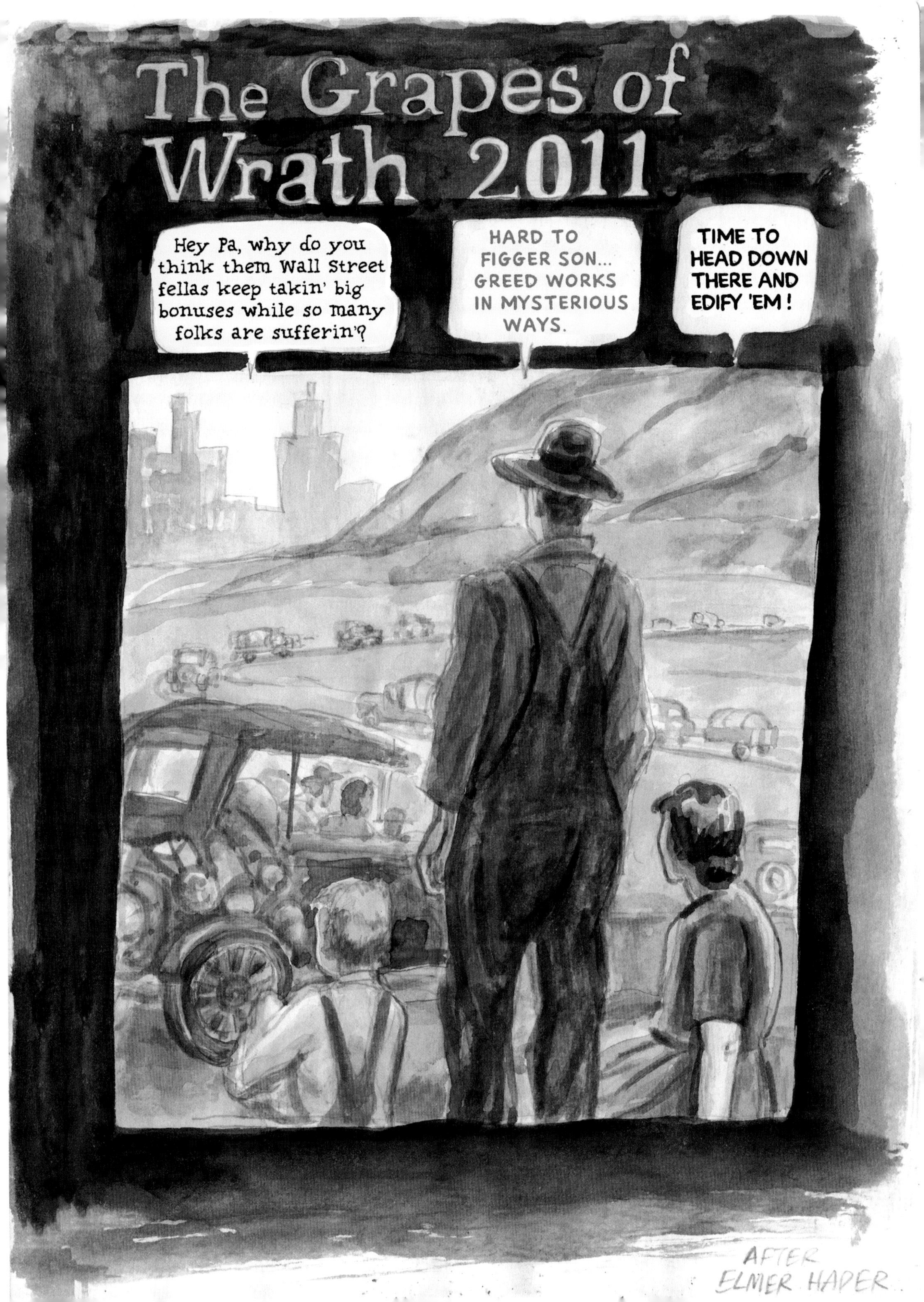
The Grapes of Wrath 2011
Hey Pa, why do you think them Wall Street fellas keep takin' big bonuses while so many folks are sufferin'?
HARD TO FIGGER SON... GREED WORKS IN MYSTERIOUS WAYS.
TIME TO HEAD DOWN THERE AND EDIFY 'EM!
AFTER ELMER HADER

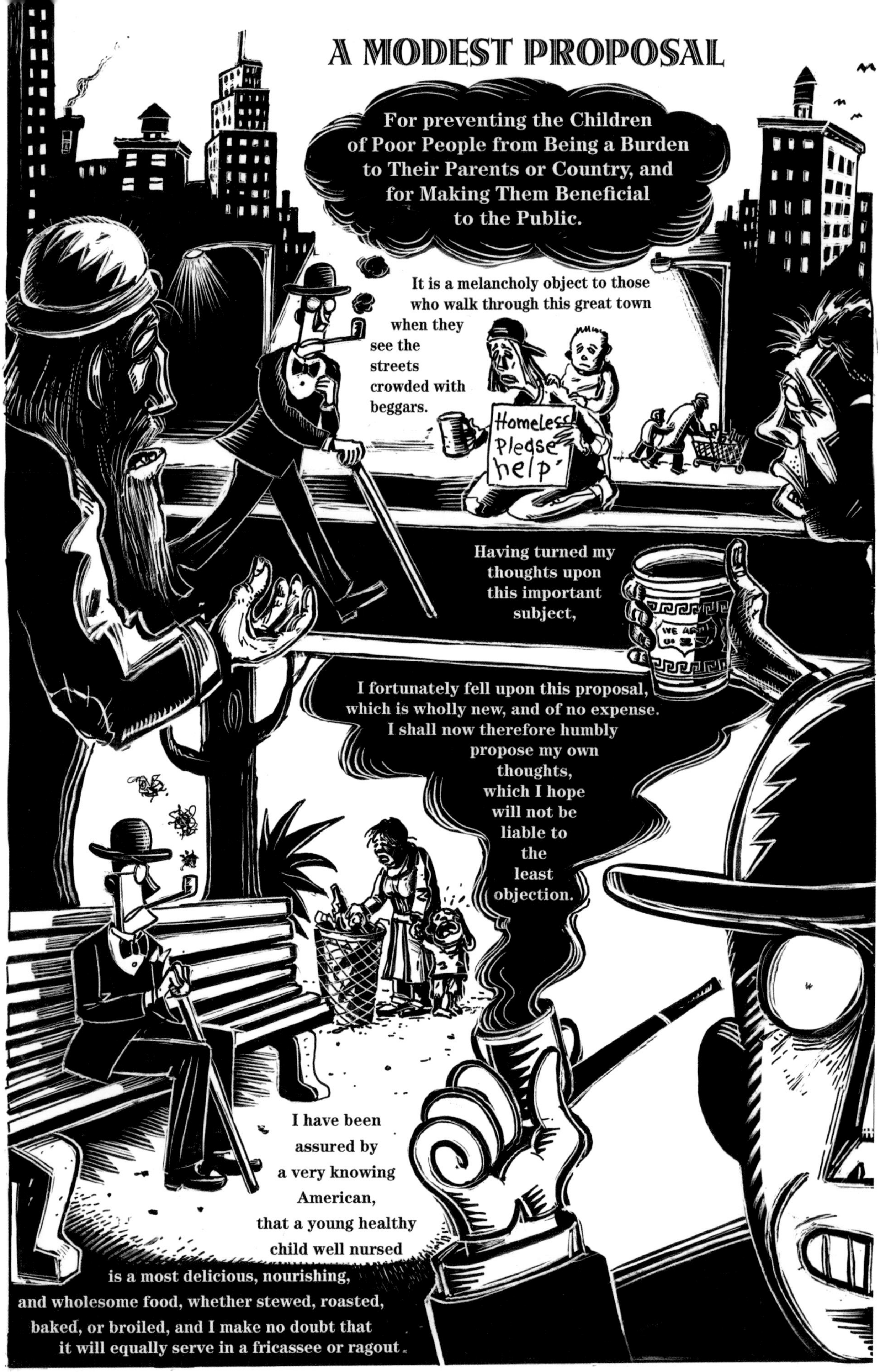
A MODEST PROPOSAL
For preventing the Children of Poor People from Being a Burden to Their Parents or Country, and for Making Them Beneficial to the Public.
It is a melancholy object to those who walk through this great town when they see the streets crowded with beggars.
Homeless Please help
Having turned my thoughts upon this important subject,
I fortunately fell upon this proposal, which is wholly new, and of no expense. I shall now therefore humbly propose my own thoughts, which I hope will not be liable to the least objection.
I have been assured by a very knowing American, that a young healthy child well nursed is a most delicious, nourishing, and wholesome food, whether stewed, roasted, baked, or broiled, and I make no doubt that it will equally serve in a fricassee or ragout.

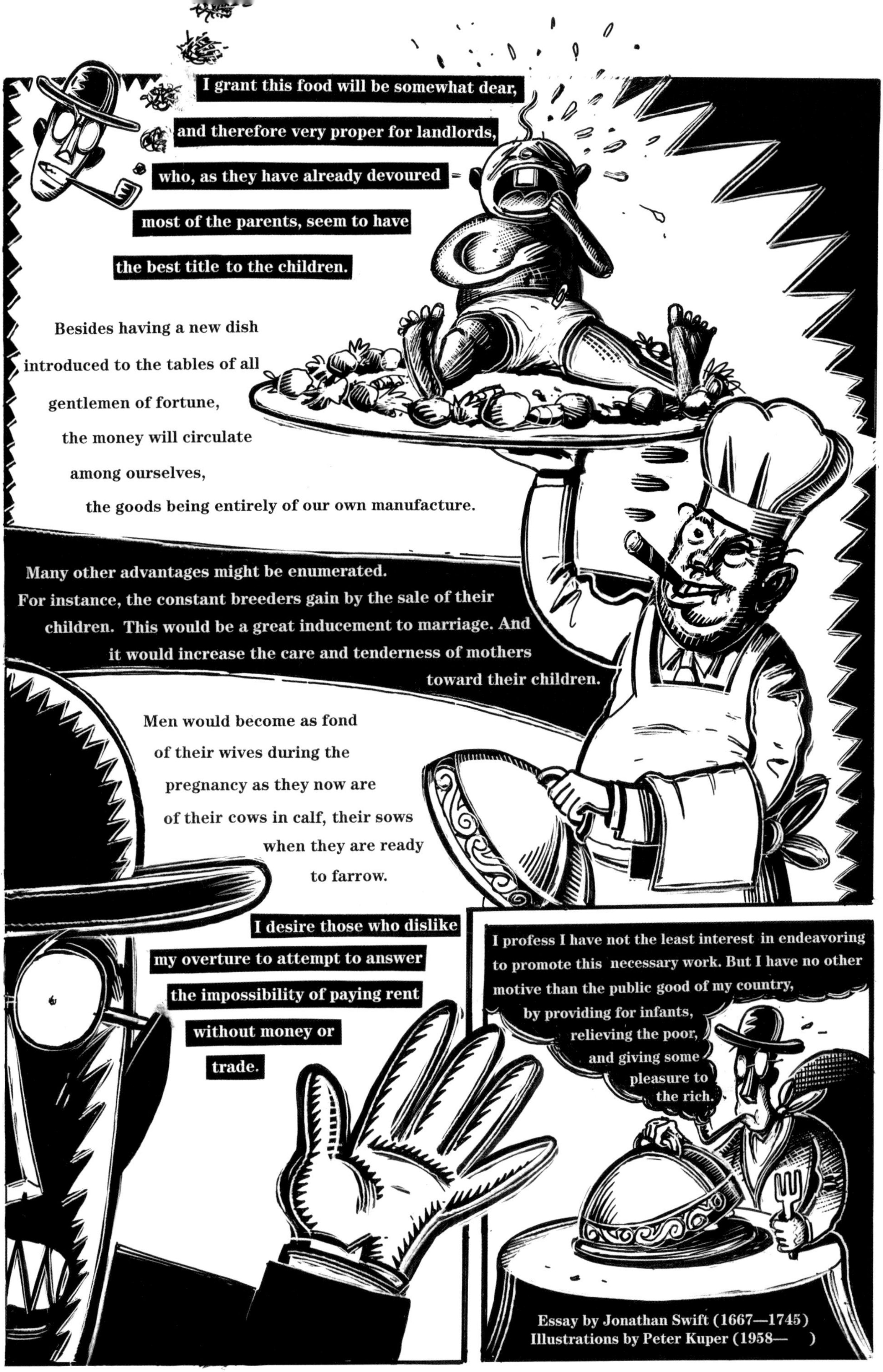
I grant this food will be somewhat dear,
and therefore very proper for landlords,
who, as they have already devoured
most of the parents, seem to have
the best title to the children.
Besides having a new dish introduced to the tables of all gentlemen of fortune, the money will circulate among ourselves, the goods being entirely of our own manufacture.
Many other advantages might be enumerated. For instance, the constant breeders gain by the sale of their children. This would be a great inducement to marriage. And it would increase the care and tenderness of mothers toward their children.
Men would become as fond of their wives during the pregnancy as they now are of their cows in calf, their sows when they are ready to farrow.
I desire those who dislike
my overture to attempt to answer
the impossibility of paying rent
without money or
trade.
I profess I have not the least interest in endeavoring to promote this necessary work. But I have no other motive than the public good of my country, by providing for infants, relieving the poor, and giving some pleasure to the rich.
Essay by Jonathan Swift (1667—1745)
Illustrations by Peter Kuper (1958—)

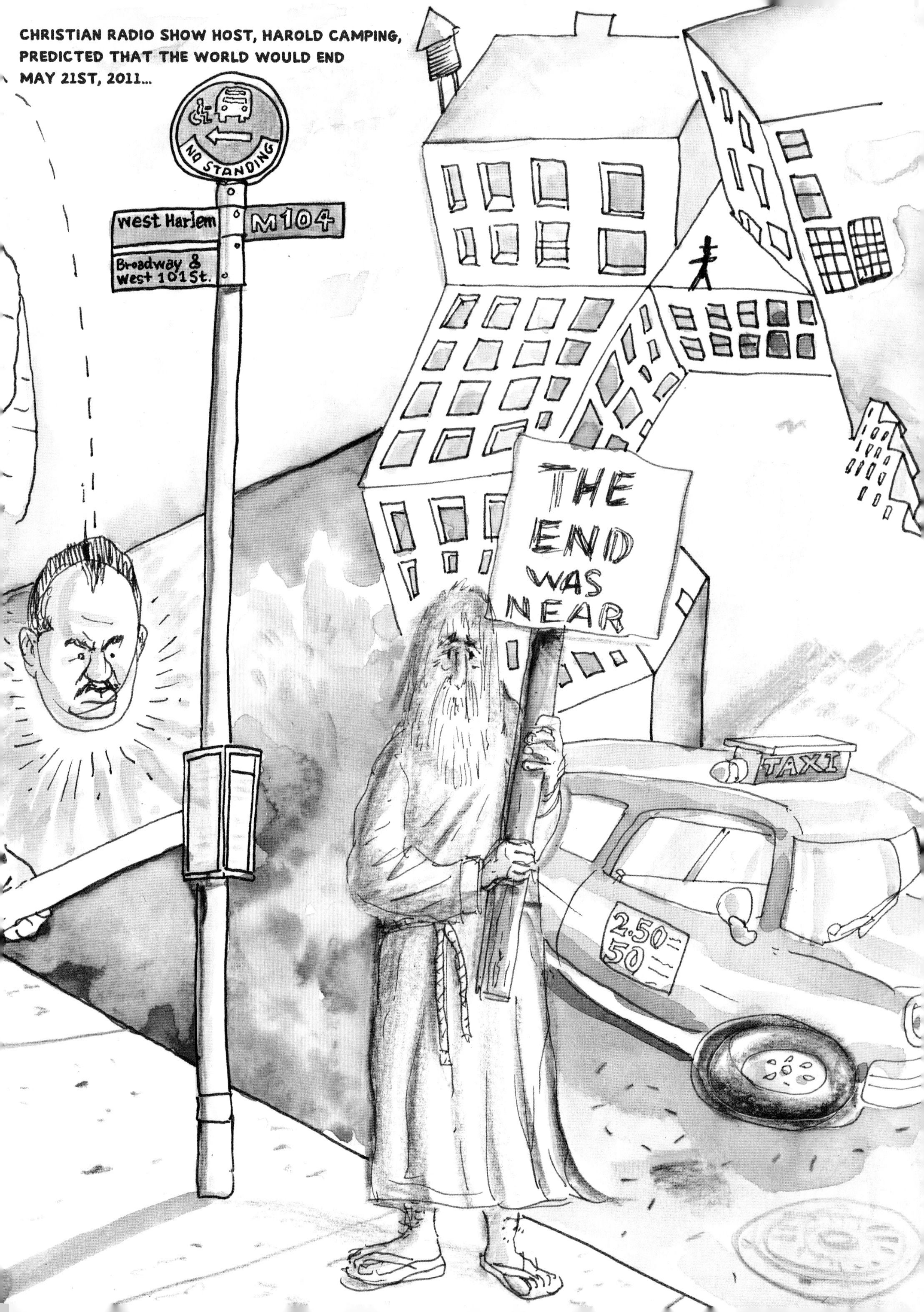
CHRISTIAN RADIO SHOW HOST, HAROLD CAMPING, PREDICTED THAT THE WORLD WOULD END MAY 21ST, 2011...
NO STANDING
west Harlem
M104
Broadway & west 101St.
THE END WAS NEAR
TAXI
2.50
50

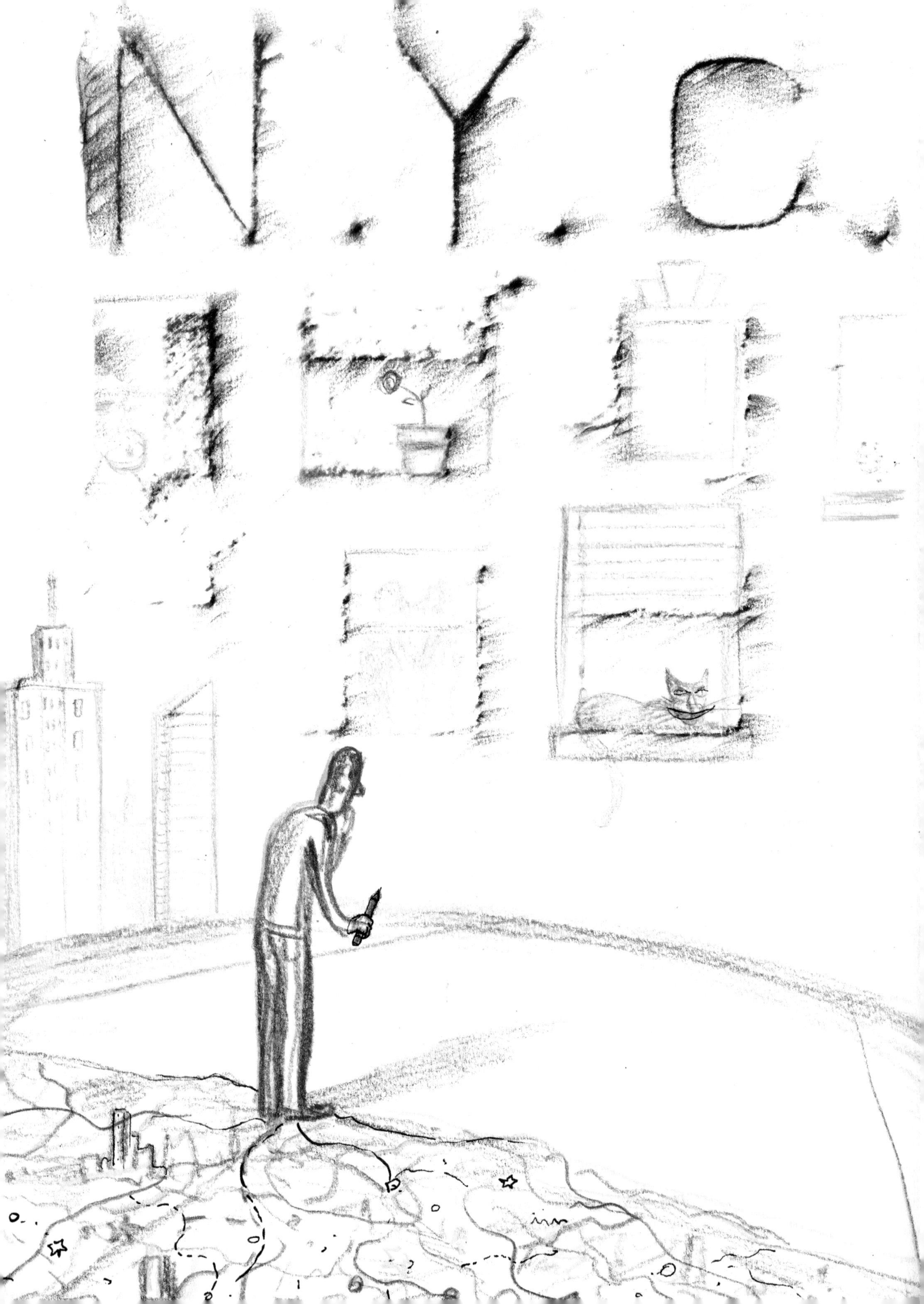
N.Y.C.

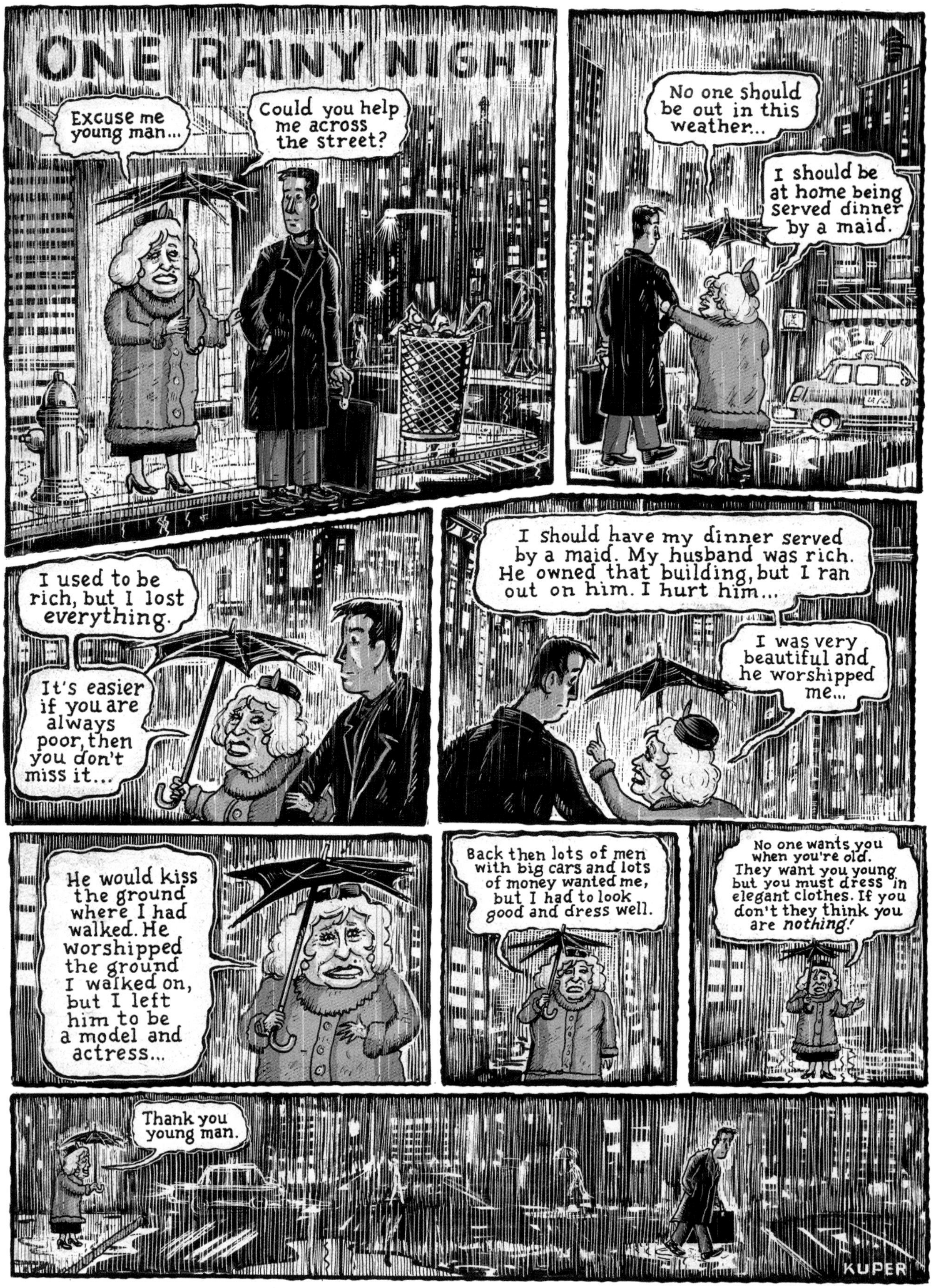
ONE RAINY NIGHT
Excuse me young man...
Could you help me across the street?
No one should be out in this weather...
I should be at home being served dinner by a maid.
DELI
I used to be rich, but I lost everything.
It's easier if you are always poor, then you don't miss it...
I should have my dinner served by a maid. My husband was rich. He owned that building, but I ran out on him. I hurt him...
I was very beautiful and he worshipped me...
He would kiss the ground where I had walked. He worshipped the ground I walked on, but I left him to be a model and actress...
Back then lots of men with big cars and lots of money wanted me, but I had to look good and dress well.
No one wants you when you're old. They want you young but you must dress in elegant clothes. If you don't they think you are nothing!
Thank you young man.
KUPER

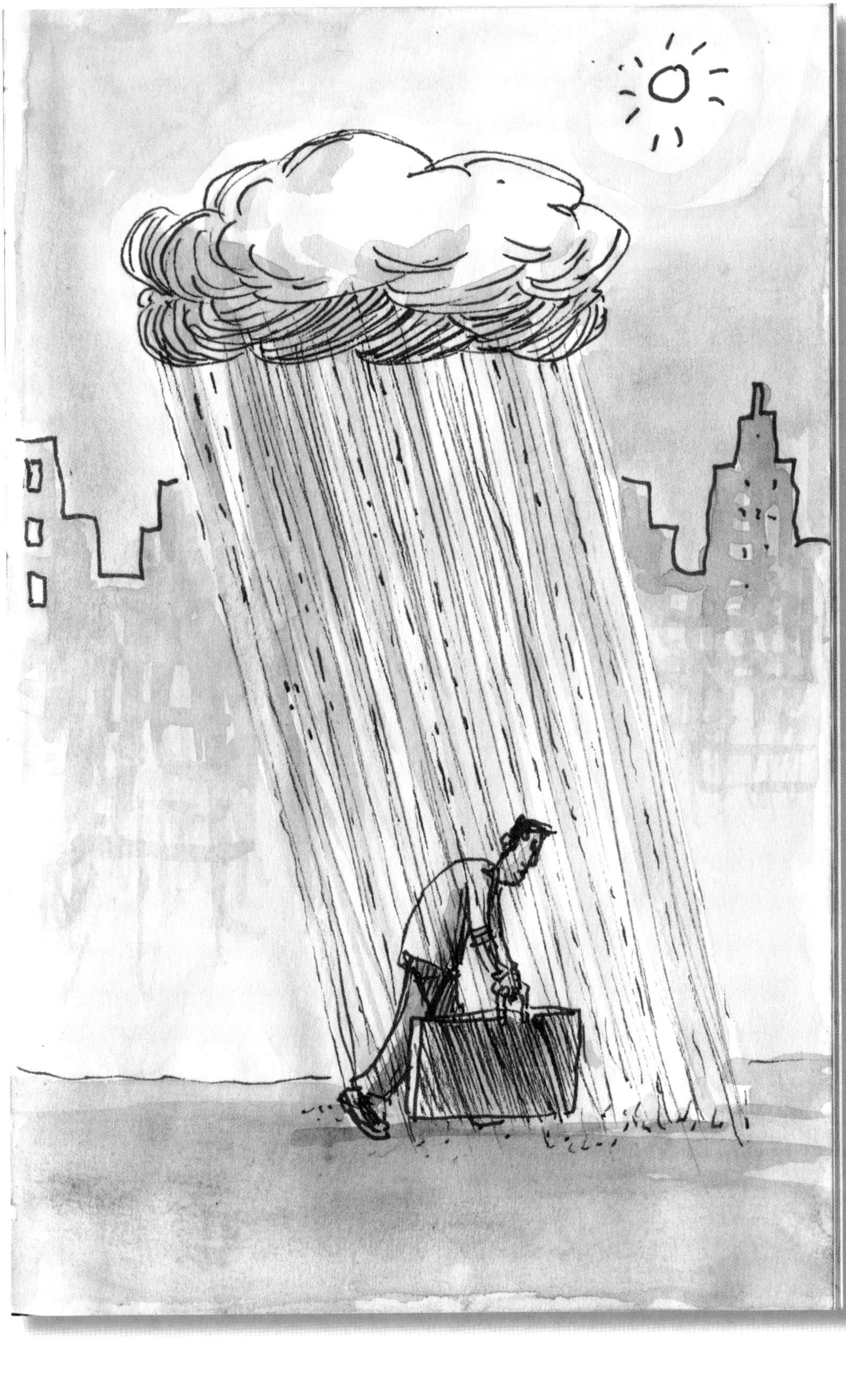

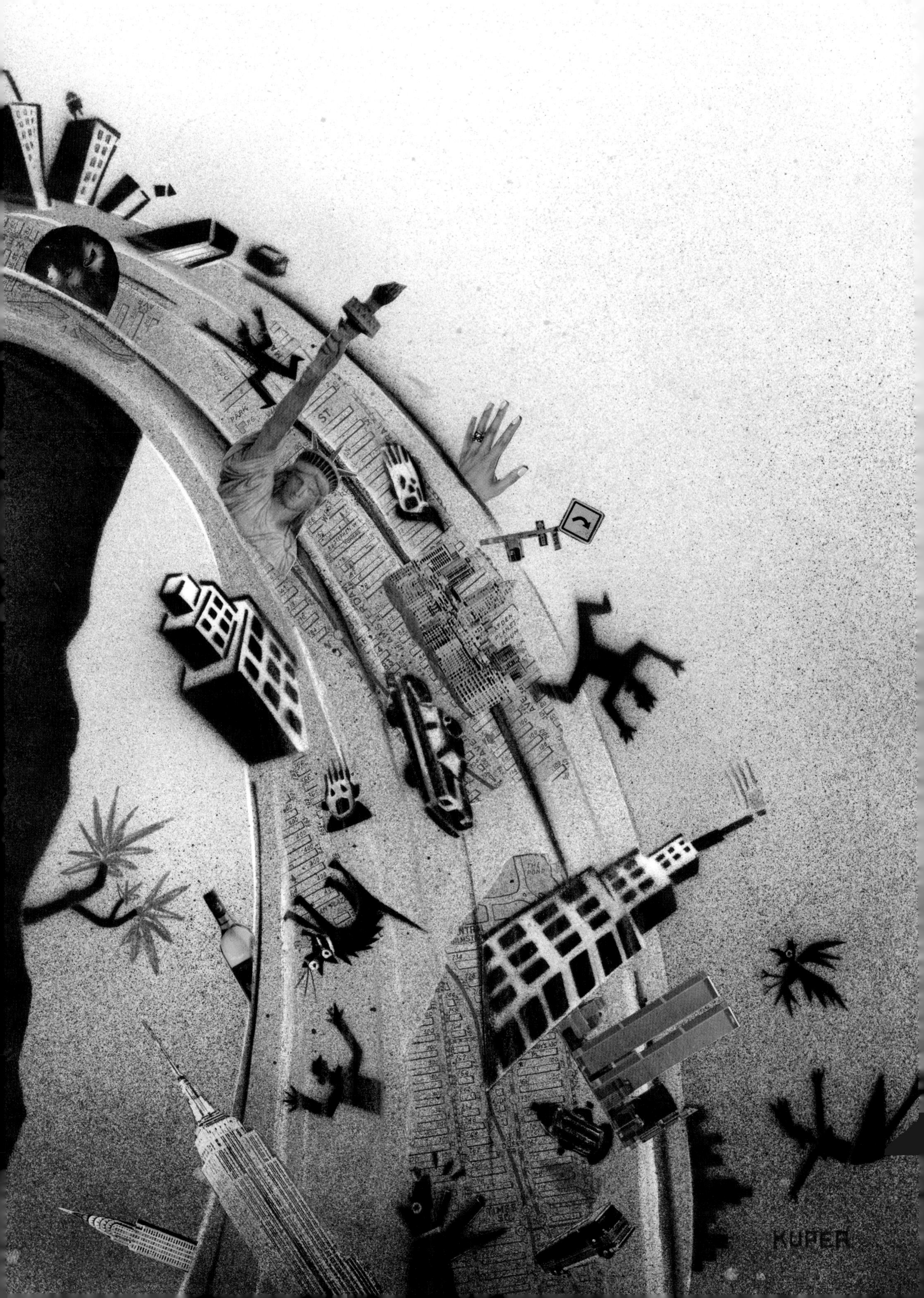
KUPER

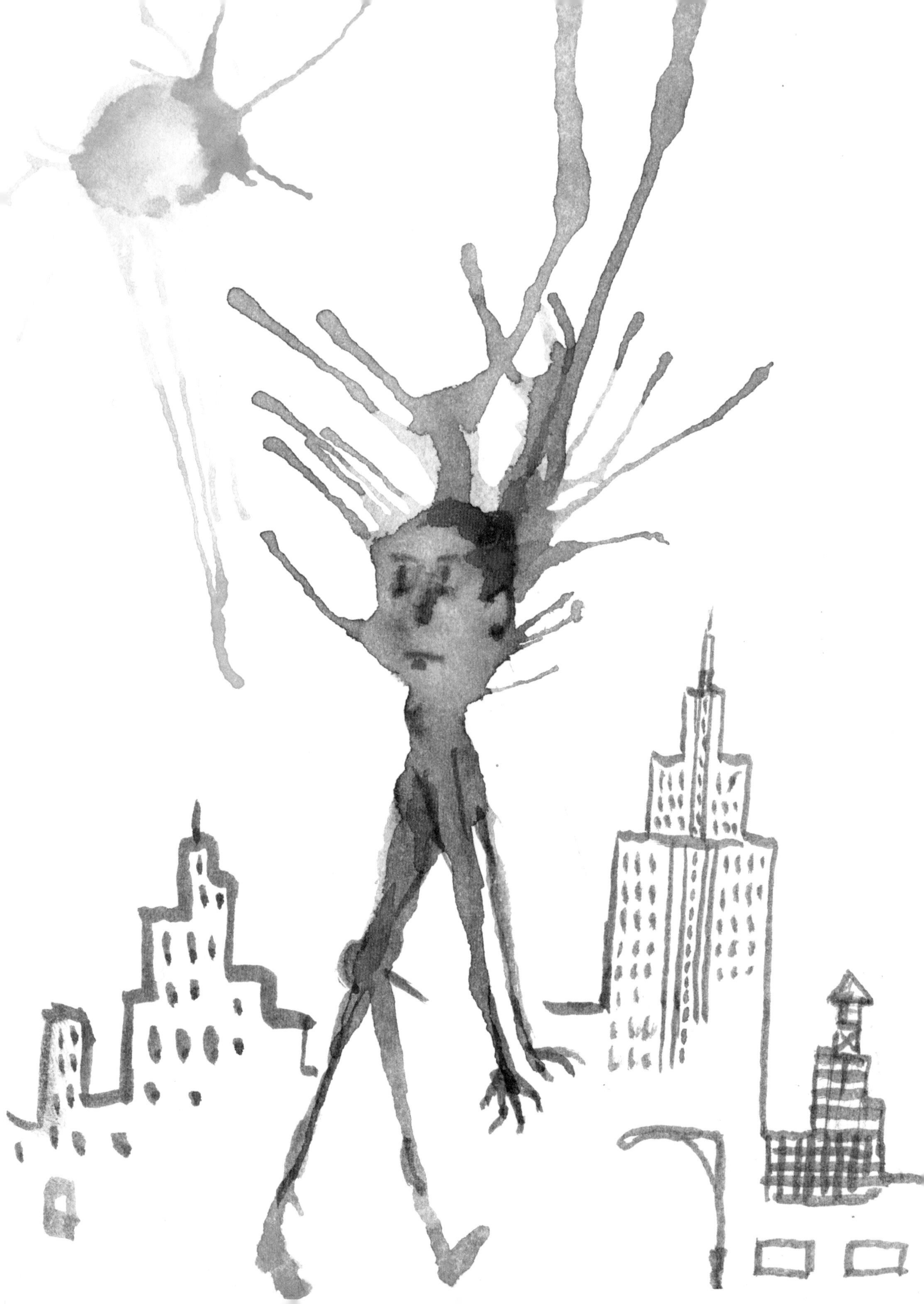

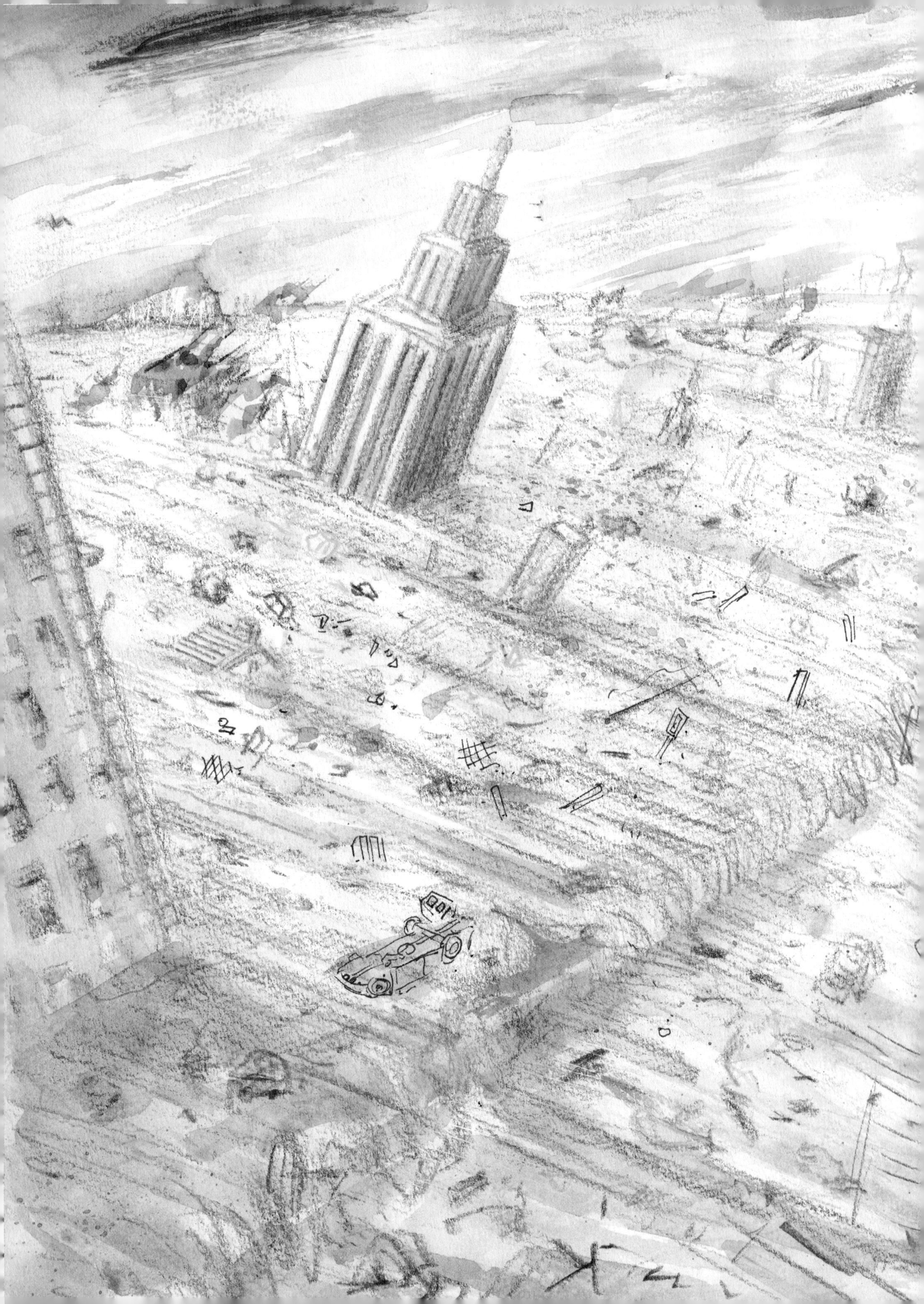

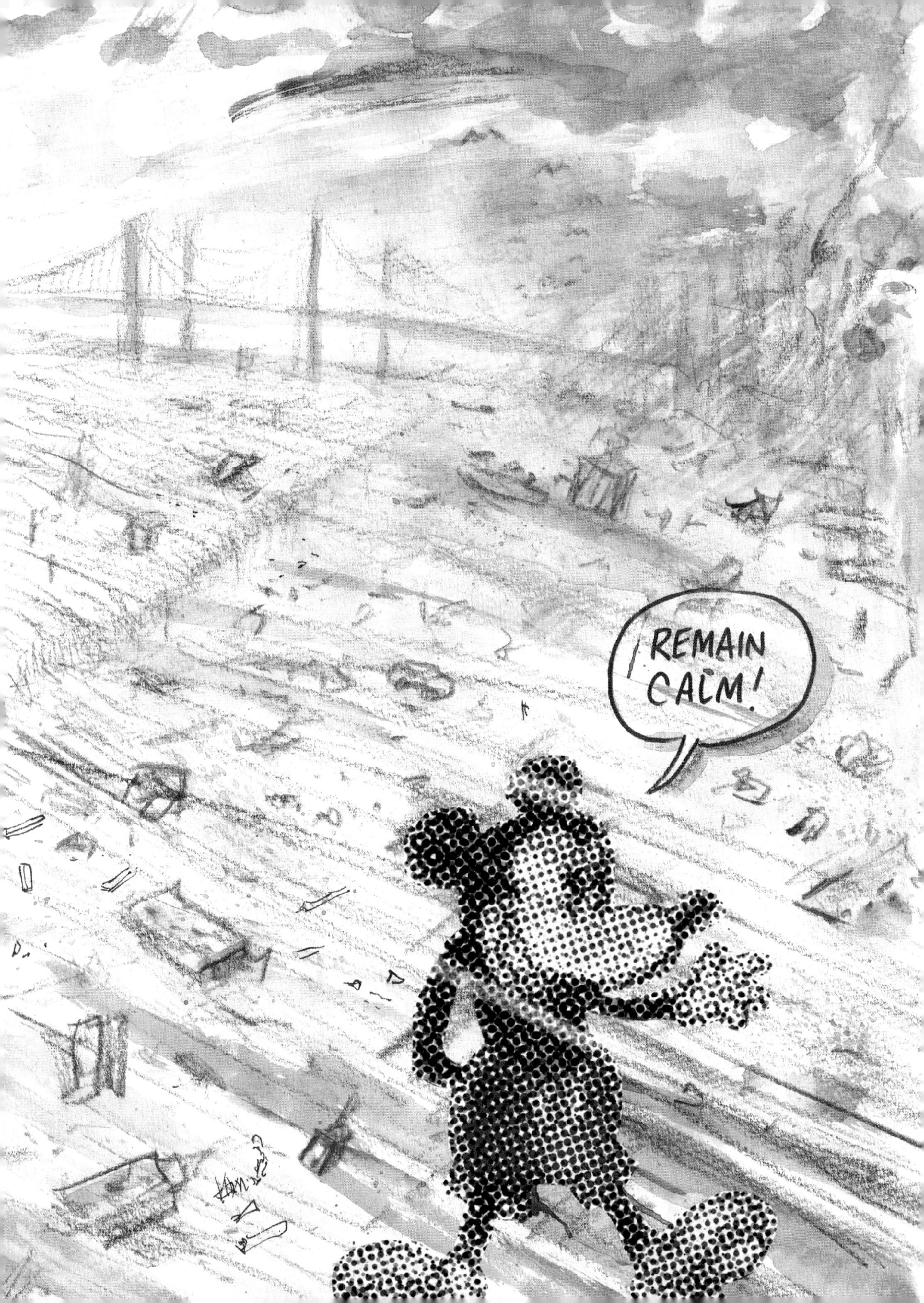
REMAIN CALM!

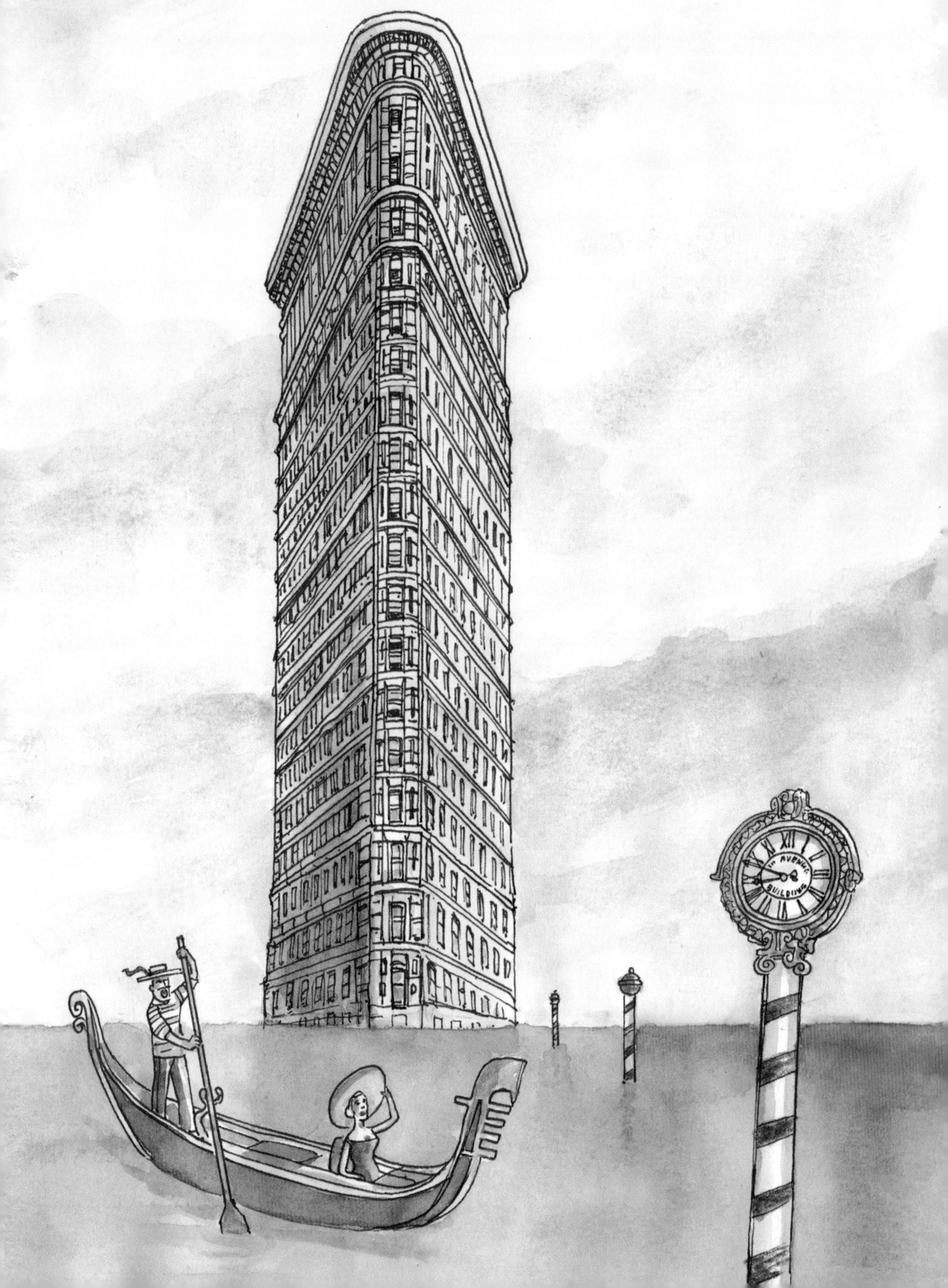
AVENUE
BUILDING

WHETHER Report

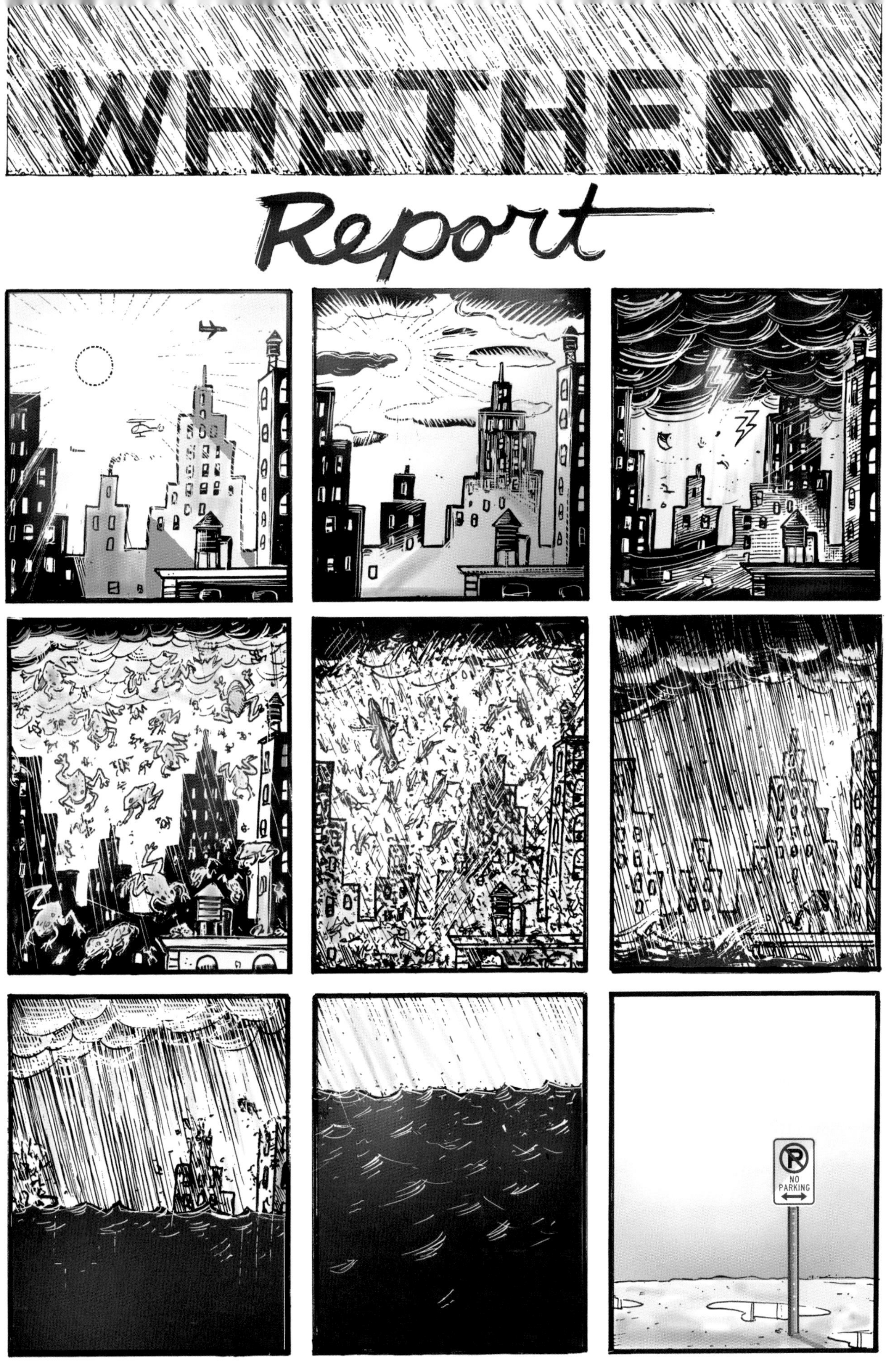
NO
PARKING

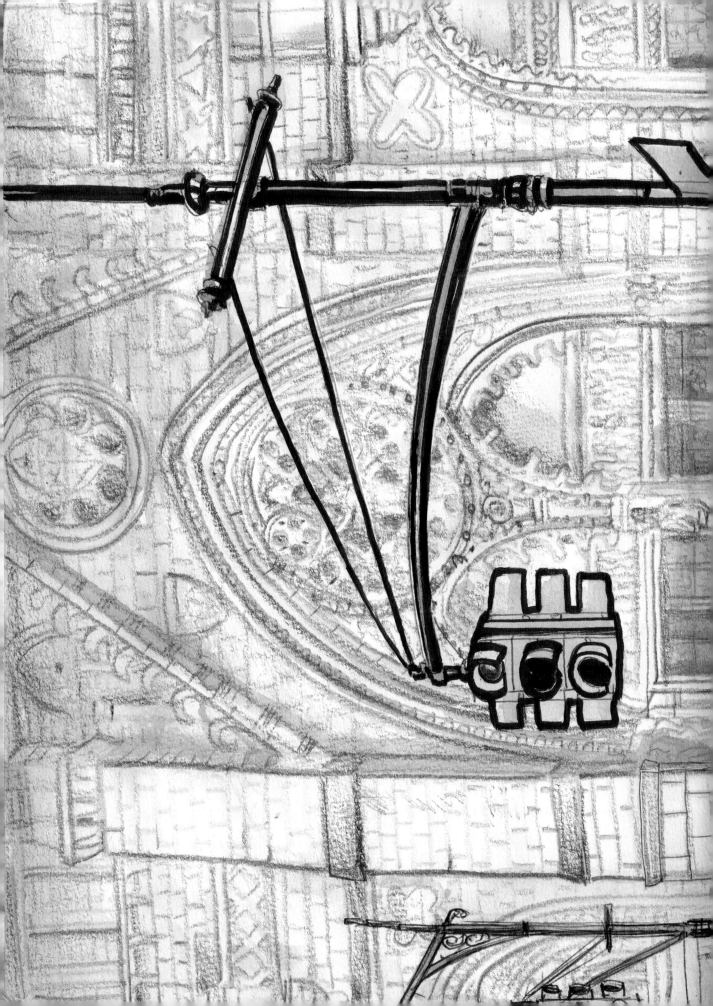

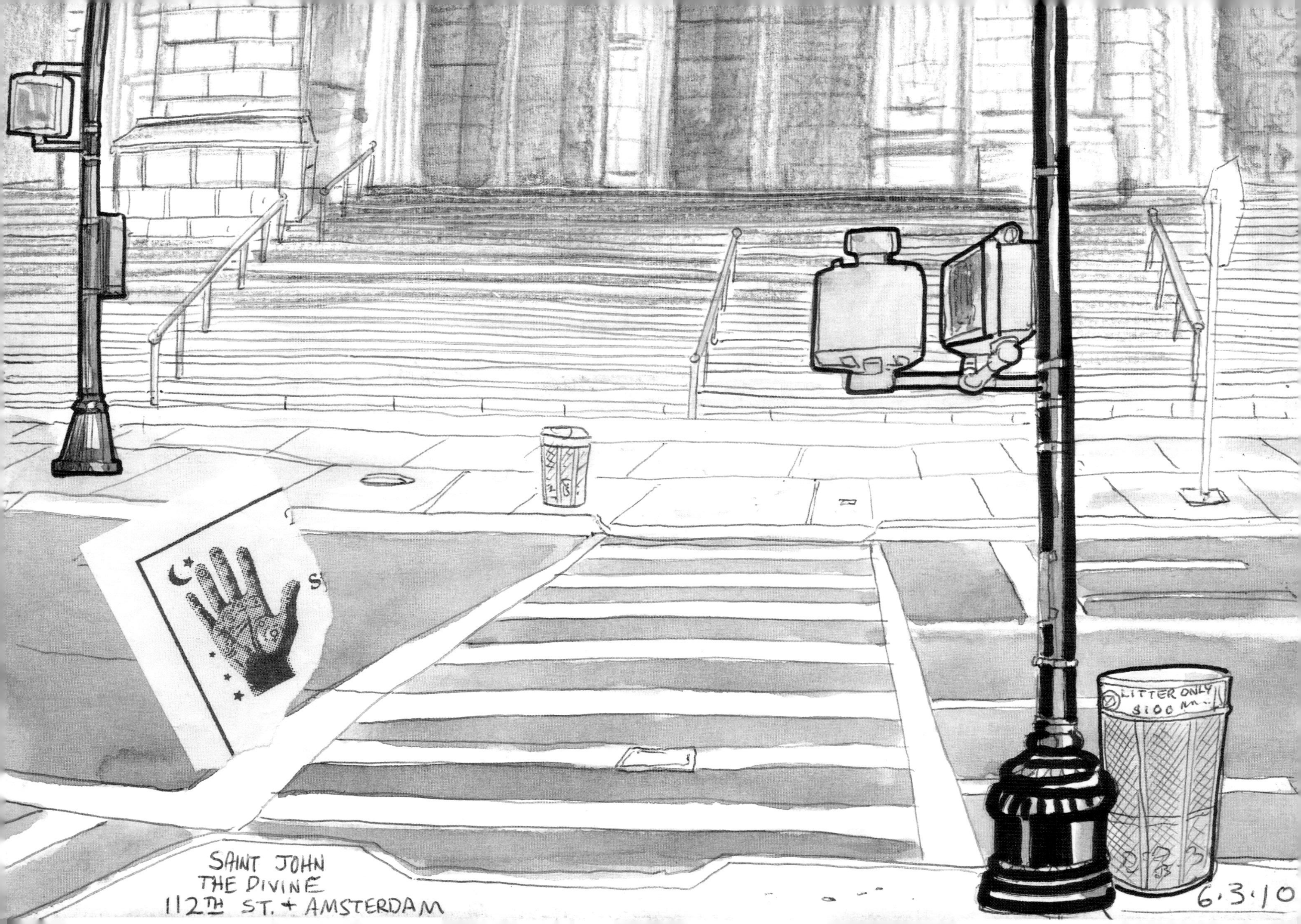
LITTER ONLY
SAINT JOHN
THE DIVINE
112TH ST. + AMSTERDAM
6.3.10

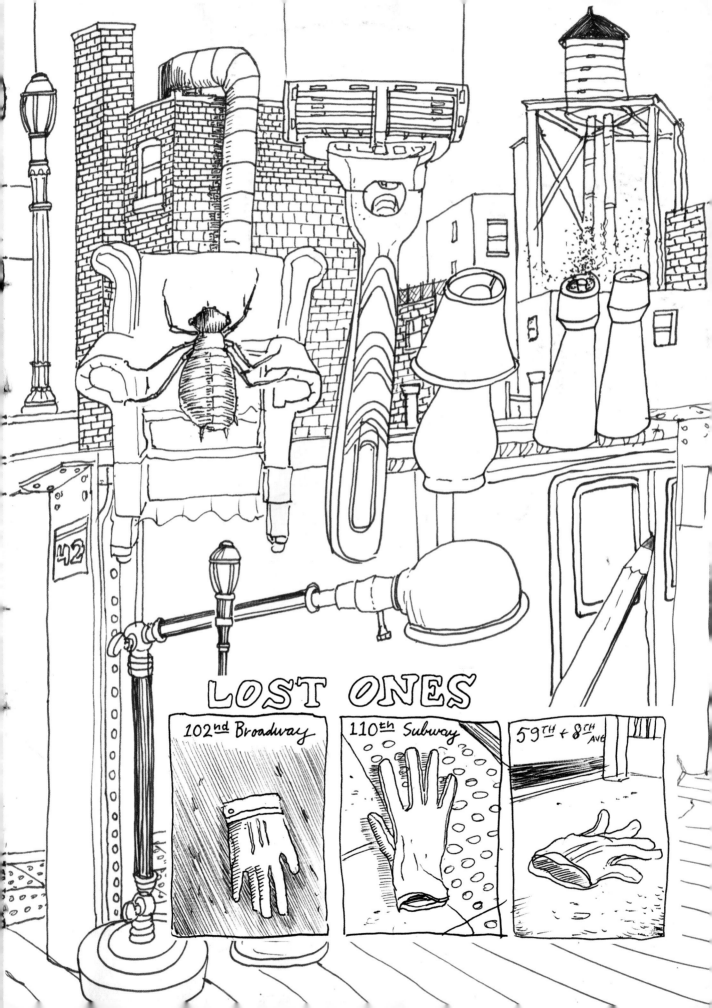

LOST ONES

102nd Broadway

110th Subway

59TH + 8TH Ave

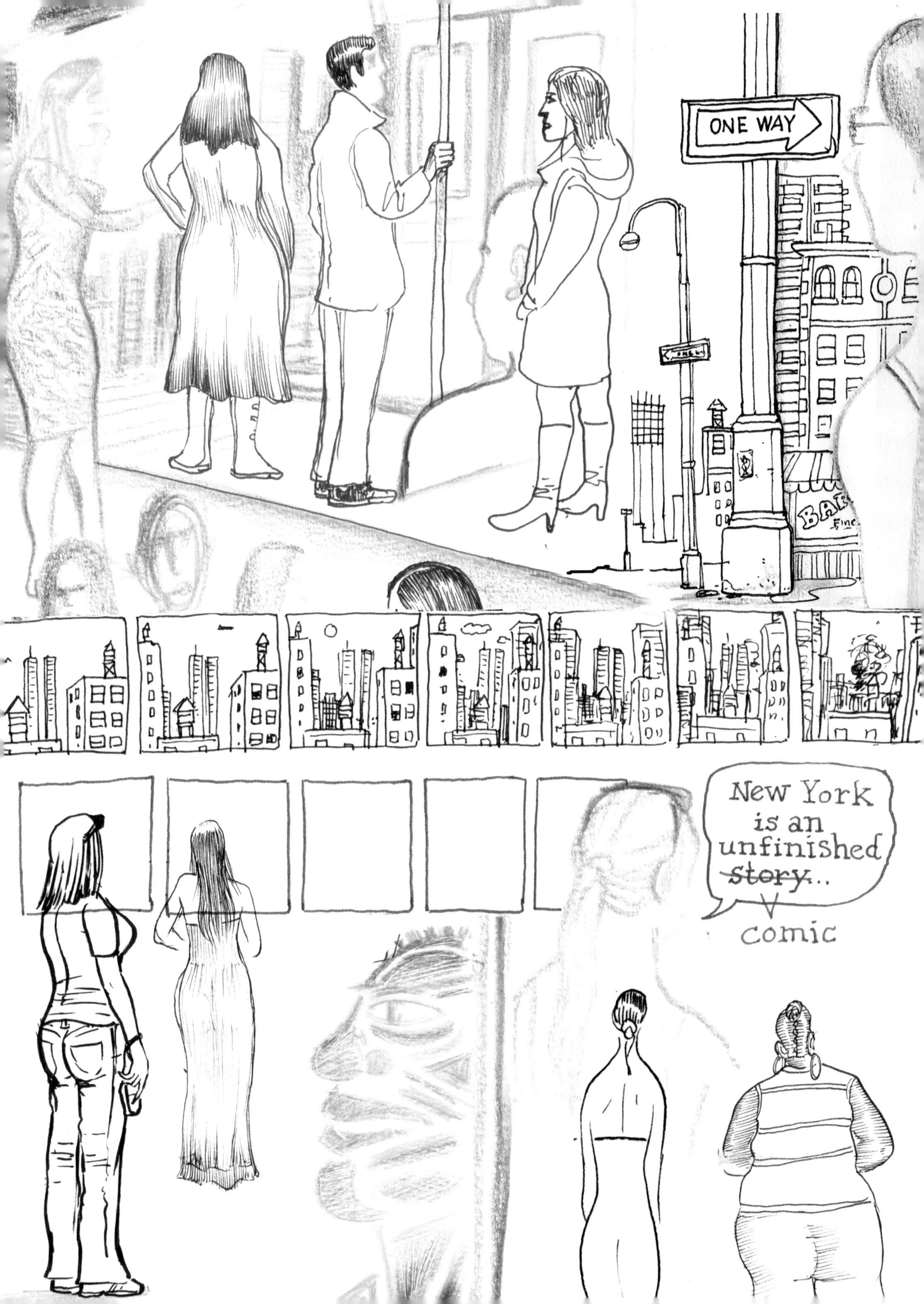
ONE WAY
New York is an unfinished ~~story~~.. comic

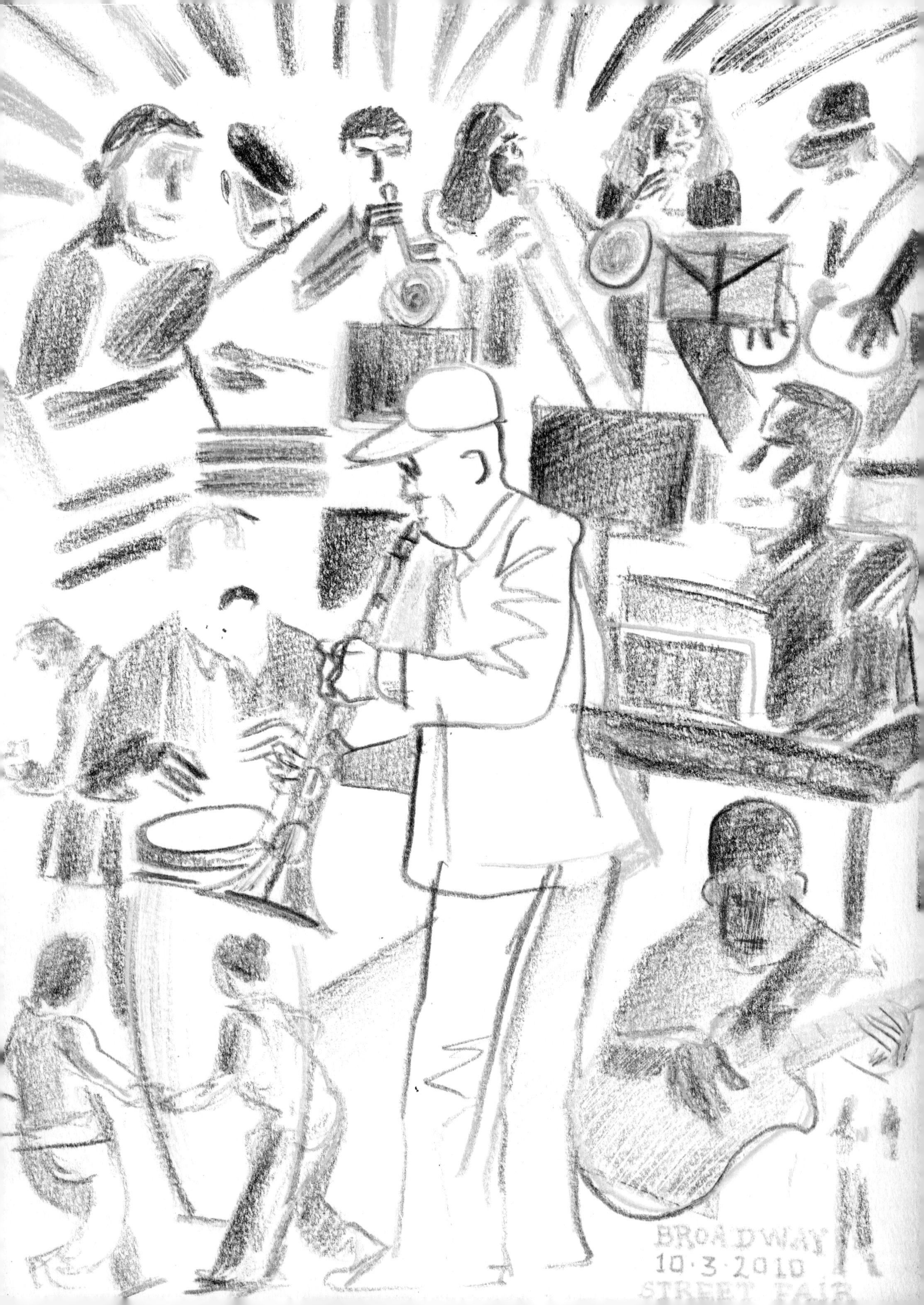
BROADWAY
10·3·2010
STREET FAIR

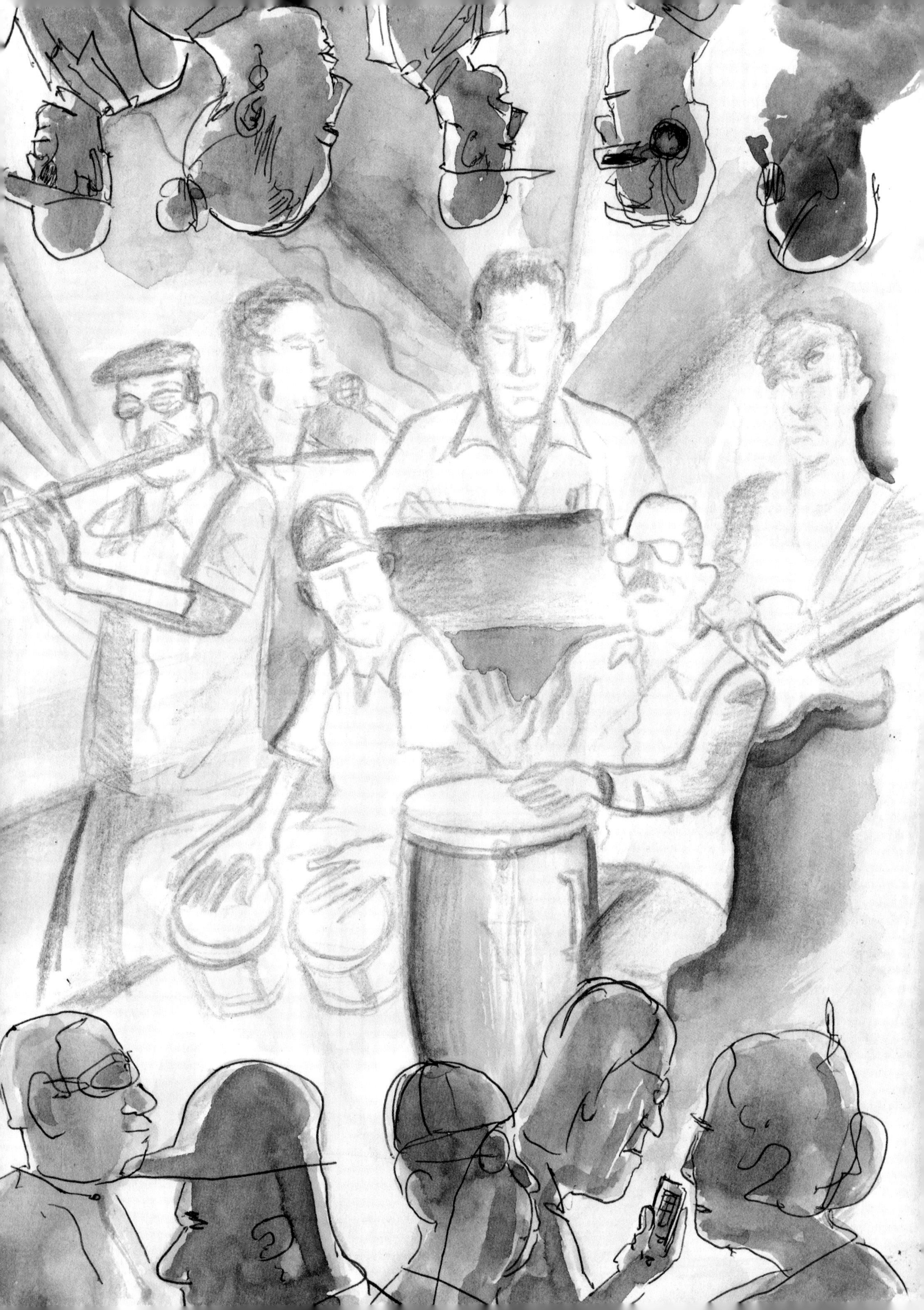

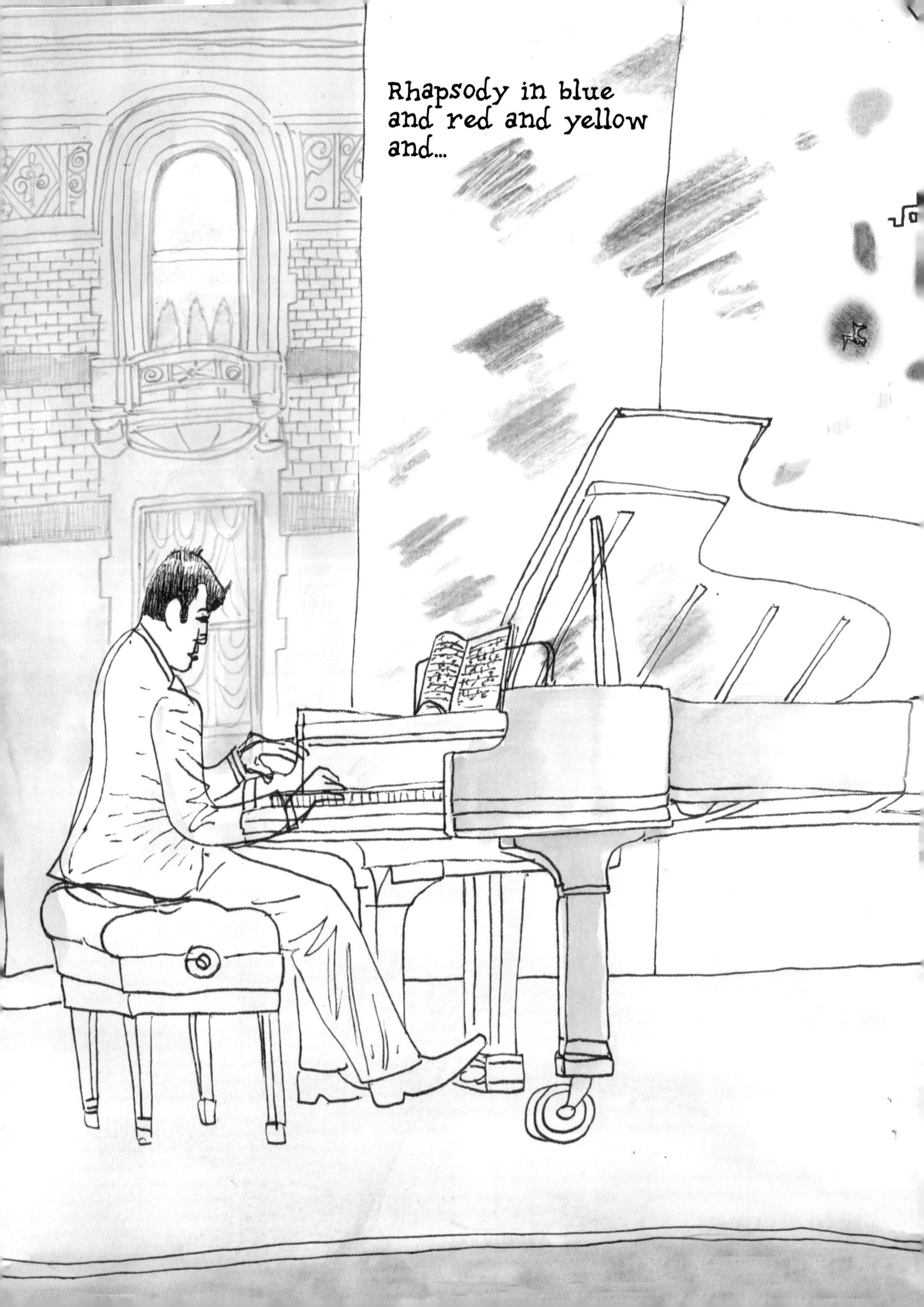
Rhapsody in blue
and red and yellow
and...

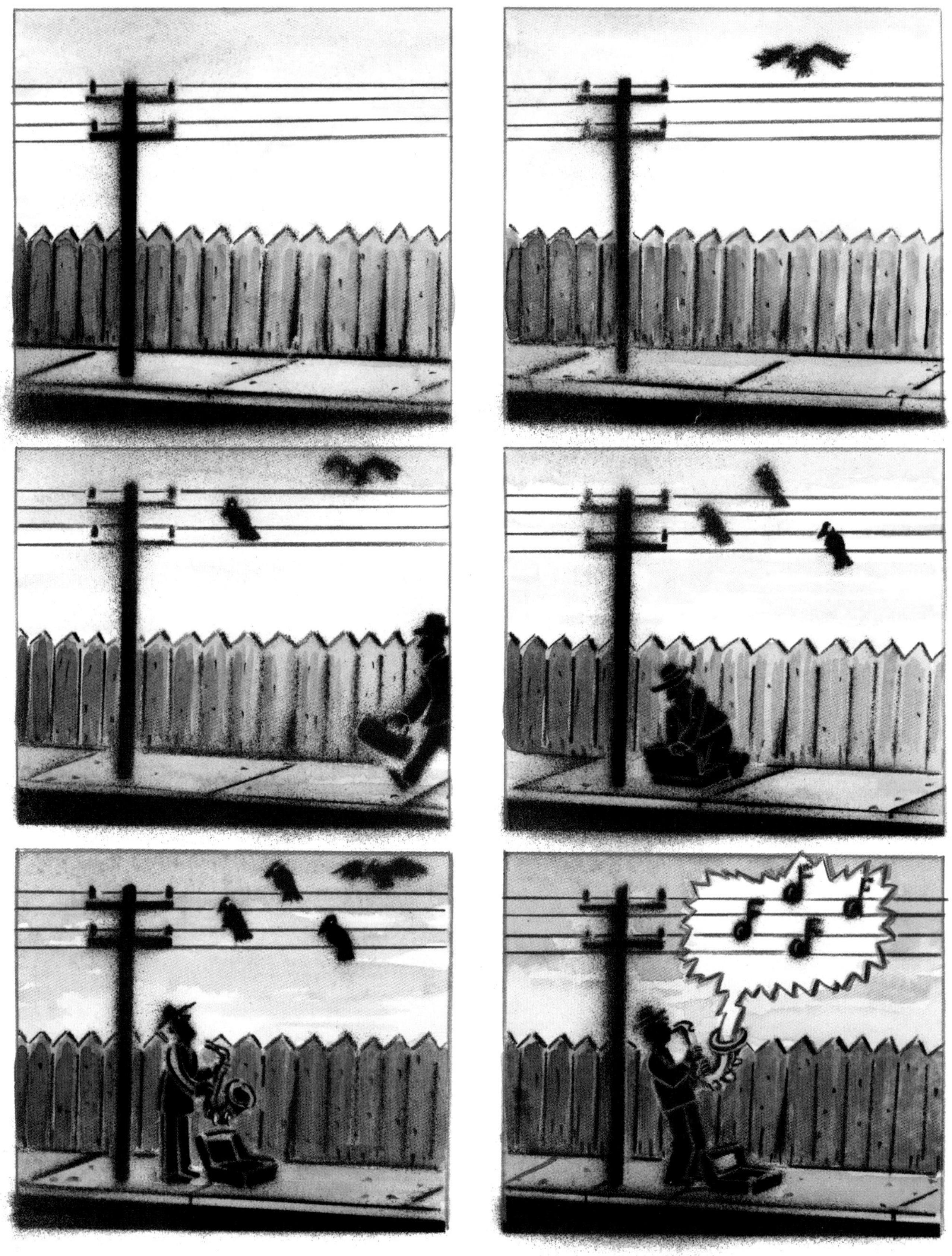

unfunnies

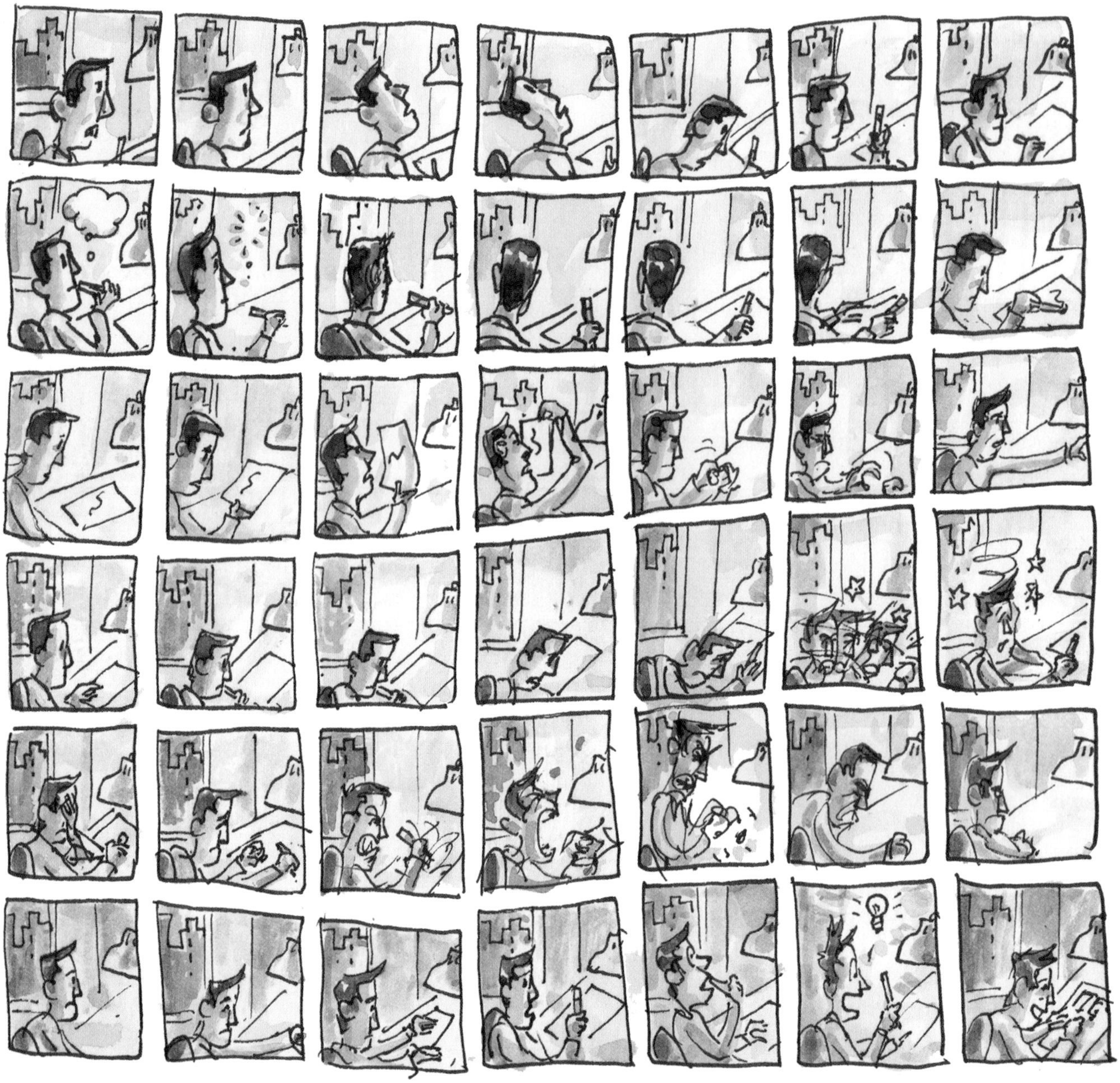

Epilogue

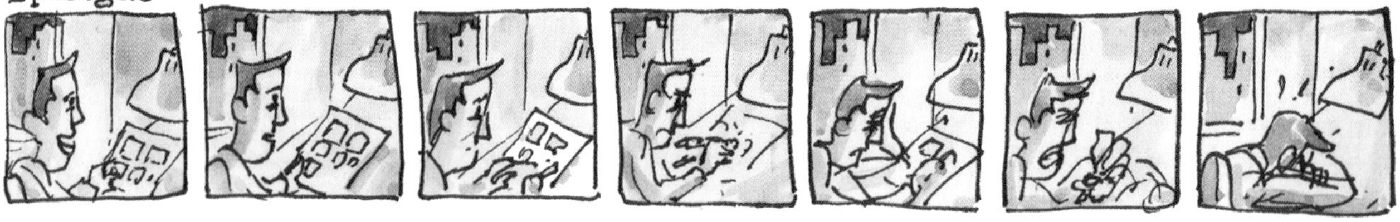

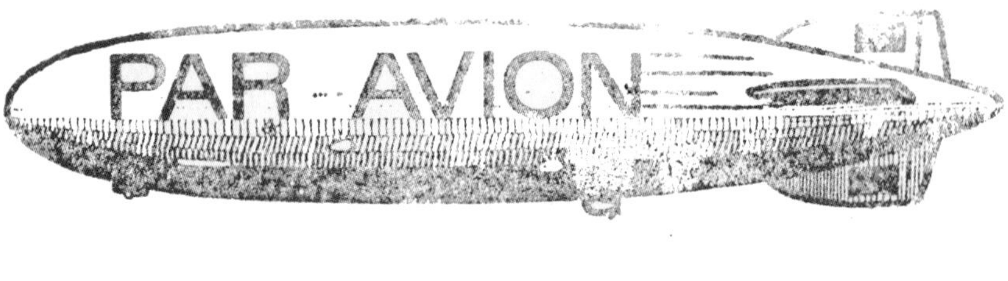
PAR AVION

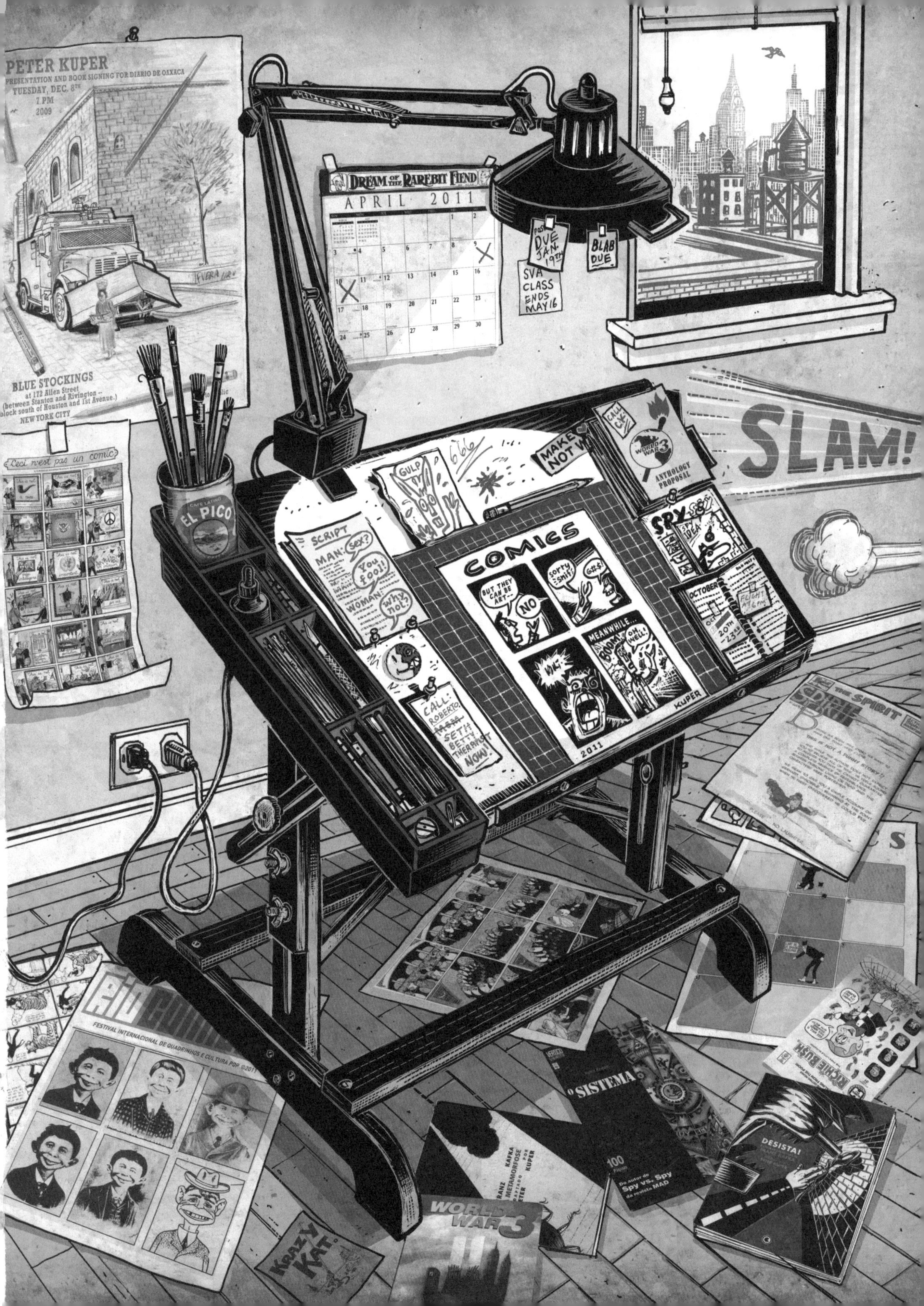

PETER KUPER
PRESENTATION AND BOOK SIGNING FOR DIARIO DE OAXACA
TUESDAY, DEC. 8TH
7 PM
2009
BLUE STOCKINGS
at 172 Allen Street
(between Stanton and Rivington --
block south of Houston and 1st Avenue.)
NEW YORK CITY
DREAM OF THE RAREBIT FIEND
APRIL 2011
DUE JAN. 19TH
BLAB DUE
SVA CLASS ENDS MAY 16
Ceci n'est pas un comic
SLAM!
MAKE NOT W
WORLD WAR 3
ANTHOLOGY PROPOSAL
SCRIPT
MAN: SEX?
WOMAN: YOU FOOL!
WHY NOT?
GULP
COMICS
BUT THEY CAN BE ART...
NO
SORRY SHIT!
MEANWHILE...
OH, WELL!
KUPER
2011
CALL: ROBERTO
SETH
BETTY
THERAPIST NOW!
SPY
OCTOBER
FLIGHT
EL PICO
CAFE LATINO
THE SPIRIT
FESTIVAL INTERNACIONAL DE QUADRINHOS E CULTURA POP ©2011
O SISTEMA
Spy vs. Spy
KAFKA
METAMORFOSE
KUPER
DESISTA!
WORLD WAR 3
KRAZY KAT
RICHIE RICH

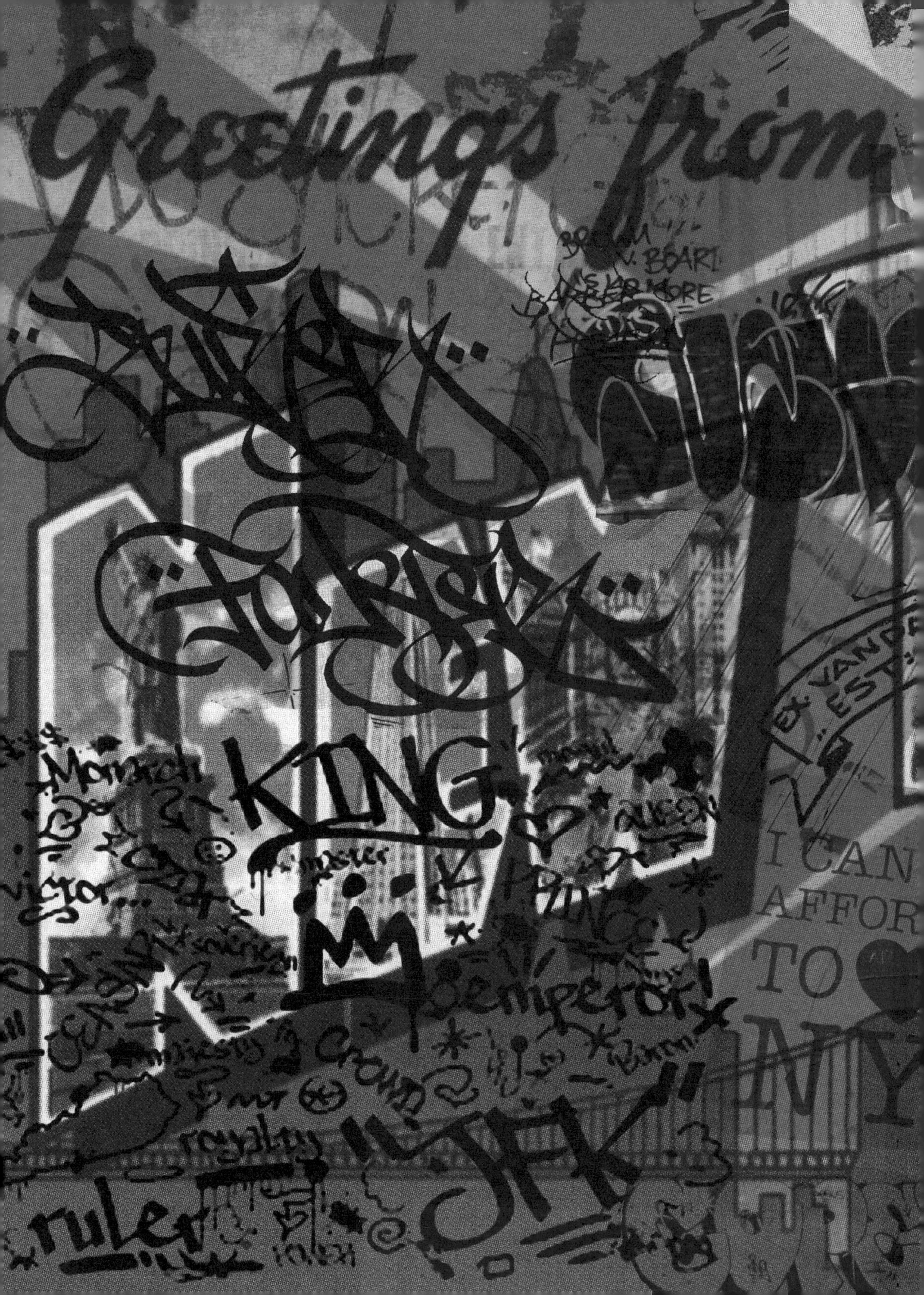

Greetings from
KING
Monarch
emperor!
crown
royalty
rules
JFK
I CAN
AFFOR
TO
NY